Knowledge and Human Liberation

Knowledge and Human Liberation

Towards Planetary Realizations

Ananta Kumar Giri

ANTHEM PRESS
LONDON · NEW YORK · DELHI

Anthem Press
An imprint of Wimbledon Publishing Company
www.anthempress.com

This edition first published in UK and USA 2014
by ANTHEM PRESS
75–76 Blackfriars Road, London SE1 8HA, UK
or PO Box 9779, London SW19 7ZG, UK
and
244 Madison Ave. #116, New York, NY 10016, USA

First published in hardback by Anthem Press in 2013

British Library Cataloguing-in-Publication Data
A catalogue record for this book is available from the British Library.

Library of Congress Cataloging-in-Publication Data
The Library of Congress has catalogued the hardcover edition as follows:
Giri, Ananta Kumar.
Knowledge and human liberation : towards planetary realizations /
Ananta Kumar Giri.
pages cm
Includes bibliographical references and index.
ISBN 978-0-85728-452-5 (hardback : alk. paper)
1. Knowledge, Theory of–Philosophy. 2. Liberation theology. I. Title.
BD161.G57 2012
121–dc23
2012042227

ISBN-13: 978 1 78308 327 5 (Pbk)
ISBN-10: 1 78308 327 1 (Pbk)

Cover illustration by Sarat Kumar Panda (Odisha, India).

This title is also available as an ebook.

For M. S. Swaminathan
S. N. Eisenstadt
Sang-Jin Han
Piet Strydom
Des Gasper
P. V. Rajagopal
Ashgar Ali Engineer
Betsy Taylor
and
Herbert Reid

who are engaged in inspiring efforts to make knowledge part of our current multi-dimensional *sadhana* and struggles for liberation.

CONTENTS

PREFACE

We should do our utmost to encourage the Beautiful, for the Useful encourages itself.

—Goethe

By their capacity for the immortal deed, by their ability to leave non-perishable traces behind, men, their individual mortality notwithstanding, attain an immortality of their own and prove themselves to be of a "divine" nature.

—Hannah Arendt, *The Human Condition* (1958, 19)

Oh People! Behold, we have created you all out of a male and female, and have made you into nations and tribes so that you might come to know one another.

—*The Quran* 49: 3

…Why should the hermeneutic model of understanding, which is derived from everyday conversation, and since Humboldt, has been methodology refined from the practice of textual interpretation, suddenly break down at the boundaries of our own culture, of our own way of life and traditions?

—Jürgen Habermas, *The Divided West* (2006, 17)

My desire for knowledge is intermittent, but my desire to bathe my head in atmospheres unknown to my feet is perennial and constant. The highest that we can attain to is not Knowledge, but Sympathy with Intelligence. I do not know that this higher knowledge amounts to anything more definite than a novel and grand surprise on a revelation of the insufficiency of all that we called Knowledge before – a discovery that there are more things in heaven and earth than are dreamed of in our philosophy. It is the lighting up of the mist by the sun… Live free, child of the mist – and with respect to knowledge we are all children of the mist.

—Henry David Thoreau "Walking" (1947, 623–4)

Human liberation is an epochal challenge now which means not only liberation from oppressive structures but also liberation from the oppressive self. It is a multi-dimensional struggle and aspiration for realizing beauty, dignity and dialogues in which knowledge – self, social as well as spiritual – can play a transformative role.

The present book in our hands, *Knowledge and Human Liberation: Towards Planetary Realizations*, undertakes such a journey of transformation and seeks to rethink knowledge vis-à-vis familiar themes such as human interest, critical theory, enlightenment, ethnography, ethnocentrism, democracy, pluralism, rationality, ethics, aesthetics, secularism, spirituality, and cosmopolitanism, among others.

The book brings together my engagement with these issues over the last two decades. In this period it has been inspiring for me to have been in communication and conversation with nine seekers of our Mother Earth who have dedicated themselves to pursuit of knowledge and human liberation in inspiring ways – M. S. Swaminathan, S. N. Eisenstadt, Sang-Jin Han, Piet Strydom, Des Gasper, P. V. Rajagopal, Ashgar Ali Engineer, Betsy Taylor and Herbert Reid. M. S. Swaminathan is the noted scientist and public intellectual of our world who has continuously striven to enrich human lives through innovations in science, technology and appropriate public policy. For Swaminathan, "We should neither worship nor discard technologies because they are old or new. What is important is to use knowledge and skills in manners that children can be born for happiness and not just for existence. We need an ecology and technology of hope and not of despair." In his dialogue with Daisaku Ikeda, *Revolutions: To Green the Environment, To Grow the Human Heart*, Swaminathan also tells us: "The movement towards multilateralism and globalization must be not merely economic, but also spiritual. What we need most is spiritual globalization… By spiritual globalization, I do not mean that every one should belong to the same religion. I am speaking of building security in the wider sense of human dignity and gender equity." In his recent works, Swaminathan talks about realization of biohappiness through "sustainable and equitable use of natural resources for more jobs and income." At 87, Swaminathan continues to embody inspiring vision and strivings. In all our meetings I have been inspired by his indefatigable energy, enthusiasm and generosity.

S. N. Eisenstadt was a great seeker of humanity who has explored so many dimensions of sociological knowledge. Until his very last moment (he passed away on 2 September 2010) he was active in his quest and he so kindly nurtured so many individuals and institutions around the world for more seeking and for thinking beyond the box. His latest project of "Multiple Modernities" has generated creative research work and debates around the world. I first met him in his home in Jerusalem in July 2002, and since then until his very last days Eisenstadt was such a kind source of support and encouragement.

Sang-Jin Han is a creative and critical sociologist from Korea who took part in the struggle for democracy there and plays a key role as a public intellectual in the post-authoritarian Korea. It has been enriching on my part to have been in communication and collaboration with him over the years. I first saw his edited book *Habermas and the Korean Debate* in the library of the University of Kentucky where I was a visiting fellow, in fact working with Betsy Taylor and Herbert Reid, in the fall of 2002. I then emailed him. We met; his work is a model of sociological engagement with knowledge giving rise to rigorous empirical work, grounded normative vision such as his concept of "middling grass-roots" (as different from mere "middle class" animated by a vision to transform existing conditions in society) and public enlightenment. Piet Strydom similarly is a model of silent dedication to sociological knowledge and the creation of a more and differently enlightened world. I first read a moving essay by him, "The Challenge of Responsibility for Sociology," in 2001. I emailed him and visited him at University College Cork in May 2002 where the lead essay of the book was presented as a seminar in his Department of Sociology. Piet continues to explore new horizons of knowledge and sociological practice and his seminal work, *Discourse and Knowledge: The Making of Enlightenment Sociology*, has been a source of inspiration to me as well as to many seeking souls around the world. He himself is an example of sacrifice for the sake of human dignity. He protested against the apartheid regime in South Africa and had to leave his mother land.

Des Gasper is an inspiring seeker of our times who has quietly and calmly dedicated himself to the pursuit of new horizons of human development, human security and development ethics. Ever since our first meeting in 1995, we have walked together many a time and have felt the call of a wider vocation of learning and scholarship. Des's range of scholarship and nurtured friendship is amazing and he continues to inspire all of us who meet him to be an embodiment of trust, integrity and devoted commitment to scholarship and human excellence.

P. V. Rajagopal and Ashgar Ali Engineer are two inspiring activists and visionaries of our times, whose vision and work assure us that even in the dark times we must not lose hope and walk together for peace, beauty and dignity. I first met with Rajagopal in the 2007 *Janadesh*, which was a month-long walk from Gwalior to Delhi for the cause of land for the landless people of India. We walked together for two days and what was touching was that, like thousands of co-walkers, Rajagopal was sleeping on the street along with his kind and inspiring wife Jill. Rajagopal continues to lead non-violent struggles for dignity and transformation in India and the world, and I have met many in Europe who are inspired by his vision and practice and have started dignity walks in their communities. For example last July (2010) I took part in the Dialogue of Humanity in Lyons, France, in which many walkers from surrounding communities took part, and they were inspired by Rajagopal. It is an example of the creative reverse globalization and planetary realization with which this book is concerned. Similarly, Ashgar Ali Engineer embodies deep commitment to knowledge and human transformations. He has been one of our most creative and inspiring practitioners and interpreters of Islam whose practice and interpretation of Islam as a religion of peace and compassion is a source of inspiration as well as a challenge for co-learning for all of us concerned. It has been enriching for me to have been in communication and grow in fellowship with this remarkable gift of the Divine, who continues to do his *tapasya* of love and transformation without fear, despite many attempts on his life.

Betsy Taylor and Herbert Reid embody a deep political and spiritual commitment to recovering our commons and transforming our existing discourse of alienation and annihilation; creating a world where we grow with beauty, dignity and dialogue. Both of them have gone beyond the domains of professional academy and have built creative bridges with the activists. Their dedicated work is a source of inspiration to me as well as many people around the world. In dedicating this book to them as well as to seven fellow dedicated practitioners of knowledge, I not only pay my personal tribute but also what we all owe to these inspiring seekers of our times who constitute the *navaratna*, the nine jewels, of our fragile Mother Earth.

I am grateful to all the friends and institutions mentioned in the following section of Acknowledgments where we have co-nurtured these thoughts. A special thank here is due to my dear friend and soul-brother Ivan Marquez, who taught at Bentley University, Massachusetts, and is currently based in Ireland, for his kind comments and generous help. I am grateful to Professor John Clammer for his kind foreword and Professor Fred Dallmayr for his inspiring afterword. I am grateful to kind and generous friends in Anthem Press, Tej P. S. Sood, Robert Reddick and Janka Romero for their nurturance of this project and to Professor Makarand Paranjape of Jawaharlal Nehru University for making initial communication between Tej and myself possible. Finally I hope this work contributes to the contemporary processes of formation of liberatory knowledge and *sadhana*, and struggles for self and social transformations.

Ananta Kumar Giri
Madras Institute of Development Studies, Chennai
15 August 2012 – Independence Day of India

ACKNOWLEDGMENTS

The chapters in this book build on essays published in different journals and presented in seminars and at conferences. I am grateful to the editors of the respective journals and the organizers of the seminars and conferences for their consideration and generosity.

Chapter One

This is the revised version of a paper first presented at the international conference on "Knowledge: East and West" held at the National Institute of Advanced Studies, Bangalore, 14–16 December 2000, and subsequently presented at: University College, Cork; University of Illinois, Urbana-Champaign; Committee on Social Theory, University of Kentucky; and the University of North Carolina, Chapel Hill. My thanks are due to all the participants in these seminars for their comments and interrogations, especially to Professors Piet Strydom, Linda Connolly, Jan Nederveen Pieterse, Betsy Taylor, Christopher Zurn, Pat Cooper, Theodore Schatazski, James Peacock, Rev. Chris Platt, Beth Powers and Arturo Escobar. This chapter was later published in the *European Journal of Social Theory* (2004) – Professor Gerald Delanty and the anonymous reviewer for the *European Journal of Social Theory* have been more than generous with their comments and encouragement and my grateful thanks are due to them.

Chapter Two

This is the revised version of a paper first presented at the international conference "Beyond East and West: Europe in a Changing World," held at Schloss-Elmau, Bavaria, Germany, 4–7 April 2004, and which now appears in *Futures* (2008). I am grateful to Professor Gerard Delanty for his kind invitation and to Piet Strydom for helping me with many of his seminal papers on evolution. I also wish to thank Dr Tattwamasi Paltasingh, then at Tata Institute of Social Sciences and presently at the Sardar Patel Institute of Social and Economic Change, Ahmedabad, for finding me some crucial books from her institute's library, and P. S. Syamala for help in word processing this essay. I am grateful to Mr Rakesh Kapoor and the anonymous reviewer of *Futures* for their comments on this paper.

Chapter Three

This chapter builds upon my introduction to *The Modern Prince and the Modern Sage: Transforming Power and Freedom* (New Delhi: Sage, 2009).

Chapter Four

This was first presented at the session "Philosophy and Anthropology: Border-Crossing and Transformations" that Terry Evens of the University of North Carolina, Chapel Hill and myself co-convened at the EASA (European Association of Social Anthropologists) biennial meeting in Vienna, 2004.

Chapter Five

I am grateful to Professor Ronald Walters of the Department of History at Johns Hopkins University for his help with and comments on this paper when it was first prepared as a term paper for a course with him on American history in the spring of 1988. This has been previously published in *Review of Development and Change* (2006).

Chapter Six

This is a revised version of a paper presented at the national seminar on "Rationality and Tribal Life" organized by the Department of Philosophy at the North-Eastern Hill University, Shillong in September 2001, and which was subsequently published in the *Journal of Indian Council of Philosophical Research* and the book *Rationality and Tribal Thought*, edited by Sujata Miri (Delhi: Mittal Publications, 2004). I am grateful to Professors Jagatpal and Sujata Miri for their very kind invitation and hospitality and to all the participants, especially to Professors Mrinal Miri, C. A. Agera, B. K. Agarwala, Archana Barua and Suryakanta Maharana for their insightful comments and enriching fellowship. This paper was revised when I was a visiting fellow at the Center of Social Studies at the Jacob-Blaustein Institute of Desert Research, Ben-Gurion University, Negev, Israel, and I wish to thank Professor Gideon Kressel and Tal for their kind hospitality.

Chapter Seven

This chapter appeared as "Rethinking Modernist Historiography" in *Creative Social Research: Rethinking Theories and Methods*, edited by Ananta Kumar Giri (Lanham, MD: Lexington Books, 2004).

Chapter Eight

This chapter was first published in the book *Rule of Law*, edited by Professor Danilo Zolo, and subsequently published in *Man & Development* (March 2002).

Chapter Nine

This chapter builds on a presentation given at a seminar at Leh, Ladakh in September 2009 on "The Role of Kashmir in the Spread of Buddhism," and has appeared in the *Journal of Indian Council of Philosophical Research* 26 (4) (2009): 137–44.

Chapter Ten

This is a revised version of an essay first presented as "Normative Pluralism and Rights and Law: The Challenge of Transformations and a Non-Dual Embodiment of Responsibility" in an international seminar on "Normative Pluralism and Human Rights" at the University of Florence, 6 December 2002. I thank Professor Danilo Zolo for his invitation and Filippo Ruschi, Helena Tagesson and other participants of the seminar for their comments and suggestions. This essay has also been presented subsequently at the Seoul National University and I thank Professor San-Jin Han and Ms Park of the Korea Foundation for their helpful suggestions and kind hospitality. This essay has been published in the *Journal of Indian Council of Philosophical Research* (2004).

Chapter Eleven

This chapter builds on my essay in *Critical Turns in Critical Theory*, a book in honor of Piet Strydom, edited by Seamus Otuama of University College Cork, Ireland, and published by I.B. Tauris in 2009. This chapter was also published in the *Review of Development and Change* (2008).

Chapter Twelve

This is a revised version of a paper presented at an international seminar on "Political Consumerism," held in Stockholm from 31 May to 3 June 2001. I thank Dr Michele Micheletti of the Department of Political Science of Stockholm University for her invitation and to all the participants for their comments and criticism. The paper was subsequently published in the *Journal of Human Values* 10 (1) (2004): 41–51.

Chapter Thirteen

This chapter builds upon my presentation at the *Hind Swaraj* centenary seminar "Social Development and Human Civilization in the 21st Century," 12–14 February 2009, organized by the Council for Social Development, Delhi. I am grateful to Professor Manoranjan Mohanty, the main organizer of the seminar, for his kind invitation and encouragement. The chapter also builds and expands on a text I wrote for an edited volume on *Hind Swaraj* edited by Vinod Chandra.

Chapter Fourteen

This is the revised version of a paper first presented at the symposium on "Civil Society and the Paths of Modernity in India" at the annual meeting of the German Sociological Association, Munich, October 2004. I thank Dr Martin Fuchs and Professor Monika Wohlrab for their kind invitation to take part in this symposium. This has been subsequently published in the *Sociological Bulletin* (2008), and I thank the anonymous reviewer and Professor N. Jayaram, its managing editor, for their comments.

Chapter Fifteen

This is a revised version of a paper presented at the seminar "Philosophy as Samvad and Swaraj" held at the Indian Institute of Advanced Studies (IIAS), Shimla, 28–30 April 2008. It builds upon my ongoing work on the subject for the last two and a half years, beginning with my presentation on the theme at the international seminar "Science and Religion in Modern India" held in New Delhi, January 2006. I thank Professors Shail Mayaram of the Center for Studies of Developing Societies, Delhi and Peter de Souza, director of the IIAS, for their kind invitation to the Shimla dialogue, and its participants for their questions, comments and reflections.

Chapter Sixteen

This chapter has been published previously in the *Sociological Bulletin* (2002).

Chapter Seventeen

This chapter was first presented at the workshop with Professor Martha Nussbaum, "Cosmopolitan Presumptions" held at Institute of Social Studies (ISS), The Hague, 10 March 2006. It was subsequently published in a special issue of the ISS journal *Development and Change* 37 (6) (2006): 1277–92. I am grateful to Professor Des Gasper for his kind invitation, Ms Phaedera Veneendaal for much help, and the participants for their stimulating conversation.

FOREWORD

John Clammer
United Nations University, Tokyo

This valuable volume brings together in one place for the first time a number of essays by one of India's (and indeed international sociology's) most innovative thinkers, and one moreover who is committed to erasing the boundaries between social theory and practice. Essentially what is suggested in the following pages is an approach to social knowledge and to positive social transformation that transcends the normal boundaries that so commonly separate sociology from philosophy and both from religion and spirituality. To a great extent the social sciences have failed to deliver on their Enlightenment promises. Perhaps this was too much to expect from them, but then as Karl Marx so effectively demonstrated, ideas do have power – they not only reflect but also shape social reality, and as we know from the history of revolutions in the past, ideas of liberatory potential can have enormous effects as the driving force of social movements that in turn transform political, economic, cultural and gendered structures, institutions and patterns of everyday practice.

While social movement theorists have largely concentrated their attentions on the material and resource mobilization basis of such movements, it is equally important to recognize that the ideas that stimulate them and motivate people to action need foregrounding. Knowledge itself in other words can be liberatory if it is of a certain kind and if it is recognized as the basis and stimulus for transformative action. In the case of individuals, this we know from studies of such phenomena as religious conversion in which a whole reformulation of identity can take place; now we also need to scale up this insight into the wider study of social transformation. This however can only be done by expanding our conception of the role of the social sciences and the self-limitations that they so frequently impose on themselves. This self-entrapment takes many forms – a preoccupation with defending disciplinary boundaries instead of crossing them; an unwillingness to face head-on the fundamental existential issues of human life and its mysteries, which in fact form the ontological basis of all cultural and social life; anthropocentric conception of the place of the human being in the wider environment and universe; a focus on the critical rather than the reconstructive; and for the most part (although there are some notable exceptions) a conception of the social sciences as essentially empirical and descriptive rather than as liberatory – as pointing to not only what is, but what might be. The latter function in the West has been largely relegated to utopianism or futurism, and as such is placed outside of the boundaries of the "serious" social sciences. This however is a profound mistake, and one that cuts the social sciences off from the possibility of contributing centrally to the goal of human emancipation, not only from external threats (the issue of social justice), but also from internal ones (psychic, spiritual and emotional emancipation). Those who address these problems are sadly more likely to be theologians, novelists or psychotherapists than they are to be sociologists or anthropologists.

There are, fortunately, some alternative voices to the conventional formulations of the scope and subject matter of the social sciences, and this book represents one of the most interesting and significant ones, as it ranges over a spectrum of not wholly integrated but highly suggestive approaches to rethinking the nature and role of a broadly based approach to social reality and ideology that refuses to recognize the standard disciplinary boundaries. It might be read as a prism through which many different facets of society can be seen, a multivocal discourse attempting to capture a range of visions about both how society might be approached and how its structures might be re-envisioned in ways that enhance and do not suppress the best qualities of being human. Here Ananta Kumar Giri suggests a number of such approaches. The first is the identification of liberatory knowledge. By no means all knowledge is liberatory – much of it can lead to or is designed to lead to greater human bondage, ecological damage and general destruction – weapons technology, nuclear energy, the motorcar, materials for biological warfare. Yet many of the most destructive forms of knowledge are paradoxically the most rewarded and funded in the distorted value systems of contemporary society, and those which can liberate – social, political, psychic and spiritual techniques – are relegated to the fringes, to the private, to the eccentric. This can be seen in any text of social theory where Marx, Weber, Durkheim and perhaps Simmel, Pareto and even Freud are given prominence, followed by the major Frankfurt School critical theorists, but no mention is made of Jung, Rudolf Steiner, Levinas, Fromm, Martin Buber, or even of seminal but now forgotten figures in mainstream sociology such as Albion Small, and certainly not of significant modern or contemporary religious, artistic or ecological thinkers. Yet it in these latter thinkers that liberatory knowledge is likely to be found, precisely because that is what they were seeking – the enhancement of life and the transformation of oppressive structures and institutions and patterns of internal psychological or emotional dependency. The hegemonic assumption in the West is that radicalism has to be political, but this is not the case: the Buddha could be argued to be far more radical than Marx. To recover this tradition and to bring it into dialogue with mainstream social science is an important project, and here a beginning is made in doing exactly that.

The second is the twofold move of on the one hand expanding the scope of what is regarded as relevant knowledge when applied to the social sciences (the incorporation of aesthetics for example into development discourse – if there can be a development ethics, why not also a development aesthetics?), and on the other of recognizing the limitations of knowledge as a category for grasping the complexities of human society. For not only is knowledge an imperfect and ever-evolving tool, but overemphasis on knowledge leads to a privileging of epistemology over ontology, and of the cognitive over the emotional and nonrational in a context in which it should be clear to any social analyst that social life is largely motivated by feelings and desires rather than by rational assessment of competing possibilities and courses of actions or choices.

To carry out this project, various outlines of which are contained in the essays that make up this book, several moves are suggested. One is the central significance of dialogue, but in this case between seemingly unlikely partners such as the German social/critical theorist Jürgen Habermas and the Indian spiritual leader and major thinker Sri Aurobindo. Another is the erasing of boundaries between what have traditionally been regarded as separate spheres – politics, rationality, spirituality, power, self-development and rights, for example. This points to new forms of creativity in social research that are not limited by the concerns of traditional academic disciplines, but are defined rather by the nature of the problems that they are addressing. A third is the movement beyond traditional critical theory as constructed by the Frankfurt School and its successors. While these seminal thinkers built a critical model out of elements largely derived from Marx and Freud, they remained, with the exception of Walter Benjamin and his aesthetic and messianic preoccupations, within a political economy framework from which the spiritual, the artistic and creative capacities, and nature and psychology beyond Freud, were excluded. Not only do we now see the limitations of this model which with its concentration on the externalities of liberation (largely the political and the economic), leaves the self untouched and has surprisingly little to say about culture, but we can also recognize that critique is only the first move in a dialectic which must also include reconstruction and the possibility of a transcendence or self-transcendence beyond the political economy model entirely. It is for this reason that Giri rightly draws attention to two vital factors: on the one hand liberation from ego as a condition of genuine socio-economic emancipation (and the failure of revolutions well attests to this fact), and on the other the exploration of social movements very different from those in which, despite his alleged demise, the ghost of Marx still lurks all too visibly – the Gandhian and Swadeshi movements in particular in this book.

These are important not only as movements of social change, but as themselves the generators of ideas about social transformation, as practical experiments as it were in the possibilities of revolution by enlightenment rather than of revolution by violence. The incorporation of these case studies also illustrates an important aspect of Giri's approach – the overcoming of the persistent Eurocentrism (or actually North American–centrisrn) of most mainstream social theory. This is not to say that other traditions do not exist – they most certainly do in India, very conspicuously, and in Japan, China and elsewhere – but they are not given much weight because of the institutional arrangements of Western universities and their frequently parochial concerns, because of lack of linguistic competence on the part of major Western scholars and, more significantly, because the concerns and methods of much non-Western social science do not accord with the accepted canons of mainstream social theory. Habermas is thus in, but Sri Aurobindo (even if most Western sociologists had ever heard of him) is out; Lenin or Gramsci are in, but Gandhi or Panduranga Shastri Athavale are not, and Seyyed Hossein Nasr or Thich Nhat Hanh are most certainly never likely to be accepted into the canon despite their profound insights into human-nature relationships and peace respectively. Here Giri makes a first step towards overcoming this dichotomy, which makes all talk of cosmopolitanism and transcivilizational dialogue hollow if it is not carried into this kind of practice. Dialogue involves actually listening to the other, of being prepared to hear not only what one might want to disagree with, but also to the possibility of the unexpected. It is not a space of argument, but of attention, and this book is a valuable tool in the expansion of that space and in the quality of listening that occurs there.

What then emerges is a new form of critical theory, one concerned with the basis of human behavior, not just its social manifestations. Giri's prism of possibilities calls for a rethinking of what we take to constitute knowledge in the social sciences and how this connects to the perennial search for liberation, not only from oppressive structures, but also from the oppressive self. To do this involves a serious reconsideration of the role of spirituality in personal and collective life and of the role of self-cultivation as a way of overcoming rather than enhancing ego. The essays in this book, in addition to introducing some lesser known or neglected thinkers, point to a greatly expanded vision of the social sciences, their very nature and what they can potentially accomplish, not as the tools of a glorified form of market research, but as liberatory means to insight, understanding, dialogue and wisdom. As Pierre Bourdieu argued, to grasp the actual conditions of one's social situation is already to be largely liberated from its determinism. He was correct, with the proviso that we acknowledge that those conditions contain the psychic, spiritual and emotional as much as the material and social in the narrow sense.

Many have argued that it is our civilization itself and its culture of greed, consumption and self-aggrandizement that has brought us to our present ecological and political impasses in which the Holocaust and its many variants could occur, where war and terrorism are the norm and social dysfunction the average, and in which respected social scientists can write widely acclaimed books on the clash of civilizations and on the end of history. Clearly a different model is needed and here, as in his extensive other writings, Ananta Kumar Giri suggests some of the key elements in this model. In addition to those outlined above, these include a movement from a Newtonian understanding of causality to a "softer" model in which participation, exploration and unexpected connections provide the frame, less for explanation than of greater insight, and that our conception of knowledge needs likewise to move from a concept of knowledge as truth to one of knowledge as process, in exactly that same conversation of participation, exploration and dialogue, not least because as Sri Aurobindo amongst others demonstrated there are limits to reason. This implies of course a transformation of sociological knowledge and of the recognition of the dialectical nature of liberation with its constant movement between the poles of the outer and the inner.

This has very practical applications, for example in the field of development studies, where while there is now a growing sub-field of development ethics, the whole notion of development should also contain an aesthetic dimension too, as development involves not only growth or material improvement, but also the issue of the quality of life and self-development without which it is merely an external phenomenon. The goal in fact could be described as "awakening" rather than as "development," from the nightmare of much of recent history despite our vaunted technological prowess into life, in which gentle action has radical implications. As Giri suggests, the purpose of our intellectual activity should be to see the world in a different way, or at least to see its possibilities and promise that correct insight can help to bring about, and to see it in ways that warm, deepen, enhance, communicate and create genuine communities. This surely is the role of the social sciences and in these essays we find a number of paths through which this goal might be achieved.

Introduction

THE CALLING OF TRANSFORMATIVE KNOWLEDGE

The prime condition for a democratically organized public is a kind of knowledge and insight which does not yet exist.

—John Dewey, *The Public and its Problems* (1927, 166)

The consideration of life itself requires that the potent reality of the soul be described in its wholeness, from its more humble to its highest possibilities.

—Wilhelm Dilthey

True, an outward battle also has to be fought, but against institutions which stand in the way of spreading the light and reign of brotherhood, not against men as unbelievers, in a spirit of understanding, of knowledge, of firm will, but also of charity for ignorance and love…

—Sri Aurobindo, *The Hour of God and Other Writings* (1972, 326)

The Adventure and Invitation of Knowledge

In the Bible we read about a woman who is wailing in the streets and her name is Wisdom.[1] She is weeping because despite her knocking we are not opening our doors. But in the human journey as well as in our contemporary world it is not only wisdom which is weeping. Knowledge is also weeping, as it has become imprisoned within a variety of structures of domination, commodification, illusion and isolation. But to know is not only to know of but to know with – a practice of knowing with which involves both self-knowledge and knowledge of the world (see Sunder Rajan 1988). It is a process of knowing where we hold each other's hands, look up to each other's faces and learn together. This helps us realize our primordial need for self-knowledge ("Know Thyself"), knowledge of the other and the world. It is in this process of knowing together that knowledge becomes a journey of co-realization, co-learning and collective learning involving both ontology and epistemology, joy as well as suffering. Suffering comes from the structures of domination imposed upon us, limiting our reality and the possibility of coming together and freely learning and sharing our hearts; joy comes from the very striving towards it, despite these imposed restrictions and fears of many kinds. Suffering also has a much deeper root, for example, suffering emerging from our lack of readiness to embrace a new definition of self and society and clinging to our earlier conception of self. Joy emerges from experiences of breaking open such boundaries and realizing liberation.

Such practices of knowing together involve both compassion and confrontation. In practices of knowing together we create a compassionate community and help each other to learn. This is also a space of solidarity, a solidarity which is always in a process of fuller realization rather than being a fixed thing. In knowing together we compassionately understand each other, our points of view, including those of the ones we confront, and in the process our points of view become circles of view capable of more generous embrace. In knowing together we also confront each other, our existing conceptions of self, nature and society – especially those conceptions which reiterate structures of domination and do not facilitate realization of our human, societal, divine and cosmic potential. But this confrontation takes a variety of forms: violent, non-violent, dualistic as well as non-dual. There are also practices of knowing together which involve compassionate confrontation, where partners of confrontation are not eternal demons; though we fight, we realize that we are part of a bigger drama of co-realization where we are not just to annihilate our enemies but create a field where transformation embraces self, other and the world.

Knowledge is at the root of realization of living and in spaces of togetherness living is nurtured and cultivated. It is in these spaces of togetherness, with all their challenges and contradictions, that life has learnt the art of living and facing the challenges of evolution. It is in the spaces of togetherness that humanity has also learnt about life, self, culture, society, Nature and the Divine. These spaces are not just collectivist spaces; they are also spaces of self-, co- and societal meditations. We find examples of such spaces of togetherness as spaces of knowledge and meditation in many different traditions of human striving – religion, art and science.

In human histories and societies we see such work on knowledge and togetherness unfolding in various fields of life including in a variety of movements – socio-political as well as socio-spiritual. These movements have presented fields in which fellow beings have come together, have learnt about themselves, each other, society, Nature and the cosmos. In these fields we have also learnt how to overcome our existing conceptions of self and social order and feel confident about new knowledge of self, society and the other that we create. For example, in our turbulent histories of the last two hundred years, workers' movements and anti-colonial and post-colonial struggles for freedom have been critical factors of transformation, and these movements have challenged existing structures of self and social formation. Workers' movements have fought for dignity of labor and against oppression by the bourgeoisie, struggling for not only their freedom but also for fuller social becoming and freedom for all. Struggles for freedom have also created new knowledge of self, society and the world, confronting the existing colonial structure of self-formation, social governance and exploitation. In Gandhi's anti-colonial and post-colonial struggle for freedom this process of knowing together transcended many boundaries. As a space of togetherness, Gandhi-inspired mobilizations, like those of Buddha and Jesus before him, created spaces of compassion and confrontation in which seeking and struggling participants knew together in struggle. This struggle brought together men and women from diverse backgrounds, including sympathetic transformers such as C. F. Andrews from the national space of the colonizers.[2]

In our contemporary world, as it was in the last half century, varieties of movements, despite inevitable and understandable human and social limitation, continue to create multiple fields of knowing together. They act as agents of self-production and challenge the available conceptions of the normal and the pathological (see Das 2003; Touraine 1977). They generate a new language of self and social imagination, urging us to realize how existing language traps us in bondage. In our contemporary world, Dalit movements, women's movements, gay and lesbian movements, differently abled movements and global justice movements, such as the World Social Forum, (see Ferrera 2006) create a field of knowing together in which social movements themselves play a key role as cognitive agents, creating new knowledge about self, Nature and society and fields to generate and sustain such knowledge. But social movements are not only cognitive agents in a narrow way, they are also spaces of emotional intersubjectivity. Spaces of togetherness from the dawn of humanity till the most recent are not only cognitive spaces but also emotional spaces of mutual nurturance and nurturance of flames of aspiration through music, art, poetry and other expressive creativities. It is not true that we find such expressive dimension only in the so-called new social movements of the last three decades or so. The workers movements also had a vibrant musical and literary engagement as do many political movements now, such as the Zapatista movement in contemporary Mexico. Fields of knowing together are multi-dimensional spaces of cognition and emotional nurturance, knowledge and art of life.

Transformative Knowledge and the Calling of a New Language

Knowledge and human liberation as it unfolds in transformative movements is also accompanied by the creation of new languages and new imaginings of self and society. Transformative movements create a space of meditative solidarity in whose lap[3] the inadequacy of the existing language of self and society is felt to be giving rise to a new language. This language is often a language of the heart[4] which is not just the reiteration of the existing language of rote utterance, grammar of life and social order. Social movements interrogate the existing language of classification, identification, punctuation and grammar and create a new language of self and social liberation.[5]

These movements in our recent global histories must be looked at as part of the entire heritage of humanity – in its multiplex histories of compassion and confrontation, the struggle to create a new language which could express the world aspired to be born. But as these movements strive to create new languages we must not romanticize these struggles nor should we be carried away by these words, forgetting the complex relationship of contestation and the need for perennial self-transformation for the realization of new social relationships suggested in the rise of new words. A perennial challenge here is the fact that both the proponents of a new language of self and society as well as their followers may just repeat such words and then continue to create and live under the illusion that such recitation alone is enough to change the existing social order which is still the house of a language of humiliation and indignity in social relations.[6]

Acknowledging these constraints and building upon our failures, including failures of traditions and experimentations with traditions, we are nonetheless challenged to realize the limits of existing language in practices of transformative knowledge, which in turn challenges us to rethink our existing and dominant conceptions of language and society. Many a time a naïve interpretation of Wittgenstein's view that language is a form of life has led to a naïve sociologism on the part of philosophers treating language as a form of life and expression of society without interrogating the structures of domination, exclusion, violence and humiliation encoded in such forms of life (see Wittgenstein 1976).[7] Philosophers are prone to a naïve sociologism because they themselves rarely do fieldwork with people who are carriers of multiple vibrant languages as unfolding streams of life. But such a naivety exists not only among philosophers but also among sociologists and anthropologists who accept Wittgenstein as a *guru* and do not explore further the challenge of exploring and realizing both the depth and the height dimension of the practice of language.[8] For example, in his autobiographical reflections *Available Light* anthropologist Clifford Geertz (2000) tells us that he considers Wittgenstein as his *guru*. But had he also considered Heidegger as his *guru* he could have developed a much deeper conception of language, social practice and the art of thick description which would have enabled him to discover a deeper stream in Wittgenstein's meditations on language and social practice.

This prompts an engagement with both Wittgenstein and Heidegger for rethinking language, social practice and the calling of transformative knowledge.[9] For Wittgenstein, "language has extensive malleability, and could accommodate other grammars to set up a differing rule. He writes with respect to a new grammar that may at first be unfamiliar: "there is nothing wrong about it, as it is a new terminology and can at any time be retranslated into ordinary language" (Luchte 2011). Wittgenstein also writes: "We shall also try to construct new notations, in order to break the spell of those which we are accustomed to" (Luchte 2011). Heidegger also tells us about the limits of looking at language as an already formulated system and urges us to understand language as a "way-making movement."[10] For Heidegger, the conventional language itself once arose as part of "singularization – a creative rule-breaking, transgression of the rule of the conventional (the prevailing restricted economy) in an expression of innovation in the grammar of existence" (Luchte 2011).[11]

Both Wittgenstein and Heidegger emphasize the significance of practice but this is neither merely practice in its usual sense nor reproduction of the status quo; it has a dimension of spiritual quest embodying a continuous critique of those existing forms and ways which hinder realization of potential and the creation of relationships of beauty, dignity and dialogues. It is helpful to realize practice in language and society as part of a broader way of spiritual pragmatics where there are meditations and struggles to create new languages in the interstices of both practical discourse and practical spirituality (see Giri 2009c). In spiritual pragmatics new languages and practices are born of multi-dimensional *sadhana*, strivings and struggles touching both the social and spiritual bases of life and society. We find elements of spiritual pragmatics in both Sri Aurobindo[12] and Martin Heidegger as well as in Wittgenstein.[13] Knowing together in compassion and confrontation, as it is challenged with the evolutionary calling of creating new languages, is confronted with this calling of a spiritual pragmatics.

The Gift of Knowledge

Spiritual pragmatics interrogates the language of knowledge as property and challenges us to realize it as a gift. Life is not a property, life is a gift. Knowledge is not a property, it is a gift. We partake in this gift of life, we stand upon the great heritage of knowledge and life and the only way we can pay back our debt to this heritage is by giving unconditionally the knowledge and life we have received. But not only today but down the ages knowledge has been bound in various ways ("Prometheus Bound") and used for domination rather than for liberation and unfolding of potential. In the past, as it is still in the present, knowledge was and is being denied to vast sections of societies – slaves, women, untouchables, low-caste, poor and the gentiles. These structures of exclusion have been challenged in some ways but yet much still remains to be done, thus, calling for the need to take part in varieties of movements of transformations.

Now we are confronted with an unprecedented challenge, in the shape of commercialization and commodification of knowledge, which starts in kindergarten and follows all the way to the portals of higher education. Even to teach one's children, on the part of a daily wage earner, one has to spend Rs 200 per month in a remote Indian village. What kind of society is this?

Today commodification of knowledge is reaching a level of obscenity and sacrilege which is an assault on the essential divine dimension of knowledge. It is an assault on both Sophia (Goddess of Wisdom in the Biblical tradition) and Sarasvati (Goddess of Learning in Indic traditions). With new weapons such as intellectual property rights, producers of knowledge are becoming slaves in the valorization of capital, losing their dignity and responsibility. Even spaces of knowledge sharing have become spaces of capital. One day I was passing through Bristol, England and met a professor who was organizing an interesting international conference the very next day. I naturally felt attracted and was prepared to sleep in the cold streets of the city just to listen to these words of wisdom but the professor told me that without paying a registration fee which ran up to hundreds of pounds I could not attend the seminar. I asked him: "You are organizing the seminar anyway. I am a passerby. Is your seminar going to suffer any loss if I do not pay? But by denying me participation are you fulfilling your sacred duty as a practitioner of knowledge? Aren't you making it a money-making machine?"

Making knowledge a gift is a continued challenge for us and it calls for multi-dimensional transformations – individual as well as structural. Knowledge is usually associated with an exclusionary elitism and expertise and here we are challenged to embody a new art of sharing and border crossing.[14] Those of us who are in paths of learning have to confront the contemporary structures of commodification of knowledge by not only giving and opening up our spaces of knowledge to all souls but also by ourselves becoming gifts of knowledge and life. We have to embody compassion and confrontation in our lives and in all the varieties of spaces of togetherness where we belong. We would also have to make our field of knowledge a fertile one, nurturing varieties of cross-fertilizations.

Knowledge, Human Liberation and Planetary Realizations

The above outlines some challenges in addressing the invitation and adventure of knowledge today and the present book in our hands explores multi-dimensional pathways of knowledge and human liberation, which involves liberation from structures of social domination as well as self-domination, such as the rule of the ego and the propensity to dominate and annihilate. Knowledge today is imprisoned not only in structures of domination but also in varieties of dualisms – expert and lay, cognitive and emotional – and we need a new art of cultivating non-duality and wholeness. The present book, continuing my quest in my earlier two efforts – *Global Transformations: Postmodernity and Beyond* (1998) and *Conversations and Transformations: Towards a New Ethics of Self and Society* (2002) – is a humble striving towards a new art of integration and politics and spirituality of liberation: individual, social as well as planetary. It seeks to nurture the garden of liberatory and transformational knowledge by presenting alternative pathways from many different locations and traditions of the world and discussing such diverse thinkers as Sri Aurobindo, Jürgen Habermas, Erasmus, Kant, Tocqueville, Gandhi, Foucault, Ramashroy Roy, Daya Krishna, Ramachandra Gandhi and Martha Nussbaum. It also seeks to rethink some important themes in contemporary discourse of knowledge such as knowledge, human interest, self-development, evolution, enlightenment, rationality, power, freedom, anthropology, democracy, history, law, *dharma*, pluralism, rights, epistemology, ontology, critical theory, development, political consumerism and responsible consumption, civil society, secularism and cosmopolitanism.

Knowledge and Human Liberation: Towards Planetary Realizations invites us to foundationally rethink and reconstitute the very terms of our conversations, such as "knowledge" and "human." Knowledge here is not confined to only what is known as knowledge in modernity, through epistemic procedures, but is linked to ontology and is also part of the interpenetrative field of action and devotion. *Gyana*, *karma* and *bhakti* – knowledge, action and devotion – constitute a multi-dimensional field of autonomy and interpretation in which our engagement with knowledge takes place. Human as well as human liberation in our book is not confined to what is typified and bounded as human in modernity, produced in an anthropocentric manner, mechanically as part of a series of dualistic operations such as an opposition between nature and society, human and non-human, and transcendence and immanence. Human liberation is not just confined to the human but is part of multi-dimensional transformative moves towards planetary realizations which involve transformation in the existing organization of society, namely the nation-state, rationality and the anthropocentric definition of the human. The "human" in this transformative quest builds upon creative post-human transformations in contemporary discourse and practice and is part of an evolving field of non-human, human and divine. Knowledge and human liberation helps us to realize ourselves as children of Mother Earth and the bigger family of the planet consisting of other beings. Human liberation is part of transformative seeking for what Dallmayr (forthcoming) calls an "Other Humanism" beyond a "high tide of old-style humanism" and embodying a "tentative resurgence of subdued, self-critical and non-Eurocentric (that is, non-hegemonic) view of human." This is also linked to animal liberation and realizing a relationship of dignity with the non-human world and a commitment to transforming suffering[15] for both the human and the non-human.

The first chapter of the book, "Knowledge and Human Liberation: Jürgen Habermas, Sri Aurobindo and Beyond," presents the pathways of transformative knowledge through a dialogue with Jürgen Habermas, the pre-eminent critical theorist of our times, and Sri Aurobindo, a multi-dimensional seeker of transformations. It pleads for going beyond knowledge and human interest and moving towards knowledge and human liberation – individual as well as structural. It nurtures many of the themes which are cultivated in later chapters of the book, such as practical spirituality and immanent transcendence. The second chapter, "Beyond West and East: Co-evolution and the Calling of a New Enlightenment and Non-duality," discusses the need to go beyond the dualism of East and West in our realization of knowledge and evolution and explores the pathways of a new enlightenment of non-duality and co-evolution. It talks about evolutionary pluralism which also resonates with many chapters of the book, especially Chapter Ten on rethinking pluralism and rights, which explores various paths of pluralism and pluralization.

This quest for finding the roots of liberatory knowledge is a key concern in Chapter Three, "The Modern Prince and the Modern Sage: Transforming Power and Freedom," which explores an alternative path of realization of power and freedom. It discusses various thinkers and movements which strive to transform power and freedom from domination into building relationships of dignity and beauty and spaces of realization of potential – individual and social. It discusses several key transformative thinkers in our human journey, such as Erasmus and Spinoza, and the way they help us to transform power and freedom. The subsequent two chapters take up this exploration of the roots of modern knowledge by discussing critically two seminal thinkers of modernity – Immanuel Kant and Alexis de Tocqueville. Chapter Four, "Kant and Anthropology," discusses the Kantian project of knowledge, especially as it constructs the field of anthropological knowledge. It discusses some of the limitations of this project of knowledge, especially its dualism. Exploration of the limits of dualism and the cultivation of paths and modes of non-duality is a key theme of the book which overflows into many chapters. Chapter Five, "Tocqueville as an Ethnographer of American Prison Systems and Democratic Practice," discusses Tocqueville's ethnographic construction of democracy and what we can learn from this superb pioneer of knowledge creation in our contemporary times. It juxtaposes Tocqueville's construction of knowledge of American democracy and knowledge of American prison system and urges us to realize how without liberatory knowledge and social transformation democracy does turn into a prison.

These five essays in Part One, "Nurturing the Garden of Transformative Knowledge: Roots and Variants," prepare the ground for the subsequent Part Two of "Rethinking Knowledge." Part Two begins with Chapter Six, which presents recent considerations of rationality, helping us to rethink rationality. It tries to overcome anthropocentrism and Eurocentrism in conceptualization of rationality. It also discusses the pragmatic reconstruction of rationality in the works of scholars such as Hilary Putnam. It pleads for a spiritual reconstruction of rationality going beyond the divide between rational and spiritual. Rethinking rationality is a key concern of the book which again overflows into several chapters, for example, the chapters on secularism and cosmopolitanism (Chapters Sixteen and Seventeen respectively). Rethinking rationality in this chapter prepares the ground for rethinking another epitome of modern knowledge: history. Chapter Seven, "Contemporary Challenges to the Idea of History," discusses contemporary challenges to the idea of history and urges us to go beyond the modernistic conception of history as power and reason. It argues that "as an enterprise of knowledge, history deals with all the three domains – power, reason and spiritual vision or politics, critical understanding and hope – but the knowledge emerging from one domain may not be compatible with another. For instance, when we look at Indian society and history, we see that knowledge of its politics and social system is incompatible with knowledge of its spiritual vision. While historical knowledge of politics and society in India gives us a picture of India dominated by a caste system and oppressive kings, knowledge of the spiritual vision gives us a story of the quest for spiritual self-realization and different *Bhakti* movements for instituting dignified relationships in society. In this field of plural knowledge, there is also a dialectic and mutual influence at work." This engagement with rethinking history in our book also calls for cultivating a realization of time as pregnant time and space as pregnant space. Pregnant spaces and times are spaces and times of emergence and help us in making a creative leap into the future, nurtured by our creative relationship with the past and memory work.

Rethinking time and modernist historiography in Chapter Seven is followed by an effort to rethink modernist law in Chapter Eight from the point of view of *dharma* (here meaning righteous conduct), in fact making a mutually interrogative and transformative dialogue between law and *dharma*. The subsequent chapter, "Compassion and Confrontation: Dialogic Experiments with Traditions and Pathways to New Futures," carries out dialogue with traditions such as Buddhism and Kashmiri Saivism to realize knowledge as a simultaneous work of compassion and confrontation. These chapters are followed by Chapter Ten, "Rethinking Pluralism and Rights: Meditative Verbs of Co-realizations and The Challenges of Transformations," which again revisits the issue of rights and discusses the challenge of pluralism. The chapter pleads for not only a plural conception of rights but to pluralize pluralist imagination itself. As Elizabeth Minnich tells us, we need to "pluralize terms so that we are less likely to forget – or collude in devaluing – the complex differences among us that remain hidden by singular terms" (Minnich 2007, 10). It also pleads for a new mode of pluralization, what it calls meditative pluralization, which resonates with the new conception of knowledge and human liberation cultivated in the book as meditative verbs of co-realizations (more on this in the following section). This is then followed by Chapter Eleven, "The Calling of a New Critical Theory: Self-Development, Inclusion of the Other and Planetary Realizations," which discusses more specifically the art of socio-cognitive critique and the practice of learning, especially collective learning. It discusses the seminal work of Piet Strydom, a contemporary creative critical theorist in this regard.

These six essays in Part Two about rethinking knowledge are then followed by six essays in Part Three on different aspects of aspirations and struggles for liberation in our contemporary world. This begins with Chapter Twelve, "Rethinking the Politics and Ethics of Consumption: Dialogues with Swadeshi Movements and Gandhi," which discusses this in the context of a key theme of our time, consumption, and carries out dialogue with the Swadeshi movement which embodied a different politics of consumption as part of the anti-colonial struggle for freedom. It also discusses what we can learn with Gandhi in nurturing a new politics, ethics and aesthetics of responsible consumption. Chapter Thirteen, "Swaraj as Blossoming: Compassion, Confrontation and a New Art of Integration" carries out a dialogue with Gandhi's *Hind Swaraj*, which reached its centenary in 2009. It reconstitutes Swaraj as blossoming and as advocating co-realizations, rather than just autonomy and self-rule as is usually conceptualized; seeing the work as animated by compassion, confrontation and a new art of integration.

The subsequent chapters discuss several aspects of struggles of conceptual and practical liberation revolving around religion, civil society, secularism and self-development. Chapter Fourteen urges us to reconstitute civil society through multi-dimensional work on self-development, thus overcoming the entrenched dualism between public participation and creative self-formation that characterizes the publicly valorized and rarely meditated discourse of civil society. The subsequent chapter, "The Calling of Practical Spirituality: Transformations in Science and Religion and New Dialogues on Self, Transcendence and Society," continues this concern and explores pathways of practical spirituality and new dialogues on self, transcendence and society, especially as we learn with two key contemporary *sadhakas* of knowledge and human liberation – Daya Krishna and Ramachandra Gandhi. Chapter Sixteen, "Spiritual Cultivation for a Secular Society," continues the quest of these two chapters and presents pathways of spiritual cultivation of secularism involving transformation of state, society and secularism. It goes beyond mere cultural critique of secularism as offered by scholars such as T. N. Madan and Ashis Nandy and defense of political secularism offered by scholars such as Rajeev Bhargava. It pleads for mutual learning between members of different religions as well as between a secular state and religious traditions, thus bringing a new perspective to contemporary engagement with a post-secular reconstruction of self and society. The concluding chapter, "Cosmopolitanism and Beyond: Towards Planetary Realizations," brings our engagement with knowledge and human liberation towards planetary realizations through a reconstitution of cosmopolitanism. The chapter seeks to transform the existing discourse of cosmopolitanism by making it part of post-anthropocentric, post-national and cross-cultural efforts to realize ourselves as members of the human and the bigger planetary family of beings.

Knowledge and Human Liberation: Building on Creative Experiments and Overcoming the Prison of Absolutism

The paths of liberatory knowledge cultivated in this book build on creative experiments in imagining and realizing knowledge in transformative ways in the dynamics of self, culture and society. This engagement reverberates with the transformative aspirations of a creative sociology of knowledge nurtured by pioneers such as Karl Mannheim, who cultivates sociology of knowledge as a multi-dimensional striving in going beyond the absolutism of both individualism and collectivism, creating a more organic society,[16] and realizing meaning beyond the logic of "optimum of adaptation" (1936, 18). Sociology of knowledge in the work of pioneers such as Karl Mannheim and recent seekers such as Elizabeth Minnich is also not imprisoned within knowledge as nouns or possessive pronouns but is open to realizing knowledge as verbs, calling for a new *yoga* of dialogue and transformations between nouns and verbs.[17] The present book, as for example is attempted in my essay on pluralism, strives to cultivate knowledge as multi-dimensional meditative verbs of self, co- and social realizations. Verbs of knowledge are not just activistic but they are also meditative. Knowledge and human liberation today calls for a new art of activistic meditation and meditative action going beyond the pervasive but rarely reflected upon dualism between noun and verb.[18]

Though Mannheim understands the significance of epistemology in modernist paths of engagement with knowledge he nonetheless challenges us to understand its limitation, which also reverberates with the spirit of the present book. For Mannheim while "all epistemological speculation is oriented within the polarity of object and subject" epistemology becomes an "analysis of the knowing subject" (1936, 12).

In Mannheim, sociology of knowledge is a striving to go beyond the absolutist point of view of both the subject and the field constructed by the knower, the observer and the participant. Writes Mannheim, "[The modern investigator] will no longer be inclined to raise the question as to which of the contending parties has truth on its side but rather he will direct his attention to discovering the approximate truth as it emerges in the course of historical development out of the complex social process" (1936, 75). He further writes:

> It may be true that every form of expression, in which we clothe our thoughts, tends to impose upon them an absolute tone. In our epoch, however, it is precisely the function of historical investigation…to analyse the elements that make up our self-assurance, so indispensable for action in immediate, concrete situations, and to counteract the bias which might arise from what we, as individuals, take for granted. This is possible only through incessant care and determination to reduce to a minimum the tendency to self-apotheosis. Through this effort the one-sidedness of our point of view is counteracted, and conflicting intellectual positions may actually come to supplement one another. (1936, 75–6)

Mannheim's sociology of knowledge makes creative use of modes of engagement such as evaluative and non-evaluative, thus cultivating the possibility of non-evaluative

evaluative stances and frames of non-judgmental judgment: "after the influence of political social position of knowledge has been accounted for there should still remain a realm of non-evaluative knowledge (not merely in the sense of freedom from partisan political judgment, but in the sense of the employment of an unambiguous and non-evaluative categorical and axiomatic apparatus)" (1936, 167). For Mannheim, "The non-evaluative insight into history does not inevitably lead to relativism, but rather to relationism... Knowledge arising out of our experience in actual life situations, though not absolute, is knowledge nonetheless... Relationism signifies merely that all of the elements of meaning in a given situation have relevance to one another and derive their significance from this reciprocal relationship in a given frame of thought" (1936, 76).

The present book continues such a relational approach to knowledge. It also nurtures the transformative agenda of sociology of knowledge by continuing to interrogate and transform the logic and structures of absolutism. While it is commonplace today to speak of plurality of knowledge, advocates of such views such as Santos and Béteille[19] rarely address the issue of how to find paths of emergent coordination and commonalty in the fields of plurality of knowledge (see Béteille 2009; Santos 2001; and also Giri 2012). In this context, as suggested in several chapters in our book, especially the chapter rethinking pluralism and rights, which I have discussed elsewhere, we need to cultivate a multi-valued logic of autonomy and interpenetration as a way to find paths of emergent commonalty in the fields of plurality of knowledge (see Giri 2006).

Liberating ourselves from absolutism is a goal shared by many seekers in the garden of transformational knowledge in societies and histories. Like Mannheim's suspicion of absolutism, Foucault shares a suspicion of totality. For Foucault, "epistemological mutation of history is not yet complete" (1972, 11). In the same spirit, the present book argues that the epistemological mutation of knowledge is not yet over and the proposed pathway of ontological epistemology of participation in the book may be considered as a move towards a new epistemological alchemy (see Marquez 2012), a step in the still-unfolding epistemological and ontological mutation of knowledge.

Foucault adopts an archaeological approach to knowledge: "Archaeological analysis individualizes and describes discursive formations [which differ from] epistemological and 'architectonic' descriptions, which analyze the internal structure of a theory" (1972, 157). For Foucault, an archaeological approach to knowledge helps us discover "tangle of interpositivitites whose limits and points of intersection cannot be found in a single operation" (1972, 160). Through archaeological analysis Foucault wants to show the "proximities, symmetries, or analogies that have made generalizations possible, in short, to describe the field of vectors and of differential reciprocity (of permeability and impermeability) that has been a condition of historical possibility for the interplay of exchanges. A configuration of interpositivity is not a group of neighboring disciplines; it is not only an observable phenomenon of resemblance; it is not only the overall relation of several discourses to this or that discourse; it is the law of their communications" (1972, 161–2). In our present book the proposed pathway of multi-valued logic of autonomy and interpretation as a mode of relationship between different domains in the field of knowledge resonates with this Foucauldian archaeological spirit of interpositivity animated by a passion for communication and at the same time seeks to make such interpositivity much more interpenetrative than what Foucault seems to attempt.

Foucault's archaeology of knowledge is critical of an archaeological approach to knowledge which reduces knowledge as document to knowledge as monument: "in our time history aspires to the condition of archaeology, to the intrinsic description of the monument" (1972, 7). The present book shares this spirit of interrogating the idea of knowledge as monument but it goes beyond just retrieving knowledge as document to understanding and creating knowledge as what Heidegger (2004) might call "way-making movement." Ontological epistemology of participation as an approach to and path of knowledge creation embodies continued transformative moves in epistemology and ontology making knowledge a continued movement.[20] Foucault is also known for his genealogical approach to knowledge which resonates with the spirit of historical contextualization in Mannheim's sociology of knowledge. But while Foucault's (1980, 117) early genealogy of knowledge gets rid of the "subject itself," the present book vibrates with the spirit of later Foucault (2005) who talks about "hermeneutics of the subject" and paths of creative subjectivation other than models of individualization offered by state and society. While Foucault's genealogy of knowledge despite promise of plurality seems to construct a linear and one-dimensional portrait of knowledge, especially modern knowledge, as disciplining discursive formations, the present book interrogates any such visible or invisible one-dimensionality and linearity[21] and seeks to understand pluralities of streams – both binding as well as liberatory – at work in any field of knowledge. The story of modern knowledge is not just a story of increasing discipline; it is also a story of struggle for liberation nurtured by emancipatory streams flowing within and across it.

Foucault talks about a "regime of truth" where truth, like knowledge, is constituted by power, and argues that "the essential political problem for the intellectual…is the possibility of constituting a new politics of truth. The problem is not changing people's consciousness – or what is in their heads – but the political, economic, institutional regime of the production of truth" (1980, 133). But in our book I talk about landscape of truth and truth realization and suggest that the challenge before us is not only a new politics of truth but a new spirituality of truth realization in the dynamics of self, culture and society involving both transformation of consciousness as well as "regimes of truth" (please see especially Chapter Fifteen on practical spirituality).

Towards an Epistemology of Awakening

The book pleads for a new relationship between power, knowledge and truth. The landscape of knowledge, power and truth provides a multi-dimensional perspective and mode of engagement and realization rather than a one-dimensional and single-point perspective. According to Boaventura de Sousa Santos, it is the "one-point perspective of Renaissance which has created an "epistemology of blindness" giving rise to "the absolute immobility of the eye and the blindness necessary to create the single view"

(Santos 2001, 266). With this epistemology of blindness modern science has discarded "all the alternative knowledges" resulting in "epistemicide" (2001, 264). In place of epistemicide we need a fertile field of epistemological efflorescence and regeneration and the present book is a humble striving in this regard.

This spirit of fertility needs a new Time realization. For Santos, in modernity, we are temporally poor, for example, most of us thinking of ourselves as only modern, divorced from tradition as well as from a notion of creative future and we need to cultivate a new "temporality of bridge" (2001, 266).[22] In cultivating paths of knowledge and human liberation we need to liberate ourselves from modernistic conceptions of linear time and experiment with different spatio-temporal formations (see Chapter Seven on history). The book pleads for cultivating pregnant space and pregnant time which can be taken further to realize time as our mother through cultivation of non-anxiety in self and society. Time is a source of much suffering in modernity. Knowledge and human liberation challenges us to go beyond the contemporary structuration of time and suffering and move towards time and healing.

In place of an "epistemology of blindness" Santos proposes an "epistemology of seeing" which involves both "creating solidarity" (Santos 2001, 270) as well "social experimentation" (2001, 273). Solidarity in "epistemology of seeing" resonates with participation in "ontological epistemology of participation" but here the language of "seeing" seems inadequate. In place of an "epistemology of blindness" we need not only an epistemology of seeing but also an epistemology of awakening which is neither simply nor solely epistemological. This epistemology of awakening is also an awakening of wholeness.[23]

For Santos, the epistemology of blindness has created many abysses, including the abyss of colonialism. In the concluding chapter on cosmopolitanism in our book I discuss the need for creating a post-colonial cosmopolis building on both post-colonial transformations and cosmopolitan aspirations. This striving for a "post-colonial cosmopolis" can build on what Santos calls "post-abyssal thinking" which is a "non-derivative thinking" as well as "ecological thinking" (2007, 23). "Ecology of knowledge is founded on the idea that knowledge is inter-knowledge" (2007, 27).

For Santos, "The first condition for a post-abyssal thinking is radical co-presence" (2007, 27). This finds a resonance in creative remembering and reconstitution of the present in the insightful recent work of Nitasha Kaul, who cultivates post-colonial paths in epistemology. For Kaul, "modernist knowledge needs to be haunted by a post-colonial memory, a re-membering, which can be instigated by placing the question of difference at the heart of the story. When one re-members, one does not simply recall – to re-member is to put it all together again. This putting together all over again is not a temporalized recitation of what happened after what. Rather it is first of all an undoing of the present… In order to re-member the present, one has to not undo simply the present, but also oneself… In this way, the post-colonial moment in epistemology is immediately also the *interpellation of knowing with re-membering*" (Kaul 2009, 116). The ontological epistemology of participation proposed in this book can also be looked at as a way of knowing with remembering and nurturing the possibility for healing, reconciliation and transformation. Kaul also urges us to realize the "epistemic violence of modernist universalism" (2009, 13) and the "violence of knowledge" itself (2009, 25). This heightens the need for going beyond the violence of modernist epistemology and nurturing non-violence in social relations and non-injury in modes of thinking. It calls for a new standpoint in knowledge participation and generation which for both Kaul and Santos is a project, "not an inheritance" (Kaul 2009, 141). We are now invited much more urgently to realize the links between emancipation and epistemology involving "an overcoming of the conventional project of epistemology itself" (Kaul 2009, 234). For Kaul, "it is the pivotal ideals of [the] conventional epistemological project – objectivity, impartiality, universality – which will need reconstruction in order to move towards transformative emancipatory projects" (2009, 234). The present book does indeed seek to reconstitute these terms of discourse, for example heightening the need to transform the language of universality to a multiverse of transversality (Chapters Six and Seventeen).

This calls for dialogue. Knowledge and liberation in quest for the post-colonial cosmopolis involves intra-cultural, cross-cultural, transcultural dialogues and planetary conversations. It involves immersion in traditions of aspirations and struggles in different locations, an involvement which seems to be missing in much of contemporary theorizing whether it is post-colonial[24] or cosmopolitan. This calls for a new pedagogy, a pedagogy of the heart, in delving deeper into our traditions of thinking and realizations (Dallmayr 2007).

Creating Transformative Resonance

In nurturing liberatory projects of knowledge we find inspiration from many fellow seekers and travellers. Piet Strydom, whose work is discussed in the book, is an inspiring contemporary critical theorist who helps us to create conditions of transformative learning involving not only double contingency of subject and object but also the triple contingency of an ever-expanding and self-reflective public (Strydom 2009). He also discusses the way knowledge can create transformative resonance. I hope presentation of different aspects of transformative knowledge and reconstitution of existing terms of discourse of knowledge in this book will contribute to creating transformative resonance in striving for knowledge and human liberation. But this striving has to interrogate and transform another structure of resonance – what William Connolly calls "The Evangelical-Capitalist Resonance Machine" (2005). Connolly discusses this in the context of coming together of American Christian fundamentalists and the neo-liberal capitalists in the last quarter century of American religion, economy and politics. This resonance machine creates "resentment against cultural diversity, economic egalitarianism, and the future" (Connolly 2005, 879). This resonance machine is at work in other parts of the world as well as the fundamentalist-capitalist-resonance machine. In this context, a challenge for knowledge and human liberation is to interrogate and transform this fundamentalist-capitalist resonance machine, and the present book suggests ways of transforming religious fundamentalism through practical spirituality which also involves transformation of existing logic of capitalism. Readers will find a sympathetic affinity between ways discussed in the chapter on practical spirituality in the book and what Connolly writes about evangelical proponents of "Open Theism" in contemporary United States who contend that "the view of God as omnipotent – and omniscient – makes God complicit in evil" (Connolly 2005, 882). In this context, Open Theism expresses a "desire to replace a spirituality infused with revenge with one inspired by care for the fragility of the world" and "pray to a limited, loving God who learns as the world turns" (Connolly 2005, 882).

But this project of creating transformative resonance is not only a political project: it involves new experiments in body, mind and soul. Building upon his earlier work on neuro-politics which also involves an unspoken project on neuro-spirituality (see Chapter Nine where Connolly talks about the need for a new mysticism), Connolly tells us: "We should experiment cautiously with body techniques that then find expression in thought and feeling… Such strategies might include visualization, priming dreams by reviewing a perplexing issue before going to sleep, lucid dreaming – meditation, and neurotherapy" (Connolly 2006, 75). Connolly hopes that "as we move back and forth among experiential awareness, media studies, knowledge of body/brain processes, and subtle technologies of body / brain intervention [in Sri Aurodinbo it would be subtle technologies of body / brain transmutation through *Yoga*], we may also gain more insight into how to confront and counteract the politics of cultural revenge that exerts so much of power…today" (2006, 75).

Through such experiments we can "tap a latent reserve of compassion," in ourselves, "a reserve that finds expression in future conduct" (Connolly 2006, 73).[25] For Connolly, this is also pertinent to the "quality of ethical life" in our world today, especially paths of the ethical nurtured by savants such as Spinoza who "deny that goodness takes the form of obedience to universal law, as claimed in the dualist traditions of Augustine and Kant," helping us realize that "command-and-obedience models of morality too often contain within them a drive to revenge against the human condition, finding expression in punitive and accusatory orientations towards the diversity of life" (2006, 73). In place of revenge, Spinoza urges us to practice love.

There is a world-wide renewal of Spinoza now and in cultivating new paths of knowledge and human liberation we can draw inspiration from him. In our chapter on transforming power and politics we briefly discuss Spinoza, especially his work on power and multitude. Here we can also learn from an inspiring work on Spinoza by Chitta Ranjan Das, where he writes: "According to Spinoza, love is the mediating link between knowledge and power. Love of humanity, love of the world, a deep faith in the unending possibilities of individuals as well as the collectives. This calls for a higher consciousness which all knowledge should congenially aim at" (Das 2009, ix).

Spinoza helps us to understand the limits of both reason and religion realizing which is an important challenge before knowledge and human liberation today. This is highlighted in the recent works of Jürgen Habermas, especially in his debate with Cardinal Joseph Ratzinger (now Pope Benedict XVI) held on 19 January 2004 at the Catholic Academy in Munich in which both agree that: "Religions and secular rationalities need to engage in a mutual process of dialogue in order to learn from each other and to protect the planet from the destructive potential of the uncoupling of faith and reason" (Heythrop Institute 2005, 2).[26] Habermas and Ratzinger term this mutual need of faith and reason for each other a co-relationality. But Ratzinger and Habermas themselves state that the co-relationality between faith and reason in the modern world, although led by Christianity, needs to "engage other cultures and religions in order to become a polyphonic co-relationality capable of providing norms and values for a global world" (Heythrop Institute 2005, 2; see also Habermas 2008).

What is striking is that in this debate Habermas acknowledges the limits of secular rationality, such as the pathology of reason, while Ratzinger acknowledges the pathology of religion, as manifested in the recent link between religion and terrorism. But pathology of religion has a much deeper root, for example, in a one-dimensional exclusivity which does not acknowledge the *apophatic* character, i.e., "the ineffable character" of our human-divine existence and the "darkness enveloping it" (Wilfred 2008, 84).[27] While the divine cannot be bound in a systemic way, all religions including the self-proclaiming open-ended religions seek to bind it, making it an exclusivist site where Divine also becomes afraid to manifest Himself or Herself leading to what is called the hibernation of God in Jewish theology. This is a foundational pathology of religion which calls for continued spiritual awakening and self-development. Similarly the pathology of reason consists of its own exclusivity and it being a hand maiden of instrumental reason and reason of the state. For overcoming the pathology of reason, Habermas (2006, 5) pleads for a "complementary learning process" in which both people of faith and those of reason take part. In this learning process "true belief is not only a doctrine, believed content, but a source of energy that the person who has a faith taps performatively and thus nurtures his or her entire life" (2006, 9).

In this dialogue Habermas and the Pope urge us to realize that what is needed at the contemporary juncture is a "correlation of reason and faith, of reason and religion, both being summoned to mutual cleansing and healing." And in this task of cleansing and healing we can walk with and draw inspiration from not only Kant – who seems to be the primary source of inspiration for Habermasian critical theory – but also Spinoza, the philosopher who worked as a doctor of human affects and pleaded for more understanding beyond quick judgment. Spinoza stressed the significance of reason in religion and challenged us to go beyond superstition. Spinoza also sought to heal the split between "natural knowledge" and "divine knowledge" with ease. For Spinoza, "'natural knowledge' attainable by all human beings through the access of their own natural faculties is really equivalent to prophecy, namely, that unique communication of 'sure knowledge of some matter revealed by God to human beings'" (Bagley 2008, 15). As Das (2009, 157) presents us Spinoza's pathways of religion:

> Reason leads us to religion. Union with men by social piety raises us to feel the spirit of God... We can only unite with them as one among them. To know this, to know oneself *sub specie aeternitatis* leads us to the intellectual love of God. This love is Spinoza's religion, and its reward is beatitude. It is that state of faith which comes after complete understanding. This religion is also a modern necessity.

Knowledge, Human Liberation and a New Art of Integration

Overcoming pathologies of reason, religion and the wider society calls for a new art of healing and integration which is integral rather than totalitarian. It is an embodiment of a new art of wholeness[28] going beyond many of our destructive polarities and specialized fragmentations.[29] Modern knowledge, guided by critical rationality and democratic mobilizations, has challenged us to realize the significance of the horizontal. Habermas's communicative rationality is part of the much needed democratic transformation for horizontal dignity, justice and equality. Religions and spiritual quests have always challenged us not to forget the significance of the vertical and depth dimension[30] of our lives. But in traditional religion and spirituality the vertical has got imprisoned within many hierarchies of domination and it has also been accompanied by world-rejecting renunciation and flight from responsible and transformative engagement with the world. Ascent has rarely been accompanied by descent and horizontal solidarity with fellow beings. But knowledge, human relation and planetary realizations today call for a new art of integration of the vertical and the horizontal as part of an ever-evolving, expanding and mutually interpenetrative circle of the vertical and the horizontal.

This art of integration is, at the same time, an art of weak integration compared to the *telos* of strong integration in modern self, society and polity. The discourse of integration in sociology as well as in the wider public discourse in modernity, for example in the discourse of nationalism and self, has been imprisoned in a logic of strong integration which has been source of much violence, suffering and annihilation of potentiality. In this place we need to cultivate an art of weak integration, where integration begins with the realization of weakness and vulnerability and where this acknowledged vulnerability becomes the lubricant and binding thread for integration as an unfolding, evolving and emergent journey of realization of connectedness and wholeness animated by a transformative interpenetration of dynamic emptiness as well dynamic harmony. The objective is not valorization of strength or mastery, especially over others, but realization of weakness and weak strength as a companion to realize our common fate and our emergent shared potentiality. Knowledge, human liberation and planetary realizations need to cultivate an art of weak integration, building upon insights from critical theories of post-nationalism and developments such as weak naturalism, weak nationalism, weak epistemology, weak ontology, weak theology and weak pedagogy.[31]

This new art of weak integration calls for self-development and transformative intellectual, social, political and spiritual mobilizations. Here we can draw upon not only seekers such as Benedict Spinoza but also Dara Shukoh, who four hundred years ago embodied the art of crossing borders. Dara Shukoh was the eldest son of Shah Jahan and translated the Upanishads into Persian. He explored common sources of both the Upanishads and the Quran, urging us to realize the "commingling of two oceans" which angered the priests as well as the Emperor to be. He was killed by Aurangzeb (Dara Shukoh 2006, also see Gandhi 2010). But in his meditations

Dara Shukoh challenges us to realize that friendship is the most important marker of a seeker of knowledge (1912).[32] This resonates with some thoughts I was shared in my recent fieldwork in Kandhamal, Odisha in Janauary 2009 where an erstwhile follower of Rastriya Swayam Sevak Sangh said that the highest religion is the religion of friendship (see. Giri 2009b). The contemporary challenge of knowledge, human liberation and planetary realization is to realize these fields as fields of friendship even as they are continuously challenged by hatred and enmity. This also urges us to be *bhikhus – gyanabhikhus, premabhikhus, jeevanabhikhus* and *viswabhikhus*.[33]

But these fields of life and knowledge implicit in it have become barren and have become graveyards of destruction of potential – individual, social as well as planetary. In this context, we need to make our grounds of knowledge and life fertile again by being earthworms ourselves.[34] We also need to tend the garden of transformational knowledge with care and courage as gardeners.[35] But we also need to develop what Peter Sloterdijk calls "avicultural skills," grow wings and become birds.[36] Being birds such as swans which can simultaneously walk on earth, swim in water and fly in the sky would help us come out of our fixation with one location and consequent exclusionary and annihilating absolutism which is a source of much violence and suffering today. Knowledge, human liberation and planetary realizations call for a new realization of human beings as simultaneously earthworms, human and swans. In cultivating fields of knowledge, human liberation and planetary realizations, embodying the spirit of multi-valued ontological epistemology of participation of the book we would have to be simultaneously earthworms, gardeners and swans nurturing the soil, making it fertile,[37] tending the garden and flying out from isolation and bondage in quest of a new poetics, politics, spirituality of knowledge, human liberation and planetary realizations.

Notes

1 Nicolaus of Cusa (1401–1464), a seeker of the inspiring pathway of what he called "knowing unknowledge" or "learned ignorance" writes: "I want to tell you that wisdom cries out in the streets, and her very cry indicates how she dwells 'in the highest'" (quoted in Dallmayr 2007, 61).

2 C. F. Andrews came as an Anglican priest to India in 1905 and got closely involved with the creative works of Rabindranath Tagore at Visvabharati, Santiniketan as well as with the freedom struggle of India. He was a close friend of Gandhi. Andrews had travelled to many parts of the world – South Africa, Fiji and others – to express his solidarity with indentured Indians and struggling laborers. He was a great "bridge builder" (see Chaturvedi and Sykes 1949; Visvanathan 2007).

3 A poem by the author, originally written in Odia and translated below, presents such a view of the birth of new languages from the lap of intimate and meditative solidarity:

I

Oh friend
You said
We need a new language
A new *sadhana* of words and *tapasya* of worlds
This is not a language of victory

Nor is one of self-advertisement and aggrandizement
Neither is it a language of doomsday
This is a language of walking our ways together
Walking our dreams, *sadhana* and struggle

II

In our co-habitations of affection
Of compassion and confrontation
Words become *mantras*
Of a new life, a new responsibility
Of wiping tears from our eyes and
Again taking each other into our laps
Renewing our strength from embrace
We create new paths by walking
We create new language
Our language is the language of walking
Stars of *mantras* leap from our lap

4 In his essay, "Language: A Medium of Expansion of Heart," written more that half a century ago, Chittaranjan Das suggests some pathways in this direction.

5 For example, Habitat for Humanity is a Christian socio-religious movement in the US which builds houses with the help of volunteers for low-income families in many communities in the US and worldwide. Habitat for Humanity interrogates the existing language of homeownership in the US, for example the existing cultural logic that homeowners are morally superior to the renters (see Giri 2002b). It strives to create a new language of home as the altar of God and builds houses with what it calls "the theology of the hammer."

6 In his recent book on Biswantha Patnaik, the leader of the land Satyagraha movement in Orissa, Chittaranjan Das asks whether Sarvodaya and constructive works are mere words (Das 2009, 16): "Are these only words?" Das also tells us how in the course of this movement new terms such as Jivanadana proliferated and slowly people tended to substitute such words for concrete social transformations and transformation in relationships.

7 Society in modernity has been conceptualized in terms of the nation-state, which is built upon annihilation of multiple languages existing in the space of the nation-state and violent enthronement of one single language as the official language of the nation-state.

8 John Clammer (1976) talks about social Wittgensteinianism as a "pseudo-sociology" based on the "insight that ordinary language embodies or reflects social usages, culture and belief."

9 Even now there is little effort to walk with both Heidegger and Wittgenstein together in thinking about language and social practice though there are remarkable exceptions such as Luchte (2011) and Rorty (1991). In the international seminar on "Language, Mind and Social Construction" at the Department of Humanities and Social Sciences, Indian Institute of Technology, Mumbai in February 2009, while there were many papers presenting Wittgenstein's views on language there was not even a single paper presented on the meditations on language of either Heidegger or Sri Aurobindo.

10 What Heidegger writes in his essay, "Way to Language" deserves our careful attention: "*What unfolds essentially in language is saying as pointing*. Its showing does not culminate in a system of signs. Rather, all signs arise from a showing in whose realm and for whose purposes they can be signs" (Heidegger 2004, 410). Furthermore, "What is peculiar to language thus conceals itself on the way, the way by which the saying lets those who listen to it get to the language" (Heidegger 2004, 413). For Heidegger, "the way to language is the...way-making movement of propriation and usage" where "propriation propriates human beings

for itself… propriation is thus the saying's way-making movement toward language" (2004, 418, 419):

> What looks more like a tangle than a weft loosens when viewed in terms of the way-making movement. It resolves into the liberating notion that the way-making movement exhibits when propriated in saying. It unbinds the saying for speech. It holds open the way for speech, the way on which speaking as hearing, hearing the saying, registers what in each is case is to be said, elevating what it receives to the resounding word. The saying's way-making movement to language is the unbinding bond, the bond that binds by propriating. (Heidegger 2004, 419)

What Heidegger speaks about language as "saying" and "way-making movement" is suggested in the tradition of people's enlightenment in Europe, namely the folk high school movement and people's enlightenment patiently cultivated by Grundtvig and Kristen Kold. Both of them challenged us to realize language as "living words" – words that could enliven and energize us. This is also akin to Sri Aurobindo's suggestion to create poems which would work like *mantra*.

11 In this context, what Luchte (2011) writes below deserves our careful attention and further realization, especially the Heideggerian notion of ecstatic temporality as the womb of birth of a new language and society:

> …this is then what Heidegger means by *world*, a thrown projection of binding commitments which has it root in ecstatic temporality and the events of world projection. We can see traces of this root most readily in Heidegger's indication of existential spatiality… Yet his *existentials* are not merely arbitrary as they themselves arose amidst the projection of world, in its meaning and its morphology. In this way, various conventional names Heidegger chose, such as *Sorge* or *Schulde*, would be seen to contain the historicity of such names as they themselves were originally projected amid an anticipatory resolution, of an individuation, or better a singularization – a creative rule-breaking, transgression of the rule of the conventional (the prevailing restricted economy) in an expression of innovation in the grammar of existence.

12 Sri Aurobindo in his *Life Divine* talks about a nobler pragmatism "guided, uplifted and enlightened by spiritual culture and knowledge" (1970). In his *Human Cycles* Sri Aurobindo also talks about spiritual vitalism. Sri Aurobindo also urges us to look at language as *mantra* and cultivate the *mantra* dimension of language. This urges us to go beyond a simplistic view of language as reflection of society. This resonates with Martin Heidegger's conception of language as way-making movement.

13 Veena Das, building upon Stanley Cavell, shares some insightful reflections here:

> When anthropologists have evoked the idea of forms of life, it has often been to suggest the importance of thick description, local knowledge or what it is to learn a rule. For Cavell [Stanely Cavell, the noted contemporary philosopher] *such conventional views of the idea of form of life eclipse the spiritual struggle of his [Wittgenstein's] investigations.* What Cavell finds wanting in this conventional view of forms of life is that it not only obscures the mutual absorption of the natural and the social but also emphasizes *form* at the expense of *life*… the vertical sense of the form of life suggests the limit of what or who is recognized as human within a social form and provides the conditions of the use of criteria as applied to others. Thus the criteria of pain do not apply to that which does not exhibit signs of being a form of *life* – we do not ask whether a tape recorder that can be turned on to play a shriek is feeling the pain. The distinction between the horizontal and vertical axes of forms of life takes us at least to the point at

which we can appreciate not only the security provided by belonging to a community with shared agreements but also the dangers that human beings pose to each other. These dangers relate to not only disputation over *forms* but also what constitutes *life*. The blurring between what is human and what is not human sheds into blurring over what is life and what is not life. (Das 2007, 15–16, emphasis added)

In her recent work, Das applies Wittgenstein's insight in his statement, "An entire mythology is stored within our language" (see Das 2011, 240) in understanding moral and spiritual strivings on the parts of Muslims of India in their everyday lives. In language in the scriptures like Quran, Hindu *sastras* and also in everyday life, there is an entire mythology stored which helps the practitioners to go beyond their religious and scriptural boundaries and relate to the others. For Das:

> I suggest that the…terms at hand such as *bhagwan*, and *khuda* which travel easily in the speech of Hindus and Muslims and are deployable in both formal and informal contexts, make it possible to imagine the practices of the other and to get on with the daily commerce of living together. Further the thought that Wittgenstein's space of a whole mythology being buried in our language should be understood to include the history of concepts, words and gestures not only as rooted within a tradition but also in the manner in which they travel and become nomadic. For instance, Iqbal Mian [a person in Das's dialogical ethnography] prides himself as one who uses *aql*, or reasoning, and thus tells me often that it is his obligation as a Muslim to understand other religions. According to one *hadith* (a saying of the Prophet) he has heard, a Mulim must tell others about the glories of Islam, but he cannot do without understanding what others hold dear in their own religion. (2011, 240)

Das shares with us such moral strivings faced by Muslims in their everyday lives:

> …how do I cultivate morality as a dimension of everyday life, when certain forms of knowing (e.g. that Hindus are characterized as *Kafirs*, as nonbelievers) somehow contradict my feelings that there are forms of being together that I can come to experience as part of my ordinary life that I wish to acknowledge but for which I should not be required to give justifications. (Das 2011, 233)

Das further writes:

> But there is a dimension in everyday life that cannot be derived from a reflection on well-honed concepts but combines different fragments from the past, improvisation on concepts that simply 'at hand,' in Wittgenstein's terms. This is neither a story of secularism nor of syncretism but rather one in which the heterogeneity of everyday life allows Hindus and Muslims to receive the claims of each other that have arisen by the sheer fact of proximity, face to face relations, and the privileging of aesthetic immediacy of emotions even over the prohibitions emanating from various authoritative discourses of Hinduism and Islam. (2011, 248)

14 In the Indian context, it challenges us to transform Brahminical exclusion of knowledge and create a new dialectic of self-realization where Brahmins and Dalits help each other to be seekers of both labor and knowledge together (see Giri 2002a). It also challenges us to overcome the exclusionary division between the expert and the layperson in practices of knowledge. Here we can build upon rich traditions of lay wisdom in pathways of the world especially in Nicolaus Cusa's the *Layman on Wisdom*, where a poor untutored layman meets in the Roman Forum a very wealthy orator whom he addresses courteously (a manner reminiscent of Socrates in the marketplace): "I am quite amazed at your pride, for even though you have

worn yourself out with the continual study of innumerable books, yet you have not been moved to humility" (quoted in Dallmayr 2007, 60). This lay tradition is characterized not only by humility but also by a "pathos of immediacy: the immediacy of concrete experience as contrasted with the mere book learning and a purely scholastic treatment of real life" and "speaking and writing in a simple vernacular idiom" (Dallmayr 2007, 61).

15 Derrida referring to Bentham's question vis-à-vis animals "Can they suffer?" writes: "the question is not to know whether the animal can think, reason or speak, etc., something we still pretend to be asking ourselves (from Aristotle to Descartes, from Descartes, especially, to Heidegger, Levinas, and Lacan)…but rather to know whether animals *can suffer*" (Derrida 2008, 27).

16 What Mannheim wrote nearly three quarters of a century ago seems prophetic today:

> Nor is it by chance that the outlook which brings together the social and the cognitive spheres emerges in a time in which the greatest exertion of mankind once more consists in the attempt to counteract the tendency of an individualistic undirected society, which is verging toward anarchy, with a more organic type of social order. In such a situation there must arise a general sense of interdependence – of the interdependence which bonds the single experience to the stream of experience of single individuals and these in turn to the fabric of the wider community of experience and activity. Thus, the newly arising theory of knowledge too is an attempt to take account of the rootedness of knowledge in the social texture. In it a new sort of life-orientation is at work, seeking to stay the alienation and disintegration which arose out of the exaggeration of the individualistic and mechanistic attitude. (1936, 29–30)

17 As Mannheim (1936, 20) writes: "The world of external objects and psychic experience appears to be in a continuous flux. Verbs are more adequate symbols for this situation than nouns." And as Elizabeth Kamarack Minnich tells us in her *Transforming Knowledge*: "We have also begun to see what turning nouns into verb forms – 'race' into 'racializing,' 'gender' into 'gendering' – may be able to do for us. Perhaps it may help us remember human agency (and so responsibility) by focusing our attention not on static things, products, abstractions but, rather, on the processes, histories, and complexly interlacing systems that create and sustain so much of our world" (Minnich 2007, 11).

We may also note here that in different philosophical, cultural and spiritual traditions, body, mind and Being are considered verbs. As Tu Wei-ming writes about body in Chinese culture and philosophy: "There's a beautiful term, *ti*, which means the body. But, that word, *ti*, can also be used as a verb. It means just my body, but also to embody. The embodiment is a process of understanding other human beings experientially as well as intellectually and spiritually" (Wei-ming 2000, 50). In his *Art and Experience*, John Dewey also writes about mind: "Mind is primarily a verb" (quoted in Elbridge 2000, 244–5). And theologian and philosopher Raimon Panikkar writes about Being: "Being is a verb, an action, and it has rhythm" (Panikkar 1995, 26). About the meaning of Being in Arabic, Lenn E. Goodman writes: "Being in Arabic is *Kawn*. Given the verbal force typical in Arabic nouns derived from verbs, the word develops the connotation of 'becoming,' in Plato's sense of coming to be *genesis*… Its Aristotelian opposite is *fasad*, corruption, again with verbal force, meaning, rotting, waiting, decomposing" (Goodman 2003).

18 In his engagement with knowledge Boaventura de Sousa Santos (2007) presents a notion of "action-with-*clinamen*." He borrows from "Epicurus and Lucretius the concept of *clinamen*, understood as the inexplicable 'quiddam' that upsets the relations of cause and effect, that is to say, the swerving capacity attributed by Epicurus to Democritus' atoms. The *clinamen* is what makes the atoms cease to appear inert and rather be invested with a power of inclination, a creative power, that is, a power of spontaneous movement" (2007, 40–41).

Santos further writes: "Unlike what happens in revolutionary action, the creativity of action-with-*clinamen* is not based on a dramatic break but rather on a slight swerve or deviation whose cumulative effects render possible the complex and creative combinations among atoms, hence also living beings and social groups" (2007, 40–41). This view of action with energy also needs to cultivate knowledge as action with meditation which in turn calls for further cross-cultural work on action, meditation and modes of energization.

19 For Béteille, an ideological approach to reality tends to present an absolutist picture, while sociology and social anthropology present us plural standpoints: "there is no one unique or privileged standpoint in the study of society and culture. Even within the same society there generally is a plurality of standpoints, varying with religion, class, gender or moral and intellectual predilection, and besides different outsiders may view the same society from different standpoints. Sociology and social anthropology cannot move forward unless the plurality of standpoints is accepted as a fundamental condition for the systematic and comparative study of society and culture. But it is one thing to acknowledge the value of, say, studying marriage from the standpoint of a woman, or discrimination from that of a *dalit*, and quite another to have the standpoint itself defined by a particular agenda" (2009, 210). Yet each of these standpoints is partial though they may claim absolutism on its behalf. Béteille would agree with this. But realizing the partial nature of one's standpoint and realizing that one's standpoint is interpenetrated or needs to be interpenetrated by others' standpoint calls for further work on self-transformation, ontological transformation and transformation of one's one-dimensional epistemology and politics. This calls for a multi-dimensional *sadhana* of multi-valued logic. Each of these standpoints is partly true and also not partly true. Moreover, each of these standpoints is also interpenetrated by the standpoint of others. For example, a Dalit standpoint on society is interpenetrated by Brahminical standpoint in the ontology of reality as a field which holds both the Dalits and Brahmins together even though both of them may deny that their standpoint is interpenetrated by the other. Similar is the situation vis-à-vis the standpoint of man and woman about society. While this is an aspect of reality which has attracted attention, our epistemological construction of it is often one-dimensional, something fuelled by an uncritical and one-dimensional commitment to a single political ideology. In this context, there needs to be communication among these plural standpoints. How do we pluralize our plural standpoints which at the levels of self, ideology and even sociological method, present themselves in a singular and exclusionary way? Pluralizing plural standpoints calls for generosity and expansion of points of view on the part of both participants and observers which is not necessarily suggested in the sociological method as it is prevalent today. This calls for spiritual work on self, method, accepting others and realizing the limits of self and one's standpoint. While Béteille helps us in understanding the limits of ideology in realizing our integral and inevitable human and social condition of pluralities, we are also challenged to probe further the limits of sociology in undertaking pluralization as a multi-dimensional process of self-becoming and social realization involving acceptance of the partial nature of one's standpoint and embracing the other (see Giri 2011).

20 Recently the philosopher Heike Kampf (2009) talks about historicization of epistemology and ontology. Ontological epistemology of participation involves historicization of both epistemology and ontology.

21 It is enriching here to think about Partha Chatterjee's recent genealogical investigation of modern normative political theory what he calls "Lineages of Political Society" (2009). Chatterjee uses lineage as a method in Foucault's genealogical sense, but like Foucault presents a unitary view of modern knowledge, in this case modern normative political theory, without exploring the plurality of streams of contestation within this constructed single field of normative theory. For example, in this normative space everybody did not justify colonialism as exception to the norm of normative political theory. Chatterjee seems

to have a singular notion of norm such as representative democracy but this single theme itself hides a plurality of streams, not to speak of well-known tension among equality, liberty and fraternity. Methodologically, lineage as an approach seeks to go beyond linearity, but this is deployed much more to tell multiples stories from "most of the world" rather than multiple streams of normative struggles, social mobilizations and contestations from the Euro-American world. The language of lineage is used to construct a linear and one-dimensional object of critique, in this case the "mythical space of" normative political theory but the object of critique has also a lineage of plurality as the historical experience of "most of the world" from which such a critique is being launched. Probably we need a new genealogical method which is equally generous to the lineages of plurality in all parts of the world and not only in colonized and post-colonial societies. This aspiration is also suggested in my cultivated pathway of a post-colonial cosmopolis in the last chapter of the book.

22 In the words of Santos: "Projects are an anticipation of reality and as such imply distance from current experience. This anticipation and distance has a specific temporality, the temporality of a bridge among noncontemporaneous courses of action through aspiration and desire. The fallacy of false contemporaneity…makes such a bridge a useless device, thus turning aspiration into conformism and desire into the desire of confirmism" (2001, 266).

23 Jack Kornfield (2000, 162) talks about the "Mandala of Awakening."

24 Partha Chatterjee envisions the challenges before "post-colonial political theory" thus: "The first is the challenge to break the abstract homogeneity of the mythical time-space of Western normative theory… The second is the even greater challenge to redefine the normative standards of modern politics in the light of the considerable accumulation of new practices [from colonial and post-colonial societies as well as from the Euro-American world]" (2009, 23). But this project does not explicitly realize the need for cross-cultural dialogue. Furthermore, this does not include the challenge of understanding and learning languages of normative thinking in traditions such as those which exist in India. For example it is said that King Janaka, father of Sita, nurtured his people as a mother. Learning much more about such languages of governance would bring new enrichment and imagination to post-colonial political and social theorizing. But how is it possible when our post-colonial advocates mostly interact with knowledge emerging from the Euro-American world and rarely go inside other traditions of thinking and realizations? The possible significance of nurturing one's subjects as a mother is explored in the following poem:

> King Janaka nurtured
> His People as a mother
> And Could not our Janakas—
> Our fathers in politics, family and religion
> Nurture us as mothers?
> Could not God and His arrogant servants
> Be a Manifestation of Creative Motherhood
> And our state and society
> A Flow of Motherhood
> In place of the machinery of violence
> > A Flow of Compassion and Transformation.

(Extracts from a poem in Odia written and translated by the author.)

25 Recent collaboration between neuroscientists and spiritual practitioners such as the Dalai Lama and his followers shows us how creative work with mind makes brain much more porous and open to transformations. See Begley (2007).

26 It must be noted that even many contemporary sociologists are talking about the emergence of a postsecular society and modernity in Europe. Consider here what Klaus Eder writes: "Secular modernity only interfered in favour of the secular claims on values and truth. It does not replace reason by belief, but it forces believers and non-believers to talk in public about their reciprocal claims and critiques. This is the only way to order an equally poly-theistic as poly-atheistic world. It requires institutions without an exclusive claim of truth. This postsecular modernity has to recognize the legitimacy of continuing dissensus on secular principles as well as on religious beliefs and it has at the same time to tame the dissension and turn it into a creative consensus" (2007, 14–15).

27 Creative theologian and social philosopher Felix Wilfred (2008) thus cultivates the paths of *apophatic* theology which finds a correspondence in paths of *apophatic* anthropology nurtured by Ivan Illich: "Apophatic anthropology is the rigor of not talking about God, but actually living as Christ enfleshed has done" (Schroyer 2009, 57). This finds a resonance with the new relationship between faith and knowledge articulated by Jürgen Habermas (2003) which primarily revolves around creative practice. See the subsequent discussion of Habermas in the succeeding paragraphs of this book.

28 In my current work on wholeness I am exploring a new logic of wholeness which realizes that the quest for as well as the field of wholeness acknowledge the many holes in our lives and building on these holes strives towards an emergent wholeness which is contingent and not closed (see Giri 2009a).

29 Specialized knowledge has the power of concentration but transformative knowledge, while acknowledging its necessity, understands its limitations and moves from fragments to emergent wholeness. In this context, what Schiller wrote long ago is full of challenging insights: "Thus, however much the world as a whole may benefit through this fragmentary specialization of human powers, it cannot be denied that the individuals affected by it suffer under the curse of this cosmic purpose. Athletic bodies can, it is true, be developed by gymnastic exercises; beauty only through the free and harmonious play of the limbs. In the same way the keying up of individual functions of the mind can indeed produce extraordinary human beings; but only the equal tempering of them all, happy and complete human beings... *It must, therefore, be wrong if the cultivation of individual powers involves the sacrifice of wholeness*" (Schiller 1982, 43). Schiller also urges us to realize that in modernity State stands for a Whole and we are chained to it as a fragment. What Schiller writes below can help us understand our predicament of fragmentariness, from which our quest for a new art of wholeness begins:

> Everlastingly chained to a single little fragment of the Whole, man himself develops into nothing but the little fragment; everlastingly in his ear the monotonous sound of the wheel he turns, he never develops harmony of his being, and instead of putting the stamp of humanity upon his own nature, he becomes nothing more than the imprint of his occupation or of his specialized knowledge. But even that meager, fragmentary participation, by which individual members of the State are still linked to the Whole, does not depend upon forms which they spontaneously prescribe for themselves...it is dictated to them with meticulous exactitude by means of a formulary which inhibits all freedom of thought. The dead letter takes the place of living understanding..." (Schiller 1982, 35)

We can here think together Schiller's reference to dead letter and Grundtvig's plea for living words.

30 In a recent insightful work philosopher A. Raghuramraju discusses the work of philosopher Chandidas on desire, knowledge and liberation and tells us how Chandidas accords a primary importance to depth dimension in liberation by which he means "routes of intensification" (Raghuramraju 2009, 132). Intensification is also close to concentration.

31 Weak naturalism as a companion in quest for weak integration helps us realize that we are part of nature but we are not determined by it and we should eschew the arrogance of human mastery and social control. This is accompanied by weak nationalism, which interrogates the construction of the nation-state as a naturalized entity propagating the cult of unitary strength at the expense of the plurivocity of beings, societies, languages, nations and cultures. Weak epistemology in this journey makes our epistemic certainty humble and urges us to realize the limits of methods in our scientific understanding as well as social life. All these are accompanied by weak ontology which urges us to realize that ontological cultivation is not only a cultivation of mastery of the self but also cultivation of its humility, fragility, weakness and servanthood facilitating blossoming of non-sovereignty and shared sovereignties (see Vattimo 1999). Weak theology as a companion in this quest for weak integration makes theology weak rather than strong, which then facilitates border crossing and dialogues between religions and theological systems. Weak theology is also facilitated by the rise of practical spirituality in religions which relativize pronounced religious beliefs and dogmas and lay stress on practice, especially transformative practice, to transform social suffering. Finally weak pedagogy helps us realize that if the project of realizing good society is a pedagogic one then as educators we cannot perpetuate the logic of strength by imposing our views on others, especially on children, and treating fellow participants and citizens as children, but must persuade them to take part in collective transformative co-learning where as educators we realize, as Sri Aurobindo challenges us to realize, that "nothing can be taught."

32 Writes Dara Shukoh:

> There is no asceticism in it, everything is easy, gracious and a free gift... Even the blessed Prophet used to call his disciples by the words companions and friends. And there was no mention of *Piri* and *Muridi* (Teacher and Disciple) between them. Therefore, whenever, in this book there occurs the word "friend," understand by it the seeker of God. (Dara Shukoh 1912, 5)

Earlier in the text, while discussing the work of Connolly, we had discussed about new possibilities for self-realization and political transformation opened by new meditative experiments with mind and body. What Dara Shukoh also writes in this book helps us understanding the link between knowledge, meditation and compassion:

> Anyone whose heart has become refined, and has awakened, sees in this world... beautiful and refined forms, hears exquisite music... But he whose heart is burdened with coarseness, and is unawakened (on the higher), sees ugly forms, and hears disgusting sounds... And he does not see anything but what exists on the physical plane...
>   Therefore, O Friend! Thou shalt practise with diligence and perseverance, the methods of meditation...the rust from thy heart will be removed, and the mirror of thy soul will become bright... (Dara Shukoh 1912, 5)

33 The Buddha has urged us to be *bhikhus*. But what is the meaning of being a *bhikhu* today? Does it mean to be a beggar? Given the negative connotation of the word begging, we have to first transform the language of begging and make it a movement of seeking. To be a *bhikhu* today is to be a seeker, a wanderer but not necessarily with a different robe and a bowl in hand. We become *gyanabhikhus*, seekers of knowledge, *premabhikhus*, seekers of love, *jeevanabhikhus*, seekers of life, and *viswabhikhus*, seekers of the world and the cosmos.

34 Socrates thought of himself as a gadfly. I submit that we need to realize ourselves as earthworms, making our fields of relationship even with powers that be more fertile and thus capable of new beginning. There is an epochal need for cross-fertilization now. In his reflection on Grundtvig, the inspiring founder of the folk high school movement in Denmark,

Fernando (2000) writes that Grundtvig worked towards people's education where one part of the society could fertilize the other. This work of fertilization and cross-fertilization is an epochal need today as there is so much exclusion all around and so little cross-fertilization. We need to be earthworms in order to fertilize and cross-fertilize ourselves, others and society.

35 During a recent discussion R. Kumaran, who teaches Sociology at Gandhigram Rural Institute, Dindigul, Tamil Nadu, very insightfully commented on the distinction between farmer and gardener. While the farmer tends to weed out the so-called unnecessary plants, the gardener tends to nurture all plants in the garden with care. Rationalist gardening in modernity however, as Stephen Toulmin (2001) would caution us, tends to make gardening too planned and it too tends to weed out the so-called unnecessary plants.

36 Anthropologist Evans-Pritchard (1940) tells us how the Nuer think of human children as simultaneously human and birds. M. N. Srinivas, the distinguished student of Evans-Pritchard, writes that among the Coorgs in South India it is believed that a cobra during the last phase of his life "develop wings" (Srinivas 2003, 168). Instead of treating it as irrational and drawing lessons from philosopher Sloterdijk as well as the spiritual traditions of humanity, we need to consider ourselves as simultaneously humans and birds. To this I would also add earthworms. If Connolly talks about experience and experiment, we need to engage ourselves in new creative experiments of imagining ourselves as earthworms, human and swans. In a spirit of planetary realizations we can also place ourselves in the positions of our non-human fellow beings and realize what it is like to be an earthworm or a bird or a snake. We can also engage ourselves in creative experiments of realizing ourselves as five elements of the universe such as earth, air, water, fire and sky. If the recent coming together of neuroscience and spirituality gives us transformative possibilities in new experiments, in undertaking an experiment where we feel like water, fire, air, earthworms and swans would help us overcome our anthropocentric fixation and move towards planetary realizations. My friend and co-traveler Professor Subhash Sharma, who is the dean of the Indus Business Academy, Bangalore and Greater Noida, is doing some such experiments with the name of what he calls osmotic meditation (see Sharma 2009).

37 Making the soil of our land, life and relationships fertile calls for cross-species collaboration and also grace from Nature and the Divine, especially as we seem to have come to a point of desertification of our land. Global warming is symbolic of the barrenness of our soil and to overcome this we need new initiatives, meditations and struggles as well as the co-work and grace of Nature and the Divine.

References

Begley, Sharon. 2007. *Train Your Mind, Change Your Brain: How a New Science Reveals Our Extraordinary Potential to Transform Ourselves.* New York: Balantine.

Béteille, Andre. 2009. "Sociology and Ideology." *Sociological Bulletin* 58 (2): 196–211.

Chatterjee, Patha. 2004. *The Politics of the Governed: Reflections on Popular Politics in Most of the World.* Delhi: Permanent Black.

———. 2009 "Lineages of Political Society." Founder's Day Lecture, Madras Institute of Development Studies, 3 April.

Chaturvedi, Badrinath and Marjorie Sykes. 1949. *Charles Freer Andrews: A Narrative.* Delhi: Government of India, Publications Division.

Clammer, John. 1976. "Wittgensteinianism and the Social Sciences." *Sociological Review* 24 (4): 25–35.

Connolly, William E. 2005. "The Evangelical-Capitalist Resonance Machine." *Political Theory* 33 (6): 869–86.

———. 2006 "Experience and Experiment." *Daedalus* (Summer): 67–75.

Dallmayr, Fred. 2007. *In Search of Good Life: A Pedagogy for Our Troubled Times*. Lexington: University of Kentucky Press.

_____. "The Return of Philosophical Anthropology." In Ananta Kumar Giri and John Clammer, eds, *Philosophy and Anthropology: Border-Crossing and Transformations*. London: Anthem Press. Forthcoming.

Dara Shukoh, Muhammed. 1912. *The Compass of Truth or Risala-In-Haq-Numa*. Allahabad: The Panini Office.

_____. 2006. *Majma-Ul-Bahrain: Commingling of Two Oceans*. Gurgaon: Hope India Publications.

Das, Chittaranjan. 2009. *Benedict Spinoza: An Appreciation*. Delhi: Shipra.

Das, Veena. 2003. "Social Sciences and the Public." In *Oxford India Encyclopaedia of Sociology and Social Anthropology*. Delhi: Oxford University Press.

_____. 2007. *Life and Words: Violence and the Descent into the Ordinary*. Berkeley: University of California Press.

_____. 2011. "Moral and Spiritual Striving in the Everyday: To Be a Muslim in Contemporary India." In Anand Pandian and Daud Ali, eds, *Ethical Life in South Asia*, 232–52. Delhi: Oxford University Press.

Derrida, Jacques. 2008. *The Animal That Therefore I Am*. New York: Fordham University Press.

Dewey, John. 1927. *The Public and Its Problems*. New York: Henry Holt & Co.

Eder, Klaus. 2007. "Secularization, Desecularization and the Emergence of a Postsecular Modernity: Making Sense of the Religious Field in Europe." Seminar paper, Humboldt University, Berlin.

Elbridge, Richard. 2000. "Dewey's Aesthetics." In M. Cochran, ed., *Cambridge Companion to John Dewey*. Cambridge: Cambridge University Press.

Ferreira, Francisco. 2006. *Towards a New Politics: What Future for the World Social Forum?* New Delhi: Vasudhaiba Kutumbakam.

Foucault, Michel. 1972. *The Archaeology of Knowledge and the Discourse on Language*. London: Tavistock.

_____. 1980. *Power / Knowledge: Selected Interviews and Other Writings*, ed. Colin Gordon. London: Harvester Press.

_____. 2005. *Hermeneutics of the Subject: Lectures at the College de France, 1981–82*. New York: Palgrave.

Gandhi, Gopal. 2010. *Dara Shukoh: A Play*. Chennai: Tranquebar.

Giri, Ananta Kumar. 1998. *Global Transformations: Postmodernity and Beyond*. Jaipur: Rawat Publications.

_____. 2002a *Conversations and Transformations: Towards a New Ethics of Self and Society*. Lanham, MD: Lexington Books.

_____. 2002b *Building in the Margins of Shacks: The Vision and Projects of Habitat for Humanity*. Delhi: Orient Longman.

_____. 2009a *Learning the Art of Wholeness: Integral Education and Beyond*. Draft report submitted to the Indian Council of Social Science Research.

_____. 2009b "Peace in Kandhamal." *Mainstream* 47 (19).

_____. 2012 "With and Beyond Plurality of Standpoints: Sociology and the *Sadhana* of Multi-Valued Logic and Living." In *Sociology and Beyond: Windows and Horizons*. Jaipur: Rawat Publications.

Goodman, Lenn. 2003. *Islamic Humanism*. New York: Oxford University Press.

Habermas, Jürgen. 2003. "Faith and Knowledge." In *Future of Human Nature*. Cambridge: Polity Press.

_____. 2006. "Religion in the Public Sphere." *European Journal of Philosophy* 14 (1): 1–25.

_____. 2008. *Between Naturalism and Religion*. Cambridge: Polity Press.

Heidegger, Martin. 2004. "The Way to Language." In *Basic Writings*. London: Routledge.

Kampf, Heike. "The Engagement of Philosophy and Anthropology in the Interpretive Turn and Beyond: Towards an Anthropology of the Contemporary." In Ananta Kumar Giri and John Clammer, eds, *Philosophy and Anthropology: Border-Crossing and Transformations*. London: Anthem Press. Forthcoming.

Kaul, Nitasha. 2008. *Imagining Economics Otherwise: Encounters with Identity / Difference*. London: Routledge.

Luchte, James. 2011. "Under the Aspect of Time: Heidegger, Wittgenstein and the Place of Nothing." This builds upon his earlier article in *Philosophy Today* in Spring 2008 and was retrieved from http://luchte.wordpress.com/under-the-aspect-of-time/ (accessed 3 January 2013).

Mannheim, Karl. 1936/1979. *Ideology and Utopia: An Introduction to the Sociology of Knowledge*. London: Routledge and Kegan Paul.

Marquez, Ivan. "Reconceiving Education and the Humanities: New Approaches to Old Questions." In Ananta Kumar Giri, ed., *Pathways of Creative Research: Towards a Festival of Dialogues*. Forthcoming.

Neilson, Brett. 2009. "Cultural Studies and Giorgio Agamben." In Gary Hall and Clare Birchall, eds, *New Cultural Studies: Adventures in Theory*, 128–45. Hyderabad: Orient BlackSwan.

Panikkar, Raimon. 1995. *A Dwelling Place for Wisdom*. Delhi: Motilal Banarasidass.

Raghuramaraju, A. 2009. *Enduring Colonialism: Classical Presences and Modern Absences in Indian Philosophy*. Delhi: Oxford University Press.

Santos, Boaventura de Sousa. 2001. "Towards an Epistemology of Blindness: Why the New Forms of 'Ceremonial Adequacy' Neither Regulate Nor Emancipate." *European Journal of Social Theory* 4 (3): 251–79.

_____. 2007 "Beyond Abyssal Thinking: From Global Lines to Ecologies of Knowledges." Text of the essay retrieved from the web which was published in *Review* 30 (1): 45–89.

Schroyer, Trent. 2009. "Illich's Genealogy of Modern Certitudes." In *Beyond Western Economics*. London: Routledge.

Sharma, Subhash. 2009. "Osmotic Meditation: A New Tool for Stress Management and Mind Expansion." *3D: IBA Journal of Management and Leadership* 1 (1).

Singh, Balmiki Prasad. 2008. *Bahudha and the Post 9/11 World*. Delhi: Oxford University Press.

Sri Aurobindo. 1972. *Birth Century Library: Set in 30 volumes – Volume 17: The Hour of God and Other Writings*. Pondicherry: Sri Aurobindo Asram.

Srinivas, M. N. 1952/2003. *Religion and Society among the Coorgs of South India*. Delhi: Oxford University Press.

Strydom, Piet. 2009. *New Horizons of Critical Theory: Collective Learning and Triple Contingency*. Delhi: Shipra.

Sunder Rajan, R. 1998. *Beyond the Crises of European Sciences: Towards New Beginning*. Shimla: Indian Institute of Advanced Sudies.

Swaminathan, M. S. 2005. *Revolutions: To Green the Environment, to Grow the Human Heart: A Dialogue Between M. S. Swaminathan and Daisaku Ikeda*. Chennai: East-West Books.

Toulmin, Stephen. 2001. *Return to Reason*. Cambridge, MA: Harvard University Press.

Touraine, Alain. 1977. *Self-Production of Society*. Chicago: University of Chicago Press.

Vattimo, Giani. 1999. *Belief*. Cambridge: Polity Press.

Visvanathan, Susan. 2007. *Friendship, Interiority and Mysticism: Essays in Dialogue*. Hyderabad: Orient Longman.

Wei-ming, Tu. 2000. "The Complex Bridges between China and the West." In Michael Tobias, J. Patrick Fitzerald and David Rothenburg, eds, *A Parliament of Minds: Philosophy for a New Millennium*, 46–59. Albany: State University of New York Press.

Wilfred, Felix. 2008. "Christological Pluralism: Some Reflections." *Concilium* 3: 84–94.

Wittgenstein, Ludwig. 1976. *Philosophical Investigations*, trans. G. E. M. Anscombe. Oxford: Basil Blackwell.

Part I

NURTURING THE GARDEN OF TRANSFORMATIONAL KNOWLEDGE: ROOTS AND VARIANTS

Chapter One

KNOWLEDGE AND HUMAN LIBERATION: JÜRGEN HABERMAS, SRI AUROBINDO AND BEYOND

An Adventure and an Invitation

Human liberation has been a key concern with humanity from the dawn of history, and in the contemporary moment, it manifests before us as an epochal challenge, as the prevalent guarantors of liberation in modernity – liberalism and socialism – have left us alone in the street. The dead end at which our familiar projects of social emancipation and human freedom are at present urges us to rethink liberation as part of a new seeking, striving, and experimental subjectivity at the level of both self and society. Human liberation means liberation from the oppressive structures of society as well as from one's ego and urge to control (which is one of the most important sources of social evils, as Teressa Brennan (1995) would tell us). It also means to relate positively and affirmatively to new schemes of being and becoming and to create alternative spaces of self-realization, intersubjectivity and solidarity. In this practice and quest of human liberation, knowledge plays an important role, and Jürgen Habermas and Sri Aurobindo, two soul-touching thinkers of our time, help us to understand the multi-dimensional pathways of linkages between knowledge, human interest and human liberation. Their pathways of seeking and striving touch us not only as cognitive schemes but as intimations of a Beyond. Though Habermas is conventionally looked at as approaching knowledge only through rational argumentation, there is a suggestion of a Beyond in him. It is no wonder then that in many of his works, as for example in *Between Facts and Norms: Towards a Discourse Theory of Law and Democracy*, Habermas (1996) talks of the need to proceed with "weak transcendental idealizations" in our practices of communication and the acquisition of knowledge (also see Habermas 2002a). Habermas (1990) himself urges us to realize that "cognition, empathy, and agape" must be integrated in our quest of knowledge and "concern for the fate of one's neighbor is a necessary emotional prerequisite for the cognitive operations expected of participants of discourse" (Habermas 1990, 182). Such a suggestion for a Beyond (whose full potential, however, is not fully explored in Habermas (2002a), though in his recent work he shows more openness to such invitation) can be deepened and broadened by a dialogue with Sri Aurobindo.

In his *Knowledge and Human Interest*, published more than four decades ago, Habermas brings to the center the significance of self-reflection in knowledge. But at this stage, self-reflection for him seems to primarily emerge from the psychoanalytic situation of dialogue between the doctor and patient, though germs of its origin in mutually validating pragmatics of communication are already visible here. In his later works, self-reflection has a broader ground of origin and nurturance, namely in our participation in processes of moral argumentation and public sphere. This practice of knowledge can be deepened by Sri Aurobindo's pathway of the yoga of integral knowledge, which enables one to have a deeper "self-awareness," "self-consciousness" and "self-realization," to discover, know and realize the transcendental dimension in self, society and Nature, and the inherent connectedness between self, other and the world (Sri Aurobindo 1992). This simultaneous dialogue with Habermas and Sri Aurobindo also touches the very core of ontology and epistemology in thinking about and practices of knowledge. In Habermasian knowledge and human interest, knowledge mainly consists of knowledge of self and society, but despite the Habermasian distinction between ego-identity and self-identity Habermas does not touch the transcendental dimension of self. Habermas does touch upon knowledge of nature through the category of sciences, but this knowledge is mainly one of technical control.

A dialogue with Sri Aurobindo helps us to bring the very conception of knowledge into a foundation-broadening and cross-civilizational dialogue; for example, thinking about knowledge of self, society, nature and god/transcendence as part of an interconnected field of autonomy and interpenetration. The relationship among them is not one of dualism alone, and though this relationship has been predominantly thought of and lived in a regime of pervasive dualism within modernity (of which Habermas still continues to be a passionate advocate), there is a non-dual dimension in their logic of constitution and embodiment characterized by what J. N. Mohanty calls "multi-valued logic," or what J. P. S. Uberoi calls "four-fold logic of truth and method" (cf. Mohanty 2000; Uberoi 2002). A dialogue between Habermas and Sri Aurobindo can not only broaden the ontology of knowledge, but also help us realize that the distinction between ontology and epistemology that has been valorized in modernity needs to be transcended by embodying what can be called an ontological epistemology of participation, taking cues from recent transformations in both epistemological and ontological imaginations such as "virtue epistemology" and "weak ontology."[1] But here a Habermasian mode needs to be ready for a foundational border crossing, for despite his critique of positivism, he is within a modernist epistemological privileging in his conception and method of knowledge and denial of ontology.[2] Even though this denial has to some extent to do with his understandable, much needed and admirable fight with the ghost of Heidegger, Habermas seems now to turn this into a new orthodoxy, thereby showing how critical theory is incapable of critiquing its very foundational presuppositions, such as valorization of rational argumentations, performative competence, validity claims, and linguistic intersubjectivity rather than emotional intersubjectivity (cf. Craib 1998). But the problem of dualism and instrumentalism does not vanish by being part of communicative action, and knowledge as human liberation, not only as human interest, calls for developing non-dual and non-instrumental modes of relationships which are not automatically guaranteed, even when we shift from positivism to a Habermasian communicative rationality (see Bhaskar 2002).

A dialogue between Habermas and Sri Aurobindo has another potential for a foundational border crossing for critical theory, and this has to do with realizing the very limits of knowledge itself. The Habermasian articulation of knowledge and human interest valorizes knowledge and communication, and here Habermas's critique of the "illusion of pure theory" does not really acknowledge the limits of knowledge itself in a foundational sense. Consider here the following lines of the *Ishopanishad*, one of the foundational texts of spiritual universality coming from India: "Andham Tamah Prabishyanti Jo Avidyam Upasate, Tato Vuya Ibate Tamah Jo Vidyaam Ratah." It means, "those who worship ignorance are steeped in darkness but those who are steeped in knowledge are also steeped in darkness." Therefore to be steeped in the valorization of knowledge and communication to the exclusion of other practices of self cultivation, such as listening, silence and self-emptying vis-à-vis one's will to power and will to arguments, and connectedness with the world – not only the human social world but also with the world of nature and transcendence – is to be steeped in blindness, and we now need a new critical theory which helps us to understand the limits of knowledge and human interests. Critical theory in its modernist incarnation started with a Marxian critique of the valorization of capital, to which the proponents of the early Frankfurt school added a helpful critique of the valorization of state and the media. But now, especially in these days of communicative revolutions, we need a new mode of critique and reconstruction which combines a critique of the valorization of capital and power with a critique of valorization of knowledge and communication, enabling us to understand the very limits of knowledge itself.[3]

Knowledge, Human Interest and Human Liberation: A Brief Introduction to Jürgen Habermas and Sri Aurobindo

Jürgen Habermas is an important interlocutor of our times. Born in 1929, he has continued to fight for the rise of a democratic Germany from the ashes of its Nazi past, and is an outstanding public intellectual. Sri Aurobindo (1871–1950) is a major seeker and experimenter who along with Gandhi and Tagore can be considered one of the three important makers of modern India, whose strivings also included the goal of a better humanity. Sri Aurobindo was the most important leader of India's freedom struggle before the arrival of Gandhi, and in many ways can be looked at as having germinated major themes which were to preoccupy Gandhi, such as "back to the villages" (Sri Aurobindo 1973; see Heehs 2008). During this struggle, he was once implicated in a bomb case and arrested. While in the prison he had a spiritual vision and gained a new calling to strive not only for India's political independence, but for a new spiritual dawn for the whole of humanity, for a manifestation of a new evolutionary consciousness. After being acquitted in the bomb case Sri Aurobindo left British India and came to Pondicherry in 1910, which was then ruled by the French. He there embarked upon a multi-dimensional journey of seeking and creativity. He edited a journal named *Arya* and wrote his major works, *The Human Cycle*, *The Life Divine* and *The Syntheses of Yoga* as regular columns in this journal. Besides these works, Sri Aurobindo had also written, among others, *Ideals of Human Unity*, *Future Poetry* and the epic *Savitri*, which chronicles the journey of a soul in her quest of overcoming death and suffering, and which was nominated several times for a Nobel Prize in literature.

Sri Aurobindo is one of the very few modern Indian thinkers who does not reject reason outright but accords it a primal place in human development and evolution. Sri Aurobindo also does not reject modernity outright; instead his *The Human Cycle* puts reason and modernity in perspective. When we read this we find similarities between Sri Aurobindo and Habermas. Sri Aurobindo here points to the crucial significance of reason in understanding the validity of traditions. Like Habermas, Sri Aurobindo also stresses the need "to universalize first of all the habit of reason," but "the reason which is to be universally applied, cannot be the reason of a ruling class: for in the present imperfection of the human race that always means the fettering and misapplication of reason degraded into servant of power to maintain the privileges of the ruling class. *It must be the reason of each and all seeking for a basis of agreement*" (Sri Aurobindo 1973, 184, emphasis added).

Like Habermas's plea for undistorted communication, Sri Aurobindo also sensitizes us to the distortion that power can introduce in the working of a rational discourse and the realization of even its inherent emancipatory potential. But for Aurobindo, even though reason is so important for moral development and evolution (both phylogenetic and ontogenetic), it cannot be a sole foundation of morality. Aurobindo accords this role to spirit. An ideal society, for Aurobindo, is not a mere "rational society" but a "spiritual society" which does not abandon rational foundation but deepens and transforms it. A society founded on spirituality is not governed by religion as a mere social custom. A spiritual society regards man not only as a "mind, a life and a body, but as a soul incarnated for a divine fulfillment upon earth, not only in heavens beyond, which after all it need not have left if it had no divine business here in the world of physical, vital and mental nature" (Sri Aurobindo 1962, 213).

Both Sri Aurobindo and Habermas are passionate critics of systems which deny human flourishing. Much of Habermas's passion can be attributed to his struggle for radical democracy and his fight against Nazism in his native Germany. Sri Aurobindo was also a critic of Nazism and contributed in his own ways as a *yogi* to the fight against the Nazis.[4] While Habermas speaks of the colonization of the life world Sri Aurobindo uses a much more passionate language of criticism, such as barbarism going beyond the familiar distinction between civilization and barbarism. Habermas (2002a) is now a critic of the marketization of the globe and his critique can be deepened by the critical perspective of economic barbarism that Sri Aurobindo outlines in his *Human Cycles*: "Just as the physical barbarian makes the excellence of the body and development of physical force…so the vitalistic or economic barbarian makes the satisfaction of wants and desires and the accumulation of possessions his standard and aim" (Sri Aurobindo 1962, 94).

While there are similarities between Habermas and Aurobindo, there are some major differences. One of this has to do with Habermas's theses of the linguistification of the sacred – the sacred has now lost its aura and is part of ordinary language. As is well known, Habermas makes a shift from philosophy of consciousness to philosophy of language and looks at the sacred linguistically. This is related to the issue of poetry and prose in thinking about language, and also to critique and reconstruction. Habermas is critical of any poetic use of language as he is afraid that it can dislocate humans from their reason and make them servile followers of tyrannical crowds, like the Nazis. But in his own work we find a poetic dimension. Consider the following lines of Habermas: "This ontology fetishizes words, bows down before their roots, believing words to be pure only in their venerated origins…" (Habermas 2002a, 65). Habermas directs his energies here against Heidegger, but poetry in Heidegger was not only a poetry of glory, it also embodied a deep "pathos of shakenness" (Shanks 2001). Sri Aurobindo, much like Heidegger, has a broader conception of language and dialogue which can be understood by reading what Derrida writes about his conversations with Levinas: "…we often addressed to one another what I would call neither questions nor answers but, perhaps a question-prayer, a question prayer that would be anterior to all dialogue" (Derrida 1999, 13). For Sri Aurobindo, poetry is a *mantra*, an invocation of self, social and world-transformation. Writes Sri Aurobindo (1948) in his legendary epic *Savitri*:

A lonely freedom cannot satisfy
A heart that has grown one with every heart
I am a deputy of the aspiring world
My spirit's liberty I ask for all.[5]

Knowledge and Human Interest: Towards Critical Dialogues

Knowledge and Human Interest is one of the earliest master pieces of Habermas which lays the ground work for his subsequent meditations. It contains Habermas's rich and multi-faceted dialogue with Hegel, Kant, Marx, Fichte, Dilthey, Nietzsche, Pierce and Freud. The main concern there is how knowledge and human interest have been conceptualized in these thinkers. But while carrying on careful dialogue with these masters, Habermas develops a point of view of his own concerning knowledge and human interest. In this we find a tilt towards both psychoanalysis and pragmatism. While psychoanalysis provides him the possibility of combining therapy and critique, pragmatism provides him an alternative to both ontology and epistemology as it urges him to focus on the "lack of alternatives to a practice in which communicatively socialized subjects always already find themselves engaged" (Habermas 2002a, 118). Pragmatism also provides him with democratic possibilities in his elaboration of knowledge-constitutive interests: "The anti-elitist, democratic, and thoroughly egalitarian attitude that shapes and penetrates the work of all the pragmatists was far more important than the *contents* of any particular essay on politics or democracy" (Habermas 2002b, 228).

Habermas wants to establish a transformative link between knowledge and human interest through the practice of self-reflection as for him "in the power of self-reflection knowledge and interest are one" (Habermas 1971, 313). The significance of *Knowledge and Human Interest* lay in initiating a break away from not only idealism but also positivistic science and epistemology; a positivistic self-understanding of science as "the sciences have retained the character of philosophy: the illusion of pure theory." However, in this supposed breaking away from the illusion of pure theory Habermas unfortunately leaves aside the whole vision and practice of theory as a mode of ideal participation (Neville 1974). Habermas tries to deal with this challenge by weak transcendental idealization, but even in weak transcendental idealization there is idealization, not only in a genealogical but in a permanent constitutive sense. Idealization is an important part of practice itself. Therefore the way out of the illusion of pure theory is not to oppose theory and practice but to understand how they are mutually constituted. Mutual constitution does not mean that there is no disjunction between them; in fact there is a disjunction between them which is not external to their relationship but lies at the very core of it. But to acknowledge disjunction is not to accept it as fate and not accepting anything as fate is a Habermasian insight *par excellence*. The calling here is to cope with this disjunction in a creative manner. One creative mode of coping is striving towards reconciliation, and here the perspective of a Beyond is helpful.

In a recent reflection, Habermas says that what has been at the core of his strivings is to lay the foundations of what he calls a Kantian pragmatism (Habermas 2002b). But this Kantian pragmatism in thinking about ontology and epistemology now needs a radical supplement of self-cultivation, self-critique and border crossing. Fallibilism as an epistemic project is dear to the Kantian pragmatism of Habermas as well as of Putnam (2001) but does it require some ontological self-cultivation such as practice of humility? Habermas himself has embodied a border crossing between Kant and pragmatism and what is called for now is a transcultural border crossing and a transcivilizational dialogue on knowledge and human interest, ontology and epistemology. This is unfortunately a major problem with Habermas, as with his pragmatic allies from the other side of the Atlantic such as Richard Rorty and Hilary Putnam (Giri 2003a). Though Habermas speaks of the inclusion of the other, he wants to include the other from the point of view of Kant, albeit a reformulated Kantianism (i.e., Kantianism with a pragmatic face). But there are some problems in the way Habermas has appropriated the pragmatic tradition, especially that of Dewey. While practices of knowledge are too disembodied in Habermas, this is not so in Dewey. Knowledge and the public sphere in Dewey are nourished by an aesthetic ecology and the agents here are not only rational but also cosmogenic (cf. Reid and Taylor 2002, 10).

But speaking of Kant, in these days of over flown boundaries, there is need for a genuine global conversation on knowledge, human interest and human liberation. Here the challenge is not to valorize either Kant or Dewey but to make them fellow partners in a transcivilizational dialogue on human liberation and Enlightenment, particularly on what Habermas calls justification and application. In this cross-civilizational dialogue, we realize that what enables justification as a mode of persuasion, and frees it from the problem of self-justification, is not only rational argumentation or even mutual validation but a new ethics of argumentation embodying love and suffering – the willingness to undertake suffering for the sake of love and truth. The capacity to suffer while looking at the face of the other is crucial not only for communicative validity but also for the realization of justice, both at the intersubjective as well as societal and global levels. This calls for not only a pragmatic translation of Kant but also a transcivilizational dialogue with him, for example, from the strivings and aspirations of a Gandhi (Giri 2002a). A transcivilizational dialogue between Kant and Gandhi can help us realize the significance of not only rational arguments but also self-suffering which is different from sadism or inflicting suffering on others. A transcivilizational dialogue between Kant and Gandhi can radically transform the very foundation of justification and application by establishing intimate links between not only suffering and justification but also between suffering and hope. In this context, what Habermas writes about the three fundamental Kantian questions deserves our careful attention: "The first question, 'What can I know?' is merely speculative. The second, 'What ought I do?' is merely practical. But the third question, 'What may I hope?' is both practical and theoretical at the same time" (Habermas 1971, 203). But the question of hope also is more than theory and practice understood in a Kantian and Habermasian sense, and here a Gandhian calling emphasizes the crucial significance of suffering with and for the love of the other for the generation and sustenance of hope (also see Chapter Four on Kant).

In this sprit of a global conversation, a key question is whether the vocabulary of interest is adequate here, and to ask ourselves whether Habermasian knowledge and human interest face the problem of not only instrumentalism but also anthropocentrism. Habermasian knowledge and human interest work within a model of mastery, performative competence and performative valorization, and here a key challenge is "exceeding the performative" and realizing our responsibility (Derrida 2001; Strydom 2000). In a related vein, Dallmayr raises the problem of humanism in Habermas, but Habermas does not want to listen as he is still deeply preoccupied with the understandable and to some extent admirable fight with the ghost of Heidegger. Habermas reduces listening to "the 'Yes' or 'No' response of a potential hearer": "The hearer must take the position of a second person, give up the perspective of an observer in favor of that of a participant…" (Habermas 2002a, 90). Thus listening here is reduced to hearing, and both of them are thought of in the frame of a valorized model of communication which does not realize its own inherent silence. Habermas is weary of "auratic silence" because of its degenerative fascist possibility and reduces all silence to auratic silence "which draws from the specific context of a more or less unmistakable meaning" (2002a, 90).

Habermas makes much of the linguistic turn, but his conception of language, as he himself admits, is formal-pragmatic and misses not only its integral dimension of silence but also what Vincent Crapanzano (1992) calls its dramaturgical character. Moreover, the apparent shift from the philosophy of consciousness to the philosophy of language does not solve all problems, much less issues of consciousness and ontology, as it just inaugurates a new vista of self-cultivation and understanding of the world. Consider here the following lines of J. N. Mohanty: "Is not 'consciousness' itself a word having its original home in a language game? Is not language –primarily as the act of speaking – a modality of consciousness? ...are not consciousness and language both unified in a third something? It is Heidegger's *Dasein* or is it Hegel's *Geist?*" (Mohanty 2002, 112).

Human interest in Habermas is mainly cognitive interest and emancipatory interest, but there is need for broadening in both the domains. Cognitive interest in Habermas is isolated from body and emotion (cf. Connolly 1999, 2002). Emancipatory interest now faces the challenge of acknowledging the limits of emancipation, of going "beyond emancipation" (Laclau 1992). A key question here is whether knowledge and human interest are entrapped within a logic of empowerment; are they servant to a will to power? What kind of self-cultivation should we be engaged in so that, in pursuing knowledge and human interest, we do not use power to coerce and dominate, and are able to realize what Heidegger calls a "power-free" state (Dallmayr 2001c)? Habermas takes the calling of self-cultivation for granted as he is confident that being part of communication we can solve this problem automatically, as doing otherwise would be an act of performative "self-contradiction." But performative self-contradiction is a narrow aspect of self-critique, and here building on the expected shame of participants, that they would suffer from the shame of self-contradiction if they do not reach out to the other in their communicative interaction, is not adequate for the realization of the task at hand.

Once we understand the limits of an emancipatory interest, especially as it is faced with the calling of self-cultivation, then we realize the other limits of the very language of emancipation. The discourse of emancipation has focused primarily on social emancipation, and now this can be deepened by emancipation from ego – in fact, the liberation of self from ego. Liberation then consists of overcoming both self-alienation and social alienation. Overcoming self-alienation is enriched by what Roy Bhaskar says, which is in tune with the perspective of Sri Aurobindo: "The dialectics of de-alienation (of re-totalisation) are all essentially the dialectic of love: of Self (>Self), of each and all (>Totality) and in both inner and outer movements, both as essentially love of God. The essence of liberated man therefore is love of God, and God, we could say, is not only love but essentially to be loved" (Bhaskar 2000, 44).

A major problem here is Habermas's earlier over-confidence in his rationalistic project and lack of participation in multiple traditions of humanity.[6] Despite his own admission that philosophy "even in its post-metaphysical form, will be able neither to replace nor to repress religion as long as religious language is the bearer of a semantic content that is inspiring and even indispensable," (Habermas 1992, 51) he can relate to other traditions only in a manner of "appropriation" (Habermas 2002a, 79). This appropriation begins with his translation of Kant. He finds Kant's actors solitary and wants to redeem this by making them part of a public discursive formation of will. Then comes his dialogue with Kierkegaard. He finds Kierkegaardian inwardness of interest but does not want to leave it at that; he wants inwardness to emerge from its participation in the public sphere (cf. Matustik 1997). Similar are his translations of theologians such as Johannes Baptist Metz. Habermas appreciates Metz's effort to create a politically responsible polycentric church and theology (Habermas 1997). Metz does this with his critique of "Hellenized Christianity" and his articulation of a pathway of what he calls "anamnestic reason," a reason which remembers the memory of struggle and resists forgetting. But in his dialogue with Metz, Habermas asserts a one-way approach. Instead of using Metz's formulations of "anamnestic reason" to broaden and deepen argumentative reason, Habermas asserts its primacy. However, Habermas retains Metz's terminology of "Hellenized Christianity," which unfortunately soon degenerates into a quick judgmental category.

This is, for example, how Habermas deals with some of the foundational questions that Dallmayr (1992, 141) raises, such as the issue of reconciliation. For Dallmayr, "… the continued invocation of subject-philosophy [in Habermas] gives rise to various splits or divisions (other terms of 'demarcations') – between human beings and nature, ego and alter, ego and id – which in turn promote various modes of mastery and control" (1992, 142). In response, Habermas writes, "I hope to have learned much from Kant, and still I have not become a Dallmayrian Kantian… It is not a higher-level subjectivity and therefore, without sacrificing a transcendence from within, it can do without the concept of an Absolute. We can dispense with this legacy of Hellenized Christianity as well as any subsequent right-Hegelian constructions upon which Dallmayr still seems to rely" (Habermas 2002a, 91).

Thus Hellenized Christianity becomes a term of labeling in Habermas. But it is unfair to throw this at Dallmayr, because Dallmayr works within a liberative tradition of Christianity. His conception of God and the Absolute emerges out of his deep participation in the emancipatory spiritual heritage of humanity, as he has personally taken part in new spiritual strivings in Islam, Hinduism, Buddhism and Christianity (Dallmayr 1996, 1998, 2001a, 2001b). But compared to this, Habermas has an ethnocentric approach to knowledge and human interest, and though he speaks of post-conventional morality and post-metaphysical thinking, his metaphysics comes from Kant on the one hand and Judeo-Christian tradition on the other – though he himself does not integrate his own opening to Jewish mystical thought to his post-metaphysical mode.[7] In a recent interview, Habermas makes it clear: "We no longer confront other cultures as alien since their structures still remind us of previous phases of our own social development. What we *do* encounter as alien within other cultures is the stubborn distinctiveness of their religious cores" (Habermas 2002a, 156).[8]

It is of course to be noted here that in his approach to his own religion Habermas has made a shift from his earlier Marxist or even pragmatist denial as he writes: "For the normative self-understanding of modernity, Christianity has functioned as more than just a precursor or catalyst. Universalistic egalitarianism…is the direct legacy of the Judaic ethic of justice and Christian ethic of love" (Habermas 2002a, 148–9). But he is anxious to de-transcendentalize religion, and though it has a continued emancipatory potential in freeing us from what Spinoza had long ago articulated as the problem of "theological illusion," the anxious reduction of all transcendence to only a "transcendence from within" calls for rethinking. There are many different conceptions of transcendence possible and the Habermasian agenda of "transcendence from within" suffers from the modernist anxiety to imprison transcendence within a familiar language and the public sphere. Consider here the following lines of Luc Ferry: " … When I hear a musical passage, it does not reduce to a series of related notes with no connection between them (actual immanence). On the contrary, it contributes – in an immanent way, apart from any rational operation – a certain structure that transcends this actual immanence, without being imposed on me from the outside like an argument from authority. This 'immanent transcendence' contains within itself, par excellence, the ultimate significance of lived experiences" (Ferry 2002, 26). In post-metaphysical and secular moments, God is referred to not to "ground truth, but comes after it, to give it a meaning" (2002, 31).

Knowledge and Human Liberation: Sri Aurobindo

For Sri Aurobindo (1992), the need for a deeper knowledge requires us to be self-conscious and not only self-critical: "In this process the rationalistic ideal subjects itself to the ideal of intuitive knowledge." Self-reflection is an important concern in Habermas and Sri Aurobondo accords this to self-knowledge; but self-knowledge here has a much deeper and broader meaning which includes the knowledge of Self as different from ego and knowledge of God: God not as a fixed structure but a creative becoming embodying and symbolizing the highest human possibility. For Sri Aurobindo, " …our knowledge is not integral if we do not make this self in the individual one with the cosmic spirit…" (1992, 347). Habermasian distinction between ego identity and self-identity gets a deeper calling in Sri Aurobindo's pathways of liberative knowledge: "Enlightenment brings to us the knowledge that the ego is only an instrument…" (Sri Aurobindo 1992, 53). Furthermore, "As we gain in clarity and the turmoil of egoistic effort gives place to a calmer self-knowledge, we recognize the source of the growing light within us" (1992, 56). Acquisition of self-knowledge "brings us face to face with the extraordinary complexity of our own being" but a seeker here does not "solve arbitrarily the conflict of his own inner members. He has to harmonize deliberate knowledge with unquestioning faith; he must conciliate the gentle soul of love with the formidable need of power…" (1992, 68, 71). The goal of knowledge here is a radical transformation of self, world and nature. Sri Aurobindo writes:

> What we propose in our Yoga is nothing less than to break up the whole formation of our past and present which makes up ordinary material and mental man and to create a new center of vision and a new universe of activities in ourselves which shall constitute a divine humanity or a superhuman nature… Life has to change into a thing vast and calm and powerful that can no longer recognize its old blind eager narrow self or petty impulse and desire. Even the body has to submit to a mutation and be no longer the clamorous animal or the impending clod it now is, but become instead a conscious servant and radiant instrument and living form of the spirit… Life is the field of a divine manifestation not yet complete: here, in life, on earth, in the body. (Sri Aurobindo 1992, 66, 68)

In his reflections on knowledge, Sri Aurobindo does not look at it only as an epistemic project. For him, "The seeker of the integral state of knowledge must be free from attachment to action and equally free from attachment to inaction" (Sri Aurobindo 1992, 332). They also face the challenge of overcoming our desire mind. In the words of Sri Aurobindo:

> Equality, not indifference, is the basis. Equal endurance, impartial indifference, calm submission to the causes of joy and grief without any reaction of either grief or joy are the preparation and negative basis of equality; but equality is not fulfilled till it takes its positive form of love and delight. The sense-mind must find the equal *rasa* (pleasure) of the All-Beautiful, the heart the equal love and Ananda for all, the psychic Prana (vital) the enjoyment of this rasa, love and Ananda (joy). This, however, is the positive perfection that comes by liberation; our first object in the path of knowledge is rather the liberation that comes by detachment from the desire-mind and renunciation of its passions. (Sri Aurobindo 1992, 339)

Overcoming the desire mind in the yoga of knowledge is accompanied by realization of Gnosis. Gnosis has the power to overcome the duality between subject and object: "Reason or intellect is only the lower *buddhi* (intellect); it is dependent for its action on the precepts of the sense-mind and on the concepts of mental intelligence. It is not like gnosis, self-luminous, authentic, making the subject one with the object" (Sri Aurobindo 1992, 458). Furthermore, the intuitive reason "acts in a self-light of the truth" which "proceeds not by intelligent but by visional concepts: it is a kind of truth-vision, truth-hearing, truth-memory, direct truth-discernment" (Sri Aurobindo 1992, 455).

For Sri Aurobindo, in the yoga of self-knowledge, "The old philosophical quarrel between Being and Becoming" is not helpful and in it "Our sense of separate existence disappears into a consciousness of illimitable, undivided, infinite being" (Sri Aurobindo 1992, 420). But Sri Aurobindo himself makes clear that realizing oneness is "our essential fact of self-knowledge" but this "unity works itself everywhere and on every plane by an executive or practical truth of duality" (1992, 418).

In his reflection on knowledge, Sri Aurobindo makes a distinction between higher knowledge and lower knowledge: the lower knowledge is the knowledge of the apparent world while higher knowledge is the knowledge which "seeks to know the truth of existence from within" (Sri Aurobindo 1992, 492). But in making this distinction he is not within the conventional scheme of hierarchy of knowledge, as he writes: "Science, art, philosophy, ethics, psychology, the knowledge of man and his past, action itself are means by which we arrive at the knowledge of the working of God through Nature and through life" (1992, 492). Thus in this scheme of interconnected integral knowledge, knowledge of society is not inferior to knowledge of God or spiritual knowledge; rather it holds the key to the latter. In his work Habermas urges us to realize the significance of empirical[9] studies of our world, especially current transformations of striving for a more dignified society, and this has an important place in Sri Aurobindo's pathways of integral knowledge as well.

In contemporary critical theory, whether it starts from Habermas or from Foucault, knowledge is often subservient to either power or mastery, but Sri Aurobindo urges us to understand the integral connection between knowledge and love: "Perfect knowledge indeed leads to perfect love, integral knowledge to a rounded and multitudinous richness of love" (Sri Aurobindo 1992, 522). But at the same time Sri Aurobindo tells us that knowledge has equal power to love, but "their method of arriving at is different" (1992, 524). This suggests that Sri Aurobindo is open to acknowledging the differential autonomy of knowledge and love as the two domains are also interconnected.

In his *Human Cycles*, Sri Aurobindo laments that the modern European idea of society is founded upon the primacy of vital dynamism and has "neglected the spiritual element in man which is his true being" (1962, 277). He is for a spiritual vitalism and spiritual realism: "spirituality will not try to slay the vitality in man by denying life but will rather reveal to life the divine in itself as the principle of its own transformation" (1962, 286); furthermore, "Our idealism is the most rightly human thing in us, but as mental idealism it is a thing uneffective [*sic*]. To be effective it has to convert itself into a spiritual realism" (1962, 301). Like Habermas Sri Aurobindo stresses on learning from our failures: "Failures must be originally numerous and difficult but the time comes when the experience of past failures can be profitably used..." (1962, 330).

Sri Aurobindo writes: "The central aim of knowledge is the recovery of the Self, of our true self-existence, and this aim presupposes the admission that our present mode of being is not our true existence" (1992). He also makes it clear that when he talks of knowledge and human liberation it is not individual salvation alone: " ...an individual salvation in heavens beyond, careless of the earth, is not our highest objective; the liberation and self-interest of others is as much our own concern –we might almost say, our divine self-interest – as our own liberation. Otherwise our unity with others would have no effective meaning."

Knowledge and Human Liberation: Transformations and Beyond

In the above paragraph, Sri Aurobindo urges us to realize the simultaneous liberation of the self as well as the other, which can be thought of together with Habermas's pathways of practical discourse. Communicative interaction is the most important part of this practical discourse. This practical discourse can be part of a practical spirituality, and Sri Aurobindo's perspective of spiritual realism is a significant part of it (Metz 1970; Vivekananda 1991). Practical spirituality, as Swami Vivekananda[10] argues, urges us to realize that "the highest idea of morality and unselfishness goes hand in hand with the highest idea of metaphysical conception" (1991, 354). This highest conception pertains to the realization that man himself is God: "You are that Impersonal Being: that God for whom you have been searching all over the time is yourself –yourself not in the personal sense but in the impersonal" (Vivekananda 1991, 332). The task of practical spirituality begins with this realization but does not end there: its objective is to transform the world. Swami Vivekananda reiterates this idea in the form of a challenge: "The watchword of all well-being of all moral good is not 'I' but 'thou.' Who cares whether there is a heaven or a hell, who cares if there is an unchangeable or not? Here is the world and it is full of misery. Go out into it as Buddha did, and struggle to lessen it or die in the attempt" (Vivekananda 1991, 353). What practical spirituality stresses is that the knowledge that one is Divine, that one is part of a Universal Being, facilitates this mode of relating oneself to the world. This knowledge is, however, not for the acquisition of power over the other; rather it is to worship her as God. In the words of Vivekananda: "Human knowledge is not antagonistic to human well-being. On the contrary, it is knowledge alone that will save us in every department of life, in knowledge as worship" (Vivekananda 1991, 353).

The realization of practical spirituality in the dynamics of self, culture, and society is as much a normative ideal as the building of a rational society or realization of a state of undistorted communication (Giri 2002c; Wuthnow 1998, 2001). The coming of a spiritual society requires both the "reflexive mobilization of self" (Giddens 1991) as well as building up of alternative communities which are founded on the principles of practical spirituality. According to Sri Aurobindo, the coming of a spiritual society begins with the spiritual fulfillment of the urge to individual perfection, but ends with the building of a "new world, a change in the life of humanity or, at the least a new perfected collective life in the earth-nature" (Sri Aurobindo 1970, 1031). "This calls for the appearance not only of isolated evolved individuals acting in the uninvolved mass, but of many gnostic individuals forming a new kind of beings and a new common life superior to the present individual and common existence. A collective life of this kind must obviously constitute itself on the same principle as life of the gnostic individual" (Sri Aurobindo 1970, 1031).

We find the glimpses of emergence of such spiritual communities in the integral education movement in India, which is a grass-roots social movement at work in building spiritually inspired integral education schools. In the state of Odisha there are now more than five hundred such schools, inspired by the ideas of Sri Aurobindo and his spiritual companion The Mother, and these schools have been a product of an earlier study circle movement. In these spaces we find the glimpses of the emergence of a new connection between knowledge and human liberation through the mediations of love, labor and mutually shared time (see Giri 2009). But its fuller potential remains unrealized because of traces of authoritarianism in the management of these schools which is sometimes brushed under or justified in the name of spirituality. Here opening up these spaces to further democratic deliberation of the kind suggested by Habermas is helpful.

Sri Aurobindo's gnostic individuals are seekers and bearers of the multi-dimensional transformation of practical spirituality. But these gnostic individuals are not Nietzschian supermen driven by the will to power; they are animated by a will to serve, and desire to transform the contemporary condition and to build a society of beauty and dignity. But their seeking nonetheless faces the challenge of what Roy Bhaskar calls the prehistory of spirituality (personal communication). Bhaskar says that we are at a prehistory of spirituality, as spiritual seeking in the past has not always embodied the collectivist struggles for human emancipation. Spiritual seekers and movements continue to face the challenge of overcoming their egoism, a narrow and self-centered view of salvation. The will to assert and participation in mutually validating discursive argumentation is a crucial step in overcoming these. Therefore, if Derrida (1998) says that we cannot authorize ourselves in the name of religion, the same is true of spiritual quest as well: we cannot authorize ourselves in the name of spirituality. In the critique of authority, including acknowledging what Gianni Vattimo (1999) calls "the contingency of the whole," there is a continued significance of a Habermasian critical perspective. Liberatory movements of even the spiritual kind continue to be entrapped in a logic of authoritarianism, and here the Habermasian practice of argumentation and mutual validation can go a long way in creating an appropriate democratic public space for spiritual evolution of self and society. As we have seen, this critical perspective for realizing its own inherent potential can learn from the pathways of a Sri Aurobindo, as his project of knowledge and human liberation can be facilitated by the movements of radical democracy and the formation of appropriate public spheres. Going beyond the facile polarity between rationality and spirituality, West and East, we can build here on this intertwined pathway of knowledge and human liberation to create a more beautiful and dignified world for all of us.

Notes

1 While in virtue epistemology there is a recognition of the ontological preparation involved in epistemological engagement (cf. Greco 2001), in weak ontology, as formulated by Vattimo and suggested in the works of Connolly, there is a deep recognition of a danger of an essentialist fixed ontology (see Vattimo 1999).

2 Habermas writes, "…as long as philosophy remains caught in ontology, it is itself subject to an objectivism that disguises the connection of its knowledge with the human interest in autonomy and responsibility" (Habermas 1971, 311). But why should this necessarily be the case? On the other hand, consider here what an uncritical primacy of epistemology does to human sciences and human action:

> The primacy of epistemology short-circuits ontological issues by assuming that once the right procedure for attaining truth as correspondence or coherence or consensus is reached, any remaining issues will either be resolved *through* that method or shown to be irrelevant. The primacy of epistemology thereby treats the ideas of subject, object, representation, and knowledge as if they were already fixed in their range of application…

The primacy of epistemology turns out itself, of course, to embody a contestable social ontology. The empiricist version, for instance, treats human beings as subjects or agents of knowledge; it treats human things as independent objects susceptible to representation, or, at least, as a medium in which the designative dimension of concepts can be disconnected rigorously from the contexts of rhetoric/action/evaluation in which they originate (Connolly 1995, 6).

3 Though some proponents of critical theory share that critical theory has been always aware of the limitations of knowledge. See for a slightly different perspective Strydom (2009).

4 Heehs (2008) tells us that even when political leaders in India had not taken a stance against Nazism Sri Aurobindo took a stance against it.

5 In *Savitri* there are many conversations between Savitri, who is trying to overcome death, and Yamaraj, the King of Death. Rev. Chris Platt of the Episcopal Church in Lexington,

Kentucky, suggests that these conversations also embody a Habermasian discursive argumentation (personal communication). I am grateful to Rev. Platt for this extremely innovative reading and am exploring it further.

6 In this context, what Sang-Jin Han writes from a Confucian perspective deserves our careful attention:

> Critical theory is required to reflect on the normative basis of its own project. Critique always presupposes normative claims which need to be reorganized as such. Critique is, in fact, derived from, and based on, cultural traditions capable of orienting human actions. (1998, 306)

7 My argument that Habermas's post-metaphysics just hides a metaphysics of Kantianism and Christianity finds a support in what Connolly writes:

> What, then, is the thought behind the thought that drives the actually existing Habermas to give singular primacy to one dimension of discourse over all others? Perhaps, at a visceral level, it is a reiteration of the Christian and Kantian demands to occupy the authoritative place of public discourse. The imperative to occupy that place of authority may be bolstered by another preliminary drive, that is, *the political* sense that a non-Kantian, religiously pluralized world fall into either disorder or religious tyranny if its participants did not endorse a single standard rational authority… (1999, 39)

8 Though in his recent works especially in his dialogue with Cardinal Joseph Ratzinger and now the present Pope, there is a slow opening to other religious traditions (see Ratzinger and Habermas 2007).

9 Consider here the following lines from one of Habermas's recent interviews: "[the issue of global justice] on the analytical level, it demands a great deal of empirical knowledge and institutional imagination" (Habermas 2002a, 166).

10 Another pioneering spiritual seeker of modern India known in the West for his interventions in the World Parliament of Religions at Chicago in 1893.

References

Aboulafia, Myra Bookman and Catherine Kemp, eds. 2002. *Habermas and Pragmatism*. London: Routledge.

Bhaskar, Roy. 2000. *From East to West: The Odyssey of a Soul*. London: Routledge.

_____. 2002. *Reflections on Meta-Reality: Transcendence, Emancipation and Everyday Life*. New Delhi: Sage.

Brennan, Teressa. 1995. *History After Lacan*. London: Routledge.

Connolly, William E. 1991. *Identity \ Difference: Democratic Negotiations of Political Paradox*. Ithaca, NY: Cornell University Press.

_____. 1995. *The Ethos of Pluralization*. Minneapolis: University of Minnesota Press.

_____. 1999. *Why I Am Not a Secularist*. Minneapolis: University of Minnesota Press.

_____. 2002. *Neuropolitics: Thinking, Culture, Speed*. Minneapolis: University of Minnesota Press.

Craib, Ian. 1998. *Experiencing Identity*. London: Sage.

Crapanzano, Vincent. 1992. *Hermes' Dilemma and Hamlet's Desire: on the Epistemology of Interpretation*. Cambridge, MA: Harvard University Press.

Derrida, Jacques. 1998. "Faith and Knowledge: Two Sources of 'Religion' at the Limits of Reason Alone." In Jacques Derrida and Giani Vattimo, eds, *Religion*. Cambridge: Polity Press.

_____. 1999. *Adieu to Emmanuel Levinas*. Palo Alto: Stanford University Press.

_____. 2001. "The future of the profession or the university without condition (thanks to the 'Humanities,' what *could take place* tomorrow)." In Tom Cohen, ed., *Jacques Derrida and Humanities: A Critical Reader*. Cambridge: Cambridge University Press.

Dallmayr, Fred R. 1992. "Critical Theory and Reconciliation." In Don S. Browning and Francis S. Fiorenza, eds, *Habermas, Modernity and Public Theology*. New York: Crossroad Publishing Company.

_____. 1996. *Beyond Orientalism: Essays on Cross-Cultural Encounter*. Ithaca, NY: Cornell University Press.

_____. 1998. *Alternative Visions: Pathways in the Global Village*. Lanham, MD: Rowman & Littlefield.

_____. 2001a. "Liberation Beyond Liberalism: New Voices from Buddhism and Islam." In Ananta Kumar Giri, ed., *Rethinking Social Transformation: Criticism and Creativity at the Turn of the Millennium*. Jaipur: Rawat Publications.

_____. 2001b. "Dialogue of Civilizations: A Gadamerian Perspective." Notre Dame, IN: University of Notre Dame Press. Manuscript.

_____. 2001c. "Resisting Totalizing Uniformity: Martin Heidegger on Macht and Machenschaft." In *Achieving our World: Toward a Global and Plural Democracy*. Lanham, MD: Rowman & Littlefield.

Ferry, Luc. 2002. *Man Made God*. New York: Columbia University Press.

Giddens, Anthony. 1991. *Modernity and Self-Identity: Self and Society in the Late Modern Age*. Cambridge: Polity Press.

Giri, Ananta Kumar. 2002a. *Conversations and Transformations: Towards a New Ethics of Self and Society*. Lanham, MA/Oxford: Lexington Books.

_____. 2002b "Spiritual Cultivation for a Secular Society." Madras Institute of Development Studies Working Paper.

_____. 2002c. *Building in the Margins of Shacks: The Vision and Projects of Habitat for Humanity*. New Delhi: Orient Longman.

_____. 2003. "The Calling of Global Responsibilities." In Philip Quarles van Ufford and Ananta Kumar Giri, eds, *A Moral Critique of Development: In Search of Global Responsibilities*. London: Routledge.

_____. 2009. "Learning the Art of Wholeness: Integral Education and Beyond." Draft of a report.

Greco, John. 2001. "Virtues and Rules in Epistemology." In Abrol Fairweather and Linda Zagzebski, eds, *Virtue Epistemology: Essays on Epistemic Virtue and Responsibility*, 117–41. Oxford: Oxford University Press.

Habermas, Jürgen. 1971. *Knowledge and Human Interests*. Boston: Beacon Press.

_____. 1973. *Theory and Practice*. Boston: Beacon Press.

_____. 1992. *Postmetaphysical Thinking*. Cambridge: Polity Press.

_____. 1996. *Between Fact and Norm: Contributions Towards a Discourse Theory of Law and Democracy*. Cambridge: Polity Press.

_____. 1997. "Israel or Athens, Or To Whom Does Anamnestic Reason Belong? On Unity in Multicultural Diversity." In David Batsone et al., eds, *Liberation Theologies, Postmodernity and the Americas*. London: Routledge.

_____. 1998. *Inclusion of the Other: Studies in Political Theory*. Cambridge: Polity Press.

_____. 2002a. *Religion and Rationality*. Cambridge, MA: MIT Press.

_____. 2002b "Postscript: Some Concluding Remarks." In Myra Bookman Aboulafia and Catherine Kemp, eds, *Habermas and Pragmatism*, 223–33. London: Routledge.

Han, Sang-Jin. 1998. "Three Tasks of Critical Theory and Korean Development." In San-Jin Han, ed., *Habermas and the Korean Debate*, 289–315. Seoul: Seoul National University Press.

Matustik, Matin J. 1997. *Postnational Identity: Critical Theory and Existential Philosophy in Habermas, Kierkegaard, and Havel*. New York: Guilford Press.

Heehs, Peter. 2008. *The Lives of Sri Aurobindo*. New York: Columbia University Press.

Neville, Robert C. 1974. *The Cosmology of Freedom*. Albany: State University of New York Press.

Mohanty, J. N. 2000. *Self and Other: Philosophical Essays*. Delhi: Oxford University Press.

_____. 2002. *Between Two Worlds: East and West*. Delhi: Oxford University Press.

Ratzinger, Joseph and Jürgen Habermas. 2007. *The Dialectics of Secularization: On Reason and Religion*. San Francisco: Ignatius Press.

Putnam, Hilary. 2001. *Three Enlightenments*. Amsterdam: Spinoza Lectures, University of Amsterdam.

Reid, Herbert and Elizabeth M. Taylor. 2002. "John Dewey's Aesthetic Ecology of Public Intelligence and the Grounding of Civic Environmentalism." Bloomington: Indiana University Press. Manuscript.

Shanks, Andrew. 2001. *'What is Truth?' Towards a Theological Poetics*. London: Routledge.

Sri Aurobindo. 1948. *Savitri: A Legend and a Symbol*. Pondicherry: Sri Aurobindo Ashram.

_____. 1962. *Human Cycles*. Pondicherry: Sri Aurobindo Ashram.

_____. 1970. *Life Divine*. Pondicherry: Sri Aurobindo Ashram.

_____. 1973. *Back to the Villages*. Pondicherry: Sri Aurobindo Asrham.

_____. 1992. *The Syntheses of Yoga*. Pondicherry: Sri Aurobindo Ashram.

Strydom, Piet. 2009. *New Horizons of Critical Theory: Collective Learning and Triple Contingency*. Delhi: Shipra.

Uberoi, J. P. S. 2002. *The European Modernity: Truth, Science and Method*. Delhi: Oxford University Press.

Vattimo, Giani. 1999. *Belief*. Cambridge: Polity Press.

Wuthnow, Robert. 1991. *After Heaven*. Princeton: Princeton University Press.

_____. 2001. *Creative Spirituality: The Way of the Artist*. Berkeley: University of California Press.

Chapter Two

BEYOND WEST AND EAST:
CO-EVOLUTION AND THE CALLING
OF A NEW ENLIGHTENMENT
AND NON-DUALITY

In [*On the Origin of Species*], Darwin had touched only incidentally on man, yet *as a man*, he placed himself – the observing scientist – outside the spectacle of nature. His own absolute superiority (and by extension, that of his kind) vis-à-vis the rest of the animal kingdom he never thought to question… In writing *the Descent of Man*, Darwin relinquished his stand outside the world and took up a position right inside it… Rather than taking for granted the preeminence of rational man (as a precondition for engaging in scientific inquiry), the question became: How did he get there?

—Tim Ingold, *Evolution and Social Life* (1986, 48–9)

The classical dichotomies between internal and external, organism and environment, face radical questions. Why must we think that one of the two polarities plays an active role (as cause), and the other plays a passive role (as environment)…and the organisms are nothing but objects this force plays upon?… Living systems are not collections of traits or characteristics that are passively subject to direction imposed on them by various environmental forces. They are autonomous and active entities that themselves contribute to the creation and modulation of these forces. Evolution is always a co-evolution.

—Gianluca Bocchi and Mauro Ceruti,
The Narrative Universe (2002, 159–60)

…the criteria of enlightenment and emancipation are themselves evolving as part of the evolutionary process…since evolution is an open-ended process, awakening, realization or enlightenment need to be relativised and conceived as in principle subject to evolution, so that they cannot be identified for any being or specific species in an absolute manner.

—Roy Bhaskar, *Meta-Reality: The Philosophy of Meta-Reality.*
Vol. 1: Creativity, Love and Freedom (2002, 25–6)

The Problem

Evolution was once a dividing mark between the "developed us" and the "underdeveloped or primitive them," but there have been certain foundational transformations in the theory and normative quest of evolution which challenge us to overcome both anthropocentrism and ethnocentrism. Developments in both the discourse and practice of socio-cultural evolution as well as biological and cosmic evolution point to the need for cultivating a new enlightenment and non-duality going beyond the dualism of environment and the organism, ontogenesis and socio-genesis and "us" and "them." Evolutionary thinking as part of Spencerian Social Darwinsim was used to rank societies in the scale of development. This is also another legacy of Western enlightenment, which continues to influence perspectives on socio-cultural evolution coming from scholars such as Jürgen Habermas who define cultural evolution in terms of rationalization. Development of ego-identity is an important mark of Habermasian ontogenetic model of societal and individual development (Habermas 1971). But both evolution and enlightenment are foundationally being re-thought now. Evolution refers now to a co-evolution of the organism and environment as part of a ceaseless journey in which man is not the endpoint of evolution. As Ingold tells us about Julian Huxley's caricaturing of the philosophical jellyfish: "...which of us is up a blind alley is something that can be judged only in evolutionary hindsight. In the present circumstances, a philosophical jelly-fish [*sic*] would have grounds for pessimism as regards the future of man" (1986, 19). And as Henri Bergson challenged us nearly a century ago:

> Intuition and intellect represent two opposite directions of the work of consciousness: intuition goes in the direction of life, intellect goes in the inverse direction, and thus finds naturally in accordance with the movement of matter. A complex and perfect humanity would be that in which these two forms of conscious activity should attain their full development. And, between this humanity and ours, we may conceive any number of possible stages, corresponding to all the degrees of imaginable of intelligence and of intuition. In this lies the part of contingency in the mental structure of our species. A different evolution might have led to a humanity either more intellectual still or more intuitive. (1912, 282)

The evolutionary challenge of the development of the mind in the direction of intuition that Bergson presents us finds a resonance in the works of Sri Aurobindo from India. Sri Aurobindo is a multi-dimensional experimenter having taken part in the Indian freedom struggle, and also subsequent strivings for the spiritual evolution of humanity. Like Bergson, Sri Aurobindo gives primacy to consciousness in the evolutionary process.[1] But this primacy is not posited in opposition to matter. Sri Aurobindo points us to the limitations of mind and the need for supramental transformation as a crucial challenge for the evolutionary transformation of humanity. Bergson and Sri Aurobindo go beyond both East and West and embody a transcendence of each of these starting points presented as the only horizons of the world. Building on their work as well as other recent works on evolution, the present essay presents co-evolution as a transformational evolutionary challenge which takes us beyond East and West. The perspective of co-evolution suggests that in evolution it is both environment and organism, that the individual and the collective are significant and urge us to go beyond a dualistic determinism. Co-evolution is also linked to the idea of emergent evolution, which suggests that evolution did not nor does proceed in accordance with any pre-conceived plan and the particular path that evolution takes at a particular point depends upon contingent circumstances and developments. Such a discourse and practice of evolution calls for a new enlightenment, one that valorizes not only ego and rationality but urges us to realize our connected self and multi-dimensional existence, where mind and intellect are part of a wider intuitive and supramental realization. As Sri Aurobindo challenges us: "The limited ego is only an intermediate phenomenon of consciousness necessary for a certain line of development. Following this line the individual can arrive at that which is beyond himself..." (1970, 58). The present chapter discusses the evolutionary challenge before self and society in terms of realizing a new enlightenment which just does not valorize rationality and dualism, but strives for realization of non-duality in manifold relations of being and becoming in self and society. This way it hopes to make a contribution to contemporary reflections on the future trajectories of our shared humanity.

The Journey of Evolution

Lamarck and Darwin are founders of modern idea of evolution. Darwin has also influenced thinking about socio-cultural evolution, particularly that of Herbert Spencer. But even though Spencer had a teleological view of evolution, Spencer himself also wrote: "Evolution does not imply a latent tendency to improve, everywhere in operation..." (cited in Ingold 1986, 17). The rank-order of societies, or for that matter the rank-order of species, is not essential to an evolutionary paradigm as there are many divergent lines of evolution. "What is essential to it is the idea that all human groups (ourselves included) are fellow passengers on the same overall movement... and hence the differences between them must be relative to where they stand" (Ingold 1986, xii).

Darwin is a key interlocutor in the modern, scientific discourse of evolution. From the point of view of our narrative it may be helpful for us to understand that in his evolutionary theory Darwin emphasized being rather than becoming. Darwin looks at evolution "within a framework of being, according to which things exist only in and for themselves, and not as instants in the unfolding of a total system" (cf. Ingold 1986, 8).[2] As we shall see with Bergson, opening ourselves to becoming and a different realization of time, where time is not external and abstract but a creative duration, is an important part of evolution. With Sri Aurobindo and Bergson, we see that overcoming the dualism of being and becoming, and the vertical and horizontal dimension of evolution, has been and continues to be an important goal of evolution.[3]

Darwin seems to have valorized struggle for existence as an important part of our evolutionary history. But even Darwin used it mostly as a metaphor, not literally.[4] Natural selection is based upon not only on competition but also on co-operation; in fact a key evolutionary challenge before us now is to overcome the dualism of competition and cooperation. As Kropotkin (1912, 31) wrote after Darwin: "...the war of each against all is not the law of nature. Mutual aid is as much a law of nature as mutual struggle." Kropotkin urges us to realize: "...natural selection continually seeks out the ways precisely for avoiding competition as much as possible. The ants combine in nests and nations; they pile up their stores, they rear their cattle; and thus avoid competition; and natural selection picks out of the ant's family the species which know best how to avoid competition, with its unavoidably deleterious consequences" (Kropotkin 1912, 61).

The Calling of Co-evolution

Co-evolution presents a mutually transforming relationship between organism and environment. Organisms and environment are not only related, but they interpenetrate each other.[5] It also presents an interacting relationship between species which influences their evolutionary trajectory; in fact it refers to reciprocal evolutionary change of interacting species. When organisms influence each other's evolution, this is a manifestation of the co-evolutionary process in Nature. Birds are often important actors in co-evolutionary systems. "For example, predation by birds easily drives... co-evolution... Some butterflies have evolved the ability to store poisonous chemicals from the food plant they eat as caterpillars, this becoming distasteful. This reduces their chances of being eaten, since birds, once they have tried to devour such butterflies, will avoid attacking them in future. Other butterflies have gradually evolved color patterns that mimic those of the distasteful butterflies (called 'models')" (Erlich et al. 1988).[6]

In such instances, we see that co-evolution is an important part of the evolutionary dynamism. "Co-evolution is the result of the fact that each interacting species is a part of the environment of the other species it interacts with. Each species 'adapts' to the other."[7] But adaptation (in inter-specific interaction as well as in the interaction between species and environment) in "co-evolution" can and does have a different meaning. In co-evolution, adaptation is not a passive reaction to the demand on the organism by the environment. In fact, in co-evolution, as compared with Darwin's principle of natural selection, the metaphor of adaptation is replaced with the metaphor of construction, which we can further extend to co-construction or co-creation. While in the model of adaptation organisms are passive objects, in modes of construction, organism and object, subject and environment are related to each other in co-creative ways, overcoming alienation between the two.[8]

This work of construction, or rather co-construction, in the interaction between organism and environment urges us to appreciate that organisms are autopoietic rather than passive; they self-reproduce rather than just reproduce.[9] It also urges us to appreciate the significance of non-adaptation: "Non-adaptive does not mean unintelligible"

(Stephen J. Gould and Lewontin, Richard, as cited in Bocchi and Ceruti 2002, 152). What does not adapt to the environment is not of less evolutionary significance; in fact it can be of enormous evolutionary significance.[10] In socio-cultural evolution, the "non-adaptive" can constitute the nurturing ground of hidden remnants which then become a source of creative evolution. Thus the calling of co-evolution is linked to the calling of autopoiesis where organisms write their own poems of creativity in a relational and emergent way.

Co-evolution suggests that evolutionary paths are not linear and one-dimensional; they are plural and contextual. It is thus linked to another recent development in evolutionary theory, namely evolutionary pluralism. A pluralist perspective on evolution as suggested by Stephen J. Gould and Richard Lewontin urges us to realize that "there are several alternative ways in which selection and adaptation can combine with each other" (Bocchi and Ceruti 2002, 151). In fact the perspective of evolutionary pluralism has emerged as a critique of dualism, urging us to realize that evolutionary journey is embedded in history.[11] Both the perspectives of co-evolution and evolutionary pluralism reiterate the significance of contingency. But for Stephen J. Gould, "Contingency is a thing onto itself, not the titration of determinism by randomness" (Bocchi and Ceruti 2002, 222). Here discoveries of fossils as well as developments in cosmology have come to our aid that rectify "the interpretation of natural history as a linear progression" and any self-confident claim about evolutionary inevitability such as the rise of Homo sapiens or even the origin of life (Bocchi and Ceruti 2002, 192). Contingency urges us to understand the complexity of history in evolutionary dynamics and acknowledge, as social theorist Nancy Weiss Hanrahan (2000) would suggest, things could have been different. Furthermore, as physicist and cosmologist Freeman Dyson tells us, even "the standard association between proteins and nuclear acids is not controlled by any a temporal need or a pre-existing design; it is highly probable, on the contrary, that it is the final result of a complex history" (cited in Bocchi and Ceruti 2002, 201). Thus evolution is not the domain of necessity; neither is it the domain of chance, but the domain of contingency. The origin of life and the present preeminence of man on earth might not have happened as well. Contingency makes evolution emergent.

Co-evolution is linked to autopoeisis. It is also linked to learning. In fact, as Kevin Kelly suggests, "co-learning might be a better term for what coevolving creatures do. Coteaching also works, for the participants in co-evolution are both learning and teaching each other at the same time" (1994).[12] But for appreciating the significance of learning in co-evolution we have to overcome anthropocentrism. Learning is not "an exclusive mark of our species": "the particles for learning lie everywhere in all inert media, waiting to be assembled (and often self-assembled) into something that surges and quivers" (Kelly 1994).[13]

Creative Evolution and Spiritual Evolution: Henri Bergson and Sri Aurobindo

The perspective of co-evolution opens up the dimensions of creativity and emergence in evolution, and here we can remember the seminal work of Henri Bergson. Bergson's

Creative Evolution is an important landmark in thinking about evolution. For Bergson, "Heredity does not only transmit characters; it transmits also the impetus in virtue of which the characters are modified, and this impetus is vitality itself" (1912, 244). Bergson gives primacy to consciousness in the evolutionary dynamics but this is not presented in a one-sided manner with an *a priori* idealism–materialism divide. As Bergson tells us: "...matter, the reality which descends, endures only by its connection with which ascends. But life and consciousness are this very ascension" (Bergson 1912, 39). As we shall see, this has a close affinity with Sri Aurobindo's perspective on evolution as involving both "ascent" and "descent." For Bergson: "...it is consciousness or rather supra consciousness, that is at the origin of life... But this consciousness, which is in need of creation, is made manifest to itself only when creation is possible. It lies dormant when a life is condemned to automatism; it wakens as soon as the possibility of a choice is restored" (1912, 275).

In our discourse and practice of evolution, Bergson (1912, 24) urges us to realize the significance of time. "Evolution implies a real persistence of the past in the present, a duration which is, as it were a hyphen, a connecting link." But this time is neither a static moment in an automation or a geometrical space,[14] nor is it a point in a pre-destined teleology. In our thought about evolution Bergson urges us to go beyond both a mechanical and a teleological binding: "The doctrine of teleology...implies that things and beings merely realize a programme previously arranged. But if there is nothing unforeseen, no invention or creation in the universe, time is useless again. As in mechanistic hypothesis, here again it is supposed that all is given" (1912, 41). Bergson elaborates this further, which suggests that his is not a simplistic critique of teleology: "But in speaking of a progress towards vision, are we not coming back to the old notion of finality? It would be so, undoubtedly, if this progress required the conscious or unconscious idea of an end to be attained. But it is really effected in the virtue of the original impetus of life; it is implied in the movement itself, and that is just why it is found in independent lines of evolution" (1912, 102). Realizing evolution in a non-teleological manner but which is not dismissive of the significance of an inspiring telos, such as a more inclusive development of consciousness, the emergence of an ecological mind (cf. Skolimowski 1984), a more beautiful and responsible human civilization or supra-mental evolution, has been and continues to be an important task. Bergson can help us in this journey. The impetus to life is crucial to evolution. There are differences between plants and animals, animals and human beings but what is important to realize is that we cannot make an essentialist, evaluative and self-valorizing judgmental distinction between them. For Bergson, "There is no manifestation of life which does not contain, in a rudimentary state – either latent or potentially – the essential characters of most other manifestations" (Bergson 1912, 12). Commenting on the issue of variation, especially as it emerges in neo-Lamarckism, Bergson tells us: "The variation that results in a new species...is not...merely an accidental variation inherent in the germ itself, nor is it governed by a determinism *sui generis* which develops definite characters in a definite direction... It springs from the very effort of the living being to adapt itself to circumstances of its existence... But the question remains, *whether the term 'effort' must not be taken in a deeper sense, a sense even more psychological* than any neo-Lamarckian supposes" (Bergson 1912, 81, emphasis added).

Bergson helps us to understand that further development of intuition in the context of the overwhelming static presence of intellect is an evolutionary challenge. For Bergson, "…intellect does not admit of the unforeseeable;" it is "skillful in dealing with the inert" and "awkward the moment it touches the living" (Bergson 1912, 172–3). For Bergson, "…intuition is mind itself, and, in a certain sense, life itself… Thus is revealed the unity of spiritual life. We recognize it only when we place ourselves in intuition in order to go from intuition to intellect…" (1912, 282–3).

Sri Aurobindo has also opened up many new vistas in the discourse and practice of evolution. In his *magnum opus*, *Life Divine*, Sri Aurobindo (1970,. 3) speaks of the evolution of "Life in Matter" and the evolution of "Mind in Matter": "Life is already in Matter and Mind in Life because in essence Matter is a form of veiled Life, Life a form of veiled consciousness." Sri Aurobindo here suggests a principle of evolution and involution, ascent and descent. For Sri Aurobindo, "Ascent or Evolution is only possible because there has been Descent or Involution. Matter can evolve because there has been a descent of spirit into matter. As with Matter, so also with Life, Soul and Mind. Each of these can evolve, because there has been an involution of spirit into it" (quoted in Maitra 2000, 69). Furthermore, "evolution is not merely an ascent from a lower to a higher state of being, it is also an integration of the higher with the lower status. This means that when a higher principle emerges, it descends into lower ones and causes a transformation of them" (Maitra 2000, 70). For example, in the evolutionary journey when mind emerges "not only does a new principle appear on the scene, but the lower principles of matter and life also undergo a transformation so that they become different from what they were before the emergence of mind" (Maitra 2000, 70). Sri Aurobindo thus urges us to understand the need for integrating the vertical with the horizontal in our evolutionary striving and discourse of evolution.

Another important dimension of evolution in Sri Aurobindo is *psychicization*, "that is to say, the opening out of the psychic being within. Evolution is not only a movements upwards and a movement downwards, but is also a movement inwards…within us dwells a spark of divinity… Evolution means the development of this psychic being…" (Maitra 2000, 71). A very different evolutionary possibility "opens if we can live within the inner being" (Sri Aurobindo 1970, 722).

Sri Aurobindo also urges us to understand the significance of the individual in the process of evolution: "In the involution of the Spirit into matter, the self was lost. Evolution, therefore, must have for its object the recovery of the self. This recovery is possible through the conscious individual being…" (quoted in Maitra 2000, 72). For Sri Aurobindo, "The immense importance of the individual being which increases as he rises on the scale, is the most remarkable and significant fact of a universe which started without consciousness and without individuality in an undifferentiated Nescience. This importance can only be justified if the Self as individual is no less real than the self as cosmic being or Spirit and both are powers of the Eternal" (quoted in Maitra 2000, 72).

Sri Aurobindo is a critic of the materialistic theory of evolution: "There is not a single creation, but a triple – material, vital and mental; it may be regarded as a composite of three worlds, as it were, interpenetrating each other" (Sri Aurobindo 1989, 4).[15] But evolution does not stop with the mental; it also involves a supramental transformation and transmutation. In the supramental stage, self and society overcome the limits of mind, especially its dualistic construction of the world, and discover the interconnectedness of existence. Sri Aurobindo states in the very beginning of *Life Divine*: "...mental consciousness may itself be only a form and a veil of higher states which are beyond mind. In that case, the unconquerable impulse of man towards God, Light, Bliss, Freedom, Immortality presents itself in its right place in the chain as simply the imperative impulse by which nature is seeking to evolve beyond mind" (1970, 3). Sri Aurobindo urges us to realize, "The animal is a living laboratory in which nature has, it is said, worked out man. Man himself may well be a thinking and living laboratory in whom and with whose conscious cooperation she wills to work out the superman, the God. Or shall we not say, rather, to manifest God" (1970, 4).

At this juncture, some comments and clarifications are in order. Despite anthropocentric suggestions, the God of Sri Aurobindo, like Sponza's, is not anthropocentric. What Bergson (1912, 262) writes also suggests a transgressive understanding of God in Sri Aurobindo: "...God has nothing of the already made; he is unceasing, life, action, freedom. Creation, so conceived, is not a mystery; we experience it ourselves when we act freely." God in Sri Aurobindo is not part of any theological system; God is part of a spiritual journey.[16] Secondly, when Sri Aurobindo speaks about superman, he makes it clear that his is not Nietzsche's superman. Sri Aurobindo appreciates Nietzsche's call for "self-exceeding" but this self-exceeding should not be an exercise in acquiring vitalistic strength over others but in helping us realize the spiritual dimension of self and society: "not the strong and enlightened vital will hymned by Nietzsche, but a spiritual self and spiritual nature" (Sri Aurobindo 1962, 224).

Sri Aurobindo makes it clear that spiritual man, not only mental and vital man, is the sign of the new evolution:

> The vital man, the mental man have had an immense effect upon the earth-life, they have carried humanity forward from the mere human animal to what it is now. But it is only within the bounds of the already established evolutionary formula of the human being that they can act; they can enlarge the human circle but not change or transform the principle of consciousness in its characteristic operation. Any attempt to heighten inordinately the mental or exaggerate inordinately the vital man – a Nietzschean supermanhood, for example – can only colossalise the human creature, it cannot transform or divinise him. (1970, 772)

Sri Aurobindo here makes a crucial argument that the next stage of evolution involving supramental transmutation and spiritualization of man calls for active cooperation and conscious participation. For Sri Aurobindo, "it has to be noted that the human mind has already shown a capacity to aid nature in the evolution of new types of plants and animals… It is not an impossibility that man should aid nature consciously also in his own spiritual and physical evolution and transformation" (Sri Aurobindo 1970, 844). "In the previous stages of evolution Nature's first care and effort had to be directed towards a change in the physical organization… But in man a reversal is possible, indeed inevitable…for it is through his consciousness, through its transmutation and no longer through a newly bodily organism that the evolution can and must be affected" (1970, 843–4).

Sri Aurobindo's emphasis on evolution involving supramental realization can be thought along with some other recent perspectives on evolution, especially that of involving the acknowledgment of and emergence of an "ecological mind" presented by Henryk Skolimowski (1984). Ecological conception of mind recognizes mind not only "as active but as co-creative: as made not only of abstract powers of reasoning but also as sensitivities of the entire body" (Skolimowski 1984, 111). It emphasizes that the mind co-creates reality, which is different from a one-sided idealistic extremism that "reality is created by mind" (Skolimowski 1984, 113). For Skolimowski, "We are an aspect of the universal mind or the total mind, and our limitations reflect the limitations of this larger mind. We can become much brighter, but only if the *total mind* as developed by the whole of humanity (through evolution) becomes much larger and brighter" (1984, 115). For Skolimowski, "The ecological theory of mind restores the power and place of mind in the universe of becoming" (1984, 116). But this does not acknowledge the need for a fundamental transmutation of the mind in the direction of the surpramental. This probably would be a major difference between Sri Aurobindo and Skolimowski, though Skolimowski very interestingly talks about a possible future post-linguistic and post-cognitive communication facilitated by further development of "spirituality [when] we shall be communicating much more directly, from spirit to spirit" (1984, 83).

Some scholars have argued that while Bergson does not have any teleology, Sri Aurobindo's perspective on evolution is teleological (cf. Maitra 2000). Yes, Sri Aurobindo does refer to teleology, but this is not such a deterministic teleology that "every step in the process [of evolution] is directed by the spirit" (cf. Maitra 2000, 68). Teleology in Sri Aurobindo is not a conventional one of giving primacy to purpose in a human sense. Rather it is the other name for an "urge of an intrinsic Truth-necessity," a "manifestation of all the possibilities inherent in the total movement" (1970, 835). Furthermore, scholars such as Maitra enthusiastically portray Sri Aurobindo as a champion of India and the East and are overzealous in their *a priori* judgmental comparison between Sri Aurobindo and thinkers such as Bergson. For them, while Sri Aurobindo gives importance to Being, Bergson emphasizes becoming. But it is not helpful to draw a radical contrast between them along such lines. Reality, for Sri Aurobindo, is beyond being and becoming.[17]

While in *Life Divine* Sri Aurobindo outlines human evolution as part of cosmic evolution, in his other major work, *Human Cycles*, he outlines his perspective on social evolution (Sri Aurobindo 1962). He is a critic of the linear approach to evolution and discusses the cycles of development of society. He discusses the movement of societies from the typal/conventional stage to an age of individualism and reason but does not make a categorical and ethnocentric distinction between civilization and barbarism. He considers primacy given to profit and money at the expense of everything else as an instance of economic barbarism (1962, 94). But what is important is that in his outline of social evolution Sri Aurobindo does not end with individualism and reason but describes the coming of a subjective age. This subjectivity has expressed itself in human history through the discovery of the nation-soul. But many a time this subjectivism through nationalism has manifested itself as an annihilationist collective ego. Sri Aruobindo urges us to realize that collective ego is more dangerous than individual ego. He distinguishes between true and false subjectivism. True subjectivism, for Sri Aurobindo, should enable us to "find out that the true individual is not the ego, but the divine individuality which is through our evolution preparing to emerge in us" (1962, 39). In *Human Cycles* Sri Aurobindo also discusses the "ideal law of social development" where individuals, communities and humanity are trying to perfect themselves:

> [T]he law for the individual is to perfect his individuality by the free development from within, but to respect and to aid and be aided by the same free development in others... The law for the community or nation is equally to perfect its cooperative existence by a free development from within, avoiding and taking full advantage of the individual, but to respect and to aid and be aided by the same free development of other communities and nations... The law for humanity is to pursue its upward evolution towards the finding and expression of the divine in the type of mankind, taking full advantage of the free development and gains of all individuals and nations and groupings of men, to work towards the day when mankind may be really and not only ideally one divine family, but even then, when it has succeeded in unifying itself, to respect, aid and be aided by the free growth of its individuals and its constituent aggregates...
>
> The true law of our development and the entire object of our social existence can only become clear to us when we have discovered not only, like modern science, what man has been in his past physical and vital evolution, but his future mental and spiritual destiny and his place in the cycles of nature. (Sri Aruobindo 1962, 63–4, 56)

Both Bergson and Sri Aurobindo point to the horizon of a spiritual evolution of humanity, but both of them acknowledge that spirituality as it is conventionally understood is not up to this task and it needs to be transformed. For Bergson, "the great error of the doctrines of the spirit has been [isolating] the spiritual life from all the rest" (1912, 293). Sri Aurobindo also urges us to realize this problem of isolated and alienated spirituality as an evolutionary difficulty to work on with, "it is true that the spiritual tendency has been individual and not collective" (1962, 885). This suggests that evolution does not just depend upon a deeper living in the inner being, it also calls for an appropriate intersubjective and collective experiment in the public sphere. Sri Aurobindo's suggestion for a spiritual evolution in cosmology, society and history can be facilitated by combining deeper seeking in and of the inner being with experiments in collective learning, creative intersubjectivity and the building of new institutions which facilitate such an evolutionary quest. This now brings us to the sphere of self and society which resonates with the dynamics of co-evolution of organism and environment that we touched upon in our previous discussion of biological evolution.

Socio-cultural Evolution: Overcoming the Dualism between Ontogenesis and Sociogenesis

Socio-cultural evolution has been the subject of much thinking in social sciences for the last one hundred and fifty years. Piet Strydom, in a remarkable assessment of recent works on evolution, points to a new European convergence on thinking about socio-cultural evolution, which seeks to combine the insights of Darwin and the communication theory of Habermas in a reflective manner. For Strydom, the perspective of evolution that emerges from both Darwin-inspired sociologists such as Bernhard Geisen and communication-oriented sociologists such as Klaus Eder is "non-reductive": "Rather than either a Darwinian selectionist or a developmental structural theory of a classical or neoclassical kind, we witness the emergence of a more complex post-classical situational theory" (Strydom 2004, 32). Strydom here particularly draws our attention to the work of Klaus Eder. For Strydom, while Parsons and Luhman "are in line with the official neo-Darwinistic interpretation which gives priority to selection or external setting," Eder shares with Habermas a pan-selectionist approach characterized by "epigenetics which emphasize internal structures, learning and the role in evolution of the organism as an autonomous entity with its own development" (Strydom 1993, 306). What is important to note here is "[t]he reflexive turn implied in the concern with internal structures and learning has had the effect of putting knowledge at the center of attention in evolutionary thinking" (Strydom 1993, 306). But is this knowledge only societal knowledge or knowledge of practical reason, or does it also involve self-knowledge that both Habermas and Sri Aurobindo in their very different ways point to?[18]

In his interestingly titled essay, "Societies Learn yet the World is Hard to Change," Eder draws our attention to the significance of learning in evolutionary process – but this learning is not individual learning but also societal learning. Eder writes, "The macro-sociological basis of evolutionary learning process has to be conceptualized not in terms of a theory of social action, but in terms of a theory of social interaction, not in terms of competent subjects, but in terms of evolving terms of intersubjectivity..." (Eder 1999, 199). Eder makes a distinction between learning and evolution: "... whereas learning carries the ontogenetic and sociogenetic development of knowledge and morality evolution evolves a change in the structural properties of practices" (Strydom 2004, 27).

Eder builds on Habermas' communicative model of socio-cultural evolution but while in Habermas, "modernity is depicted as the telos of moral evolution," for Eder social evolution has to be "retrieved from the web of universal history in which it got stuck virtually from the start with a view to focusing on the contexts of the utilization of knowledge and moral representation made available by collective learning processes" (Strydom 1992, 316). In emphasizing collective learning process, Eder seems to be overcoming the supposed "ontogenetic fallacy" of Habermas. For Eder, the evolution of practical reason focuses on "the social praxis that serves as the vehicle of practical reason" (Strydom 1992, 316). But is this social praxis only collective and intersubjective? In subsuming social praxis under collective learning and the "triple contingency" of the public, Eder and Strydom may be committing a sociogenetic fallacy. The challenge before the discourse and practice of socio-cultural evolution is to avoid the dualism of ontogenesis and socio-genesis and to realize that it is a work of co-evolution.

Overcoming the dualism of ontogenesis and socio-genesis calls for development and evolution in both self and society. In Habermas such an overcoming is facilitated by the development of post-conventional moral development in individual and society. Habermas's perspective on the post-conventional comes closer to the coming of the subjective in Sri Aurobindo, but while in Habermas there is no radical call to overcome "ego-identity,"[19] Sri Aurobindo makes transcending the separative existence of ego and mind and discovering the universal/transcendental dimension in self, society and cosmos a key part of his evolutionary appeal. The perspective on socio-cultural evolution has to overcome the dualism of the developed and the developing, West and East, modern and traditional, ontogenetic and sociogenetic, and come to terms with the new evolutionary challenge of spiritual and supramental transformation which in turn calls for a new enlightenment and non-duality.

The Calling of a New Enlightenment and Non-duality

Enlightenment in the West has been thought of primarily as rational enlightenment, and recent rethinking of it does not interrogate this foundational constitution and telos. Though Foucault's critique of Kantian enlightenment has the suggestion of going beyond this rational foundation, it does not go all the way in embodying the pathway of a new enlightenment which consists of recognizing the non-dual foundation or dimension of the dual existence of self and society. From the other side of the Atlantic, philosophers such as Hilary Putnam (2001) and Richard Rorty (1999) talk about a "pragmatist enlightenment" or practical enlightenment which emphasizes learning and "reflective transcendence," but this proposal is immanent only within practice and does not want to touch the transcendental or spiritual dimension. Such a lack impoverishes the project of "pragmatist enlightenment," which does not want to transcend the banality of patriotism and Western ethnocentrism and take part in a transcivilizational dialogue on realization of Enlightenment which involves both rational criticism as well as spiritual transformations (cf. Dallmayr 2002, Giri 2002). Pragmatist enlightenment thus becomes reduced to a self-confident political act in the public sphere which then can be deployed to categorize individuals and societies. Such models of public enlightenment do not include processes of self-cultivation. The calling of a new enlightenment urges us to realize the significance of self-cultivation as an aspect of both self-striving (or what is called in Indian spiritual traditions *sadhana*) and socio-political struggles. Buddha, Gandhi and Sri Aurobindo point to the need for such a new enlightenment. In critical philosophy and social theory, Roy Bhaskar articulates it in his recent transformation of critical realism into a philosophy of meta-reality. Writes Bhaskar, "If I become a better person then I am necessarily going to act better, have better effects on all planes of social being. So the principle of self-referentiality is entirely consistent with what I have called practical mysticism, that is being a non-dual being…" (Bhaskar 2002, xxxvii).

In the first chapter of his *Meta-Reality: Creativity, Love and Freedom*, interestingly titled "The Vedanta of Consciousness: Transcendence, Enlightenment and Everyday Life," Bhaskar describes three main aspects of processes of non-duality: transcendental identification, reciprocity and co-presence: "What happens in the non-dual moment is that you are immediately present. So in the non-dual moment you are there and there is you, that is your transcendentally real self, not your ego or some aspects of your embodied personality, but its ground state" (Bhaskar 2002, 10). Bhaskar outlines the pathway of a new enlightenment and self-realization thus: "…self-realization is you (as an embodied personality) *becoming* one with you (as your transcendentally real self)" (2002, 18). "You dis-identify with everything which is not your ground state, that is you… For enfolded within your ground state is the totality of the cosmic envelope, including the ground states and alethic truths of all other beings and aspects of the cosmos" (2002, 20).

Co-presence includes both space and time and it has implications for rethinking enlightenment as well as evolution. Co-presence as an aspect of non-dual realization and transformation means that enlightenment calls for realization that the other is co-present in me. And in so far as evolution is concerned, "…the theory of co-presence means that the process of evolution is open for species as well as the beings belonging, at any moment of time, to them. If everything is implicit on any one object, then there are enormous possibilities of awakening, unfolding or consolidating or in-building new powers in the evolutionary process. This encompasses something akin to the alchemical transmutation of species, or elements, something which evolution of necessity, even as currently understood, implies" (Bhaskar 2002, 25). Going beyond an anthropocentric and arrogant conception of enlightenment calls for a new enlightenment of realization of non-duality and *co-presence*. As Bhaskar would challenge us, which is in tune with the perspective of co-evolution and emergent evolution suggested in this essay:

For if mankind is implicit in an amoeba, then self-realization for that amoeba can mean anything from maximum fulfillment for an amoeba (of its particular type, always potentially unique), to attaining the level of self-realization for an explicitly conscious and potentially self-conscious being such as man, into which that amoeba may evolve through various levels and thresholds of realization, some of which may depend upon the wakening of powers and potentials, which are at present only in implicit in man and only awakened in species of which we have no knowledge or awareness. (Bhaskar 2002, 26)

Bhaskar presents realization of non-duality in a world of duality as a great challenge before enlightenment and evolution. Here it is helpful to go back to our earlier discussion that the strivings of co-evolution also embody an attempt to overcome dualism of many kinds, mainly environment and organism, external and internal. It is also helpful for us to note that non-duality has been an aspiration and striving with humanity and has expressed itself in myths, symbols, philosophies[20] and rudiments of social formations. For example, in earlier phase of our human history, during the time of the Mother Goddesses in Eurasian world, symbols such as spiral and the double helix were widespread, which point to mixing of dualities, transcendence and reveal how "unity, being transformed into duality, reaches a new and deeper unity" (Bocchi and Ceruti 2002, 20).[21]

Beyond West and East: The Spiritual Evolution of Humanity and the Calling of Transformations

Thus the whole humanity is confronted with the challenge of a new evolutionary transformation, one that confronts all of us in the planet transcending the familiar and even now the entrenched dualities of West and East, animal and man. Overcoming the ethnocentrism of both Orientalism and Occidentalism, as well as anthropocentrism is an epochal challenge. Spiritual evolution of humanity as suggested by Bergson and Sri Aurobindo is an important evolutionary task. But now the prevalent discourse and practice of spirituality needs to be transformed along multi-dimensional trajectories involving both food and freedom, self-development and social transformation, animated by a project and aspiration of universal self-realization. The transformational challenge now is to realize that self-realization cannot be narrowly conceptualized in individualistic terms: it involves liberation of all; it is indeed a project of universal self-realization and co-realization. As Roy Bhaskar (2002, 26) urges us to realize, "At a more quotidian level it could be argued that in Buddha's day, merely individual self-realization did make sense, in that it was possible to conceive of a complete and free being, independently of large chunks of socialized earth... However in our day, the, so to speak, contingent but very central interconnectedness of all human beings means that merely individual self-realization is impossible, in the sense that it can only be attained if all other human beings on the planet, and other species too, are liberated from the systems, which humankind has created, which oppress them."

But while it might have been possible to conceive of self-realization in isolated individual terms in Buddha's time, Buddha himself did not take this route. Buddha's pathways of strivings and struggles involved a project of liberation of all beings, not only human. This is the outstanding legacy of the legend and myth of Bodhisattva.[22] We need to be part of a "memory work" (cf. Dallmayr 1998) of bringing to our life the life and struggles of Buddha, the myth of Bodhisattva as well as many myths around the world about evolutionary struggles and aspirations. These myths can speak "to us today of other stories; stories they are not just before history, but that contain some possibilities that could be and never were, and infinite possibilities that are still waiting to be created in our present and in our future" (cf. Bocchi and Ceruti 2002, 257).

The spiritual strivings of Buddha were not bound to any theology and his project of enlightenment included rational deliberations with others, especially the downtrodden and excluded sections of society (cf. Carrithers 1983). Buddha worked with people and reasoned with them not to accept anything blindly because it has been the custom. Buddha worked in people's language and contributed to the generation of a democratic public sphere of spiritual enlightenment. It is this aspect of the legacy and aspiration of Buddha which finds a correspondence in collective learning, "triple contingency" and the democratic public sphere passionately advocated by inspiring interlocutors from contemporary Europe such as Jürgen Habermas, Klaus Eder and Piet Stydom. Spiritual imaginations and strivings in both conventional West and East have suffered from authoritarianism, feudalism and hierarchy. Though some changes seem to have been made in the West in terms of democratic transformation of authoritarianism, spirituality still continues to be bonded to many kinds of authoritarianism in many parts of the East, including India. In this context, generation of a democratic public sphere as an integral part of a project of the spiritual evolution of humanity is an important lesson that seekers and scholars from the East can learn from experiments in collective learning and democratic public sphere in the West. Our friends in the West too can learn that the public sphere does not involve only the public, and without a project of a new enlightenment and self-realization, the discourse of democracy, evolution and the public sphere can turn out to be new ghosts.

By Way of Conclusion

This inquiry into a new path of evolution and enlightenment yields important insights in terms of the discourse and practice of both biological as well socio-cultural evolution. Co-evolution is the crucial challenge here that calls for a new enlightenment and non-duality going beyond the dualism of organism and environment, individual and society. Our engagement has also explored pathways of creative and spiritual evolution drawing upon the seminal strivings of Bergson from Europe and Sri Aurobindo from India. This has shown us similarities between them going beyond the dualism of East and West. Thus this chapter has explored new ways of cultivating our soil for our emergent future going beyond varieties of entrenched dualisms such as ethnocentrism and anthropocentrism. In the sphere of socio-cultural evolution the present chapter pleads for simultaneous self-transformation and the democratic formation of will in the public sphere. This has significant implications for self, culture, society and polity, especially for practices of policymaking, institutional nurturance and creativity. Socio-cultural evolution is not a linear path but institutions preserve some key evolutionary insights such as dignity of self and other; now not only for the humans but also for the non-human. For example, new social institutions embodying dignity for humans have to be transformed so that they also embody dignity for other life forms and non-human animals. The plea for overcoming dualism such as human and non-human and ethnocentric dualism between West and East has important policy and practical implications in terms of the generation of appropriate consciousness, as well as institutional spaces where these insights can be cultivated, nurtured and preserved. This also has implications for generating spaces of self as well as collective learning. In this context, Sri Aurobindo has challenged us to realize that it is through an alternative integral education that we have to prepare for a new evolution. The present chapter has offered us glimpses of a new evolutionary journey which has significant implications for future studies, and this initial engagement is an invitation to all of us concerned to explore and embody further its integral and practical implications, as well as a new social and spiritual imagination.

Notes

1 The primacy of consciousness in the evolutionary journey is being recognized by many, from philosophers to anthropologists. In this context what Ingold, an anthropologist, writes deserves our careful attention: "The fundamental premises of an evolutionary cosmology are that there is but one world, that this world is not a collection of inert things but a continuous and creative movement, and that as conscious subjects, we human beings are a part of it. Consciousness must, therefore, be understood as an active force within the world, rather than as its projection into an other-worldly microcosm." He also tells us: "…consciousness is neither material nor ideal; it is no kind of substance but a movement or process" (1986, 298).

2 Ingold further argues: "The ideas of *continuity* and *temporality* are both the crucial components of the Darwinian conception of evolution. Yet for Darwin they had connotations quite different from those they had for Lamarck and his predecessors. For the continuity of 'descent without modification' is not a real continuity of becoming but a reconstituted continuity of discrete objects, each of which differs minutely from what comes before and after" (1986, 8).

3 We may note here, as Ingold tells us, "whereas Lamark was concerned with the vertical dimension of evolution, Darwin stressed its horizontal dimension. Thus, for example every individual is an 'incipient variety' every variety an incipient subspecies" (1986, 8).

4 In this context, Bocchi and Ceruti tell us that for Darwin "the metaphor of struggle for existence must be understood in a nonliteral way" (2002, 111). In a recent reflection on Darwin, Chitta Ranjan Das (2006) also argues that now the metaphor of struggle for existence must be transformed into a struggle for excellence.

5 In this context Bocchi and Ceruti draw our attention to the pioneering work of Sussan Oyama and Richard Lewontin:

> Susan Oyama has developed the most radical and far-reaching consequences of the idea of co-evolution. Neo-Darwinism was based on a root metaphor, the metaphor of the internal and the external. Natural selection is an external factor that is dependent on the environment; variations are internal raw materials, dependent on organisms. By contrast, in Lewontin's co-evolutionary concept, organisms and environment are at all times interrelated by definition. Oyama adds something more to this: organism and environment are not separable. At the individual level, the unit of evolution is the system of development. (2002, 160–61)

6 This draws on an article on co-evolution on the web by Erlich et al. Available at http://www.stanford.edu/group/stanfordbirds/text/essays/Coevolution.html

7 From a lecture on co-evolution posted on the web, now unavailable.

8 Richard Lewontin (cited in Bocchi and Ceruti 2002, 160) who is one of the recent proponents of the perspective of co-evolution, tells us:

> The metaphor of adaptation must be replaced with the metaphor of construction, a metaphor that has very specific implications for the form of evolutionary theory.

According to the concept in which organisms are passive objects of autonomous forces, evolutionary change can be represented by two parallel systems of differential equations. The first describes the manner in which an organism O evolves in response to the environment... The second is the law of autonomous change of environment, only as a function of environmental variables... A constructivist perspective overcoming the alienation between the organism-object and the subject-environment must instead be expressed with two coupled differential equations, in which you have the co-evolution of the organism-environment couple.

9 Chris Lucas, "Autopoiesis and Coevoultion." Available at http://www.calresco.org/lucas/auto.htm

10 In this context, Bocchi and Ceruti (2002, 153) tell us: "Of all the DNA found in chromosomes, only a minimal fraction participates in the syntheses of proteins: on human beings it does not reach 2 percent." The rest are the junk DNA. "Whatever their origin and their type might be, the function of junk DNA sequences is invaluable: it is the principal reservoir of variability on which species can count in future evolution."

11 As Bocchi and Ceruti (2002, 194) tell us: "Isolated factors do not transform organisms and species: their interaction does. And their interaction is always different. Each time, it is a new history."

12 Kevin Kelly's article on co-evolution posted on the web: http://www.kk.org/outofcontrol/ch5-e.html

13 In this context, what Kevin Kelly writes deserves our attention: "The dethronement of learning is one of the most exciting intellectual frontiers we are now crossing. In a virtual cyclotron, learning is being smashed into its primitives. Scientists are cataloguing the elemental components for adaptation, induction, intelligence, evolution, and coevolution into a periodic table of life. The particles of learning lie everywhere in all inert media..." See http://www.kk.org/outofcontrol/ch5-e.html

14 In this context, Bergson (1912, 47) tells us that "we are born artisans as we are born geometricians." Skolimowski (1984, 96) also tells us that one of the challenges of evolution is to acknowledge that different geometries are possible: "...starting with the womb in which we were conceived and in which the evolution of our species has been taking place – our being has been determined by amorphous and irregular shapes, round and female. This is the original geometry of nature. But then with the rise of civilization a different kind of geometry was forced upon us: linear, angular, straight."

15 Sri Aurobindo (1989, 8) tells us that "instead of a mechanical, gradual rigid evolution out of the indeterminate Matter by Nature-Force we move towards the perception of a conscious, supple, flexible, intensely surprising and constantly dramatic evolution by a Super-Conscient knowledge which reveals things in Matter, Life and Mind out of the unfathomable Inconscient from when they arise."

16 In this context, scholars such as Skolimowski (1984, 773) may have to rethink their position that insofar as evolution is concerned, Sri Aurobindo like Teilhard de Chardin has a divided loyalty "to the inexorable, creative and transforming power of evolution on the one hand, and to traditional perfect, finished God on the other." But while Teilhard de Chardin's evolutionary end point, Omega Point, may be a return to Christ, Sri Aurobindo's evolutionary journey does not return to any "finished God." Sri Aurobindo's *Brahman* is not a finished God.

17 Consider here also what Skolimowski (1984, 154) writes: "evolution is becoming which continually explodes into being. The forms of being are flowers of becoming."

18 While self-knowledge in Habermas refers to knowledge of oneself as an "ego identity" and also post-conventional moral consciousness, in Sri Aurobindo self-knowledge also involves the knowledge of oneself as a universal self or transcendental self.

19 To be fair to Habermas, Habermas does present us with glimpses of a higher self which is much more than an ego.

20 Speaking of philosophical manifestation of non-duality what Bocchi and Ceruti (2002, 47) deserves our careful attention:

> The dialogical and dynergic cosmology symbolized by the union of Shiva and Shakti and manifested in Yoga has given rise to many philosophical systems of the two great spiritual traditions of classical India: Hinduism and Buddhism. Beyond all their differences and disagreements, they express a principle [of] "duality within non-duality." The ultimate reality of the universe, the "noumen," is defined precisely as "non-dual": a-dvaita (a Hindu term) or a-dvaya (a Buddhist term).

21 As Bocchi and Ceruti tell us, "The spiral is a symbol of evolution of universe, cosmic energy, breathing, development and the unlimited potentials of becoming. In the art of the Mesolithic and Neolithic (found in France, Ireland, and England) it represents above all transcendence. Often it is associated with the bull, whose horns are nothing more than stylized spirals... The double helix is the symbol of mixing of dualities. It is a dynergic symbol...to show the generative power of complementary opposites" (2002, 20).

22 Here we need to understand the difference between two strands of Buddhism, *Hinayana* and *Mahayana*. As Bocchi and Ceruti (2002, 48) tell us:

> The ethical ideal of *Hinayana* was that of a personal salvation, egoistic and private. The *Mahayana* developed around the doctrine of the universal and unconditional liberation of all creatures, without any exception. Personal realization and illumination had to be used in the service of others. The suffering felt by others was one's own, and personal well-being was the well-being of everyone. Those who embraced this ideal were called *bodhisattva*: creatures whose essence (*sattva*) is illumination (*bodhi*).

References

Bergson, H. 1912. *Creative Evolution*, trans. Arthur Mitchell. London: Macmillan.

Bhaskar, Roy. 2002. *The Philosophy of Meta-Reality. Vol. 1: Creativity, Love and Freedom.* Delhi: Sage.

Bocchi, Gianluca and Ceruti, Mauro. 2002. *The Narrative Universe*, trans. Luca Pellegrini and Alfonso Montour. Cresskill, NJ: Hampton Press.

Carrithers, Michael. 1983. *Buddha*. Oxford: Oxford University Press.

Dallmayr, Fred. 2002. *Dialogue Among Civilizations: Some Exemplary Voices*. New York: Palgrave Macmillan.

Das, Chittaranjan. 2006. *Veera Jodha Kari* [Being a Heroic Warrior]. Bhubaneswar: Suhrut Prakashani.

Erlich, Paul R., David S. Dobkin and Darryl Wheye. 1988. "Coevolution." Available at http:// www.stanford.edu/group/stanfordbirds/text/essays/Coevolution.html (accessed 12 April 2012).

Eder, K. 1999. "Societies Learn yet the World is Hard to Change." *European Journal of Social Theory* 2 (2): 195–215.

Giri, Ananta Kumar. 2002. *Conversations and Transformations: Towards a New Ethics of Self and Society.* Lanham, MD: Lexington Books.

Habermas, Jürgen. 1971. *Knowledge and Human Interests*. Boston: Beacon Press.

———. 1979. *Communication and the Evolution of Society*. Boston: Beacon Press.

Hanrahan, Nancy W. 2000. *Difference in Time: A Critical Theory of Culture*. Westport, CT: Praeger Publishers.

Ingold, Tim. 1986. *Evolution and Social Life*. Cambridge: Cambridge University Press.

Kelly, Kevin. 1994. "Coevolution." *Out of Control: The New Biology of Machines, Social Systems, and the Economic World*. Available at http://www.kk.org/outofcontrol/ch5-e.html (accessed 12 April 2012).

Kropotkin, Peter. 1912. *Mutual Aid: A Factor of Evolution*. New York: Alfred A. Knopf.

Lucas, Chris. 2000/2005. "Autopoeiesis and Coevolution." Available at http://www.calresco.org/lucas/auto.htm (accessed 12 April 2012).

Maitra, S. 2000. *The Meeting of the East and West in Sri Aurobindo's Philosophy*. Pondicherry: Sri Aurobindo Asrham.

Putnam, Hilary. 2001. *Three Enlightenments*. University of Amsterdam, Spinoza Lectures.

Rorty, Richard. 1999. *Philosophy and Social Hope*. London: Penguin.

Skolimowski, Henry. 1984. *The Theatre of the Mind: Evolution in the Sensitive Cosmos*. Wheaton, IL: The Theosophical Publishing House.

Sri Aurobindo. 1962. *Human Cycles*. Pondicherry: Sri Aurobindo Ashram.

———. 1970. *Life Divine*. Pondicherry: Sri Aurobindo Ashram.

———. 1989. *Evolution*. Pondicherry: Sri Aurobindo Ashram.

Strydom, Piet. 1992. "The Ontogenetic Fallacy: The Immanent Critique of Habermas's Developmental Logical Theory of Evolution." *Theory, Culture & Society* 9: 65–93.

———. 1993. "Sociocultural Evolution or the Evolution of Practical Reason: Eder's Critique of Habermas." *Praxis International* 13 (3): 304–21.

———. 2004. "The Theory of Evolution in Contemporary Sociology: A New European Convergence?" University College Cork, Ireland, Department of Sociology. Later published in *New Horizons of Critical Theory: Collective Learning and Triple Contingency*, Delhi: Shipra Publications, 2009.

Chapter Three

THE MODERN PRINCE AND THE MODERN SAGE: TRANSFORMING POWER AND FREEDOM

The entire tradition of political theory seems to agree on one basic principle: only "the one" can rule, whether that one be conceived as the monarch, the state, the nation, the people, or the party. The three traditional forms of government that form the basis of ancient and modern political thought – monarchy, aristocracy, and democracy – reduce, from this perspective, to one single form. Aristocracy may be the rule of the few, but only in so far as these few are united in one single body or voice. Democracy, similarly, can be conceived as the rule of the many or all, but only insofar as they are unified as "the people" or some such single subject. It should be clear, however, that this mandate of political thought that only the one can rule undermines and negates the concept of democracy. *Democracy, along with aristocracy in this respect, is merely a façade because power is de facto monarchical.*
—Michael Hardt and Antonio Negri, *Multitude: War and Democracy in the Age of Empire* (2004, 328–9, emphasis added)

When my powers clash with the powers of another man they are reduced to nothing; and this is due to the fact the other is, as it were, another me – a creature belonging to the same species that I do and thus endowed with capacities and means that are essentially equal to my own.
—Poitr Hoffman, *The Quest for Power: Hobbes, Descartes and the Emergence of Modernity* (1996, 5)

In human life, Suffering is the antithesis of Power, and it is also a more characteristic, and more fundamental element in Life than Power is… Suffering is the essence of Life, because it is the inevitable product of an unresolvable tension between a living creature's essential impulse to try to make itself into the center of the Universe and its essential dependence on the rest of creation and on the Absolute Reality on which all creatures live and move and have their being. On the other hand, human power, in all its forms is limited and, in the last resort, illusory. Therefore any attitude towards Life that idolizes human power is bound to be a wrong attitude towards Suffering and, in consequence, a wrong attitude towards Life itself.

—Arnold J. Toynbee, *An Historian's Approach to Religion* (1956, 74)

The Modern Prince and the Modern Sage: Introduction and Invitation[1]

The prince has been the dominant archetypal model of being and becoming in modernity, and despite the supposed beheading of the kings in the modern world, as Machiavelli (1981) and Antonio Gramsci (1957), among many others, tell us it is the values of the prince, namely his will to power, that guide us in the modern world, rather than the values of an unconditional ethical obligation of the self to the other. Power, politics and empowerment have provided determinant frames of self-constitution and social emancipation in the modern world, and they have provided the singular definition of freedom as well. Modernity has been characterized by the ascendancy of politics and a power-model of the human condition over all other modes of being and values of life such as those of virtue, *shraddha* (reverence and love) and *tapashya* (loving meditation for transformation). There of course has been a shift in the locus of power in the evolution of modern society. If earlier power was embodied in the prince as an individual, in the course of history this locus has shifted to institutions and systems of society. But the institutionalization of power in the modern and late-modern world does not mean that it has ushered in more freedom for the subjects, since in both the cases (i.e. in the case of the prince and in case of the modern prince) the modern institutionalized locus of power, not only Gramsci's political party – it is power as domination, or in Max Weber's phrase, "the ability to carry over one's own will against the will of others," which has guided our thought, practice and conduct.

In fact, the modernist preoccupation with politics and power has been accompanied by very little realization of transformation beyond the capture of power, despite thinkers such as Gramsci challenging us: "An important part of the Modern Prince will have to be devoted to the question of intellectual and moral reform..." (Gramsci 1957, 139). Those savants in the modern world such as Erasmus, who have provided us with an alternative challenge of being and becoming and have urged us to strive for freedom and radical reflection without the capture of power and authority and through "faith in man," have been totally sidetracked by other leaders in religion and politics whose main objective has been the capture of power, and through this assurance of human emancipation.[2] It is the *weltanschauung* and the will to power of these leaders which is noticeable in all movements of emancipation in the modern world, whether it is the movement of the liberals or the communists. But after hundreds of years of experience and experiments with such power models of emancipation, freedom and the human condition, we are slowly realizing that the capture of power is neither the be all or end all of life, and it is certainly not a guarantee for the attainment of a dignified life and the establishment of a "good society." It is, perhaps, for this reason that commentators such as Anthony Giddens (1991) urge us to make a distinction between power politics and life politics, where life politics is a politics of self-actualization and is concerned with the question, "how we should live our lives in emancipated social circumstances."

However Giddens cannot explore the logic of self-actualization without the addendum of politics, as is the case with another commentator, Seyla Benhabib (1987), who cannot proceed even a step further in her meditation on norms and utopia without the adjective and the noun;political and politics without the words such as "politics of fulfilment" and "politics of self-transfiguration." This shows the hegemony of the power model of the human condition and the prince's will to power in our current thought and practice. This "hegemony of a power" perspective on the human condition has recently received a new lease of life from contemporary master interlocutors such as Michel Foucault, whose disciples assert that there is no escape from the circle of power and counter-power, and any project of a "good life" which is determined to put power in its place and strives to actualize an unconditional ethical obligation of the self to the other is doomed to failure to begin with. But in Foucault himself, we also find a realization of the limitation of power in ensuring human emancipation as he himself writes: "In fact, I have especially wanted to question politics – the questions I am trying to ask are not determined by a pre-established political outlook and do not tend to the realisation of some definite political project" (Foucault 1984, 376). For Foucault, "In short, it is a matter of starting out search of a different critical philosophy: a philosophy that does not determine the conditions and limits of a knowledge of the object, but the conditions and undefined possibilities of the subject's transformation" (Foucault 2005, 526). In his posthumously published work, *The Hermeneutics of the Subject*, Foucault urges us to realize that "The political, ethical, social, philosophical problem of our day is not try to liberate the individual from the state and its institutions but to liberate us both from the state and the type of individualisation linked to the state. We have to promote new forms of subjectivity…" (Foucault 2005, 544).

This chapter in our engagement with knowledge and human liberation is concerned with the questions of rethinking and transforming power as a theme in itself and in the light of contemporary transformations in discourse and society. It is born out of a realization that interrogating the modernist faith in politics and power as sole guarantors of human well-being and freedom constitutes an epochal challenge before us in this new century and in our new millennium. It seeks to explore how we can transform power in the late-modern condition of the systematization and institutionalization of power. For example, one key question now is whether only either the route of individual asceticism or democratic transformation of institutions is enough to transform power, or does it call for simultaneous work on self-transformation and structural transformation. The present essay seeks to explore how we can rethink power and realize its transformative meaning. It seeks to explore the resources it can derive from many different sources – traditional philosophies, religions, spiritual movements, and alternative quests within modernity – in this task of rethinking and reconstruction. For example, when an interlocutor such as Hannah Arendt (quoted in Cohen and Arato 1992, 178) writes that to have power is "acting in concert, on the basis of making and keeping promises, mutually binding one another, covenanting," it provides us another mode of being vis-à-vis power – one of "power with" rather than "power over."

While exploring the transformative contours of power, the present chapter does not propose a simple polarity between power and virtue, the prince and the sage, power as "evil" and wisdom as "good," but explores transformation in the context of the complex multi-dimensional reality and possibility of power. As Stellan Vinthagen (2008) echoes the spirit of nuanced transformative engagement with power, "power is many-faceted and…even the will, body and the mind of the resistance fighter is not free from power." This points to our implication in the field of power. For Judith Butler, power shapes the formation of subjectivity: "Power not only *acts on* a subject but, in a transitive sense, enacts the subject into being" (Butler 1997, 13). Though the indispensable force of power in the shaping of subjectivity in many conditions (which makes Butler write: "No individual becomes a subject without first becoming subjected to or undergoing subjection") cannot be summarily dismissed in the name of any *a priori* spiritual enthusiasm, at the same time it does not exhaust all the possibilities of the subject, including her transformational and transcendental dimension. Our implication in the field of power does not lead only to the double subjectivity that Butler talks about: our subjugated subjectivity and our emergent subjectivity shaped by power. It is also the very field for transforming the logic of power and working towards a transformational self and society where the goal is realizing what Dallmayr, building on Heidegger, calls a "power-free" existence (cf. Dallmayr 2001). Butler's view of the subject even in her double subjectivity does not give enough attention to the transcendental dimension of the subject which, while being subjugated by power, still refuses to surrender but strives for transformation. Instead of proceeding with a polarity between the subjugated and transformative view of self and power, an acknowledgment of our complex implication in the field of power is an indispensable and helpful companion to our political and moral struggles to transform power. In this context the insights of Foucault can be brought transformationally together with insights of experimenters such as Erasmus, Eckhart, Gandhi and Subcommandate Marcos of the Zapatista movement, who challenge us to go beyond the trappings of power and counter-power.

An important challenge here is also to transform power into what Antonio Negri (1991), building upon Spinoza, calls "constituent power" in which it is freely constituted by the multitude. Constituent power is not "power over" but "power with," as "power over" obstructs the unfolding of potential of not only the dominated but also the dominating.[3] The idea of the multitude is neither just the mass nor the people, it is a web of existence which is characterized by the simultaneous work of singularity, as well as the emergent commonality among singularities self-aware of one's common condition as well as the need for transformation. Constituent power is linked to ongoing democratic transformations of society in which the sovereign power which rules in the name of the One is subjected to the power of the Multitude going beyond the polarity and dualism of the One and Many. As Michael Hardt writes about Negri's interpretation of the very significant transformative reconstitution of power in the hands of Spinoza,

> [For Spinoza] [d]emocracy is to be the absolute, unlimited form of government, because in it the Supreme Power is fully constituted by the power of the multitude. Spinoza's democracy is to be animated by a constituent Power, a dynamic form of popular authority… In effect democracy is a return to a plane of the *Ethics*: Power (*potentia*) does not exist in Spinoza's democracy except to the extent that it is a constituent Power completely and freely constituted by the power of the multitude… If *Ethics* reduces the distinction and subordinates Power (Sovereign Power, for example) to power in the idealistic terms of its utopian vision, the *Political Treatise* poses the real tendency toward a future reduction of the distinction, when a democratic power would be completely constituted by the power of the multitude. (Hardt 1991, xvi)

But is this process of democratic transformation only political or is it at the same time a multi-dimensional work on self-transformation and collective transformation?[4] As Ramashroy Roy poses this problem in a provocative way in his *Beyond Ego's Domain: Being and Order in the Vedas*:

> [Public order is threatened by the split between] man's concern for his own good and that for the good of others. But can this threat to the public order be mitigated, if not completely eliminated, by the installation of the Polis?… For Aristotle, transcendence of self-interest is consequent upon participation in public affairs [but] the shortcomings associated with personal character cannot be expected to be rectified by the public realm, if it lacks necessary support from individuals reborn as citizens. To be reborn as a person who, rising above his self-interest, becomes attentive to and actively seeks to pursue collective good, is, then, to willingly accept a life dedicated to the cultivation of *dharma*. (Roy 1999, 5)

For fuller democratic realization, Roy here points to the need for being reborn as persons and citizens and cultivating *dharma*, which here can be understood as nurturing a mode of dutiful and compassionate engagement which helps the self, society, the commons and the cosmos to blossom. Negri's interpretation of constituent power lacks this simultaneous engagement with political and spiritual transformation of self, society and polity, and the present book seeks to carry out such a connected inquiry, interrogation and transformation.

As we are confronted with the task of transforming power, we are also confronted with the task of transforming freedom, here again as a theme in itself and in the light of contemporary transformations in discourse and society. The current discourse of freedom, like the discourse of power, is at a dead end. It is certainly nice to hear from a thinker such as Ernesto Laclau: "We are today coming to terms with our own finitude and with the political possibility that it opens. This is the point from which the potentially liberatory discourses of our post-modern age have to start. We can perhaps say that we are at the end of emancipation and at the beginning of freedom" (Laclau 1992, 137). But Laclau does not tell us how we can rethink freedom today and have an integral realization of it, a realization which transcends the familiar dichotomies in thinking about and striving towards freedom: economic and political, food and freedom, and political and spiritual. Our task of transformation is made enormously difficult by the fact that in the current euphoria about global democratization and civil society, we proceed with a narrow view of freedom, where we are primarily concerned with freedom from authoritarian structures and the individual's freedom of choice. The work of Isaiah Berlin (2000) and Amartya Sen (1999) as they make a distinction between negative freedom and positive freedom promises a step forward in the current impasse, especially out of the current libertarian capture of the calling of freedom but the promise of recovery, even in this agenda is an illusory one as neither Berlin nor Sen tells us how we can transcend the dualism between negative and positive freedom. They are silent about the ontological and aesthetic preparation we need to have at the level of self and society so that the devotion to freedom becomes an integral one and the individual in her own life is able to ensure liberty for herself and at the same time becomes an agent of well-being in the life of others. Though Sen's challenge of linking food and freedom is important, the lack of ontological preparation in such rethinking of freedom is still a crucial gap for us to fill.

To put it succinctly, the current reflection on freedom again reflects the modernist preoccupation with power and political freedom, and has not given enough attention to the challenge of spiritual freedom as an ideal and practice at the level of both self and society, nor to the aesthetic dimension of freedom. By having a view of freedom as a spiritual and aesthetic[5] process of transformation and the agent of freedom as a transformative self, which begins with self-control over one's lower self and cultivation of one's higher self, we can go beyond good and evil, positive and negative. It is crucial here to realize that despite our use of words such as "lower" and "higher," which is a reflection of our inescapable human finitude, especially the finitude of language, lower and higher self here, as it is in many spiritual traditions of the world, do not point to a hierarchical fixation. Lower self, for example, is not the self which just wants to have sex, and higher self meditating under the bush. Rather, lower self points to a self which is bound to itself, its ego understood in a narrow way, and with maximization of one's pleasure even when it involves slitting the throats and spilling the blood of others while the higher self points to a seeking for relationship[6] and transformation, transforming the quality of our desire no matter what we desire, flesh or God.[7] Transforming freedom is thus confronted with the task of transformation of self from lower to higher (understood in a non-dual and non-hierarchical way) and embodiment of responsibility (cf. Levinas 1974, 1990). For instance, Sri Aurobindo (1962) argues that standards of conduct and the practice of freedom must be anchored in a spiritual plane where the goal of freedom is not only to have the freedom to choose but also to transform our needs and desire. A spiritual seeking also helps us to discover the emergent universal ground within us where the social distinction between individual and collective, negative and positive freedom gets a new frame of reference for criticism and transcendence.

An aesthetic and spiritual engagement with freedom helps us transform our dominant conceptions of governmentality where self-governance becomes the foundation and model of governance. This is the spirit of Gandhi's striving for Swaraj and Foucault's later engagement with self-government. The key issue here is that for self-governance the very machinery and telos of governance has to be changed, as rule in self-rule is not the same as we know in familiar machineries of rule. It calls for more persuasion and transformation rather than just repression and the application of force.[8]

Transforming Power and Freedom

Transforming power and freedom has been the subject of a recent book, *The Modern Prince and Modern Sage: Transforming Power and Freedom*, where nearly 30 contributors from different disciplines, fields of engagement and parts of the world offer valuable insights (Giri 2009). In our engagement with these issues we can draw upon the insights of some of these contributors. The book seeks to transform power and freedom by exploring the contours of a new politics and spirituality emerging in our times which contribute to self-transformation, world transformation and cosmic transformation. The first part of the book, "Reconstituting Power and Freedom: Modernity and Beyond," begins with a foundational essay on the reconstitution of the political in modernity by S. N. Eisenstadt (2009). For Eisenstadt, modernity began with an emphasis on the autonomy of man, and this new ontological conception not only led to the breakdown of traditional legitimization but loss of traditional markers of certainty. Social movements of various kinds played an important role in the reconstitution of the political in modernity. Social movements became bearers of utopian visions carrying the "roots of modern political programme in the heterodox Gnostic traditions of Medieval Europe." For Eisenstadt, "The Great Revolutions [of modernity] can indeed be seen as the first or at least the most dramatic, and most successful attempt in the history of mankind to implement on a macro-societal scale utopian visions with strong Gnostic components." Furthermore, "Such visions became closely connected with the second major component or orientation of the political programme of modernity – namely the recognition of the multiple interests and of multiple conceptions of the common good, slowly extending also to the realm of (religious) beliefs." But this reconstitution of the political in modernity along with the axes of pluralism had its limits in authoritarian regimes which "tended to espouse a very restricted, limited conception of citizenship and a highly regulated access of civil society to the state." But in the very formative moment of European modernity there was a deep contestation of authoritarianism in religion and politics and striving for a new mode of relationship, and Erasmus embodied this. As Felix Wilfred (2009) writes in the second chapter of the book, "Erasmus' positive vision of the humankind marked a significant departure from the medieval Christian tradition insisting on human sinfulness and frailty – a tendency Luther carried to the extreme. The modernity was a rejection of such a conception, which it replaced with a more trusting attitude in the human and its abilities."

The French Revolution was the paradigmatic act of breaking away from authoritarian foundationalism and in his contribution, "Political Symbolism: Or How to Stay on the Surface," historian and philosopher Frank R. Ankersmit (2009) helps us in understanding the significance of anti-foundationalism for the sake of continued political reconstitution and representative democracy. For Ankersmit, "The French Revolution was not such a decisive social and political caesura because it had discovered the absolutely sound foundation for a wholly new political order – it could only be such a revolutionary event, because it did away with the very notion of foundations in general... Both French Revolution and representative democracy presuppose the rejection of political foundationalism." In this creative anti-foundational strivings, political symbolism plays an important role, but for this politics should not be left reduced only to issues of management. Ankersmit makes a distinction between politicians and political managers and urges us to continue to nurture anti-foundational political symbolism, especially at the contemporary juncture, as politics is increasingly being reduced solely to problems of management.

But the French Revolution was only a beginning in the direction of needed multi-dimensional transformation. While its slogans of equality and liberty became orthodoxies, in the political movements of liberalism and socialism, fraternity is still crying in the streets around the world. Of course, today fraternity means both brotherhood and sisterhood, a part of what Binod Kumar Agarwala (2008) in his subsequent contribution on Kant calls belonging. Agarwala critically interrogates as well as interprets Kant in a novel way as concerned with the calling of belonging. For Agarwala, the "Kantian ruler is as absolute as the Hobbesian sovereign, but Kant succeeds in evading this from the readers by claiming that the sovereign is not the head of the state...but a public law, act of a public will." But in his *Critique of Judgment*, Kant was fascinated with the calling of belonging to community where authority is based on "knowledge – knowledge as virtue, not power." For Agarwala, we can overcome this antinomy between power and liberty by belonging to the nation and state. But given the complicity of both nation and state in a violent project of homogenization and exclusion, it is helpful to transform Agarwala's proposal into a community of virtues which also celebrates colors of pluralism.

Agarwala's contribution points to the limits of power and liberty in modernity, and the subsequent contribution of Philip Quarles van Ufford, "The Power of Modernity and the Tail of the Devil," explores these limits in a very foundational way in both the European home and outside the colonized world. In European home, modernity has asserted its power by banishing the devil from the world, but Quarles van Ufford (2009), taking cues from Goethe's *Faust*, urges us to realize that the devil has performed a disappearing act himself. In this context, for Quarles van Ufford, "...we may discern the tail of the devil in everyday life in the form of exaggerated forms of optimism and overly facile promises of social order." Violence becomes indispensable in such a project of abolition of evil and establishment of order, as Quarles van Ufford shows remarkably with examples of Dostoevsky's Grand Inquisitor and Arthur Koestler's party executioner. With colonialism this project of killing is let loose globally but the fire that burns other's homes finally comes back and engulfs the home of European modernity as well (see Uberoi 2002). With the help of Conrad's *Heart of Darkness* Quarles van Ufford shows us how this devastation comes home.

In this context, a great challenge of dealing with the power of modernity and modernistic power is confronting violence and coercion and the subsequent contributions of a philosopher and a sociologist are highly instructive. In her contribution, "Rethinking Power: Aesthetics, Dialogue, Hegemony," Kanchana Mahadevan (2009) discusses insightfully the seminal works of Hannah Arendt, Michel Foucault and Antonio Gramsci. For Mahadevan, "...violence is an indifference to the point of view of the other" but building on Arendt she argues that power cannot be equated with violence. Rather, "Arendt's notion of power promises to be a constructive endeavour towards evolving new forms of solidarity." Mahadevan ties this notion of power as the "art of public dwelling" from Arendt with conceptions of struggles building on Foucault, Habermas and Gramsci and argues that "politics is the struggle for public discourse." But is this struggle only political? Doesn't it involve self-transformation and ethical-moral and spiritual transformation of societies? While Giri explores the challenge of self-cultivation that power is confronted with in the third section of the book, sociologist and cultural theorist Jan Nederveen Pieterse (2009) presents us the empirically as well as normatively challenging issue of the metamorphoses of power. One important aspect of the metamorphoses of power in society and history is a very fragile shift from coercion to cooperation. Pieterse challenges us to go beyond the reversals in contemporary *real politik* and to acknowledge both cooperation and coercion in the working and trajectories of power. Pieterse (2009) discusses several trends towards a democratic and cooperative regulation of power over time, such as, among others:

1. Over time the exercise of power is increasingly normatively regulated. Political and military power generally since the era of the French Revolution and the "age of democratic revolution" have been increasingly subject to constitutional and legal structures;
2. In most countries there is a shift from government to governance and towards interactive decision-making and decentralisation in public administration...

But Pieterse himself urges us to realize that this is by no means a generalized trend: "A countertrend is the growing global and domestic inequality and concentration of income and power at the top, which in the United States increasingly takes the form of plutocracy." For Pieterse, "Nevertheless the empirical circumstances that underlie these trends – growing demographic densities, global interdependence and growing human capacities – are structurally significant. This makes greater cooperation likely."

But the likelihood of this realization is dependent upon varieties of transformative struggles, and the part two of the book *The Modern Prince and the Modern Sage*, "Beyond the Modern Prince: Varieties of Struggles and New Intimations," presents some of these. It begins with Stellan Vinthagen's discussion of non-violent movements and the challenge of the management of power. As has been already discussed, through exploring non-violent resistance Vinthagen goes beyond a simplistic view of power and resistance and urges us to understand their complex constitution as well as differentiation by presenting power as subordination and resistance as disobedience. Power as subordination is not totally subjection: it is dependent upon the willful participation of those who are part of it, including their acts and potential for disobedience. While explicating non-violent resistance with an example from Gandhi, Vinthagen (2009) urges us to realize that "The Gandhian non-violence involves a simultaneous resistance against the oppressive role of the counterpart and a cooperation with the same counterpart as a human being and part of a unity of humanity."

Vinthagen's explorations are followed by Bernard Adeney-Risakotta who, in his essay, "Power From Below: Indonesian Reflections on the Paradigm of Power," also discusses the issue of non-violent resistance to power. Beginning with a discussion of the issue of the similarity and differences between Javanese and Western approaches to power, Adeney-Risakotta (2008) also challenges us to understand the distinction between power and violence. Building on the non-violent struggles to overthrow the autocratic regime of Suharto and other such movements in society and history, especially the non-violent struggle for freedom led by Gandhi, Adeney-Risakotta (2009) writes: "...the classic, almost universal paradigm of power as domination based on violence, generates more misunderstanding than clarity. Power is very diverse and distributed in different ways among the people. Power is not primarily the possession of a small elite but rather is located in the people. Power is the ability of the people to act together to achieve their aims. Powerlessness is the inability to initiate real change in human social reality." We can relate this to Spinoza's constituent power that we discussed before.

Adeney-Risakotta's reconstitution of power is carried forward to a new height and depth in the subsequent contributions in the section. Sang-Jin Han (2009) describes democratic transformation in contemporary Korea in which "middling grassroots" play an important role: "...the middling grassroots are those who are part of the middle class objectively, yet distinctive in that their identity as part of 'people,' not the 'power-bloc.'" Jose Jowel Canuday (2009) helps us understand the creative potency of humans even in the most difficult situations of war and devastation. Canuday tells us how people caught in between armed conflicts in Mindanow, Philippines and subjected to evacuations "carry themselves with dignity as they struggle and initiate ways to survive and recover." The displaced people come back to their lands and villages and cultivate their lands. The issue of land is a crucial issue for people all over the world, and in his contribution in this section Piet Strydom tells us about search for structures of cooperation in the land reform dispute in the post-apartheid South Africa. Mateo Mier y Terán G. C. (2009) tells us about the walking rebellion of the Zapatistas in Mexico, which challenges the taken-for-granted foundations of economy, polity and society by striving for autonomy and radical democracy. At the core of this is a project to transform power in a foundational way through its principle of "commanding by obeying," which has enkindled creative and radical imagination world-wide.[9]

Commanding by obeying involves an aesthetic transformation of the modernist cult of mastery to an ethics and aesthetics of servanthood where we relate to each other not as masters but as friends (cf. Giri 2002, Ruskin 2004).[10] In their contribution in this section, "Globalisation, Democracy and the Aesthetic Ecology of Emergent Publics for a Sustainable World: Working From John Dewey," Herbert Reid and Betsy Taylor (2008) present us engaging and inspiring gifts from John Dewey for transforming power and freedom, namely what they call "an aesthetic ecology of public intelligence." Going beyond corporate power, elitism and various divides, Dewey pleads for a vibrant democratic participation nurtured by an aesthetic ecology and an ecological ontology. Dewey also brings a new emergent dimension to the work of self and society which goes beyond conventional pragmatism: "...Dewey does not mean an Aristotelian notion of potentiality as the emergence of a *fixed* end which the individual actualises. Rather, he means an *emergent* quality of co-creation between individual and world." An important part of the challenge of transforming power and freedom, for Reid and Taylor, is to nurture a participatory logic and to overcome the "logic of fungibility" "...which reduces beings to an assemblage of predefined traits." For Reid and Taylor, "Fundamentalism of all sorts operate by locking individuals to pre-given categories that are fetishized as immanent to their substantive being, rather than emergent from relational processes of co-creation between individual and matrix." Participatory logic helps us to "reclaim democratic politics" from space-based logics of fungibility to place-based logics of democratic public inquiry. "Participatory reason moves scientists from the laboratory into the field, moves citizens from media-spectatorship into place-based inquiry, moves pedagogy and professionalism from classrooms into civic engagement and public debate, moves art from commodified fashionable reactions to risky and original encounters within history and life-world."

In their essay, Reid and Taylor tell us of new global social movements for generating global commons, and we are fortunate to have in our midst reflections from Helena Tagesson, a participant in one such movement, namely Attac (Association for the Taxation of Financial Transactions for the Aid of Citizens), a movement for global justice. Tagesson shows us from example of her own participation in Attac how such movements embody a yearning of the heart for a new politics and spirituality. Tagesson (2009) also discusses the issue of disappointment in working with liberatory struggles and different possible ways of working with it. This resonates with Terán's discussion of difficulties of social change in the communities in which Zapatista works.

Contributions in the third section of the volume, "Transforming Power and Freedom: New Horizons," continue this exploration of new horizons of politics and spirituality in transforming power and freedom. It begins with the insightful contribution of Akop P. Nazaretyan (2009) on power and wisdom in the history of social behavior. For Nazaretyan, "While weapon's killing power and people's concentration have been successfully growing for millennia, war victim's ratio has not." For Nazaretyan, this is a fragile suggestion of work of wisdom in history vis-à-vis the power to annihilate. Nazaretyan calls it the "technohumanitarian balance" which states that "the higher production and war technologies' power, the more refined the behaviour-regulation means that is required for self-preservation of society." This balance, like Pieterse's discussion of the metamorphoses of power, is tenuous and calls for continued work on inner liberation on the part of both self and society. Theologian Dietmar Mieth (2009) presents us glimpses of this calling of power and inner liberation from the inspiring life and works of mystic Meister Eckhart from Europe. With a radical interpretation of the meaning of Christ as well as the vocation of being a Christian, Eckhart challenges us to understand the power of inner liberation: "Christ reveals both the compassion of God as the inner structure of the world and solidarity as the inner structure of the human being" (Meith 2009). Eckhart's power of inner liberation was accompanied by continued striving for justice or "ardour for justice." Eckhart preached in the vernacular and was inspired by as well as supported the feminine spirituality of the Beguines: "The Beguines were free groups of women who, often following deaths of their husbands, in times of war or in times of surplus in general, or perhaps in times of a new emancipation of women, joined together to lead a simple religious life in poverty." Probably this feminine spirituality inspired Eckhart to envision each human being as a mother. For Eckhart we are continuously called upon to give birth to God at each moment of our lives.

Eckhart's critique of power as domination and continued search for multi-dimensional inner liberation in self and society finds a parallel in the life and thoughts of Erasmus. Erasmus explored new dimensions of human and social transformation beyond the dominant logic of power. It is in this context that philosopher and transformative thinker Fred R. Dallmayr's (2009) subsequent contribution on Erasmus, "War Against the Turks? Erasmus on War and Peace," helps us address the challenge of war and peace as an integral part of transforming power and freedom (see Hardt and Negri 2004). Dallmayr begins his essay: "Today, democracy is joined by another fugitive: everywhere peace seems to be in retreat or on the defensive… In such grim surroundings, Erasmus continues to offer inspiration and solace – a solace nurtured by his close familiarity with the perennial follies of humanity." For Erasmus, "we are betrayed by our lust for power." Machiavelli, a contemporary of Erasmus, had described this lust for power in *The Prince*. In his contribution, Sapir Handelman (2008) challenges us to go beyond *The Prince* and understand the crucial significance of leadership responsibility. For Handelman, holders of power have to embody responsibility, especially in situations of intractable conflicts such as Israel and Palestine. But this calls for bathing in streams of wisdom and not only drinking from the cups of lust of power, and in his subsequent contribution Christian Bartolf presents us gifts of wisdom from Tolstoy's last major work, *A Calendar of Wisdom: Daily Thoughts to Nourish the Soul*. Bartolf concludes with Etienne de La Boétie's seminal contribution, *Discourse on Voluntary Servitude* in which La Boétie, a contemporary of Machievelli, had challenged us to first acknowledge our voluntary servitude[11] and then strive to transform this. La Boétie had written way back in 1548, "Obviously there is no need of fighting to overcome this single tyrant, for he is automatically defeated if the country refuses consent to its own enslavement" (La Boétie 1548, 22). This is also the spirit of Gandhi's refusal in one's own enslavement, though Gandhi here emphasizes the need for non-violent resistance. Gandhi also challenges us to go beyond the trappings of power as determined destiny. As Mrinal Miri (2009) interprets the Gandhian pathway in his subsequent contribution to the book "Gandhi and Empowerment": "What we must strive for is not a tenuous, uneasy equilibrium of power, an equilibrium which is always on the brink of being upset. Gandhi's preferred word here is 'fellowship' – fellowship between communities and individuals."

Gandhi speaks about fellowship beyond the logic of power, and this finds a correspondence in our mutual implication as suggested in Robert Bernasconi's (2008) elaboration of Sartre's ontology of freedom as "none is free until all are free." Sartre ties freedom to responsibility. As Bernasconi tells us, "Freedom is ultimately for Sartre not freedom over other man or woman: the meaning of freedom for Sartre is responsibility, or, more specifically, it is for each of us *my* responsibility. My ontological freedom is responsibility for everything, except my responsibility itself, which is given." In his *Notebooks for An Ethics*, Sartre tells us: "…if one had a full intuition of one's own freedom, one would see it as requiring universal freedom and one would not be able to destroy the freedom of others." Mark Lindley then discusses this calling of responsibility in an urgent field of our times namely our planetary ecology. He also discusses the challenge of rethinking freedom in the face of ecological crises.

This mutual implication and imperative of responsibility is taken up in the subsequent contribution of Ananta Kumar Giri, "Power and Self-Cultivation: Aesthetics, Development Ethics and the Calling of Poverty," who joins the discussion of transformation of power and freedom by exploring the challenge of self-cultivation that confront both. In exploring the challenge of self-cultivation that the logic and holders of power face, Giri discusses the other Foucault, who talks of care of the self. Giri also explores several alternative traditions, namely the Indian tradition of sharing food, the European tradition of *Bildung* and the Confucian tradition of self-formation. Giri carries out this exploration of power and self-cultivation with specific reference to the field of development and discusses the issue of aesthetics, ethics and poverty, pleading for how all these transgress boundaries and call for a new politics and aesthetic ethics of sharing.

Giri discusses the challenge of development ethics and poverty, and the subsequent contribution of Thahn-Dam Truong (2009) explores this through a discussion of human security from a Buddhist perspective. Truong's explorations of security and peace and his quest to "open the space for inter-paradigmatic learning" resonate with the earlier contribution of Dallmayr. For Truong, "the human security project cannot succeed if based on neo-liberal individualism;" it calls for "the search for a communicative non-identitarian subject with a heart." Truong challenges us to understand the connection between dualism and violence and the significance of non-dualism for transforming power and freedom. At the same time, Truong self-critically acknowledges that Buddhism does not offer a theory of social power and has not addressed the issues of social and gender hierarchies. Nevertheless its epistemology of connectedness and wisdom is crucial for transforming power and freedom: "One conceptual error, if not corrected, leads to imbalanced action, causing imbalanced responses leading to other conceptual errors, and the chains of error and imbalanced action continues. The will of mind (determination) in Buddhist thought is not geared towards power and control but towards understanding through meditative techniques to develop a wholesome mind. A wholesome mind is the key to the release of compassion and non-violence. In this regard, ontological security is not derived from the notion of fixed stable self (socially or morally defined). It is derived from the ethical ideal to perceive oneself in relation to others and as others."

This volume on transforming power and freedom concludes with a provocative essay by John Clammer, "Beyond Power: Alternative Conceptions of Being and the Reconstitution of Social Theory." Clammer (2009), building upon Buddhism as well as Gandhi, challenges us: "The key to understanding models of power/anti-power is a question of ontology. Anti-power that is simply a struggle against power can never succeed: what is necessary is to deconstruct the notion and necessity of power itself and the impoverished conception of humankind upon which power theories are based, one that suggests in fact that humans cannot act ethically or outside of a framework of pure interest." Clammer makes clear: "The issue here, as for Gandhi, is not the abnegation of power, but its transformation from a means of domination and mechanism of violence to a force for the positive remaking of human and natural life, the harnessing of the energy (in Japanese *ki*) that flows throughout the universe but which can be focused, concentrated and utilised for healing and never for destruction." This calls for personal revolution in self and science, along with structural transformation, a point stressed by Chitta Ranjan Das – a heart-touching critic and transformative experimenter of our times – in his afterword. For Das, "...to be and not merely to know is the real thing, the real catalyser."

Transforming Power and Freedom: Co-suffering and Shared Sovereignties

Clammer challenges us never to use power for destruction but for healing; but in major traditions of thought and practice, power has been instrumentally used to inflict suffering on self, other and society (2009). Much of this has been inflicted not only on humanity but also on the non-human world in the name of sovereignty: the cult of sovereignty which wants to control all in the name of the Sovereign One – the Lord, the Man, self, and the nation-state. In this context there is an epochal challenge now to transform sovereignty, which is based upon bare life and violated bodies and souls, into shared sovereignties animated by a multi-valued logic of autonomy and interpenetration (cf. Agamben 1998; Giri 2005). Practice of shared sovereignties has the potential to help us overcome the violence of sovereignty which we see in intractable battles over ego and territories at the level of both self and nation-state. Shared sovereignty is facilitated by postnational transformations of nation-states and postegotistic transformations at the level of self. This is also facilitated by the work of what Dallmayr (2005) calls "sacred non-sovereignty" where a sovereign self or society is not preoccupied with power and mastery but with an ethics and spirituality of servanthood. This transforms *The Prince* in religion, politics and now in many domains of our lives into little princes and princesses where we are able to laugh at those who just want to sit on their thrones and those who spend their whole life in counting coins.[12] Practice of shared sovereignty and "sacred non-sovereignty" also transform our Gods into small gods, helping us co-walk in the evolutionary tryst of this fragile cosmos of ours.

Shared sovereignty and sacred non-sovereignty call for shared suffering for realization of our potential – self as well as collective, societal as well as cosmic.[13] But apart from democratic transformation, this also calls for the need to undertake suffering on the part of the self, to touch the heart and soul of the other, including that of sovereign power. Transforming power and freedom thus calls for preparation to undertake and embody suffering as a mode of being and relationship (including political struggle) which is neither sadistic nor masochistic, but a participation in the joys of transformation and for building a collective and ontological foundation of dignity and for multi-dimensional human, societal and cosmic flourishing.

Undertaking suffering here is an act of love as exemplified in the life of martyrs[14] in visions and history, from Antigone to Ken Saro-Wiwa to Chhattisgarh Mukti Morcha,[15] Socrates to Gandhi, but love here is neither a reduction of the self and other but discovery of each other's mystery. Transforming power and freedom thus brings us back as well as forward to our originary and ever-present constitutive poetics and politics of love. It is no wonder then that two critical thinkers of our times conclude their fascinating political treatise on our times with love. Michael Hardt and Antonio Negri write in their *Multitude*: "The new movements demanding global democracy not only value the singularity of each as a fundamental organizing principle but they also pose it as a process of self-transformation, hybridisation, and miscegenation. The multiplicity of the multitude is not just a matter of being different but also becoming different. Become different than you are! These singularities act in common and thus form a new race, that is, a politically coordinated subjectivity that the multitude produces. The primary decision made by the multitude is really the decision to create a new race or, rather, a new humanity. When love is conceived politically, then, the creation of a new humanity is the ultimate act of love" (Hardt and Negri 2004, 358).

But the creation of a new humanity is not only a matter of "biopolitical production," as Hardt and Negri would suggest, but also of spiritual generation. Transforming power and freedom through the poetics and politics of love challenges us to overcome the modernist primacy of both the productive and the political and be engaged with love and politics in infinitely generative ways, beginning with love as a mystery of communion rather than just production. As Luce Irigaray would challenge us:

Carnal sharing becomes then a spiritual path, a poetic and also a mystical path… Love takes place in the opening to self that is the place of welcoming the transcendence of the other… The path of such an accomplishment of the flesh does not correspond to a solipsistic dream…nor to a fin-de-siècle utopia, but to a new stage to be realised by humanity… Nature is then no longer subdued but it is adapted, in its rhythms and necessities, to the path of its becoming, of

its growth.[16] Caressing loses the sense of capturing, bewitching, appropriating…
The caress becomes a means of growing together toward a human maturity that
is not confused with an intellectual competence, with the possession of property…
nor with the domination of the world. (2002, 115–17)

Notes

1 Unless otherwise indicated, all quotations in this chapter are drawn from Ananta Kumar
   Giri, ed., *The Modern Prince and the Modern Sage: Transforming Power and Freedom* (Delhi: Sage
   Publications, 2009).
2 Here we can think of Martin Luther who, after the success of his Protestant revolt, sided
   with the kings in suppressing the peasant revolts in Germany. He even did not mind sending
   one of his co-Protestant fighters, Thomas Munster, to the gallows for supporting peasant
   revolt. See Chitta Ranjan Das' (1989) essay on Luther and Erasmus in his *Shukara o Socrates*
   (*The Pig and Socrates*).
3 As Arne Naess inteprets Spinoza, "Power over others tends in the direction of limiting
   others' right to unfold their nature" (Naess 1999, 49). For Spinoza, "The more we unfold the
   manifold (or many-side [*sic*]) of our nature, the more we are in ourselves (*in suo esse*), and the
   higher degree of freedom we achieve. This kind of development is experienced by joy, one's
   world is coloured by joy, or more precisely is more joyful" (Naess 1999, 48).
4 Spinoza calls for a simultaneous spiritual and political transformation. In his unpublished
   thesis on Spinoza submitted to Visva-Bharati in Shantiniketan, India in 1948, Chittaranjan
   Das explores both the spiritual and political dimensions of Spinoza's work and struggles. In
   the meantime, this work has been published (see Das 2009).
5 Here the following lines of Frederik Schiller are significant:

> Es die schoonheit ist durch
> > welche Man zu der Freihieit
> [It is beauty through which man makes his way to freedom]

6 It is helpful here to read the following fascinating interpretation of Freud that Reisner
   presents in his *Death-Ego and the Vital Self: Romance of Desire in Literature and Psychoanalysis*:

> [In his fourth chapter of *Beyond the Pleasure Principle*, Freud talks about binding and
> unbinding.] We can take binding and unbinding as a dynamic way of describing
> the transformation of id into ego. This is an internal acquiring of culture, the
> development of the civilisation of the self. Binding is achieving a certain internal
> form, putting drives into coherent patterns, making them accessible and controllable.
> Fastening the neurobiological to the psychological and, ultimately, to the ethical
> dimension of existence, Freud addresses himself to dreams and says that *we return to
> the unbound in order to bind*; it is for this purpose that we obsessively, fanatically return
> to the area of the unbound. In one of his last works, *An Outline of Psychoanalysis*,
> Freud returns to the question of binding and unbinding on a metapsychological
> scale. Then on he finds desire to be the final binding force, the aim of Eros to
> "establish ever greater unities and preserve them…to bind together." The same
> essay finds that "destructive instincts" work to undo connections and so to destroy
> things. (Reisner 2003, 234)

7 It is interesting here to remember solitary points of illuminations of scholars such as Claus
   Offe, himself a political sociologist, challenging us to realize that democracy confronts us

with the challenge of distinguishing between our "more desirable desire" and "less desirable desire" (cf. Offe 1991).

8 As Foucault writes, "It is not a matter of governing oneself as one governs others, seeking models in military command or the domination of slaves, but when I have to govern others, I can only do so on the model of the first, only decisive, essential, and effective government: the government of myself" (Foucault 2005, 544).

9 As Subcommandant Marcos tells us:

> We thought that we needed to reformulate the question of power. We will not repeat the formula that to change the world you need to seize power, and once in power you will organise it the way it is the best for the world, that is, what is the best for me, because I am in power. We thought that if we conceived a change in the premise of the question of power, arguing that we did not want to take it, this would produce a different form of politics, another kind of politicians, other human beings who could make politics very different to the one practised by the politicians we suffer today along the whole political spectrum.

10 Consider here what John Ruskin (2004, 17) wrote more than a century ago: "I know not if a day is ever to come when the nature of right freedom will be understood, and when men will see that to obey another man, to labour for him, yield reverence to him or to his place, is not slavery."

11 What La Boétie writes deserves our careful consideration:

> But o Good Lord! What strange phenomenon is this? What name shall we give to it?… To see an endless multitude of people not merely obeying, but driven to servility? Not ruled, but tyrannised over? These wretches have no wealth, no kin, nor wife nor children, not even life itself they can call their own. They suffer plundering, wantonness, cruelty, not from an army, not from a barbarian horde, but from a single man… Too frequently this same little man is the most cowardly and effeminate in the nation, a stranger to the power of battle and hesitant on the sands of tournament; not only without energy to direct men by force but with hardly enough virility to bed with a common woman! (1548, 7)

La Boétie concludes his treatise: "…there is nothing so contrary to a generous and loving God as dictatorship" (1548, 22).

12 We can here recall the heart-touching journey of the little prince in Antoine de Saint Exupéry's *The Little Prince*. But we have to co-walk in this journey as both little princes and princesses. A foundational question to this project of ours on the *Modern Prince and the Modern Sage* was raised by Yale Handelman, a heart-touching singer and dreamer of life, and wife of Sapir Handelman, a contributor in our volume. During a conversation in Freiburg, Germany, Yale asked like a little princess of de Saint Exupéry: what about a modern princess? I agree with her that in our book we could have done more on recording the contribution of the women's movement in transforming power and freedom and the significance of creative feminine politics and spirituality. But at the same time we have to ask whether the feminist movement embodied the values of the Princess and her will to power, and whether this needs to be now transformed into a simultaneous will for dignity and solidarity.

13 For realizing the significance for potential, especially my existence in the context of yours, mine and our potentiality, note the following thoughts of a novelist and a philosopher. Writes Imre Kertész in his Nobel Prize–winning novel, *Kaddish for a Child Not Born*: "Yes, my existence in the context of your potentiality… Now I no longer have doubts–it is in the clouds where I make my bed. And this question – my life in the context of the potentiality

of your existence – proved to be a good guide" (2002, 12). And writes philosopher Georgio Agamben in his *The Coming Community*:

> The recognition of evil is older and more original than any blameworthy act, it rests solely on the fact that, being and having to be only its possibility or potentiality, humankind fails itself in a certain sense and has to appropriate this failing–it has to exist as potentiality. [The only ethical experience is] the experience of being [one's own potentiality]. The only evil consists instead in the decision to remain in a deficit of existence, to appropriate the power to not-be as a substance and a foundation beyond existence; or rather (and this is the destiny of morality), to regard potentiality itself, which is the most proper mode of human existence, as a fault that must always be repressed. (1993, 44)

14 Here J. P. S. Uberoi's thoughts about the loving self-sacrifice of the martyrs of the world are noteworthy. For Uberoi, the elementary structure of martyrdom is "manifestly the non-dualism of loving self-sacrifice...but equally it is the responsibility of 'arising to bear witness" on the duality of the true and false, religion and irreligion, liberation and bondage" (1996, 130). Furthermore, "[t]he martyr is one who must love his enemy in some sense since he or she is the perfect witness (*saheed-ul-kamil*) that God, who at this time takes an interest in history and politics, does not want his servant to suppose, as the dualist would, that Satanism has any true independent existence, and so *dharmayudhya*, the righteous war, can be transformed into *satyagraha*" (1996, 124). What Uberoi writes about Antigone, the first martyr of the world, deserves our careful attention as it is linked with the project of martyrdom in both Gandhism and Sikhism:

> I think that perhaps the world's first martyr of truth and non-violence was a Greek, Antigone, a European and a woman, best known to us as depicted by Sophocles, c.500 B.C. Antigone, who preceded both Socrates and Jesus, wanted the integration of religion and society to be upheld by her *freedom of conscience* and immemorial usage, the custom of civil society, while Creon, the King, wished his reasons of state to be separate from, and to override, both religion and society. I will not attempt to decide which of the two points of view is modern for Europe, but it is Antigone's that is closest to Sikhism and Indian modernity. She had established the truth that no power on earth can make the self do anything against its nature, except indirectly confer martyrdom on it, which is also the basis of Gandhism in politics. (1996, 88)

15 Ken Saro-Wiwa is the martyr from the Ogoni tribe of Nigeria who was executed on false charges for his struggle against the multinational Shell and for the dictatorship of Nigerian nation-state. See Saro-Wiwa (1995). The martyrdom of Shankar Singh Guha Niyogi, the founder of Chhattisgarh Mukti Morcha, which fights for the dignity of workers and people, is also exemplary here. Niyogi was gunned down by the hired goons of the industrialists while he was asleep. What is striking is that even now in the face of murder and much violence Chhattisgarh Mukti Morcha continues the path of non-violent struggle. As Chandhoke writes about Chhattisgarh Mukti Morcha, "Despite the fact that CMM used only non-violent means of protest, such as peaceful demonstrations, *dharnas*, strikes, *morchas* and petitions – all of which are permissible in civil society–their protests were savagely put down. During a conversation with one of the CMM's leaders, I wondered whether it was not legitimate to use violence in a society where the regime virtually used violence against its own people. His answer was an emphatic no; violence, he argued, would impoverish the movement and denude it of any spirit of commitment" (Chandhoke 2003, 206).

16 Such a transformational relationship with Nature is crucially significant as much of modernist emancipatory politics including the so-called post-modern emancipatory project of Hardt

and Negri under the rubric of "biopolitical production" does not involve a foundational interrogation and transformation of anthropocentrism. Though we have not been able to engage ourselves fully with this issue in our volume, overcoming and transcending anthropocentrism is an important part of the political and spiritual struggle to transform power and freedom.

References

Adeney-Risakotta, Bernard. 2009. "Power from Below: Indonesian Reflections on the Paradigm of Power." In Ananta Kumar Giri, ed., *The Modern Prince and the Modern Sage: Transforming Power and Freedom*. Delhi: Sage.

Agamben, Georgio. 1993. *The Coming Community*. Minneapolis: University of Minnesota Press.

———. 1998. *Homo Sacer: Sovereign Power and Bare Life*. Stanford: Stanford University Press.

Agarwala, Binod Kumar. 2009. "Control of Power through Freedom: An Issue in Kant's Political Philosophy." In Ananta Kumar Giri, ed., *The Modern Prince and the Modern Sage: Transforming Power and Freedom*. Delhi: Sage.

Ankersmit, F. R. 2009. "Political Symbolism or How to Stay on the Surface." In Ananta Kumar Giri, ed., *The Modern Prince and the Modern Sage: Transforming Power and Freedom*. Delhi: Sage.

Benhabib, Seyla. 1987. *Critique, Norm and Utopia*. New York: Columbia University Press.

Berlin, Isaiah. 2000. *The Power of Ideas*. Princeton: Princeton University Press.

Bernasconi, Robert. 2009. "None is Free until All Are Free: Sartre's Ontology of Freedom and His Politics." In Ananta Kumar Giri, ed., *The Modern Prince and the Modern Sage: Transforming Power and Freedom*. Delhi: Sage.

Butler, Judith. 1997. *The Psychic Life of Power: Theories in Subjection*. Stanford: Stanford University Press.

Canuday, Jose Jowel. 2009. "Beyond Powerlessness: Celebrating the Power of the Displaced." In Ananta Kumar Giri, ed., *The Modern Prince and the Modern Sage: Transforming Power and Freedom*. Delhi: Sage.

Chandhoke, Neera. 2003. "When the Voiceless Speak: A Case Study of the Chhattisgarh Mukti Morcha." In Rajesh Tandon and Ranjita Mohanty, eds, *Does Civil Society Matter? Governance in Contemporary India*, 198–242. New Delhi: Sage.

Clammer, John. 2009. "Beyond Power: Alternative Conceptions of Being and Reconstitution of Social Theory." In Ananta Kumar Giri, ed., *The Modern Prince and the Modern Sage: Transforming Power and Freedom*. Delhi: Sage.

Cohen, Jean and Andrew Arato. 1992. *Civil Society and Political Theory*. Cambridge, MA: MIT Press.

Dallmayr, Fred R. 2001. "Resisting Totalizing Uniformity: Martin Heidegger on Macht and Machenshaft." In *Achieving Our World: Towards a Global and Plural Democracy*, 189–209. Lanham, MD: Rowman & Littlefield.

———. 2005. "Empire and Faith: Sacred Non-Sovereignty." In *Small Wonder: Global Power and Its Discontents*. Lanham, MD: Rowman & Littlefield.

———. 2008. "A War Against the Turks? Erasmus on War and Peace." In Ananta Kumar Giri, ed., *The Modern Prince and the Modern Sage: Transforming Power and Freedom*. Delhi: Sage.

Das, Chitta Ranjan. 1948. Unpublished thesis. Shantiniketan: Visva-Bharati.

———. 1989. *Shukara o Socrates* [*The Pig and Socrates*]. Berhampur, Orissa, India: Pustak Bhandar.

———. 2009. *Benedict Spinoza: An Appreciation*. Delhi: Shipra.

Eisenstadt, S. N. 2009. "Modernity and the Reconstitution of the Realm of the Political." In Ananta Kumar Giri, ed., *The Modern Prince and the Modern Sage: Transforming Power and Freedom*. Delhi: Sage.

Foucault, Michel. 1984. "Politics and Ethics: An Interview." In Paul Rabinow, ed., *The Foucault Reader*. New York: Pantheon.

———. 2005. *The Hermeneutics of the Subject: Lectures at the College de France, 1981–82*. New York: Palgrave.

Gramsci, Antonio. 1957. *The Modern Prince and Other Writings*. London: Lawrence and Wishart Ltd.

Giddens, Anthony. 1994. *Beyond Left and Right: The Future of Radical Politics*. Cambridge: Polity Press.

———. 1991. *Modernity and Self-Identity: Self and Society in the Late Modern Age*. Cambridge: Polity Press.

Giri, Ananta Kumar. 2002. *Conversations and Transformations: Towards a New Ethics of Self and Society*. Lanham, MD: Lexington Books.

———. 2005. "Creative Social Research: Rethinking Theories and Methods and the Calling of an Ontological Epistemology of Participation." Madras Institute of Development Studies, working paper.

Giri, Ananta Kumar, ed. 2009. *The Modern Prince and the Modern Sage: Transforming Power and Freedom*. Delhi: Sage Publications.

Han, Sang-Jin. 2009. "Social Transformation in Contemporary Korea: Three Prime-Movers in the Contested Civil Society." In Ananta Kumar Giri, ed., *The Modern Prince and the Modern Sage: Transforming Power and Freedom*. Delhi: Sage.

Handelman, Sapir. 2009. "Machievelli, *The Prince* and Leadership Responsibility." In Ananta Kumar Giri, ed., *The Modern Prince and the Modern Sage: Transforming Power and Freedom*. Delhi: Sage.

Hardt, Michael. 1991. "Translator's Foreword." In Antonio Negri, ed., *The Savage Anomaly: The Power of Spinoza's Metaphysics and Politics*. Minneapolis: University of Minnesota Press.

Hardt, Michael and Antonio Negri. 2004. *Multitude: War and Democracy in an Age of Empire*. London: Penguin Books.

Hoffman, Piotr. 1996. *The Quest for Power: Hobbes, Descartes and the Emergence of Modernity*. Atlantic Highlands, NJ: Humanities Press.

Irigaray, Luce. 2002. *Between East and West: From Singularity to Community*. New York: Columbia University Press.

Kertsez, Imre. 2002. *Kaddish for a Child Not Born*. Evanston, IL: Northwestern University Press.

La Boétie, Etienne de. 1548. "Discourse on Voluntary Servitude." Published under the title *The Anti-Dictator*. New York: Columbia University Press. Available at http://www.constitution.org/la-boitie/serve_vol.htm (accessed 23 May 2006).

Laclau, Ernesto. 1992. "Beyond Emancipation." In Jan N. Pieterse, ed., *Emancipations, Modern and Postmodern*. London: Sage Publications.

Levinas, Emmanuel. 1974. *Otherwise Than Being or Beyond Essence*. Dordrecht: Kluwer Academic Publishers.

———. 1990. *Difficult Freedom: Essays on Judaism*. London: Athlone.

Machiavelli, Niccolo. 1520/1981. *The Prince and Other Political Writings, Selected and Translated with introduction and notes by Bruce Penman*. London: Dent Everyman's Library.

Mahadevan, Kanchana. 2009. "Rethinking Power: Aesthetics, Dialogue, Hegemony." In Ananta Kumar Giri, ed., *The Modern Prince and the Modern Sage: Transforming Power and Freedom*. Delhi: Sage.

Mieth, Dietmar. 2009. "Meister Eckhart: The Power of Inner Liberation." In Ananta Kumar Giri, ed., *The Modern Prince and the Modern Sage: Transforming Power and Freedom*. Delhi: Sage.

Naess, Arne. 1999. *Det frie menneske* [The Free Human Being]. Oslo.

Nazaretyan, Akop P. 2009. "Power and Wisdom: Does World History Have a Moral Dimension?" In *The Modern Prince and the Modern Sage: Transforming Power and Freedom*, ed. Ananta Kumar Giri. Delhi: Sage.

Negri, Antonio. 1991. *The Savage Anomaly: The Power of Spinoza's Metaphysics and Politics*. Minneapolis: University of Minnesota Press.

Offe, Claus. 1991: "Democratic Institutions and Moral Resources." In David Held, ed., *Political Theory Today*. Cambridge: Polity Press.

Pieterse, Jan N. 2009. "Metamorphoses of Power: From Coercion to Cooperation?" In Ananta Kumar Giri, ed., *The Modern Prince and the Modern Sage: Transforming Power and Freedom*. Delhi: Sage.

Quarles van Ufford, Charles. 2009. "The Power of Modernity and the Tail of the Devil." In Ananta Kumar Giri, ed., *The Modern Prince and the Modern Sage: Transforming Power and Freedom*. Delhi: Sage.

Reisner, Gavriel (Ben-Ephraim). 2003. *The Death-Ego and the Vital Self: Romance and Desire in Literature and Psychoanalysis*. Cranbury, NJ: Associated University Presses.

Reid, Herbert and Taylor, Betsy. 2006. "Globalization, Democracy and the Aesthetic Ecology of Emergent Publics for a Sustainable World: Working from John Dewey." *Asian Journal of Social Sciences* 34 (1): 22–46.

Roy, Ramashroy. 1999. *Beyond Ego's Domain: Being and Order in the Vedas*. Delhi: Shipra Publications.

Ruskin, John. 2004. *On Art and Life*. London: Penguin.

Saro-Wiwa, Ken. 1995. *A Month and a Day: A Detention Diary*. London: Penguin Books.

Sen, Amartya. 1999. *Development as Freedom*. Oxford: Oxford University Press.

Sri Aurobindo. 1962: *Human Cycles*, Pondicherry: Sri Aurobindo Ashram.

Tagesson, Helena. 2009. "A Yearning of the Heart: Spirituality and Politics." In Ananta Kumar Giri, ed., *The Modern Prince and the Modern Sage: Transforming Power and Freedom*. Delhi: Sage.

Terán G. C. and Mateo Mier. 2009. "The Walking Rebellion: The Zapatista's Struggle for Autonomy and the Difficulties of Social Change." In Ananta Kumar Giri, ed., *The Modern Prince and the Modern Sage: Transforming Power and Freedom*. Delhi: Sage.

Toynbee, Arnold J. 1956. *A Historian's Approach to Religion*. New York: Oxford University Press.

Truong, Thanh-Dam. 2009. "Reflections on Human Security: A Buddhist Contribution." In Ananta Kumar Giri, ed., *The Modern Prince and the Modern Sage: Transforming Power and Freedom*. Delhi: Sage.

Uberoi, J. P. S. 1996. *Religion, Civil Society and State: A Study of Sikhism*. Delhi: Oxford University Press.

————. 2002. *European Modernity: Truth, Science and Method*. Delhi: Oxford University Press.

Vinthagen, Stellan. 2009. "Power as Subordination and Resistance as Disobedience: Non-Violent Movements and the Management of Power." In Ananta Kumar Giri, ed., *The Modern Prince and the Modern Sage: Transforming Power and Freedom*. Delhi: Sage.

Wilfred, Felix. 2009. "Play of Power and Struggle for Freedom in Renaissance Humanism: Erasmus between Scylla and Charybdis." In Ananta Kumar Giri, ed., *The Modern Prince and the Modern Sage: Transforming Power and Freedom*. Delhi: Sage.

Chapter Four

KANT AND ANTHROPOLOGY

In this chapter, we explore the challenge of rethinking modernist knowledge by looking at Kant's conception of anthropology. Kant taught courses in both anthropology and physical geography, and his book *Anthropology from a Pragmatic Point of View* was published nearly thirty years after his initial engagement with anthropology. While his lectures embodied Kant's crisis of identity as a professional philosopher, thus facilitating a border crossing between philosophy and anthropology, *Anthropology from a Pragmatic Point of View* was far short of his earlier critique of metaphysics and wanted anthropology to play by universal principles if not be totally subordinated to metaphysics. This book is especially interesting from the point of view of border crossing: "In this work Kant comes as close possible to combining the qualities of English and continental philosophy. The power of the intellect and the attraction of the imagination both merge into a system of common human concern which has more relevance today then it had before" (Zammito 2002). The word "pragmatic" in the text is important, and nearly two hundred years later new democratic possibilities seem to have arisen from border-crossing dialogue between traditions of American pragmatism and Kantian traditions, as in the works of Karl-Otto Apel and Jürgen Habermas (as suggested in Chapter One). As we shall see in the case of the master himself (i.e. Kant), Rousseau was a major influence who inspired Kant to use the project of philosophical anthropology for the education of mankind. Thus Kantian engagement with anthropology embodies several border crossings, first between different intellectual and philosophical traditions, and second between academic philosophy and popular philosophy.

Kant begins his *Anthropology*: "All cultural progress which represents the education of man, aims at putting acquired knowledge and skill to use in the world" (Kant 1978, 314). He contrasts the physiological and pragmatic approaches to anthropology: "The first offers a conceptualization of what nature makes of man, while the latter presents what man 'does, can and make himself.'" Kant pleads for the pragmatic considering the physiological approach a waste of time. At the same time, the pragmatic study must be systematic and universal: "Universal knowledge will always precede local knowledge as long as it is to be arranged and guided by philosophy, without which all acquired knowledge can provide nothing but fragmentary groping, and no science at all" (Zammito 2002, 301).

Though Kant seems to subordinate local knowledge to universal knowledge, there are important local details in his pragmatic anthropology about different peoples, nations and characters. Though Kant did not travel much beyond Königsberg, he had an anthropological eye, suggested in the title of his other border-crossing text – one which in fact represented a certain self-critical turn from pure metaphysics to anthropology – *Observations on the Feelings of the Beautiful and Sublime*. His attention to observation is borne out both in his anthropological and philosophical vocations. Notable is his following observant eye, though problematic from the point of view of justice and fairness: "A young wife is always in danger of becoming a widow, and this leads her to distribute her charms to all men whose fortunes make them marriageable; so that, if this should occur, she would not be lacking in suitors" (Kant 1978, 218). "As for the scholarly women, they use their books somewhat like a watch, that is, they wear watch so that it can be noticed that they have one, although it is usually broken or does not show correct time" (Kant 1978, 221). But Kant is not simply male chauvinist as he himself writes: "Woman is the monarch and man, the cabinet ministers" (1978, 224).

As to the significance of observation in his philosophical vocation, Kant's *Observations on the Feelings of the Beautiful and Sublime* represented a contribution to the analysis of feeling and the role of observation is quite central here. As one observer writes, "Kant clearly considered anthropological inquiry *propaeudetic* to fundamental moral philosophical inquiry" (Zammito 2002, 110). Furthermore, "In *Observations* Kant had abandoned scholarly elitism and accepted Rousseau's call for philosophers to become the "educators of mankind." But "…there could never be any question of a primitivist reception of Rousseau. The dynamic of social development was programmed into natural man, for Kant" (Zammito 2002, 116). Though Kantian anthropology tries to fulfill man's potential, there is nonetheless an ethnocentric bias as illustrated in the following comments:

> Patience of a particular kind is shown by the Indians in America who throw away their weapons when they are encircled and, without begging for pardon, let themselves be slain quietly. Does this indicate more courage than the Europeans display, who in such a situation tend to defend themselves to the last man? To me it seems to be just barbaric vanity intended to preserve the honor of the tribe so that the enemy could not force them to lament and beg as vindications of submission. (Kant 1978)

Though Kant's pragmatic anthropology is full of problematic ethnocentric statements and perspectives, at times he gives rather spectacular results of his pragmatic anthropology: "Drink loosens the tongue. But it also opens the heart wide, and it is a vehicle instrumental to moral quality, that is openheartedness" (Kant 1978, 61).

Ethnocentrism is not the only challenge in Kantian pragmatic anthropology. Anthropocentrism is another. "The most important object of culture, to whom such knowledge and skill can be applied, is Man because he is his own ultimate purpose. To recognize him, according to his species, as an earthly creature endowed with reason deserves to be called knowledge of the world, even though he is only one of all the creatures on earth" (Kant 1978, 314).

Kant does not have a disciplinary view of anthropology as he writes in the very second paragraph of his book: "Such an anthropology understood as knowledge of the world, has to be continued after the formal education is over" (1978, 4). Such an anthropology "is not yet properly pragmatic so long as it contains extended knowledge of the things in the world, such as animals, plants, and minerals in various lands and climates. It is properly pragmatic only when it incorporates knowledge of Man as a citizen of the world" (1978, 4). Despite Kant's anthropocentric limitations, such a view calls for a new kind of global or cosmopolitan anthropology beyond the imprisonment in culture, society and nation-state. And if it can cross the borders of anthropocentrism, such a pragmatic anthropology could also transform itself into a planetary and cosmic anthropology involving a fundamental critique and transformation of *anthropos* as well. Such a project would continue the explorations of Kant beyond Kant as Kant not only gives supremacy to reason but also extends its limits. For Kant, "man's rational capacity alone is not sufficient to constitute his dignity, and elevate him above the brutes" (Dowdell and Rudnick 1978, x).

What is important to note is that Kant's pragmatic anthropology contains a critique of egoism and appreciation for pluralism: "Egoism can only be contrasted with pluralism which is a frame of mind in which the self, instead of being entrapped in itself as if it were the whole world, understands and behaves itself as a mere citizen of the world. The above is all that belongs to the world."

Kant and Anthropology: Some Contemporary Considerations

The frequent occurrence of the word "world" in Kantian pragmatic anthropology should caution us about the multi-dimensional nature of the world itself – beyond this world being just a "citizen's world." As J. N. Mohanty (2000) would suggest, there are worlds and worlds. It is in this context that Keith Hart's elaboration of a Kantian project of anthropology deserves our attention. For Hart, "Kant saw that the world was moving towards war between a coalition of nation-states; yet he posed the question of how humanity might construct a 'perpetual peace' beyond the boundaries of state, based on principles we all share" (Hart 2000, 3). "In order to pursue this goal," for Hart, "the world has to be imaginatively reduced in scale and our subjectivity expanded so that a meaningful link can be established between the two" (2000, 3). Furthermore, for Hart, "We need to feel more at home in the world, to find the means of actively resisting alienation" (2000, 3). But feeling more at home in the world today cannot be pursued in a matter of certainty or mastery; it has to acknowledge the fundamentally fragile character of our home and the world, and calls for a border crossing between home and homelessness, worlds and worlds, immanence and transcendence. This calls for a spiritual transformation of Kantian pragmatic anthropology as an anthropology of the world.

As Keith Hart and David Harvey have argued, perpetual peace and cosmopolitanism are important legacies of Kant and important sources of inspiration for a planetary anthropology emerging out of simultaneous engagement with philosophical reflections and fieldwork (see the concluding chapter "Cosmopolitanism and Beyond: Towards Planetary Realizations" in this volume). But Kantian cosmopolitanism is facilitated by deepening and broadening our engagement and conversations. For Kant, "Peace will be attained through the inevitable spread of the institutional and legal structure of a 'perpetual federation' among independent republican states, each of which respects the basic rights of its citizens and establishes a public sphere in which people can regard themselves and others as free and equal 'citizens of the world.'" For Kant, establishment of "strict publicity, further ensured by the presence of an enlightened, critical, and educated world public" would facilitate the realization of peace. For Gandhi, alongside this we need the development of capacity for *ahimsa* (non-violence), love and Satyagraha. Peace is not just public; it calls for appropriate self-cultivation.

A simultaneous engagement with Kant and Gandhi suggests interesting possibilities for an alternative planetary anthropology. Gandhi's conception of anthropology was not just anthropocentric. Both Kant and Gandhi urge us to understand the significance of moral duty. This would help us transform the current discussions in anthropology about ethics and the ethics of anthropology, as well as anthropological practice. For Kant, realization of moral duty "would often require self-denial" (Kant 1964, 75). But Kant does not explore sufficiently the ontological preparation for self-denial. He does not show us how "self-denial" constitutes a source of happiness, or what Gandhi calls "joy" for moral agents: "A life of sacrifice is the pinnacle of art and is full of true joy" (Iyer 1990, 382). Gandhian suffering can redeem Kantian pure reason, as Gandhi tells us, "The conviction has been growing upon, that things of fundamental importance to the people are not secured by reason alone, but have to be purchased with their suffering... Suffering is infinitely more powerful...for converting the opponent and *opening his ears* which are otherwise shut to the voice of reason" (Gandhi as quoted in Narayanan 1968, 202). This suffering is not inflicted on the other but it is the self-sacrifice of moral agents with the other for the sake of love and justice.

Gandhi reiterates the significance of undertaking suffering for the sake of justice and it is a challenge for Kantian approaches to justice starting from Rawls to Habermas. However, while both Rawls and Habermas look at justice from the point of view of the primacy of the political, both Kant and Gandhi offer a fundamental critique of politics as the project of a desirable anthropology that is most often articulated solely in political terms. Both Kant and Gandhi call for a moral transformation of politics, which should inspire us to transform our predominantly politically-engaged anthropology. While for Kant, the ultimate objective of moralization of politics is to conquer "the crafty and far more dangerously deceitful and treason principle of evil in ourselves," for Gandhi it is to bring about "self-regulation" and a state of enlightened anarchy where "everyone is one's ruler." Gandhi calls this Swaraj and it calls for aspiration and struggle for truth, or what Gandhi calls Satyagraha. But while in the Gandhian struggle for autonomy and truth seeking, Swaraj and Satyagraha, there is emphasis on self-transcendence and self-transformation, this seems to be missing in the Kantian ideal of autonomy (see also Chapter Fourteen in this book on Swaraj).[1] The transformation of anthropology calls for a dialogue between Kantian autonomy and Gandhian Swaraj and Satyagraha.

Thus Kantian pragmatic anthropology as an anthropology of the world is now in need of transcivilizational dialogues and planetary conversations, and here a dialogue with Gandhi, to begin with, can help us to broaden, deepen and transform Kantian anthropology from a pragmatic point of view. Such a dialogue has a great significance for the whole project of philosophical anthropology as it is in its dominant version, narrow (i.e. mainly Euro-American and Western) in its source and inspiration (see Giri and Clammer, forthcoming). Anthropologists who cross over to philosophy in the Euro-American world only look at their own local gods, thus Clifford Geertz (2000) considers Wittgenstein as his *guru*, and Bourdieu (2000) Wittgenstein and Pascal. But the need for planetary conversations here cannot be reiterated strongly enough.

Another important challenge for *Anthropology* which is tied up with the Kantian legacy is the challenge of overcoming dualism. Dualism has been an entrenched heritage of modern anthropology, as for example in the works of Durkheim and Dumont, and transformation of modernist anthropology calls for multi-dimensional strivings for the realization of non-duality both as an epistemic as well as an ontological engagement. But like Kant's striving for perpetual peace, overcoming dualism is a perpetual journey. Much of anthropological logic is dualistic. While at one point it reflects our human existence of finitude, inescapable duality and limits of language, dualism is at the same time is not our destiny. It is possible to cultivate non-dual approaches to understanding our simultaneous condition of non-duality and duality. Kant sought to connect the dualism of pure reason and practical reason through aesthetic judgment. Aesthetics has the potential to cross over boundaries, especially those of entrenched dualism, and now it can be accompanied by spiritual cultivation and transformations.

Note

1 As Martha Nussbaum argues:

> Kant does think that we can hope for peace, in part because it is to the advantage of all; but he does not think that we can hope for benevolence that supports basic life opportunities for all the citizens of the world, or even for all in a given nation. This lack of moral ambition is surprising, given that all these thinkers are surrounded by, and in some cases adherents of, a Christian culture that predominantly advocated spiritual reform and self-change in respect of benevolence and other basic sentiments. (2006, 410)

References

Bourdieu, Pierre. 2000. *Pascalian Meditations*. Cambridge: Polity Press.
Dowdell, Victor Lyle and Hans H. Rudnick. 1978. Introduction to Immanuel Kant, *Anthropology from a Pragmatic Point of View*. Carbondale: Southern Illinois University Press.
Geertz, Clifford. 2000. *Available Light: Philosophical Reflections on Anthropological Topics*. Princeton: Princeton University Press.
Giri, Ananta Kumar and John Clammer, eds. *Philosophy and Anthropology: Border-Crossing and Transformations*. London: Anthem Press. Forthcoming.
Hart, Keith. 2000. "Reflections on a Visit to New York." *Anthropology Today* 16 (4): 1–3.
Iyer, Raghavan, ed. 1990. *The Essential Writings of Mahatma Gandhi*. Delhi: Oxford University Press.

Kant, Immanuel. 1978. *Anthropology from a Pragmatic Point of View*. Carbondale: Southern Illinois University Press.

_____. *Observations on the Feelings of the Beautiful and Sublime*.

_____. 1964. *Groundwork of the Metaphysics of Morals*, trans. H. J. Patton. New York: Harper Torch Books.

_____. 1795/1957. *Perpetual Peace*. New York: The Liberal Arts Press.

Mohanty, J. N. 2000. *Self and Other: Philosophical Essays*. Delhi: Oxford University Press.

Narayan, Shriman, ed. 1968. *The Selected Works of Mahatma Gandhi; Vol. 6: The Voice of Truth*. Ahmedabad: Navajivan Publishing House.

Nussbaum, Martha. 2006. *Frontiers of Justice*. Cambridge, MA: Harvard University Press.

Zammito, John H. 2002. *Kant, Herder, and the Birth of Anthropology*. Chicago: University of Chicago Press.

Chapter Five

TOCQUEVILLE AS AN ETHNOGRAPHER OF AMERICAN PRISON SYSTEMS AND DEMOCRATIC PRACTICE

Even so there is irony in the fact that... Tocqueville came here to study the wonderful ways in which America incarcerated human beings, not how democracy freed them.

—Ronald Walters (1986, 4)

Already in his own time Tocqueville was rightly considered to be the greatest thinker on democracy. Now that democracy at the end of the millennium seems to be beginning its triumphal procession over our entire globe, Tocqueville is still our best guide if we wish to understand democracy. Tocqueville has an undeniable right to such praise, since no other political thinker has been more deeply aware of the paradoxes and the sublimity that are forever the glory of democracy.

—F. R. Ankersmit (1996, 343)

Tocqueville followed a method that strove for a theoretically grounded comparative analysis of political formations, but one in which each formation also had to be situated within deep and complex structures of their own historical evolution. He did not think of historically constituted political formations as mere cases of comparative theoretical types, or of variants within a type, as though one formation might just as easily be exchanged for another of the same type. Consequently his study of democratic institutions in the United States, as well as his comparative reflections on political institutions in France, is marked by detailed empirical observations that were drawn, as we would say today, from long and arduous fieldwork using a variety of textual and oral methods, followed by theoretical work seeking to draw sustainable formulations belonging to a general comparative order while respecting the historical specificities of each institutional form...

The great attraction of a Tocqueville-inspired method for us is that it offers the possibility of partial and contingent normative theories based on the configurative study of specific political institutions in two or more countries without resorting to totalizing notions of "stages of civilization" or "levels of development." We believe

it is possible to engage in comparisons of political formations that do not assume any particular form of democratic modernity, either existent or hypothetical, as the *telos* of development. Even if Tocqueville believed that democracy was being driven by an irresistible historical force, his analytical method makes it clear that its particular forms were the result of specific historical configurations of causes.
—Partha Chatterjee and Ira Katznelson (2012, 2, 4)

The Problem

Alexis de Tocqueville is one of the most influential interlocutors of modernity whose reflections on democracy continue to inspire, engage and haunt us as we are supposedly in an age of global democratization. Tocqueville's work on democracy, *Democracy in America*, was published between 1835 and 1840. Around this period, European society was making a transition from an ancient regime to a form of social and political system whose full contours were yet to emerge. Not only the transition from feudalism to democracy but also other lines of transition, such as the transition from feudalism to the industrial and the capitalistic order, were subjects of profound concern for both the laymen and the concerned commentators of the existing condition. During this period, we have in Europe the emergence of such powerful observers of this transitional society as Saint Simon, Karl Marx and Hegel – to name the most influential among them. In the history of political and social thought, these powerful commentators of the European transition have their own schools and trajectories of influence. We have the more familiar schools built around Marx and Hegel. What is interesting is that there is also a school built around Tocqueville and that Tocqueville was a great system builder of democracy.

Tocqueville wrote about institutions of democracy in America. He was also concerned with the impact of these institutions on other institutions and cultural relations in America. When one reads Tocqueville as an ethnographer and as an anthropologist, not as a partisan social theorist,[1] one is not sure whether Tocqueville intended to build a system of democracy as a political system or whether his work is an ethnography of American democratic practice. Ethnography believes in a critical description of the complexities of life and stresses the limits of *a priori* theoretical determination and ideological assertions in the understanding and articulation of the dynamics of life. However, students of Tocqueville take a variety of positions on this issue. For some, Tocqueville belongs to a continental tradition of deductive method and theorizing, and the description of facts about American democratic practice interested him to the extent that it could lead to a coherent theoretical statement. As Melvin Richter writes, "Montesquieu's theory had provided the categories by which Tocqueville sought to explain what he had discovered by his empirical research in America. Tocqueville's own intellectual style determined in part the use he made of Montesquieu. But there can be no question that theory guided heuristically Tocqueville's explorations in person and later in his sources, just as it contributed to the ultimate shape it took in his final version" (Richter 1970, 101). Cushing Strout argues that Tocqueville has a double analytical task in *Democracy in America*: to describe America in particular while setting forth in general the abstract outlines of the egalitarian society (Strout 1969, 87). Raymond Aron, whose interpretation of Tocqueville portrays him as a counter figure to Marx, provides a somewhat different reflection: "*Tocqueville…was a sociologist who never ceased to judge while he described.* [For him], a description can not be faithful unless it includes those judgments intrinsically related to description…" (Aron 1965, 204; italics added).

But the above interpretations of Tocqueville have been subjected to a recent foundational critique by F. R. Ankersmit. In his provocative essay, "Metaphor and Paradox in Tocqueville's Writings," Ankersmit tells us that "Western political thought knows few texts so conspicuous for lack of consistency as those of Tocqueville" (Ankersmit 1996, 295). For Ankersmit, Tocqueville has no "theory of democracy" and a close reading of his texts suggests that "Tocqueville's major insights can only be found at what one might call the micro-level" (Ankersmit 1996, 295). Tocqueville's work does not carry any model of historical inevitability or certainty, and he uses paradox as an important tool of description and understanding.[2] For Ankersmit, "… both the form and the content of Tocqueville's work are a protest against the attempt to objectify democracy, to look at it from a certain distance in order to develop a theory of it" (Ankersmit 1996, 295).

Controversies exist not only around the issue of theory versus description but the implication of Tocqueville's theory for the wider question of ideology and revolutionary social transformation. Sociologist Tom Bottomore (1979) argues that the history of modern political philosophy can be characterized by two contending socio-political visions: one emphasizing the significance of economic democracy and the dismantling of capitalist class inequality for the emergence of real political democracy, the other stressing the power of democracy as a socio-political system in reducing class antagonism, leading to real social equality. In this dialogue between Marx and Tocqueville, it is assumed and sometimes explicitly argued that Tocqueville was building a theory of democracy as a political system suitable for the emerging industrial polity. It is argued that Tocqueville was looking forward to democracy as a panacea for class and corporate conflict engendered by the conflict between capital and labor in industrial society. Raymond Aron makes this fight with the ghost of Karl Marx clear: for Tocqueville, industrial wealth is mobile and not concentrated in the families. "Thus American society can provide, not a model, but a lesson to European societies by showing them how liberty is safeguarded in a democratic society" (Aron 1965, 193). Even in terms of style, for Aron, Tocqueville was writing in a literary style rather in terms of explicating concepts.

The interpretation of Tocqueville's work as providing an alternative to Marxian analysis of social transformation and as a builder of democracy as a total system obscures the real Tocqueville: Tocqueville the ethnographer. When we look closely at Tocqueville's work not as an enthusiastic ideologue, but as an open-minded ethnographer, his rich, thick but critical description of the American democratic practice strikes us. As Abraham Eisenstadt helps us understand,

> In trying to understand the tendency of his times, he kept his vision wide and his reason flexible. He did not fit them to a procrustean chronology… Tocqueville built

the grand structure of *Democracy in America* out of three elemental ideas – democracy, revolution, and liberty. He explored these elements in all their permutations and combinations, ceaselessly contemplating, ruminating, speculating. Writing a variety of scripts for the evolving future, he never insisted on the inevitability of any one of them. He kept his options open, intently resisting dogmatism. This mind-set gives the *Democracy* its special nature. It is in many respects an intellectual log book in which Tocqueville takes the reader on a shared, almost personal adventure of inquiry about the new democracy. In sum, the broad scale of his inquiry, his starting intuition, his refusal to dogmatize, his unremitting questions, his persistent hypothesizing: these formed the premises of *Democracy*, giving it a sustained importance for the generations that followed Tocqueville. (Eisenstadt 1988, 6–7)

Such an open-ended approach to Tocqueville is facilitated by historian Ronald Walters's argument that Tocqueville was never shy of placing tensions and inconsistencies at the heart of his analysis (Walters 1986, 18).

In this context of conflict of interpretations and different ways of reading Tocqueville, the present article seeks to bring the ethnographic Tocqueville to the center of our understanding of him. It argues that in order to understand the significance of Tocqueville's work, we have to be cautious in imputing our system building and political enthusiasm into Tocqueville, the ethnographer who describes the work of democracy in America rather than present a coherent theory of it. It pleads for reading *Democracy in America* not solely as a theory of democracy but as an ethnography of the American democratic practice. It submits that even to understand Tocqueville as a theorist of democracy, it is essential to remember and take seriously the fact that the young French aristocrat had come to America to study the American prison system. Its main objective is to understand Tocqueville's ethnography of American prison systems and American democratic practice, to explore the links between these two ethnographic universes, and finally to look into the significance of this ethnographic link for understanding Tocqueville's model, theory and vision of democracy.

Tocqueville's Ethnography of the Penitentiary System in America

It is not entirely clear when Tocqueville first thought of writing a book about America. In 1831–2, the official mission of the young French magistrate and his colleague, Gustav de Beaumont, was to prepare a report on American prison system, and they stayed in America for nine months. Even though they wanted to stay longer, the French government was pressing for an end to their mission and a quick return to France.

Tocqueville and Beaumont point to the aspects of solitary confinement in American prisons. They discuss two models of the penitentiary system: a) the principle of isolation practiced in Philadelphia prisons, and b) emphasis on the labor of the prisoners as in the Auburn system. Both penitentiary systems are based on the isolation of the prisoners (Tocqueville and Beaumont 1964, 55). These prisons rest upon the united principles of solitude and labor. In Philadelphia, perfect isolation secures the prisoners from all "fatal contaminations." On the other hand, in the Auburn system, prisoners labor together silently during the day. What strikes them in the American penitentiary system is the solitary confinement of prisoners in prisons.

The attitude of these two observers is anything but unambiguous. On the one hand, they refer to the danger in the refuge houses and the difficulty of keeping a house of refuge in the proper medium between a school and a prison. They also refer to "the unhappy condition of the working class who are in want of labor and bread…" (Tocqueville and Beaumont 1964, 34). But there is also much to suggest that "in many ways they were pessimistic about reform. Although criminal behaviour for the authors is primarily the result of indolence and idleness, they see no simple reformation of the criminal" (Tocqueville and Beaumont 1964, viii). Even before leaving for America, both Tocqueville and Beaumont had grand designs for studying more than criminal codes and penitentiary scheme. "We are rearing with the intention of examining in detail and as scientifically as possible all the mechanism of this vast American society about which everyone talks and no one knows" (Schleifer 1980, 1). Moreover this book on the penitentiary system is crucial in the construction of the argument in *Democracy in America*. Tocqueville's notebooks on the prison system are mostly filled with observations on political, social and economic matters that were later to furnish the data for Tocqueville's work on democracy. As Walters argues:

> To some extent there was a tie between Tocqueville's interest in American jails and his assessment of American democracy. The most striking characteristic of the penitentiary system that drew the interest of the French was its use of extreme measures – including enforced silence and solitary confinement. As convicts suffered through the prison yards, they were in a perverse way the logical extreme of Tocqueville's democratic man, each part of an undifferentiated mass, yet driven in upon himself, "shut up in the solitude of his own heart." (1986, 4–5)

Tocqueville's Ethnography of the American Democratic Practice

It is essential to look into Tocqueville's *Democracy of America* to find out what picture of the democratic man and the democratic society comes out in his ethnography. But before coming to terms with the ethnographic Tocqueville, it has to be made clear that Tocqueville was also engaged in the somewhat broader design of finding the image of democracy in American society. As he puts it clearly, "I confess that in America, I saw more than America; I sought the image of democracy itself, with its inclinations, its characters, its prejudices, and its passions in order to learn what we have to fear or hope from its progress" (Tocqueville 1945, xxxii).

In America, nothing struck him more forcibly than the general equality of conditions. "The more I advanced in the study of American society, the more I perceived that the equality of conditions is the fundamental fact from which all others seem to be derived, and the central point at which all my observations constantly terminated" (Tocqueville

1945, xvii). For him, the coming of the democratic age was inevitable not because of any inexorable law of social change but because of the supervening role of Providence. "He took this as a given, on the basis of a highly sensitive intuition rather than of extensively amassed evidence" (Eisenstadt 1988, 6).

Tocqueville attributes the working of the American democracy to the mores of the people, what he calls "habits of the heart." For him, the mores are even more significant than the laws. By mores, Tocqueville not only refers to manners that constitute the "character of social intercourse" but also to "the various notions and opinions current among men, and to the mass of those ideas which constitute their character of mind" (Tocqueville 1961, 354). In the operation of town meetings in America, Tocqueville observes the growth of a democratic temper. In New England, townships were constituted as early as 1650. The independence of the township is the nucleus around which the local interests, passions, rights and duties clung. Tocqueville describes how in Massachusetts, the mainspring of public administration lies in township. Outside of New England, the importance of the town is gradually transferred to the county, which becomes the intermediate power between the government and the citizen. For him, the prominent feature of the administration in the US is its excessive local independence. Moreover, people of America like this form of governance. As Tocqueville tells us, "In America, I know of no one who does not regard provincial independence as a great benefit" (Tocqueville 1961, 99).

In the working of American democracy, Tocqueville attributes great importance to the power of the judiciary. He writes, "Few laws can escape the searching analysis of the judicial power for any length of time" (Tocqueville 1961, 104). He looks at the legal profession as the most powerful existing security against the excesses of democracy. The language of law pervades popular consciousness in America. "All parties are obliged to borrow even the language usual in judicial proceedings" (Tocqueville 1961, 330). Lawyers, for him, form a cultural class and provide an equivalent to aristocratic temper in a democratic society. They have nothing to "gain from innovation, which adds a conservative interest to their natural taste for public order" (Tocqueville 1961, 328). The jury in America facilitates the communication between the judges and the citizens.

Political associations form the bedrock of American democracy. For Tocqueville, political associations are peaceable in their intentions and strictly legal in the means which they employ. He also discusses the function of the Federal Government. The President and the Cabinet are excluded from Congress. He finds two dangers to democracy in the way the Federal Government operates: a) the complete subjection of the legislative body to the caprices of the electoral body, and b) the very complex nature of the means which the Federal Government. employs to conduct its execution. He analyses the principal causes which tend to maintain the democratic republic in America. He shows how religion provides support to American democracy. Religion also facilitates the use of free institutions. As Tocqueville writes, "Upon my arrival in the United States, the religious aspect of the country was the first thing that struck my attention" (Tocqueville 1961, 365).

The features of democracy depicted above have been described in Tocqueville's *Volume One*. Many observers have attempted to make a distinction between the optimism in Tocqueville's portrayal of Democracy in 1835 and the dark pessimism in his second volume in 1840. As Arthur Schlesinger Jr observes:

> Looking at America in the 1835 *Democracy*, Tocqueville returned a rather hopeful answer. Religion, voluntary associations, local government, federalism, the free press, the machinery of justice, the traditions of the people…all held out the prospect of keeping private interest under social control. Above all, he was impressed and reassured by the national ardor for civic participation… Participation was both stimulated and guaranteed by political freedom. The 1840 *Democracy*, as we all know, presented a less cheering picture. Here Tocqueville introduced his theory of individualism. By individualism, Tocqueville…meant something close to the modern sociological concept of "privatization." For Tocqueville individualism meant not self-assertion, but self-withdrawal – the disposition of each member of the community to "sever himself from the mass of his fellows, and to draw apart with his family and friends, so that he forms a little circle of his own, he willingly leaves society at large to itself." (Schlesinger Jr 1988, 98)

Schlesinger attributes this perspectival difference between the two volumes to Tocqueville's close exposure to the democratic practice at home and his journey to Britain. This distinction between the optimism of the first volume and the pessimism of the second volume is a useful starting point to understanding Tocqueville's critical ethnography of the American democratic practice. However, Schlesinger himself argues that this distinction cannot be pushed too far. Tocqueville is critical of the pretensions of American people and their democratic practice in both his volumes. In both the volumes, he encounters the American condition as an aristocrat and also as a European. He is critical of many of the social, cultural and political practices of the Americans: from their literary life to how they adore their bodies. "Even in the first volume itself, the balance between virtue and self-interest remained precarious and he identified an array of dangers" (Schlesinger Jr 1988, 97). In the first volume itself, Tocqueville pointed to the tyranny of the majority and the American love for money.

In the first volume itself, Tocqueville's ethnographic mind brings him into critical encounter with much of American democratic practice. He writes, "I do not say that tyrannical abuses frequently occur in America at the present day; but I maintain that no sure barrier is established against them" (Tocqueville 1961, 307). Contrary to the familiar interpretation of Tocqueville as emphasizing mores and ignoring the material relations of social life, he argues, "No great change takes place in human institutions, without involving against its causes the law of inheritance" (Tocqueville 1961, 435).

As a superb ethnographer of the cultural condition of another people, Tocqueville presents many of the broad features of American society and culture in the context of which American democracy operates. He writes, "The Anglo-Americans are not only united together by their common opinions, but they are separated from all other nations by a feeling of pride." Throughout his text, he never misses a single chance to point to the mediocrity of the Americans in all aspects of their cultural and social life. The comparison between the Americans and the Europeans is always in his mind. For him, the "Europeans do not think of the ills they endure, while they [the Americans] are forever brooding over advantages they do not possess" (Tocqueville 1945, 136). Tocqueville is full of sarcasm about the literary and intellectual life in America. Insofar as the production of text is concerned, some students of contemporary cultural forms have made a distinction between authors and writers (Geertz 1988). For Tocqueville, in America, there are neither authors nor writers, but only journalists (Tocqueville 1945, 56). He also captures the ahistoric nature of the American character and its intellectual concerns: the only historical remains in the US are the newspapers (Tocqueville 1961, 243). The books he finds in American bookstores remind him of American pragmatism and insensitivity. Whatever books he finds interesting in America are imported from Britain. Authors in democratic societies will "aim at rapidity of execution more than at perfection of detail" (Tocqueville 1945, 59). As shall be discussed later, Tocqueville points to the paradoxes in democracy, more particularly in American democracy: the tensions between despotism and democracy, individualism and equality, equality of conditions and individualistic competitiveness and between equality and inequality. All these tensions have to be situated in the context of his observations about the general cultural attitude of the American people. In his discussion of the paradoxes of the American democratic practice, he attributes a lot of problems to the narrow self-interest of the Americans. What is interesting is that Tocqueville puts forward similar sarcastic comments on American moral standards: "The American moralists do not profess that men ought to sacrifice themselves for their fellow creatures because it is noble to make such sacrifices, but they boldly aver that such sacrifices are as necessary to him who imposes them upon himself as to him for whose sake they are made" (Tocqueville 1945, 122).

Corollary to the Anglo-Saxon pride, the fact of religious insanity strikes him. But by religious insanity, Tocqueville does not have in mind the contemporary problem of religious fanaticism and bigotry. Here he is referring to a sort of "fanatical spiritualism," "certain momentary outbreaks…when their souls seem suddenly to burst the bonds of matter by which they are restrained and to soar impetuously to heaven" (Tocqueville 1945, 134). But for him, this fanatical spiritualism is the inevitable outcome of a socio-cultural life that puts so much emphasis upon material prosperity and individual self-interest. To quote him, "I should be surprised if mysticism did not soon make some advance among a people solely engaged in promoting their worldly affairs" (Tocqueville 1945, 135). From all these observations, what comes out clearly is the derision and the sarcasm with which he looks at American society and culture.

For him, in no country in the civilized world is less attention paid to philosophy than in the United States. Americans always tend to the results without being bound to the means. "America is therefore one of the countries where the precepts of Descartes are least studied, and are best applied. Nor is this surprising. The Americans do not read the works of Descartes, because their social conditions deter them from speculative studies; but they follow his maxims, because this social condition naturally disposes their minds to adopt them" (Tocqueville 1956, 143). Starting from the realms of fundamental outlook to such areas of life as art, he only finds mediocrity and non-seriousness. "In aristocracies, a few great pictures are produced; in democratic countries, a vast number of insignificant ones" (Tocqueville 1956, 169). What also strikes his derisive aristocratic temper is the way Americans adore their bodies and their physical well-being. Anthropologist Robert Murphy's work on the disabled people in American culture also shows how American culture celebrates eternal youth and despises the old and the physically handicapped (Murphy 1987). Constance Perin shows how this adoration of youth in American culture is manifested in a negative and derisive attitude towards the children (Perin 1988).

To come from the realm of culture to the arena of democratic practice, Tocqueville starts with the tension between equality and liberty. He argues that democratic nations show a more ardent love of equality than of liberty. The passion for equality is produced by the equality of conditions prevalent in the democratic societies. For him, "the principle of equality may be established in civil society, without prevailing in the democratic world" (Tocqueville 1956, 189). He further adds, "The taste which men have for equality and that they feel for liberty, are in fact, two different things; and two unequal things" (Tocqueville 1956, 190). Compared to aristocratic societies, democratic societies take equality as an ultimate value, but this is not necessarily accompanied by freedom. Democratic communities have a natural taste for freedom. "But for equality, their passion is ardent, insatiable, incessant, invincible: they call for equality in freedom; and if they cannot obtain that, they still call for equality in slavery" (Tocqueville 1956, 192).

What is to be noted here is that Tocqueville is making a distinction between equality as a value and equality as a practice. In the so-called social condition of equality, he finds a passion for tyranny, arbitrariness and inequality among the American people. "An American is forever talking of the admirable equality which prevails in the United States…but in secret, he deplores it for himself; and he aspires to show that, for his part, he is an exception to the general state of things which he vaunts. There is hardly an American to be met with who does not claim some remote kindred with the first founders of the colonies" (Tocqueville 1956, 225). When equality is pursued to its ultimate extreme, it only creates a social condition of inequality. The corollary value, which generates inequality in the process of a pursuit for equality, is the value of individualism. In democratic societies, citizens "perpetuate, in a state of equality, the animosities that the state of inequality created" (Tocqueville 1956, 101).

Tocqueville's conception and description of individualism in democratic societies in general and in American democracy in particular is complex. Tocqueville points to the irresistible process of the emergence and growth of individualism in democratic societies. But this does not mean that Tocqueville provides unqualified support for individualism as a value to be strived for and fought over. Nor does he build a utopia around the value of individualism. As in the case of his broader presentation of the democratic society, Tocqueville's vision of an individualistic society contains more elements of "dystopia," to borrow a term from cultural psychologist Ashish Nandy, than of utopia (Nandy 1987). Cushing Strout notes that Tocqueville's vision of a society of individualism contains a possible anti-utopia that any one has ever made (Strout 1969). He is not only skeptical about the pursuit of individualism to its extreme but also is sensitive to the varieties of manifestations it can take. His notion of individualism is complex and his vision of a future individualistic society lacks his unqualified support. Like his idea of democracy, his view of individualism has ethnographic richness that can hardly be translated into a formal theory of individualism and an enthusiastic political doctrine. In this context, it is helpful to note the distinction between aristocratic individualism and apathetic individualism that Abraham Eisenstadt finds in Tocqueville's *Democracy* (Eisenstadt 1988). For Eisenstadt, in the first volume, Tocqueville confronts active individuals in American democracy who take a very active role in its public and political life: building schools, creating churches and participating in the local town meetings. But in the second volume, Tocqueville confronts apathetic individuals in American democracy: individuals who are withdrawn within themselves, individuals who live through a form of solitary confinement, individuals so busy in the pursuit of their own interests that they have hardly any concern for or commitment to public issues. This individualistic apathy makes them vulnerable to the majoritarian pressure of numbers in democratic societies; it is the basis upon which the tyranny of the majority is founded.[3] Tocqueville writes: "The same equality which renders him independent of his fellow-citizens, taken severally, exposes him alone and unprotected to the influence of the great number" (Tocqueville 1956, 148). For Tocqueville, the line of separation between egoistic selfishness and democratic individualism is thin and there is no historical destiny in this dyad. In his words:

I have shown how it is that, in ages of equality, every man seeks for his opinions within himself: I am now to show how it is that, in the same ages, all his feelings are turned towards himself alone… Selfishness blights the germ of all virtue: individualism, at first, only saps the virtue of public life, but, in the long run, it attacks and destroys all others, and is at length absorbed in downright selfishness. Selfishness is a vice as old as the world, which does not belong to one form of society more than to another: individualism is of democratic origin, and it threatens to spread in the same ratio as the equality of condition. (Tocqueville 1956, 193)

This complex relationship between individualism and equality comes out clearly in Tocqueville's discussion of the differential impact of the Protestant and the Catholic individualism upon the practice of democratic equality. For him, the Catholics constitute the most democratic class of citizens who exist in the United States. He writes, "If Catholicism predisposes the faithful to obedience, it certainly does not prepare them for inequality: but the contrary may be said of Protestantism, which generally tends to make men independent, more than to render them equal" (Tocqueville 1961, 356).

Tocqueville also points to egotistic competitiveness accompanying individualism and equality. Individualistic competitiveness, in the long run, undermines the practice of social equality. This pursuit of individualistic competitiveness, for Tocqueville, is a product of insatiable "desire," giving rise to an ambition in the individual that "he is born to no common destinies" (Tocqueville 1945, 138). "But this is an erroneous notion which is corrected by daily experience" (Tocqueville 1945).

Both Cushing Strout and Arthur Schlesinger Jr argue that by individualism Tocqueville refers to the modern sociological concept of "privatization" (Schlesinger Jr 1988; Strout 1969). Schlesinger argues that by individualism Tocqueville meant something very different from Emersonian self-reliance or Darwinian rigid individualism. But when we read Tocqueville's description closely, he also brings to the fore the operation of rugged individualism. This is especially true when he speaks about mad competitiveness and the limitless pursuit of money and business interests.

Tocqueville was not only struck by the emerging social conditions of equality in American democracy, he was also not insensitive to the emerging patterns of industrial inequality in America. Walters has argued that it is not simply fortuitous that Tocqueville discusses the emergence of aristocracy among the manufacturers in America. For Tocqueville, in democratic societies, as the conditions of men become more and more equal, the demand for manufactured commodities becomes more extensive. The manufactures, in democratic societies, have both capital and intelligence (Tocqueville 1956, 218). "While the workman concentrates his faculties more and more upon the study of a single detail, the master surveys an extensive whole..." In this manufacturing process, "the art advances, the artisan recedes" (Tocqueville 1956, 218). In manufacturing, the worker "no longer belongs to himself, but to the calling which he has chosen" (Tocqueville 1956, 217). The manufacturers are more powerful than "manners and laws." The theory of manufacturers assigns the worker a "certain place in society, beyond which he can not go: in the midst of universal movement, it has rendered him stationary" (Tocqueville 1956, 218).

In American democracy, as Tocqueville argues, the manufacturer asks nothing of the workman "but his labor; the workman expects nothing from him but his wages" (1956, 219). For Tocqueville, the manufacturers create a small aristocracy in democratic societies. Unlike those who are aristocrats by birth, these aristocrats do not form a class. Tocqueville's provocative portrayal of the manufacturing relationship in American democracy instantaneously reminds one of Marx's analysis of the capitalistic society. Tocqueville's discussion of the condition of the worker comes close to Marx's discussion of the alienation of the workers in capitalist society. Though Tocqueville himself has written, "To say the truth, though there are rich men, the class of the rich men does not exist; for the rich individuals have no feelings or purposes in common" (1956, 219), which may be interpreted as the anti-Marxian stance of Tocqueville, at the same time, his sensitive and sympathetic portrayal of the condition of the working class in democracy brings him closer to the critical insights of Karl Marx.

Tocqueville was also perturbed by an ominous trend in the American democratic practice: the problem of the tyranny of the majority. Interpreters of Tocqueville as early as John Stuart Mill have pointed to Tocqueville's arguments regarding how the sovereignty of the majority creates a tendency on their part to abusively exercise their power over all minorities. Tocqueville accounts for this tyranny by both the mediocrity of the men of power and the apathy of the citizens. For him, merit is common among the governed and rare among the governors. Individuals do not form their own authentic opinions on issues, rather they are swayed by the pressure of the numbers. Tocqueville's dark passages about the tyranny of the majority predates the most critical observations of mass society.

Tocqueville's description and evaluation of the American democratic practice – the mediocrity of its rulers, their lack of purpose and an aristocratic sublimity – has been influenced by his background, both as an aristocrat and as a European.[4] European observers of the American condition have always been critical of the shallowness of the social roots and mores in America. At a fundamental level, it reflects the way Europeans have had to come to terms with the ascendancy of America and its supersession of Europe. To place Tocqueville's critique of the democratic mediocrity in proper perspective, Ortega y Gasset's critique of mass society is helpful here (1932/1985). Ortega y Gasset makes a distinction between the uncommon aristocrats and the common masses in modern society. The uncommon aristocrats have an elevated moral and historical responsibility; they are those who have chosen for themselves a much larger commitment. On the other hand, the masses are bound by their own interest and characterized by an apathy to issues larger than their self-concern. In the same book, interestingly enough, Ortega y Gasset laments the way America supersedes Europe.

Tocqueville's Ethnography and Interpreting Tocqueville

Two broad interpretations of Tocqueville which I want to specifically encounter in this portrayal of the ethnographic Tocqueville concern the issues of his method and politics. The first interpretive problem concerns Tocqueville's method in his *Democracy in America*. In the introduction to this essay, mention is made of the way students of Tocqueville discover a systemic and formalistic method in his study. Such an argument is justified on the basis of Tocqueville's introductory remark that in America, he saw more than America; he saw the image of democracy. Robert Nisbet quotes this same line to justify his interpretation of Tocqueville's method. For him, "...the important features of Tocqueville's mind were not experimental or experiential; they were Cartesian to the hilt" (Nisbet 1988, 183). For Nisbet, Tocqueville was so obsessed with formulating an abstract and general model of democracy that "he saw more than America; and in the process he saw less than America" (Nisbet 1988, 173). This abstract mind was supposedly not interested in the particularities of the American life. Nisbet also thinks that Tocqueville's work on democracy is an exercise in ideal-type par excellence. "Tocqueville holds his two great ideal-types, Aristocracy and Democracy, in a kind of dynamic tension, a dialectical opposition, quite as Marx and Weber do with their paired opposites" (Nisbet 1988, 188). For Nisbet, Tocqueville, like Marx, had a teleological view of history: "…in Marx, socialism and communism; in Tocqueville, equality and homogeneity" (1988, 190).

Nisbet's reading of Tocqueville is an illustration of the way Tocqueville's method and political vision has usually been interpreted. Such an interpretation of Tocqueville's method can be traced, at least, back to James Bryce's classic work, *The American Commonwealth* (1888). For Bryce, Tocqueville was looking for the essence of democracy in America. Bryce contends that Tocqueville did not present "Democracy in America," but his own theoretic view of democracy illustrated by America. For Bryce, the "problem with Tocqueville's Democracy was that it was an exercise in deductive logic" (Eisenstadt 1988, 240). But in the context of this familiar interpretation of Tocqueville's method, this chapter wants to make a plea for Tocqueville's non-reductive method. Tocqueville's work on Democracy is an example of a superb ethnography; it is the best reflection of an ethnographic mind which does not believe in reducing the complexity of the human condition into certain principles. Of course, Tocqueville has a view of democracy, but in his ethnography his exercises are never of a deductive nature. As a superb cultural anthropologist, his objective is to understand the working of American democracy in the context of American mores. He was not thinking in terms of a few abstractions.[5] Had it been the case, he would not have taken it his objective to place the working of the American polity against the background of its mores, by which he meant both the principles of social structure and the fundamental assumptions of culture. The test of an ethnographic mind is the ability to see connections to larger issues in what are often dismissed as trivial things. As a sensitive ethnographer, Tocqueville took notice of trivial aspects of American life which he thought could provide some clue to the understanding of American mediocrity. Whether in a bookstore or in a museum, or in the way the individualism of democratic individuals degenerated into downright selfishness; Tocqueville had a sensitivity to observe the superfluousness of the American people. His title confirms what he had in mind: "Democracy in America" was meant to be an ethnography of democratic practice in America.

James Schleifer argues that Tocqueville used to think in terms of contraries. But it has to be stressed that Tocqueville did not have only the contrary pair of aristocracy and democracy with him. He was keen to depict the tensions between the elements which are usually interpreted to be harmonious parts of a deductive system of democracy. Tocqueville discussed in which context the fundamental elements of democracy – individualism, equality and liberty – can be in irreconcilable tension with each other. He discusses how the pursuit of individualism, in the process, may undermine the value of equality, how the pursuit of equality may lead to both "equality in freedom" and "equality in slavery." While Schleifer's argument has the potential to undermine Nisbet's attribution of essentialism to Tocqueville's method, still a very convincing case can be made for Tocqueville's ethnographic method. The epidemic of French structuralism has swayed us so much that our search for complexity can go only to the realm of the tension between the binary opposites. But the complexity of the human situation is much more than polarities in structuralist oppositions. Tocqueville had in mind not only the tension between the two historical forces – aristocracy and democracy – but the tension among the elements internal to democracy and the permutation and combination of forms that this tension can take. This is an ethnographic method, not a Cartesian one.

Tocqueville's distinction between "equality in slavery" and "equality in freedom" is indeed an insightful distinction which reminds us of Simmel's distinction between "individualism of equality" and "individualism of inequality" (cf. Béteille 1986). Setting these two pairs of distinctions in conjunction is essential to fight against another familiar interpretation of Tocqueville: namely his views on the positive relationship between individualism and equality. In his comparative reflections on India and the modern West, anthropologist Louis Dumont has made so much of Tocqueville's distinction between aristocracy and democracy (Dumont 1980), which has led him into another major contrasting pair: hierarchy and individualism. For Dumont, Tocqueville presents a symbiotic and mutually reinforcing relationship between individualism and equality. But a close reading of Tocqueville shows that Tocqueville, even at a conceptual level, is clear about the thin line of separation between individualism and selfish competitiveness that may lead to inequality. At the level of ethnography, he has many examples to make his case for a complex and non-teleological relationship between individualism and equality.

A brief comment on this debate on individualism and equality can shed further light on the clouds surrounding Tocqueville's familiar interpretations. The noted Indian social scientist Andre Béteille takes Dumont to task for forwarding the premise that "individualism entails equality" (Béteille 1986, 123). To subject this premise into examination, Béteille takes recourse to George Simmel. For Béteille, when Simmel was talking of "Individualism of inequality," he was referring to the "individual that had thus become independent also wished to distinguish himself from other individuals" (Simmel 1950, 78). Both for Simmel and for Béteille, "this inequality was posed from within" (Béteille 1986, 126). To see the tension between individualism and equality, Béteille not only goes to George Simmel but also to "the Catholics, Conservatives, socialists and various others" who have expressed some "misgivings about overemphasis on the individual" (1986, 122). But Béteille does not realize that it was Tocqueville who had also expressed his strongest misgivings about the abuse of individualism and the consequent overemphasis on the individual. Of Tocqueville, Béteille writes, "Alexis de Tocqueville was one of the first to argue that individualism and equality were both new values and that they were inseparably linked in their origin and development" (1986, 121). Yet Tocqueville's rich ethnography shows how individualism is not inseparably linked to equality: for example, how Catholic individualism can promote equality and Protestant individualism, inequality. His sarcastic comment on the American self-interest is the clearest illustration of his "misgiving of the overemphasis on the individual." Béteille finds problem with Dumont, but if he pursues his critical inquiry a little further into Tocqueville's ethnographic mind, he can find in it the same tension between individualism and equality, the tension that he finds in Simmel.

It is not clear from Tocqueville's ethnography that he had a teleological view of history – that democracy is going to replace aristocracy as an irresistible historical force.

To start with, unlike Marx's political enthusiasm for communism, Tocqueville was not personally or politically enthusiastic about democracy. Hence the fight between Marx and Tocqueville that the various liberal interpreters have conducted is a "metasocial commentary" upon the politics of these commentators than that of Tocqueville. It has to be stressed again that Tocqueville's analysis of wage-labor under the aristocracy of the manufacturers is not simply metaphorical. Among the major European thinkers, the one with whom Tocqueville has a close parallel is not Karl Marx, but Max Weber. Unlike Nisbet's argument, this parallel is not based on Tocqueville's use of ideal-types. It is based upon the fact that both Alexis de Tocqueville and Max Weber were not personally or politically enthusiastic about the historical processes and the ethnographic universes they were discussing. While writing about bureaucratic rationalization, Weber never accepted this as an "ultimate value" for him. Bureaucracy was an iron cage for him, and his ultimate value was based on charisma. Tocqueville, similarly, was a cautious and aristocratic observer of the democratic practice and was worried about the tyranny internal to democracy.

Critics of Tocqueville's ethnography argue that he was thinking about Europe while writing about America. It is pointed out how his ethnography missed a whole lot about America, such as the American education system. His ethnography is compared with Harriet Martineau's *Society in America* and judged to be less realistic, especially in its portrayal of "women and family life" (Nisbet 1988, 174). Critics of Tocqueville point out how the elements of democracy – localism, decentralization, etc. – were originally conceived by the French social observer, Lamennais (Nisbet 1988). But these criticisms do not undermine the significance and value of his ethnography. Even if Tocqueville might have been biased by Lamennais' ideas of localism and decentralization, this does not undermine his own contribution in presenting us with an ethnographic portrayal and critique of democracy in America.

Tocqueville's ethnographic mind cautions us to have models of certainty and finality not only about democracy but also about every aspect of human socio-cultural reality. It is probably for this reason that Ankersmit writes: "...writing a conclusion to an essay on Tocqueville is a task fraught with dangers... What is really interesting in Tocqueville...is not what lends itself to a reduction to consistency, coherence and logical arguments, but rather the paradoxes and inconsistencies that resist such a reduction" (1996, 341). There is an elective affinity between Tocqueville's ethnographic method and mind and the dynamics of democracy as an unstructured and emergent process, which resists *a priori* fixation and determination. The appropriate dynamics of democracy expect of us a style of understanding and writing which is not determined by any *a priori* formulation and is ever attentive to complexities, contradictions and emergent processes. As Ankersmit again helps us understand:

...if Tocqueville is correct in saying that democracy has no center, that it has neither essence nor nature of its own, this requires us to adopt a style that bestows on the text exactly the *same* characteristics... Tocqueville's texts are an implicit suggestion about which manner or style we ought to adopt if we wish to say something useful about democracy. In a curiously oblique way Tocqueville's texts show that its antitheoretical, antimetaphorical, and paradoxical style is the only key to the secrets of democracy. In contrast to relatively crude political systems like feudalism, aristocracy, or absolutism, the philosophical web of democracy is so subtle that we will tear it apart if we approach it with an unsuitable stylistic apparatus. (Ankersmit 1996, 342, 296)

Notes

1 Insofar as partisan social theorizing is concerned, it is important to note that Tocqueville writes at the beginning of his *Democracy*: "The book is written to favor no particular view, and in composing it I have entertained no design of serving or attacking any party" (as quoted in Ankersmit 1996, 324).

2 Ankersmit argues:

> Tocqueville's break with the historiographical traditions of his (and our own) time mainly consists in his abandonment of metaphor in favor of paradox. And surely we may expect a penchant for paradox in an author who, like Tocqueville, presents to his readers the French Revolution as being no revolution at all or who describes democracy as being, in fact, a despotism of the multitude and as a political system that is essentially conservative. (1996, 330)

3 Ankersmit also writes the following about the Tocquevillian interpretation of democracy:

> Democratic citizens will become more and more isolated from one another in their search for private well-being, and ever less capable of solving either individually or in mutual co-operation what they experience to be the problems of their social and political life. It is the democratic state to which they will therefore unanimously turn. (1996, 338)

4 In this context, we may note what Tocqueville writes about himself:

> Intellectually I can approve of democratic institutions, but I am an aristocrat by instinct. I passionately love liberty, legality, the respect for rights; but not democracy. That is the essence of my personality. (Quoted in Ankersmit 1996, 336)

5 It may be noted here that Tocqueville argues that there is a passion for abstraction in democracy and "Tocqueville ruefully concedes that his own use of the term 'equality' shows how much he himself has fallen victim to democracy's fatal love of abstractions" (Ankersmit 1996, 299).

References

Ankersmit, F. R. 1996. *Aesthetic Politics: Political Philosophy Beyond Fact and Value*. Stanford: Stanford University Press.

Aron, Raymond. 1965. *Main Currents of Sociological Thought*. New York: Basic Books.

Béteille, Andre. 1986. "Individualism and Equality." *Current Anthropology* 27 (2): 121–34.

———. 1987. "Equality as a Right and as a Policy." *LSE Quarterly* 1 (1): 75–98.

Bottomore, T. B. 1979. *Political Sociology*. London: Hutchinson.

Bryce, James. 1888. *The American Commonwealth*. London.

Chatterjee, Partha and Ira Katznelson. 2012. "Introduction: The Anxieties of Democracy." In Partha Chatterjee and Ira Katznelson, eds, *Anxieties of Democracy: Tocquevillian Reflections on India and the United States*, 1–19. Delhi: Oxford University Press.

Dumont, Louis. 1980. *Homo Hierarchicus: The Caste System and its Implications*. Chicago: University of Chicago Press.

Eisenstadt, Abraham 1988. "Bryce's America and Tocqueville's." In Abraham Eisenstadt, ed., *Reconsidering Tocqueville's Democracy in America*. New Brunswick and London: Rutgers University Press.

Geertz, Clifford. 1988. *Works and Lives: The Anthropologist as Author*. Stanford: Stanford University Press.

Murphy, Robert. 1987. *The Body Silent: The Different World of the Disabled*. New York: Henry Holt & Co.

Nandy, Ashis. 1987. *Tradition, Tyranny and Utopia: Essays in the Politics of Awareness*. New Delhi: Oxford University Press.

Nisbet, Robert. 1988. "Tocqueville's Ideal Types." In Abraham Eisenstadt, ed., *Reconsidering Tocqueville's Democracy in America*. New Brunswick and London: Rutgers University Press.

Ortega y Gasset, José. 1932/1985. *The Revolt of the Masses*. Notre Dame, IN: University of Notre Dame Press.

Perin, Constance. 1988. *Belonging in America: Reading between the Lines*. Madison: University of Wisconsin Press.

Richter, Melvin. 1970. "The Uses of Theory: Tocqueville's Adaptation of Montesquieu." In M. Richter, ed., *Essays in Theory and History: An Approach to the Social Sciences*. Cambridge, MA: Harvard University Press.

Schleifer, James. 1980. *The Making of Tocqueville's Democracy in America*. Chapel Hill: University of North Carolina Press.

Schlesinger, Arthur, Jr. 1988. "Individualism and Apathy in Tocqueville's Democracy." In Abraham Eisenstadt, ed., *Reconsidering Tocqueville's Democracy in America*. New Brunswick and London: Rutgers University Press.

Simmel, George. 1917/1950. "Individual and Society in Eighteenth and Nineteenth-Century Views of Life." In K. Wolff, ed., *The Sociology of George Simmel*. Glencoe: Free Press.

Strout, Cushing. 1969. "Tocqueville's Duality: Describing America and Thinking of Europe." *American Quarterly* (Spring): 87–100.

Tocqueville, Alexis de. 1945. *Democracy in America*, vol. 2. New York: Alfred A. Knopf.

_____. 1956. *Democracy in America, Specially Edited and Abridged for the Modern Reader by Richard D. Heffner.*

_____. 1961. *Democracy in America*, vol. 1. New York: Schocken Books.

Tocqueville, Alexis de and Gustav de Beaumont. 1833/1964. *On the Penitentiary System in the United States and its Application in France*. Carbondale: Southern Illinois University Press.

Walters, Ronald. 1986. "Reforming Tocqueville." Department of History, Johns Hopkins University. Unpublished manuscript.

Part II

RETHINKING KNOWLEDGE

Chapter Six

SOME RECENT RECONSIDERATIONS OF RATIONALITY

…the opposition of self and other is mediated by the emergence of the other self and the common human language of "oneself." This human language is the real and true non-dualist locus of culture, labor and politics, whether the other should be God, non-human nature, the world or other human selves, masculine or feminine, native or foreign.

—J. P. S Uberoi, *The European Modernity: Science, Truth and Method* (2002, 113)

The world as we understand it at present may be the same world as it always was but we no longer look to Physics to underpin the Myth of Stability, and provide the same comforts as before. The claims of contemporary sciences, both natural and human, are a good deal more modest, seeking neither to deny nor to explain away the contingency of things.

—Stephen Toulmin, *Return to Reason* (2001, 209–10)

Perhaps the names of persons whose *saying* signifies a face – proper names, in the middle of all these common names and common places – can resist the dissolution of meaning and help us to speak. Perhaps they will enable us to divine, behind the downfall of discourse, the end of a certain intelligibility and the dawning of a new one. What is coming to a close may be a rationality tied *exclusively* to the being that is sustained by words, the *Said* of the Saying.

—Emmanuel Levinas, *Proper Names* (1996, 4–5)

The Problem

The concept of rationality has been subjected to numerous critiques in the history of modernity, and all these critiques have been helpful in opening rationality to cross-cultural translations and examinations. Despite numerous anthropological critiques of a Eurocentric notion of rationality which looks at other people such as the tribal people having a primitive mind, a modernistic and West-centric view of rationality is still very much on the throne. This situation seems to be slightly altering in the realm of philosophical discourse with some recent foundational interrogations of rationality offered by thinkers such as Alasdair MacIntyre and Stephen Toulmin, who urge us to realize that the discourse of rationality should not be a servant either to the discourse of anthropocentrism or Eurocentrism (MacIntyre 1999; Toulmin 2001). Their reconsiderations help us overcome the anthropocentric and Eurocentric temptations to use rationality as a differentiating and discriminatory criterion. The present chapter begins with these reconsiderations and then adds to them Foucault's critique of the hegemonic universalism of Kant, Putnam's elaborations of a Deweyan approach to rationality, and Tambiah's contribution to the reconsideration of rationality from transdisciplinary concerns of anthropology and philosophy (Foucault 1984; Putnam 2001; Tambiah 1990). In elaborating these reconsiderations, it also discusses the agenda of a Pragmatic Enlightenment offered by Hilary Putnam in place of the rationalistic Enlightenment of an earlier era. But the problem with this path of Pragmatic Enlightenment is that it leaves uninterrogated the Enlightenment division between the Natural World and the human-social world, and between society and the world of transcendence. But in order to understand rationality in its inherent multiplicity we need to overcome this Enlightenment black box and understand the unfolding of reason and life; not only in the black box of "cogito ergo sum," but in a relational pathway in which reason relates not only to a separate ego but helps in relationship between ego and the world (world here means not only human social world but also the world of nature and the world of transcendence).

Reconsiderations of Rationality and Extension of Our Understanding: Overcoming Anthropocentrism

It is helpful to begin with the famous debate between Peter Winch and Alasdair MacIntyre on language and rationality. Peter Winch held that there is no reality independent of language games, but for MacIntyre to successfully describe the rules of use of another culture, the anthropologist applies the "standard of rational criticism as applied in the contemporary West" (quoted in Tambiah 1990, 121). To this Peter Winch's reply was, "Since it is we who want to understand the Zande category, it appears that the onus is on us to extend our understanding so as to make room for the Zande category, rather than to see in terms of our own ready-made distinction between science and non-science" (Tambiah 1990, 121). This task of extending our understanding vis-à-vis language and rationality is undertaken in a much more radical manner by MacIntyre in his *Dependent Rational Animals* (1999). In this book MacIntyre offers a foundational critique of the tendency to use rationality as a tool of discrimination and domination, especially as it relates to relationship between humans and animals. MacIntyre writes in the very first pages of his book: "...Aristotle's account of human beings as distinctively rational has sometimes been interpreted as though he meant that rationality itself was not an animal property but rather a property that separates humans from their animality" (MacIntyre 1999, 5). But for MacIntyre, "Aristotle did not of course make this mistake. *Phronesis*, the capacity for practical rationality is a capacity that he – and after him Aquinas – ascribed to some nonhuman animals in virtue of their foresight, as well as to human beings" (1999, 5–6).

To illustrate the point about rationality of animals, MacIntyre gives the examples of dolphins. MacIntyre tells us, building on studies carried out with the dolphins, that dolphins exercise the capacity for "perceptual recognition, for perceptual attention, for a range of different responses to what is perceived and recognized as the same individual or kind of individuals and for a range of varying emotional expressions" (MacIntyre 1999, 23). Furthermore, "The activities involved in perceptual learning and in then putting to use what they have learned render dolphins no mere passive receptors of experience. And, like human beings, dolphins take pleasure in those activities which are the exercise of their power and skills. When Aristotle says that there is pleasure in all perceptual activity and that pleasure supervenes upon the completed activity, what he asserts seems to be as true of dolphins as of human beings" (MacIntyre 1999, 26). McIntyre further tells us that dolphins of a variety of species flourish "only because they have learned how to achieve their goods through strategies concerned with members of different groups to which they belong or which they encounter" (MacIntyre 1999, 22).

Overcoming Eurocentrism

MacIntyre quotes Wittgenstein: "Animals come when their names are called just like human beings." Stephen Toumin, one of the most creative students of Wittgenstein, uses the same Wittgensteinian spirit to overcome another formidable binding in thinking about rationality, namely the binding of Eurocentrism. Toulmin shows how rationality as stability and mathematical certainty achieved its distinctive and dominant status under specific historical circumstances in modern Europe. But this is only one manifestation of rationality in history, culture and society and in thinking about rationality one should not be a slave to this particular construction. Toulmin writes, "Historically, the enthronement of mathematical rationality was just one aspect of broader intellectual response to the loss of theological consensus following Luther's and Calvin's success in enrolling craftsmen and other members of the newly literate laity into Protestant congregations" (Toulmin 2001, 205). This loss of consensus led to the infamous religious war in Europe between 1618 and 1648, and the Westphalian system of the nation-state emerging in this specific historical context was to ensure certainty and stability in this chaotic situation. For Toulmin, the Cartesian approach to certainty and rationality gained ascendancy in this specific historical circumstance. Theorists clung to Cartesian rationality because it provided them with certainty. But this came at a great price, too. Preoccupation with stability and certainty as part of a commitment to Cartesian rationality led to the construction of impermeable boundaries between different realms of human experience, knowledge and disciplines. Later on, with colonialism and imperialism, this impermeable border was constructed as a tool of discrimination and domination between Western and non-Western peoples, at the core of which lay the Eurocentric discourse of rationality.

Reconsideration of rationality in this context entails going beyond clinging to certainty and stability: to "redress proper balance between theory and practice: ...to recognize legitimate claims of 'theories' without exaggerating the formal attractions of Euclidean reasoning and to defend the lessons of actual practice without denigrating the power of theoretical argument" (Toulmin 2001, 171). Reconsideration of rationality also now calls us to live with uncertainty as "in a world of complexity, chaos and other 'non-linear' ways of theorizing, the old alliance of State, Church, and Academy has lost the secure foothold" (Toulmin 2001, 205).

In his reconsideration of rationality Toulmin makes a distinction between reason and reasonableness. While Cartesian reason may have been developed in the West, there are different ways of being reasonable even in the West. As a way of moving beyond the Cartesian agenda of rationality, Toulmin urges us to be in dialogue with Wittgenstein and John Dewey. For Toulmin, "If René Descartes is a symbolic figure marking the beginning of Modern Age, we may take Ludwig Wittgenstein as marking its end" (Toulmin 2001, 206). One aspect of this culmination is the help the late Wittgenstein provides us in freeing us from a rationalistic approach to language and a linguistic approach to rationality. For Wittgenstein, "Our imaginations are particularly open to metaphysical yearnings at the point where language 'goes on holiday'… Our yearnings begin at a time when meanings are no longer bounded by the demands of workday disciplines or responsibilities, and language finds fulfillment in the High Holy Days. Then we are free to speak in ways that expand outside those boundaries to an unlimited extent: after all, as he put it, *die Sprache ist keine Käfig* – Language is not a Cage" (Toulmin 2001, 201–2).

Wittgenstein's openness to metaphysics in thinking about language of course has a celebrated companion in the ground-breaking work of Heidegger. For Heidegger, "The human world is not the product of linguistic games which allow the denotation of things: it originates…out of the essential unfolding of Being" (Kovacs 2001, 46). Furthermore, for Heidegger, "The word tells something about human being as *Dasein* that goes beyond the idea of human being as rational animal" (Kovacs 2001).

Both Heideggerian and Wittgensteinian meditations help us rethink language and rationality, and point to the spiritual horizons of self in our reconsiderations of rationaltiy (cf. Monk 1990). It is such a horizon which is missing in the pragmatist reconsiderations of rationality and in Foucault's critique of Kant. But before we come to the issue of spiritual dimension of rationality, it is helpful to get a glimpse of the path of reconstruction and the reconsideration of rationality suggested by pragmatism.

Pragmatism and the Reconsideration of Rationality: A Third Enlightenment or a Pragmatic Enlightenment?

Toulmin presents us with both Wittgenstein and Dewey as a way of moving beyond Descartes in our reconsideration of rationality. This is how Toulmin introduces the pathways of John Dewey and pragmatism: "With the decline of Cartesian foundationalism, claims to self-validation do not carry their earlier weight: we need not choose between knowledge based on experience and knowledge based on claims to self-evidence. In this respect, Dewey was right to suggest that Pragmatism is not just one theory on a par with all others. Rather, it represents a change of view, which puts theorizing on a par with all other practical activities" (Toulmin 1990, 172).

But the significance of Dewey and pragmatism lies in not only helping us to look at theory as practice, but also in reconstituting certain prevalent ways of going about rationality. In his works, Hilary Putnam helps us understand this. For Putnam (1994), while in Carnap the scientific method is reconstructed as a method of computation, for Dewey the issue is not only one of computation but co-operation. In Putnam's words: "For Dewey, inquiry is co-operative human interaction with an environment; and both aspects, the active intervention, the active manipulation of the environment, and the cooperation with other human beings are vital." In his essay "Dewey's Logic: Epistemology as Hypotheses," Putnam urges us to understand the wider significance of the silent revolution – the revolution of procedural deliberation – initiated by Dewey. Dewey finds "traditional empiricism in its own way as aprioristic as traditional rationalism" (Putnam 1994). Dewey does not speak of reason but of the application of intelligence to problems, and it can be well appreciated here that once we pose the problem of rationality in terms of application it is difficult to hold it as the exclusive possession of either the human being or modern Enlightenment. Furthermore, Dewey and the pragmatists lay stress on procedure and they urge us to acknowledge fallibility in talking about and being part of rationality. This acknowledgment of fallibility is a crucial step in our reconsideration of rationality, as the latter has been too confident of itself, and in this overconfidence has inflicted unspeakable cruelty and suffering in human history. It must be noted here that it is acknowledgment of human vulnerability that has also been the motivation behind MacIntyre's (1999) effort to overcome anthropocentrism in thinking about language and reason.

But the stress on procedures of argumentation in pragmatism, on which Jürgen Habermas of our recent times also lays crucial significance and in the process presents us with a communicative model of rationality, has an important moral implication. It becomes an aid in co-operative living of people despite foundational disagreements. In the words of Putnam, "Pragmatism anticipated an idea that has become a commonplace in contemporary moral philosophy, the idea that disagreement in individual conception of good need not make it impossible to approximate (even if we never finally arrive at) agreement in just procedures and even agreement on such abstract and formal values as respect for one another's autonomy."

In a later work Putnam (2001) suggests the pathway of a Third Enlightenment or Pragmatic Enlightenment whose claims of reason and progress are more fallible than was allowed in the Second Enlightenment; that is, a modern Rational Enlightenment (the First Enlightenment for Putnam is the one opened up by Plato). The Pragmatist Enlightenment for Putnam puts stress on inbuilt criticism of any claim, criticism emanating from the sphere of deliberations and leading to what Putnam calls "reflective transcendence" (Putnam 2001).

At this juncture it is helpful here to bring to our conversations Foucault's critique of the Kantian agenda of Enlightenment. In place of the Kantian agenda of universalistic Enlightenment, for Foucault, we should have "vernacular Enlightenment" (cf. Dallmayr

1998) which is sensitive to localities and to the contingencies of space and time and also to disjuncture in our experience and knowledge. Foucault endorses Kant's dreams of Enlightenment but does not share his faith in the possibility of a coherent body of knowledge – knowledge related to politics, hope and scientific understanding. Knowledge emerging from these different domains may not fit and rationality has to learn how to acknowledge this (cf. Quarles van Ufford and Giri 2003). The discourse and practice of rationality, especially when it becomes a tool in rational planning, development or "Applied Enlightenment," has to acknowledge, come to terms and cope with disjunctures and incompatibilities between different bodies of knowledge and between knowledge and action. Like Toulmin's, Foucault's critique of the Kantian agenda of Enlightenment urges us to cope with uncertainties and contingencies in the discourse and practice of rationality. But Foucault's critique of Kantian universalism and plea for what Dallmayr calls vernacular Enlightenment is not a support for parochialism. Rather it has the potential for a radical hermeneutics by being open to localities and open to cross-cultural and global conversations. In the words of Dallmayr:

> ...wedded to interrogation and self-transformation, hermeneutics refuses the trap of parochialism and instead encourages ongoing self-critique carried on by Foucault's "specialized" or situated intellectuals... Most importantly, hermeneutical engagement supports and enables the kind of learning experience that alone holds the promise of genuine global cooperation and co-being. (Dallmayr 1998, 7)

Foucault's "vernacular Enlightenment" is further illumined by anthropologist Stanley Tambiah's and philosopher Mrinal Miri's reflections on the issue of rationality and science. Tambiah presents us with Malinowski's arguments that "all human beings are reasonable..." (Tambiah 1990, 67). (Tambiah also presents us Leach's arguments, which show the affinity between Malinowski's functionalism and the philosophy of pragmatism of William James.) In talking about science, Tambiah initially speaks about two modes of science: participation and causation, and then goes on to point to their intertwining existence: "...the elements of participation are not lacking in scientific discourses, and features of causality are not necessarily absent in participatory enactments" (Tambiah 1990, 109–10). This enables us to realize that we need a participatory approach to science and causation. As R. Sunder Rajan (1998) tells us in his *Beyond the Crisis of European Sciences*, to know is not only "to know of" but "to know with."

Our reconsiderations of rationality are enriched by the reflections of philosopher Mrinal Miri, who like Tambiah embodies a transdisciplinary conversation between anthropology and philosophy. Miri writes, "For me...an important part of the task of understanding the tribal situation is that of understanding the great divide between modern science and what may be called pre-science." While the modern vision for Miri entails an exclusion of the transcendent in the name of science and rationality, this is different in the case of tribes. In the tribal vision, "the transcendent understood no doubt in a variety of ways is what breathes life into reality." The focus on transcendence here is accompanied by a focus on the "inter-relatedness of things – on a holistic rather than fragmentary, atomistic, granular vision."

Further Challenges: The Calling of Spiritual Transformations in our Reconsiderations of Rationality

Tambiah's and Miri's interpenetrative reflections of anthropology and philosophy help us broaden the perspective of rationality. At the same time, it calls for further rethinking and reflections. While the issue of transcendence is a missing discourse in the recent philosophical reconsiderations of rationality and Miri's pointer to this is a welcome move, Miri's distinction between science and pre-science is not tenable in the light of the transformations taking place in modern science, which blur the distinction between participation and causation. As I have already argued, building on Tambiah and Sunder Rajan, we need a participatory mode in thinking about causation, science and rationality.

But the issue of transcendence raised by Miri based on the world of tribal life urges us to move further and deeper, involving foundational interrogations and self-transcendence, in our reconsiderations of rationality. Our reconsiderations of rationality are still very much part of an immanent critique where transcendence is dismissed as unnecessary, or the very mention of it raises a lot of anxieties (cf. Hardt and Negri 2000). Thinkers such as Putnam talk about reflective transcendence but do not explore the pathways of ontological transcendence that facilitates this (cf. Bhaskar 2002). But with Heidegger's and Wittgenstein's overture towards metaphysics, we can get the inspiration to go beyond "rationality" in our reconsiderations, and to explore, realize and live by what Sri Aurobindo calls the "supra-rational" dimensions of our "rational" existence. But this calls for a foundational reevaluation and revolution in contemporary critical philosophy which still continues to assertively and self-confidently present itself as a "post-metaphysical" undertaking (cf. Habermas 1992; Vattimo 1999).[1]

Note

1 Habermas himself notes the limits of a confident post-metaphysical move:

> In the wake of metaphysics, philosophy surrenders its extraordinary status. Explosive experiences of the extraordinary have migrated into an art that has become autonomous. Of course, even after this deflation, ordinary life, now fully profane, by no means becomes immune to the shattering and subversive intrusion of extraordinary events. [These elude] the explanatory force of philosophical language and continues to resist translation into reasoning discourses. (Habermas 1992, 51)

References

Bhaskar, Roy. 2002. *Reflections on Meta-Reality: Transcendence, Emancipation and Everyday Life*. New Delhi: Sage.
Dallmayr, Fred. 1998. *Alternative Visions: Pathways in the Global Village*. Lanham, MD: Rowman & Littlefield.

Foucault, M. 1984. "What is Enlightenment?" In Paul Rabinow, ed., *The Foucault Reader*. New York: Pantheon.

Giri, Ananta Kumar. 2002. *Conversations and Transformations: Towards a New Ethics of Self and Society*. Lanham, MD: Lexington Books.

Habermas, Jürgen. 1992. *Post-Metaphysical Thinking*. Cambridge: Polity Press.

Herdt, Michael and Antonio Negri. 2000. *Empire*. Cambridge, MA: Harvard University Press.

Kovacs, George. 2001. "Heidegger in Dialogue with Herder: Crossing the Language of Metaphysics toward Be-ing-historical Language." *Heidegger Studies* 17: 45–63.

Levinas, Emmanuel. 1975/1996. *Proper Names*. Stanford: Stanford University Press.

MacIntyre, Alasdair. 1999. *Dependent Rational Animals: Why Human Beings Need the Virtues*. Chicago: Open Court.

Miri, Mrinal. 1993. "Introduction." In Mrinal Miri, ed., *Tribal Situation in India*. Shimla: Indian Institute of Advanced Studies.

Monk, Roy. *Wittgenstein: The Duty of Genius*. London: Vintage.

Putnam, Hilary. 1994. *Words and Life*, ed. James Conant. Cambridge, MA: Harvard University Press.

———. 2001. *The Three Enlightenments*. Amsterdam: Spinoza Lectures.

Giri, Ananta Kumar and Phillip Quarles van Ufford, Phillip Quarles, eds. 2003. *A Moral Critique of Development: In Search of Global Responsibilities*. London: Routledge.

Rorty, Richard. 1999. *Philosophy and Social Hope*. London: Penguin.

Sunder Rajan, R. 1998. *Beyond the Crisis of European Sciences*. Shimla: Indian Institute of Advanced Studies.

Tambiah, Stanley. 1990. *Magic, Science and Religion, and the Scope of Rationality*. Cambridge: Cambridge University Press.

Toulmin, Stephen. 2001. *Return to Reason*. Cambridge, MA: Harvard University Press.

Vattimo, Giani. 1999. *Belief*. Cambridge: Polity Press.

Uberoi, J. P. S. 2002. *The European Modernity: Science, Truth and Method*. Delhi: Oxford University Press.

Chapter Seven

CONTEMPORARY CHALLENGES TO THE IDEA OF HISTORY

The inclusion of cyclic time is not a characteristic of cultures which are historically stunted but an indication of historical complexity. This complexity is reflected in the perceptions of the past in pre-modern times, the premises of which were different from the writing of history today.

—Romila Thapar, *Time as a Metaphor of History: Early India* (1996, 44)

Historical consciousness finds itself in an impasse. Historical consciousness seeks its fulfillment in the future, but the internal logic of an economy of profit and growth, unlike a lifestyle of contentment and self-sufficiency, inherently obliges one to mortgage the future.

—Raimundo Panikkar, *The Cosmotheandric Experience: Emerging Religious Consciousness* (1998, 114)

Authenticity implies a relation with what is known that duplicates the two sides of historicity: it engages us both as actors and narrators. Thus, authenticity cannot reside in attitudes towards a discrete past kept alive through narratives…even in relation to the past our authenticity resides in the struggles of our present. Only in that present can we be true or false to the past we choose to acknowledge.

—Michel-Rolph Trouillot, *Silencing the Past: Power and the Production of History* (1995, 151)

The Problem

In his inaugural address at the 61st session of the Indian History Congress at Calcutta, Amartya Sen develops and defends a view of history as an enterprise of knowledge. Sen takes issue with postmodern critiques of knowledge in general and historical knowledge in particular, and argues that though all of us have our own perspectives and points of view, yet it does not preclude the possibility of arriving at "an integrated and coherent picture" (Sen 2001, 86). Sen goes on to argue: "…describing the past is like all other reflective judgments, which have to take note of demands of veracity and the discipline of knowledge. The discipline includes the study of knowledge formation, including the history of science and also the history of history" (Sen 2001, 86). But though Sen is open to history of science in his engagement, he does not engage himself with history of history. Sen does not look into the issue of cultural presuppositions of the enterprise of knowledge we call history. Nor does Sen look into the different domains in the enterprise of history such as history as power, history as reason and history as vision. It is Amartya Sen who, nearly twenty years ago in his "Tanner Lectures on Human Values," had stirred our minds with the question: equality of what? In the same vein, if history is an enterprise of knowledge, then the key question is knowledge of what? Does history as an enterprise of knowledge deal with knowledge of power, of reason, or of spiritual vision? A related question here is whose knowledge? Is it the knowledge of the sovereign or the subaltern?

While the rise of subaltern studies has brought to the center the question of whose knowledge, in this chapter I want to argue that knowledge of what is also equally important in thinking about history. I want to argue, building on Immanuel Kant and Michel Foucault, that knowledge is concerned not only with power and reason but also with hope (cf. Giri and van Ufford 2001). To put it in the words of R. Sundar Rajan: "There are three thematic principles of history. History as Power, History as Reason and History as Vision" (Sunder Rajan 1996, 192–3). These three themes correspond to three questions Kant asked us long ago – what can we know, what should we will and what may we reasonably hope for; but unlike Kant and Sen, it is difficult for us to arrive at a unity among these three domains of knowledge. As an enterprise of knowledge, history deals with all three domains – power, reason and spiritual vision, or politics, critical understanding and hope, but the knowledge emerging from one domain may not be compatible with another. For instance, when we look at Indian society and history, we see that the knowledge of its politics and social system is incompatible with the knowledge of its spiritual vision. While the historical knowledge of politics and society in India gives us a picture of a caste system and oppressive kings, the knowledge of the spiritual vision gives us a story of the quest for spiritual self-realization and different *bhakti* movements for instituting dignified relationships in society. In this field of plural knowledge, there is also a dialectic and mutual influence at work. Sunder Rajan helps us understand this: "The themata of history not only cover the whole domain of phenomena but they seek to frame the other thematic principles, giving an interpretation of those interpretive devices themselves. Thus, within the historiography of power, there is a specific placement of vision and power" (1996, 192). But Sen's view of history as an enterprise of knowledge is not sensitive to this mutually transformative dialectic between power/knowledge and spiritual visions. Sen also does not interrogate the foundations of history itself as an enterprise of knowledge.

In this chapter in our engagement with rethinking knowledge, I undertake the task of a foundational critique of history as an enterprise of knowledge by discussing the work of G. C. Pande and Ashis Nandy, who draw our attention to ethnocentrism in modernist history and historiography. Then I discuss the issue of space and time by arguing how modernity privileges time – a teleological time – over space. I discuss how the temporalization of space in modernity is crucial to capitalism, imperialism and colonialism, and how history's uncritical preoccupation with linear time makes it part of what Ashish Nandy (1995) calls "the imperialism of categories." But the progression from the temporalization of space to the spatialization of time gives us two contradictory though interrelated processes – spatialization of time as speed, a process where both time and space run ever faster for the realization of capitalist profit, and the spatialization of time as a space of resistance (also of hope and alternative imagining and becoming) where spaces refuse to be swallowed up by the teleological time of both the modernizing nation-state and the dictatorship of the proletariat. In talking about space and time I discuss both Marx and Heidegger, particularly Heidegger's distinction between "clock time" and "lived time," and between building and dwelling. I plead that history should be self-critical about the modernist privileging of time over space, and now take part in both an ontological and epistemological border crossing by being attentive to both space and time, and by striving for a "spatio-temporal utopianism" (cf. Harvey 2000) where there is not only a creative interpenetration of space and time but also of past, present and future. As Dallmayr presents the outline of such a creative historiography, building on Heidegger, "At the interstices of past and future lies the lived present – a present conceived no longer as an indefinite now-point, but as a task to be shouldered by existence. Nurtured by the past and illumined by future possibilities, the present becomes the locus of practical engagement and resolute care" (Dallmayr 2000, 8–9).

Contemporary Challenges to the Idea of History: Some Foundational Critiques

G. C. Pande is a thoughtful interlocutor of contemporary India who urges us to be sensitive to the problem of cultural presuppositions in historiographies of civilizations. For Pande, modern historiography is essentially ethnocentric (i.e. Western) and its two presuppositions are: a) human civilization constitutes a linear, evolutionary process, and b) the basic feature of human civilization is the power it gives man "to control his physical environment enabling him to increase his success in the struggle for existence and the search for maximizing satisfactions" (Pande 1996, 34). But Pande asks us to ponder: "But is the idea of linear evolution of human civilization a generalization established by historical inquiry or is it just a hypothesis?" (1996, 34). For Pande, "The prevailingly modern Western view as reflected in contemporary historiography of civilization is to make scientific humanism the real value of all civilizations. The human self is here regarded as social and rational" (Pande 1996, 34). But can these cultural presuppositions about man and society be universalized? For Pande, "Positive knowledge and practical skill have always been prized and cultivated but in the earlier ages they were prized within the bounds of cultural ethos which looked beyond the merely earthy life of man to his heavenly destiny" (Pande 1996, 34). But the modern historian "even though he is not a scientist, finds it incumbent on him to endorse not merely the empirical truth of natural sciences but also an attitude of skepticism towards traditional beliefs" (Pande 1996, 45). For Pande, "This is simply a consequence of the historian's acceptance of values which define modern culture, it is not relevant to his task as a historian pure and simple" (1996, 45).

So, in being engaged with the enterprise of knowledge one has to take note of different values rather than just assert one value, for instance modern Enlightenment values of self and society. The existence of plural values with which history as an enterprise of knowledge has to deal, for Pande, does not necessarily create a situation of radical incommensurability. But to overcome the apparent and existential incommensurability, if any, what is needed is not only "positional objectivity"[1] of the kind put forward by Sen (1994) but also a participation in different worldviews and value themes in the spirit of a Gadamerian fusion of horizons. In the words of Pande, "The plurality of cultures and relativity of values does not, however, mean any radical incommensurability in the sense of mutual non-comprehension or non communication. The task of the historiography of civilization ought to be to provide a bridge for genuine cross-cultural understanding" (Pande 1996, 41).

Ashis Nandy also raises some foundational questions about the enterprise of history. For Nandy, "…the aim of history is to unravel secular processes and the order that underlie the manifest realities of past times" (Nandy 1995, 48). As an "authentic progeny of seventeenth century Europe, history fears ambiguity" (Nandy 1995, 48). Nandy laments that in contemporary epistemology, "there is no fundamental skepticism towards history as a mode of world construction" (1995, 52). For Nandy, "History not only exhausts our idea of the past, it also defines our relationship with our past selves" (1995, 54).

But this triumph of history when "historical consciousness owns the globe" (cf. Nandy 1995, 46) is recent, and Nandy urges us to realize that even in the modern West not so long ago "historical consciousness had to co-exist with other modes of experiencing and constructing the past." All societies do not have the same mode of constructing the past and here Nandy makes a broad distinction between historical and ahistorical societies around the distinction between myth and history. For Nandy, while "historical consciousness cannot take seriously the principle of forgetfulness" myths work through "the principle of principled forgetfulness" (1995, 47). While history provides certitudes, myths, legends and *puranas* provide us with a painful awareness of contingency. This is easily understood when we look at the epic of *Mahabharata*, which does not give us any final winner or loser but deep pangs and suffering. There is also a difference here with regard to time. For Nandy, "traditional India lacks the Enlightenment's concept of history" and the "construction of time in South Asia may or may not be cyclical, but it is rarely linear or unidirectional" (1995, 63). Attitude to time "including the sequencing of the past, the present, and the future – is not given or pre-formatted. Time in much of South Asia is an open-ended enterprise" (Nandy 1995, 63). It is this open-ended nature of time and the interpenetratation of time and eternity that modern historical consciousness finds puzzling and threatening. The historically minded are also hostile to horizons of transcendence intimately invoked in non-historical societies.

The nationalist interlocutors of India in the nineteenth century lamented that India lacked a historical consciousness like as that of the modern West. In order to respond to this perceived lack, they were eager to show that India had a historical consciousness comparable to the modern West. For Vinay Lal (1996), this was the case with Bankim Chandra Chatterjee, the great nineteenth century novelist from Bengal. Bankim sought to compete with modern West in showing that India had a historical consciousness, and he also wanted to use history as a guide to action. He was eager to show that India's historical tradition also had an important martial tradition. Hence in the past Indians were not wanting in anything compared to modern Europeans, who with their martial power were able to colonize the world. As Vinay Lal argues: "Bankim's interest in history was derived partly from a desire to demonstrate that the past of India, and particularly his native Bengal was one of martial traditions" (Lal 1996, 124).

But while Bankim wanted to compete with modern West in showing that India had a comparable historical consciousness, Gandhi followed a path of autonomy. For Gandhi, history is not the only guide to action. As Lal helps us understand, "Gandhi knew only too well that his attempt to apply non-violence on a mass scale in India's fight for freedom and thereby to induce the social transformation of Indian society was altogether unprecedented. History could be no guide to action in the present" (Lal 1996, 124). Furthermore, while to Bankim Krishna was a historical figure and Mahabharata a historical text, Gandhi's approaches were different. Thus Gandhi writes in 1924: "The Mahabharata is not to me a historical record. It is hopeless as a history. But it deals with eternal verities in an allegorical fashion" (Lal 1996, 125). "Gandhi would have considered the resort to history as another facet of the attempt of educated Indians, and particularly of the modernizing and urbanized elite which constituted a vanguard, to enter into a race with the West..." (Lal 1996, 126). For Lal, we can look at Gandhi as an "instance of why we should believe that the absence of historical inquiry suggests an acute presence of mind and why this lack, an alleged grave fault, must be revalorized and turned to advantage" (Lal 1996, 128).

Insider's Challenge to the Idea of History: Towards a Critique of the Privileging of Time in Modernity

G. C. Pande, Ashis Nandy and Vinay Lal make a critique of history from outside the empire, as it were. Now, we can turn our attention to some fundamental critics of history from within the modern West. Human geographer David Harvey noted for his works, *Social Justice and the City*, *Urbanization of Capital*, and *Consciousness and the Urban Experience* is one such. Harvey laments that in modernity "there has been a strong and almost overwhelming predisposition to give time and history priority over space and geography" (Harvey 1989, xiii). Marx, Weber, Durkheim, and Marshall – all of them have this in common. Marx also privileged time, and while describing the conquest of space through time that takes place under capitalism, he seems to have endorsed this particular annihilation of space through time. Marx had no particular remorse for the less advanced spaces of production and consumption being swallowed up by more advanced forces of production; for instance, the peasant by the industrial. However, for Harvey, "Marx had given primacy to historical time in part as a reaction to Hegel's spatialized conception of the ethical state as the end-product of teleological history" (Harvey 1989, 273).

Romila Thapar makes a perceptive point about history: "Our readings both of time and history have mutations, but the metaphor remains" (Thapar 1996, 44). But now while thinking of history, we have to think not only with the metaphor of time but also with space. This shift of metaphor has been made possible by new intellectual movements which urge us to understand the significance of space in the dynamics of history and society. Foucault (1986) makes this clear in his essay, "Of Other Spaces":

> The great obsession of the nineteenth century was, as we know, history: with its themes of development and of suspension, of crisis and cycle... The present epoch will perhaps be above all the epoch of space. We are in the epoch of simultaneity: we are in the epoch of juxtaposition, the epoch of the near and far, of the side-by-side, of the dispersed. We are at a moment...when our experience of the world is less that of a long life developing through time than that of a network that connects points and intersects with its own skein. (1986, 22)

But in the trajectory of modernity, there has been a move from the temporalization of space to spatialization of time. While in the former space was conquered by teleological time, a time on the march to triumph, in the spatialization of time, spaces resist being run over by the time of capitalism and modernity. We can look at various anti-colonial, anti-imperialist movements, and now ethnic movements, as instances of the spatialization of time where teleological time has stood still and given way to the assertive and resistant logic of spaces and places.

But the spatialization of time does not mean only the space-time configuration of becoming. It also means the further speeding up of the process of capitalist appropriation. Social theorist Teressa Brennan, who builds upon Lacan, offers such an understanding in her work *History After Lacan*: "Space will take the place of time by the denomination common to both: namely, speed. For to the extent that capital's continued profit must be based more and more on the speed of acquisition, it must centralize control and accumulation more, command more distance and in this respect space *must* take the place of generational time" (Brennan 1993, 147).

Rethinking History and the Challenge of Coping with Contingencies

The shift from time to space and a realization of a tension between them is best reflected in the following lines of David Harvey: "The opposition between Being and Becoming has become central to modernizing history. That opposition has to be seen in political terms as the tension between the sense of time and the focus of space" (Harvey 1989, 205). The shift and subsequent realization prepares an appropriate ground for appreciating the significance of contingency in historical thinking. Both Jürgen Habermas and Michel Foucault help us in this rethinking of history from the vantage point of the appreciation of the role of contingency in self and society. In his essay, "Coping with Contingencies: The Return of Historicism," Habermas tells us, "Until the eighteenth century, history had served as a repository for exemplary stories which supposedly can tell us something about the recurring features of human affairs…" (Habermas 1998a, 7). But with the rise of historical consciousness "the focus of attention shifts from the exemplary to the individual…this historical consciousness gave birth to an evermore intense awareness of evermore widely spreading contingencies" (Habermas 1998a, 7). For Habermas, while "since Aristotle history had always been conceived as the paradigmatic sphere of the contingent," some philosophers in modernity such as Hegel have felt threatened by "the spreading of historical contingencies" (Habermas 1998a, 7).

To be aware of contingency, for Habermas, is to realize that history is not only a story of progress but also a story of shattered expectations and the failure of traditions. In a provocative essay, "Can we learn from history?" Habermas writes, "In unobtrusive ways, we are constantly learning from major traditions, but the question is whether we can learn from events that reflect the failure of traditions" (Habermas 1998b, 12). What Habermas writes deserves careful attention:

> History may at best be a critical teacher who tells us how we ought *not* to do things. Of course, it can advise in this way only if we admit to ourselves that we have failed. In order to learn from history, we must not allow ourselves to push unsolved problems aside or repress them; we must remain open to critical experiences – otherwise we will not even perceive historical events as counter-evidence, *as proof of shattered expectations*. (Habermas 1998b, 13)

Foucault in recent times has also been a major voice in drawing our attention to the challenge of contingencies in the study of society and history. Foucault questions Kant's construction of a harmonious fit between the three domains of knowledge – scientific, political and religious. Foucault criticizes the view (attributed to Kant) that it is possible to constitute a universal rational body of knowledge. He posits contingency in the dynamics and work of these three bodies of knowledge. Each body of knowledge emerges in specific domains and in specific historical contexts. Each therefore must be seen as contingent. Foucault endorses the distinction between three bodies of knowledge – scientific, political, and religious/ideological; or hope, politics and critical understanding – as made by Kant, but urges us to perceive each of these as distinctive, as historically contingent. Each body of knowledge arises from a historically situated pursuit of answering one of the three specific questions – what can I know, what should I will, and what may I reasonably hope for. Considering the central preoccupation with history as an enterprise of knowledge in the present-day discourse, Foucault's critique of a unifying body of rational knowledge lays the foundations of an alternative historiography. In his essay "Nietzsche, Genealogy and History," Foucault (1977, 144) tells us that a genealogical approach "will never confuse itself with a quest for the 'origins'…on the contrary, it will cultivate the details and accidents that accompany every beginning." Foucault draws our attention to the work of emergence: "As it is wrong to search for descent in an unprecedented continuity, we should avoid thinking of emergence as the final term of an historical development (Foucault 1977, 148).

There is a relationship between awareness of contingency and openness to the dynamics of emergence in the work of self, society and history. Contingency tells us of the limits of *a priori* laws, formulations and determinations and looks at any hegemony with suspicion. Since there is no messianic solution to the problems of history by either the state or the Prophet or God, contingency calls for development of responsibility on our part. Therefore it is no wonder that in a recent critical work on historiography, *An Ethics of Remembrance: History, Heterology, and the Nameless Others,* Edith Wyschogrod brings responsibility to the heart of history. For her, the historian has a responsibility to describe the life of those who were silenced in the past. But she makes it clear that, "In speaking for dead others, the historian enters into a temporal zone that is neither past, present nor future" (Wyschogrod 1998, 248).

Prelude to a Creative Historiographical Engagement: Reconstruction of Time and Nurturance of Spaces of Reconciliation and Hope

The task before historiography now is to go beyond the one-sided privileging of time in modernity and of space in postmodernity. In such an overcoming of the one-sided privileging of either space or time, Heidegger provides us with some helpful resources. He makes a distinction between clock time and lived time where the latter is the time of authentic human experience. This lived time requires an appropriate place, in fact the place of dwelling in place of the place of building. For Heidegger, "Dwelling is the capacity to achieve a spiritual unity between humans and things" (Harvey 1996, 301). While building provides shelter, dwelling provides a home, and in the world of increasing homelessness there is an urgent need to "recover a viable homeland in which meaningful roots can be established. Place construction should be about the recovery of roots, the recovery of [the] art of dwelling" (Harvey 1996, 301).

But it is a tragic fact that in his recovery of art of dwelling, Heidegger failed to free himself from the temptations of the Nazi aestheticization of space and power. But this should not prevent us from building on the other Heidegger, whom even the Marxist geographer David Harvey finds inspiring. Writes David Harvey in his recent *Justice, Nature and the Geography of Difference*: "Marx regards experience within the fetishism as authentic enough but superficial and misleading, while Heidegger views that same world of commodity exchange and technological rationality [as being] at the root of an inauthenticity in daily life which has to be repudiated. This common definition of the root of the problem (though specified as peculiarly capitalist by Marx and modernist – i.e, both capitalist and socialist – by Heidegger) provides a common base from which to reconstruct a better understanding of place" (Harvey 1996, 315).

In recent times, there are some further helpful reconsiderations of space. For example, Deleuze and Guattari "employ a spatiality that appears divorced from the positivity of identity. Rather than earth, ground and fixity in a location grid, this space evokes air, smoothness and openness" (Gibson-Graham 1997, 314). In this context, Gibson-Graham speaks of a pregnant space which is a space of exploration, creativity and possibility, rather than just a space of overdetermination. Along with a pregnant space, we have to now invoke a pregnant time. Both pregnant spaces and pregnant times are spaces of reconciliation, overcoming the binding of the past and making a creative leap into the future. In the global community, 1944–1947 was one such space and time, when old rivalries were forgotten and many radical steps into future were taken, such as the declaration of universal human rights.

The Truth and Reconciliation Commission of South Africa is a recent example of a creative confrontation with the past and creation of the future. This commission calls for *ubuntu* "which means a generosity of spirit" (Lapsley 1998). As Michael Lapsley presents the voices of participants in such reconciliation process, "While opting for truth and not for revenge, for *ubuntu* and not for victimization, what we are seeking to do is to break the chain of history, the chain that in so many countries means that the oppressed in one generation becomes the oppressors in the next. It is true whether you talk about Africans in South Africa who survived the concentration camps invented by the British in the beginning of the century or relationship between Jewish people and Palestinians in Israel."

Edward Said (2000) also provides us with a similar creative challenge of reconciliation. For Said, "Israelis and Palestinians are now so intertwined through history, geography and political activity that it seems to be absolutely folly to try and plan the *future* of one without that of the other." The creation of this common future depends on identifying with the suffering of each other. But for Said,

> Most Palestinians are indifferent to and often angered by stories of Jewish suffering… Conversely most Israelis refuse to concede that Israel is built on the ruins of Palestinian society… Yet there can be no possible reconciliation, no possible solution unless these two communities confront each other's experience in the light of the other… There can be no hope of peace unless the stronger community, the Israeli Jews, acknowledge the most powerful memory for Palestinians, namely the dispossession of an entire people. As the weaker party Palestinians must also face the fact that Israeli Jews see themselves as survivors of the Holocaust, even though that tragedy cannot be allowed to justify Palestinian dispossession. (Said 2000)

Thus the crucial task before us in order to overcome the binding of the past is to be ready to suffer for the sake of our shared destiny. Here we can get help from both Gandhi and Levinas. For Levinas, the ego must be prepared to "undergo the suffering that comes to [them] from non-ego" (Levinas 1974, 123). But Kant, Habermas and Amartya Sen are silent on the need to suffer in order to overcome the bindings of the past, and their approaches to history can be redeemed by a Gandhian and Levinasian emphasis on undertaking suffering for the sake of others.

Historiography and the Calling of Creative Transformations

Thus when we speak of history we should not be confined only to the metaphor of time but must be open to space. But embracing space, we should go beyond either a temporal or spatial determinism and realize that history is an unfolding spatio-temporal journey. History as an enterprise of knowledge is neither unitary nor solely rational. It is helpful for us to have a relational and differentiated view of historiography which is concerned with power, reason and spiritual vision. The problem with current historiography is that it mostly privileges either power or reason (or both) to the exclusion of spiritual vision. But as Sunder Rajan tells us: "The different historical styles contest each other but at the same time, they also illumine each other revealing unsuspected dimensions of each other" (Sundar Rajan 1996, 193). "Since each of these schemes can reveal a truth about the other which they themselves cannot achieve by themselves, their interaction is not merely a situation of conflict and contestation but also necessary for our own awareness" (Sundar Rajan 1996, 194). Furthermore, "…within a given historiographical scheme itself, we must find a place for the political, the philosophical and the ethico-religious frames of understanding" (Sundar Rajan 1996, 194).

Sunder Rajan tells us that historiography has to take part in the threefold transformation that is sweeping the world now – the linguistic, the feminist and the ecological. To this I would like to add another triple transformation that calls for our creative response. This is outlined by Portuguese social theorist Boaventura de Sousa Santos. For Santos, we are now confronted with a triple transformation where power becomes shared authority, "despotic law becomes democratic law," and "knowledge as regulation becomes knowledge as emancipation" (Santos 1995, 482). But for the realization of this triple transformation there is the need for the realization of a new subjectivity: the task is to invent a "subjectivity constituted by the topos of a prudent knowledge of a decent life" (Santos 1995, 489). The "emergent subjectivity" of history lives in the frontier, and to "live in the frontier is to live in abeyance, in an empty space, in a time between times" (Santos 1995, 491). Living in an empty space and empty time calls for realizing the dialectic between time and eternity, tradition and modernity, and here openness to emptiness as an integral dimension of space, time, being and society can help us in deconstructing modernist formulations of space and time and laying the grounds of an alternative historiography.

Note

1 Against the postmodern deconstruction of objectivity, Sen provides the agenda of positional objectivity thus: "…positionally dependent observations, beliefs, and actions are central to our knowledge and practical reason. The nature of objectivity in epistemology, decision theory and ethics has to take adequate note of the parametric dependence of observation and information on the position of the observer" (Sen 1994, 126). But the realization of a transpositional point of view requires transcendental engagement and work on the self. However, the lack of an ontological striving in Sen does not enable us to realize the full potential of such a promising epistemology.

References

Brennan, Teresa. 1993. *History After Lacan*. London: Routledge.
Dallmayr, Fred R. 2000. The International Seminar on "Future of Traditions." *The Future of the Past*. December. Aurangabad.
Foucault, Michel. 1977. "Nietzsche, Genealogy, History." In Donald F. Bouchard, ed., *Language, Counter-Memory, Practice: Selected Essays and Interviews*. Oxford: Basil Blackwell.
———. 1986. "Of Other Spaces." *Diacritics* 16: 22–7.
Gibson-Graham, Julie Kathy. 1997. "Postmodern Becoming: From the Space of Forms to the Space of Potentiality." In George Benko and Ulf Strohmayer, eds, *Space and Social Theory: Interpreting Modernity and Postmodernity*. Oxford: Basil Blackwell.
Habermas, Jürgen. 1998a. "Coping with Contingencies – The Return of Historicism." In Jozef Niznik and John T. Sanders, eds, *Debating the State of Philosophy: Habermas, Rorty, and Kolakowski*. Westport, CT: Praeger.
———. 1998b. "Can We Learn from History?" In *A Berlin Republic*. Cambridge: Polity Press.
Hanrahan, Nancy W. 2000. *Difference in Time: A Critical Theory of Culture*. Westport, CT: Praeger.
Harvey, David. 1989. *The Condition of Postmodernity: An Enquiry into the Origins of Cultural Change*. Cambridge, MA: Basil Blackwell.
———. 1996. *Justice, Nature and the Geography of Difference*. Cambridge, MA: Basil Blackwell.
———. 2000. *Spaces of Hope*. Edinburgh: Edinburgh University Press.
Hawthorn, Geoffrey. *Plausible Worlds: Possibility and Understanding in History and the Social Sciences*. Cambridge: Cambridge University Press.
Lal, Vinay. 1996. "History and the Possibilities of Emancipation: Some Lessons from India." *Journal of Indian Council of Philosophical Research*, Special Issue: Historiography of Civilizations (June): 95–137.
Lapsley, Michael. 1998. "Confronting the Past and Creating the Future: The Redemptive Value of Truth Telling." *Social Research* 65 (4): 741–58.
Levinas, Emmanuel. 1974. *Otherwise than Being or Beyond Essence*. Dordrecht: Kluwer Academic Press.
Nandy, Ashis. 1995. "History's Forgotten Doubles." *History and Theory*, Theme Issue 34 (World Historians and their Critics): 44–66.
Pande, G. C. 1996. "Historiography of Civilizations and Cultural Presuppositions." *Journal of Indian Council of Philosophical Research* (January–April) 31–49.
Panikkar, Raimundo. 1993/1998. *The Cosmotheandric Experience: Emerging Religious Consciousness*. New Delhi: Motilal Banarasidass.
Said, Edward. 2000. "Invention, Memory, and Place." *Critical Inquiry* 26 (Winter): 175–92.
Santos, Boaventura de Sousa. 1995. *Toward a New Common Sense: Law, Science and Politics in the Paradigmatic Transition*. London: Routledge.
Sen, Amartya. 1994. "Positional Objectivity." *Philosophy & Public Affairs* 22 (2): 126–45.
———. 2001. "History as an Enterprise of Knowledge." *Frontline*, 2 February, 86–91.
Soja, Edward. 1996. *Third Space: Journeys to Los Angeles and Other Real-and-Imagined Places*. Cambridge, MA: Basil Blackwell.
Sunder Rajan, R. 1996. "Notes Towards a Phenomenology of Historiographies." *Journal of Indian Council of Philosophical Research* (Jan–April): 187–207.
Thapar, Romila. 1996. *Time as a Metaphor of History: Early India*. Delhi: Oxford University Press.
Trouillot, Michel-Rolph. 1995. *Silencing the Past: Power and the Production of History*. Boston: Beacon Press.
Wilson, Richard A. 2000. "Reconciliation and Revenge in Post-Apartheid South Africa: Rethinking Legal Pluralism and Human Rights." *Current Anthropology* 41 (1): 75–98.
Wyschogrod, Edith. 1998. *An Ethics of Remembering: History, Heterology and the Nameless Others*. Chicago: University of Chicago Press.

Chapter Eight

RULE OF LAW AND THE CALLING OF *DHARMA*: COLONIAL ENCOUNTERS, POST-COLONIAL EXPERIMENTS AND BEYOND

Dharma really means something more than religion. It is from a root word which means to hold together; it is the inmost constitution of a thing, the law of its inner being. It is an ethical concept which includes the moral code, righteousness, and the whole range of man's duties and responsibilities.

—Jawaharlal Nehru

[The modern legal system in the West] is a system which fits an egalitarian and individualistic society... It starts with individuals and is a manifestation of their own picture of the social order. The classical legal system of India substitutes the notion of *authority* for that of legality. The precepts of *smruti* are an authority because in them was seen the expression of a law... But it has no constraining power by itself. Society is thus organized on the model of itself.

—Robert Lingat, *The Classical Law of India* (1973, 258)

Whatever might have been the emphasis of traditional Indian culture, both equality and the individual are central concerns in the contemporary constitutional and legal systems; and it is impossible to understand what is happening in India today without taking into account Constitution, law, and politics.

—Andre Béteille, *Society and Politics in India* (1997, 218)

In the Indian epics, as in most pagan world views, no one is all perfect, not even the gods. Nor is anyone entirely evil; everyone is both flawed and has redeeming features. [For Radhabinod Pal, the only dissenting judge of the international tribunal judging Japanese war crimes, the] name of justice should not be allowed only for the prolongation of vindictive retaliation.

—Ashis Nandy, "The Other Within: The Strange Case of Radhabinod Pal's Judgment of Culpability" (1995, 53)

Prelude: *Dharma* and the Rule of Law in Classical Indian Traditions

The classical Indian traditions had a different conception of both rule and law as compared to modern Western traditions. While the constraining power of legality is central to modern Western traditions, in India it is moral authority which is at the core of the rule of law (Lingat 1973). The classical law of India is characterized not by positive law and legality but by moral authority and duty which is called *dharma*. *Dharma* refers to the totality of duties which are incumbent on individuals. It also signifies eternal rules which maintain the world. The rule of law entailed in the rule of *dharma* in classical Indian traditions was part of a transcendental engagement. God or the Creator was considered the ultimate source of law. But *dharma* was a point of connection between the transcendental realm, the life-world and the societal world of individuals. The object of *dharma* was to create a better world where individuals and societies could attain divine self-realization. As Robert Lingat tells us: "...the law which the *sastras* (sacred texts) communicate to us does not arise from the will of men. The rules of conduct and the duties which it enunciates are preconditions for the realisations of social order as it was intended by the Creator. These rules preexisted the expression of them" (Lingat 1973, 176). Rules in classical India were thought to be of divine origin but in the Western tradition law has been thought of as part of conscious deliberation of individuals in societies. Unlike law, custom is a "purely human development in the sense that it develops at the level of human groups involved" (Lingat 1973, 177). However, unlike Roman jurisprudence, the origin of custom in classical Indian traditions "eludes human memory, which confers upon it an almost sacred character and gives it a force which it neither had nor has in Western civilisations" (Lingat 1973, 177).

In classical India, institutions of law and polity were subordinated to an ideally conceived spiritual authority. At the empirical level, the working of such a rule of law did not provide respectful treatment and equality to everybody, but at the ideational realm, the subordination of political power to spiritual authority provided a frame for "ideal participation" to individuals (Lingat 1973, 259). Deviation from this ideal path was the cause of the onset of disorder, anarchy or what is called *arajakata* in classical Indian thought. The onset of anarchy was caused by the deviation of people from the path of *dharma*, or righteous conduct. Anarchy does not here refer to an external power vacuum in society, say the interregnum between "the death and succession of kings" but to that condition "when the weak are oppressed and exploited at the hands of the strong" (Roy 1999, 8). *Arajakata* refers to the condition when *matsyanyaya*, or the law of the fish, prevails: when the strong swallow the weak without either any guilt of conscience or societal punishment. Both order and anarchy are thought of normatively in classical Indian tradition, more particularly in the traditions of reflections and practice initiated by the *Vedas* and the *Upanishads*. In his recent thought-provoking work, *Beyond Ego's Domain: Being and Order in the Vedas*, the preeminent Indian political theorist Ramashroy Roy tells us that deviation from the path of *dharma*, which causes the rise of anarchy or *arajakata*, is caused by greed and "the tendency ingrained in every individual to acquire for himself as much of worldly goods as possible to the detriment of others" (Roy 1999, 2).

In the Vedic perspective, as in the Platonic, establishment of order in the public has to go hand in hand with the establishment of order in the life of the self. This in turn involves overcoming greed, passion and egotism in one's life and developing a capacity for otherness and the public good. Such a process involves "attuning one's soul to the divine ground of being by turning around from passion" (Roy 1999, 221). "This turning around is necessary because when passions seize control of the individual's life, his soul gets afflicted with disorder" (Roy 1999, 221). But transcendence of one's passion and propensity to control others which, as the modern theorist Teressa Brennan (1993) tells us, constitute the core of social evil, cannot be overcome by just participation in the polis. "The shortcomings associated with personal character cannot be expected to be rectified by the public realm" (Roy 1999, 5). Rather it calls for our rebirth as citizens; citizens of not only the polis, but of the community of good and of the Kantian "kingdom of ends," and this in turn calls for following the life of *dharma*, or righteous conduct – "to willingly accept a life dedicated to the cultivation of *dharma*" (Roy 1999, 5). For Roy, "Without the discipline of *dharma*, *matsya nyaya* (the law of the fish where big fishes eat the small ones) becomes a harsh reality and public order becomes difficult to maintain" (1999, 5). Establishment of order is predicated on following the path of *dharma* in the life of both self and society, and deviation from it leads to lawlessness, anarchy (*arajakata*) and disorder in society.

Thus in thinking about order, which in a decent society means an appropriate frame of co-ordination in the lives of individuals and societies, there is the need for appropriate self-preparation (Giri 2002). The classical Indian perspective on order and the rule of law has always stressed the centrality of appropriate self-preparation and self-formation, and the limit of external legislation in establishing order. "[The] curbing and controlling of unruly passions depends not so much on external regulations and sanctions as on generating a psychic force" which promotes "individual salvation and social concord through the development of the sense of sociality that sustains the individual's commitment to *dharma*" (Giri 2002, 13). In classical Indian traditions the rule of law is for those who are "unable by themselves to develop the source of order in their psyche and need the constant persuasion of *nomos* and the sanctions of law" (Giri 2002, 282).

Dharma, or the path of duty or righteous conduct, is at the core of thinking about the rule of law in Indian traditions. But the rule of *dharma* is not confined only to the psychic realm, to the effort of overcoming passion and generating appropriate psychic motivation. The rule of *dharma* needs an appropriate social and institutional arrangement. The interaction between the society which embodies "the principles constituting the rule of *dharma*," and its members is characterized by "reciprocal responsiveness" (Giri 2002, 13). It "devolves upon the individual to consciously and actively uphold its integrity" and makes it "incumbent upon the social order to safeguard individual integrity and dignity" (Giri 2002, 13). In "reciprocal responsiveness," the goal is not merely to establish compatibility between individual and society at an external level but at a deeper level. This is emphasized by both Sri Aurobindo and Coomaraswamy, two great savants of Indian tradition and thought in the modern world. For Sri Aurobindo, "For as it is the right relation of the soul with the supreme, while it is in the Universe, neither to assert egoistically its separate being not to blot itself out in the Indefinable, but to realize its unity with the Divine and the world and unite them in the individual, so the right relation of the individual with the collectivity is neither to pursue egoistically his own material or mental progress or spiritual salvation without regard to his fellows, nor for the sake of the community to suppress or maim his proper development, but to sum up in himself all its best and completest possibilities and pour them out by thought, action and all other means on his surroundings so that the whole race may approach nearer to the attainment of its supreme personalities" (1948, 17). For Coomaraswamy, "The individual is no longer enslaved by his own desires, but has found an infallible guide and mentor in the person of the *Dharma* or Indwelling Spirit" (1978, 84–5).[1] Central to politics and self-realization in this pathway is "self-government" or Swaraj, which depends upon self-control (*atmasamyama*) (Coomaraswamy 1978, 84–5). But it may be noted that in self-rule or self-governance, rule and power are of a qualitatively different kind compared to what is at work in the rule of law in the public domain. While the rule of law in the public domain can afford to proceed only with a controlling, regulative and domineering approach, in self-rule the rule that is at work cannot work only with the model of power as control and domination, characterized by the Nietzchean and Weberian will to carry out one's will against the will and resistance of others, but has to work with a newly transmuted and transfigured understanding of rule and power. Power and rule in self-rule and self-governance call for a new relationship with the self, a relationship of persuasion and dialogue, and such a dialogical self-rule is a helpful companion for the realization of dialogical democracy in the public domain (Dallmayr 1997).

In classical Indian traditions, it was believed that the king as the executive of political power must be subordinated to the priest, the *purohita*, the Brahman. Ananda Coomaraswamy puts this as the principle of the subordination of temporal power to spiritual authority. This is different from the conventional notion of the rulers of classical India as oriental despots. For Coomaraswamy, "The kingship envisaged by the Indian traditional doctrine is thus as far removed as could well be from what we mean when we speak of an 'Absolute Monarchy' or of individualism" (Coomaraswamy 1978, 86). Even "the supposedly Machiavellian *Arthasastra* flatly asserts that only a ruler who rules himself can long rule others" (Coomaraswamy 1978, 86). This imperative of self-rule on the part of the rulers in classical Indian tradition is akin to what Plutarch advises in his book *To an Uneducated Ruler* to the rulers of classical antiquity in the West: "One will not be able to rule if one is not oneself ruled. Now, who there is to govern the ruler? The law, of course; it must not however be understood as the written law, but rather as reason, the *logos*, which lives in the soul of the ruler and must never abandon him" (quoted in Foucault 1986, 88).

Therefore in the traditional conception of the rule of law, the practice of self-rule is at the core, and this has an epochal significance now as we are face to face with the limits of the law as the foundation of a good life and as we suffer from the apathy of legal minimalism. But one difficulty with the traditional conception of law and its model of ideal participation, self-formation and the creation of a public order around the *path* of *dharma* is that institutions in traditional Indian society did not match up to such an ideal model of self-formation and social order. *Manusmriti* or the Laws of Manu have been an important source of law in traditional Indian society. *Manusmriti* supported distinctions of caste and gender in law: "In ancient India, the Brahmans were considered to be the superior class. As such, they had in law and in fact privileges and prerogatives not held by other sections of Hindu society" (Spellman 1964, 111).

There were two sources of law in classical India – the texts of law, or the *Smritis* as they were called, such as *Manu Smriti*, and custom. The *sastras* or the sacred texts were sources of written law, and customs, unwritten laws. "The *sastra* incorporated numerous customs, inevitably, since it was itself the fruit of custom systematized…" (Derrett 1968, 158). Furthermore, since the *sastra* was based on "usage, in particular in its practical (*vyavaharic*) chapters, usage may be cited to explain written law" and the *sastras* (sacred texts concerning law) offered an umbrella "under which various judicial forms could shelter" (Derrett 1968, 160). The relationship between *sastric* written laws and unwritten customs was complex. There were many instances when customs contradicted written laws, and rulers and judges of society had to accept custom as grounds for valid law. Both the *sastras* and customs were presented as constant and eternal, but in reality both changed. However, both of these resisted absolute codification and were subject to interpretation. In the West, law is associated with fixity and not much amenable to interpretation, which makes Zygmunt Bauman (1987) observe that law is characteristic of modernity and interpretation of postmodernity. But in classical Indian tradition it was interpretation which was at the core of the rule of law. This openness towards interpretation was related to a sensitivity to contexts in Indian traditions which is different from the context-transcendent character of modern law (cf. Ramanujan 1989).

While the *sastras* and customs provided the sources of law, the actual juridical administration was carried out by the law of the courts. In the administration of justice, the king was the highest appellate court, but there was autonomy for judges. The classical law of India, transformed through the passage of time, continued for many centuries, and when Muslims began their rule in India it instituted Islamic law in its jurisdiction. But the Muslim rule did not alter the fundamental structures of classical law in India. Lingat helps us understand this: "The system which the invaders imported was fundamentally similar to that of the Hindus… In either case the authority of the law rested not on the will of those who were governed by it, but on divine revelation, on the one hand *The Koran* and the *Sunna*, and on the other hand the *Vedas* and *Smriti*" (Lingat 1973, 261). The Islamic law was applied only to believers, while Hindus were ruled by the *Dharmasastras*. In both Hindu and Islamic laws interpretation had the same importance, and custom held a significant (if not the same) role, "even though in principle it could not contradict a revealed text" (Lingat 1973, 261). But a major transition in law and society took place when Indian society was subjected to British colonialism. Though the initial period was one of mutual stocktaking where even the ruling British did not want to put an alien rule on the native soil, soon this gave rise to efforts to replace indigenous law with modern law. This is the story of colonial encounter in the rule of law in Indian tradition and society, and there is a need to understand this at great length as the foundations of modern law laid during colonialism continue to influence and determine the relationship between law and society in contemporary India.

The Rule of Law and the Colonial Encounter

The onset of British rule in India was a major watershed in Indian society and history. The East India Company, which ruled parts of India in the eighteenth century, took steps to introduce autonomous judicial and political administration in its territories. As historical anthropologist Bernard Cohn tells us, "In the second half of the eighteenth century, the East India Company had to create a state through which it could administer the rapidly expanding territories acquired by conquest or accession. The invention of such a state was without precedent in British constitutional history. The British colonies in North America and the Caribbean had from their inception a form of governance that was largely an extension of the basic political and legal institutions of Great Britain" (Cohn 1997, 57). But in its rule over India the British had to create a separate system of political and juridical administration. The early British rulers were careful not to introduce English rules in Indian soil; they did not want to interfere in the working of the native society. At the same time, the British felt the need to create new instruments of rule in colonial India which would be in tune with the local ethos. In this effort, India also provided a laboratory for experimenting with new models of rule and governance emerging in Great Britain, for instance the ones proposed by the utilitarians. As Erik Stokes tells us in his instructive historical study, *English Utilitarians and India*: "The British mind found incomprehensible a society based on unwritten customs and on government by personal discretion, and it knew only one sure method of marking off public from private rights – the introduction of a system of legality under which rights were defined by a body of formal law equally binding upon the state as upon its subjects" (1982, 82).

In the introduction of rules of law in Indian society during the early days of colonialism, there were two important considerations: first to create a rule of property in the native land, and second to create rules of adjudication. In creating an appropriate rule of adjudication, there were two streams of efforts and consciousness: one which emphasized that the new rules should be based on the existing rules of Indian society; and another which found the native rules too chaotic and so in need of formalism and codification. While Warren Hastings, the first Governor-General of Bengal, and scholars of the Early British Raj in India (known as Orientalists), who had much more respect for the native Indian tradition, wanted the new rules to be in tune with the rules of the *Dharmasastras*, others such as Thomas Macaulay and James Mill, who were influenced by the contemporary regnant ideology of utilitarianism, were much more in favor of a formal law along the lines of English Law.

Warren Hastings was appointed in 1772, under a new parliamentary act, to the newly created position of Governor-General, and was instructed by the Board of Directors to place the governance of Bengal on a stable footing. Hastings had spent some time in the court of the last of the Muslim rulers of Bengal and from his personal knowledge of the working of the administration he could not share the prevalent British view that Indian rules were despotic (Cohn 1997, 61). Hastings believed that "Indian knowledge and experience as embodied in the varied textual traditions of Hindus and Muslims were relevant for developing British administrative institution" (Cohn 1997, 61). He encouraged a group of younger servants of the East India Company to "study the 'classical' languages of India – Sanskrit, Persian and Arabic –as part of a scholarly and pragmatic project aimed at creating a body of knowledge that could be utilized in the effective control of Indian society" (Cohn 1997, 61). The objective here was to help "[the] British define what was Indian and to create a system of rule that would be congruent with what were thought to be indigenous institutions. Yet this system of rule was to be run by Englishmen and had to take into account British ideas of justice and the proper discipline, form of deference, and demeanor that should mark the relations between rulers and ruled" (Cohn 1997, 61).

One of the people who helped Hastings the most in this task was Sir William Jones (1746–1794), a classical scholar who studied Persian and Arabic at Oxford. Jones and his colleagues believed that there was historically in India a fixed body of laws which were inscribed in the texts of Hindus and Muslims. William Jones, like Hastings, rejected the idea that "India's civic constitution was despotic" and believed that "in antiquity in India there had been legislators and lawgivers of whom Manu (the protagonist of the famous and most important *Manusmriti*) was not only the oldest but also the holiest" (Cohn 1997, 72). Based on Jones's dedicated work on the laws of the *Dharmasastras*, his successor H. T. Colebrook published "The Digest of Hindu Law on Contracts and Succession" in Calcutta in 1798. The digest codified Hindu laws which were made invariant, compared to the "flexible" laws of the Hindus. In the adjudication of justice, "initially the courts looked to scriptures for domestic and social norms and rested heavily on the interpretation of *pundits* (traditional Hindu scholars) for the Hindu law. These interpretations reflected a Brahminical view of society, which saw its influence in terms of immutable religious principles" (Washbrook 1981, 653).The canonized Hindu law during the early phase of colonial rule "expanded its authority across large areas of society which had not known it before or which, for a very long period, had possessed their own more localized and non-scriptural customs" (Washbrook 1981, 653). According to David Washbrook, "The rise of the Hindu law was one of many developments of the period which made the nineteenth century the Brahmin century in Indian history and perhaps helps to explain why the twentieth century was to be the anti-Brahmin century" (1981, 653). During the early days of the colonial rule the British were enthusiastic "patrons of the *sastras*" (cf. Derrett 1968) and believed that the original or earliest legal text was the most authentic. However, in such Orientalist constructions of India and the law, "the dynamic interaction between textual law and non-textual custom, which had gradually evolved in pre-British India was hypostatized" (Nair 1996, 21).

The search for a formal code in regulation and adjudication followed the introduction of a more secure rule of private property in India. Cornwallis, the Governor-General of Bengal succeeding Hastings, introduced the *zamindari* system there in 1793, which was called Permanent Settlement. Permanent Settlement offered land ownership to the *zamindars*, or landlords, for a fixed yearly payment to the government. The fixation of this fee ensured regular revenue to the colonial rulers. Introduction of private property was "perceived as the fundamental means for ordering Indian agrarian society" and for establishing "an ideologically coherent and functionally systematic basis for revenue collection" (Dirks 1986, 300). If the *zamindars* defaulted on their fixed yearly payment, then their estates were to be put up for auction. But Henry Munro, the Governor-General of the Southeastern Presidency of Madras, disagreed with Cornwallis' rule of property for Bengal and introduced the *ryotwari* system where land ownership was conferred upon individual tenants or the *ryots* rather than on one landlord. Such a rule of property established a direct relationship between the colonial state and the cultivators, and Munro argued that such a rule of property was much more in tune with the ethos of traditional Indian society. His critique of Permanent Settlement, the other rule of property introduced by Cornwallis, is instructive: "We have, in our anxiety to make everything as English as possible in a country which resembles England in nothing, attempted to create at once throughout extensive provinces a kind of landed property which had never existed in them" (quoted in Dirks 1986, 318). Munro gave ownership to individual tenants and took for his principle of assessment of land revenue "the traditional criterion of good Indian rulers that the state share of produce should not exceed one-third" (Stokes 1982, 84). Like William Jones, Munro was much more sympathetic to the native institutions, and wanted to restore the jurisdiction of the village *panchayats*, or customary tribunals, composed of village elders, "invest the village headman with limited powers in petty civil and criminal cases, to appoint new grades of Indian 'native judges' with greatly extended jurisdiction; and to limit the right of people from the lower courts" (Stokes 1982, 141).

During the British colonial rule, the rule of law and the rule of property proceeded hand in hand, but the conferral of permanent property rights on big landlords in the system of Permanent Settlement devastated the Indian countryside instead of developing it. "Far from defining and protecting existing rights Cornwallis had thrown all into confusion by vesting an almost absolute property right in the great *zamindars* (landlords) and leaving all subordinate interests undefined. The mass of litigation which had ensured from the Permanent Settlement was left to be dealt with by a judicial organization wholly inadequate in scope and arrangement" (Stokes 1982, 141). Furthermore, "The length and cost of the judicial process had grown so huge as to be tantamount to a virtual denial of justice and a 'destructive anarchy'" (Stokes 1982, 141). Historical anthropologist Nicholas Dirks writes about the impact of this rule of property on Indian society: "The permanent settlement provides one of the clearest examples of the British reification of their concept of old regime within the framework of a new 'progressive' system governed by the overarching principles of order and revenue... Boundaries became fixed, relationship became bureaucratically codified... The fixity of the revenue demand was both a metaphor of this change and the fundamental cornerstone of the new regime. To maintain both the revenue demand and local social order, Kings – and Kingdoms – were subordinated to the institutional structures of the new colonial legal system" (Dirks 1986, 330).

What is to be understood at this point is that pre-British ownership of land did not approximate the British idea of fixed and permanent ownership. There were varieties of ownership right in pre-British India, including communal ownership, and in parts of India such as Tamil Nadu in the eighteenth century, "between 60 and 50 percent of all cultivable land was given away under the category of *inam* (tax-exempt) land" (Dirks 1986, 312). Unlike the new colonial masters, the kings ruled not by "administrating a land system in which land owed its chief value from the revenue it could generate but by making a gift" (Dirks 1986, 312). But "The British, with a very different view of property rights, misunderstood all this. When they attempted to sort out who owned the land, they assumed opposition, not complimentarity: the owner, they thought must be either the cultivator or the king, thus creating many of the classificatory problematic of the land systems..." (Dirks 1986, 311).

To come back from the rule of property to the rule of law, we must realize the step by step displacement of traditional law in the colonial period, a displacement which also continued in post-independent India. We must remember that when Sir William Jones and his colleagues gave the digest of Hindu laws, these codified Hindu laws were already displaced from the way they had been conceptualized and worked out before. As Archana Parashar writes, "These judges, even though applying the rules of Hindu and Islamic laws, interpreted them according to their understanding and training. Moreover, the rules of procedure and evidence were alien to the systems of Hindus or Islamic laws and when applied to these systems of laws they had the result of transforming them in unforeseen directions" (Parashar 1992, 72). The British sought to formalize and systematize law in colonial Indian society. "In pre-British India there were innumerable overlapping local jurisdictions and many groups enjoyed one or another degree of autonomy in administering law to themselves... The relation of the highest and most authoritative parts of the legal system to the 'lower' end of the system was not that of superior to subordinate in a bureaucratic hierarchy... Instead of systematic imposition, of 'higher' law on lesser tribunals, there was a general diffusion by the filtering down (and occasionally up) of ideas and techniques" (Galanter 1989, 16). But the British formalized the higher and the lowers ends of justice and sought to make the latter centralized and systematic.

Thomas Macaulay, a member of the Law Commission established in 1835, played a crucial role in this task of codification and formalization. His important and lasting contribution to Indian law and jurisprudence was the establishment of the Indian Penal Code. In 1835 Macaulay instructed the Law Commission to "frame a complete criminal code for all parts of the Indian Empire which should not be a digest of existing laws but should embrace all reforms thought desirable" (Stokes 1982, 222). Macaulay refused to take any of the existing Indian criminal law system as the basis for the penal code, as he marshaled a wealth of evidence regarding the despotic and chaotic nature of the existing penal codes. At this point in time, Hindus and Muslims were governed not only by different civil codes and personal laws but also by different penal codes. Macaulay could sense that establishing a uniform civil code would be difficult as it would touch upon the jurisdiction of the Hindu and Islamic religions. So he sought to create a uniform penal code. But it has to be borne in mind that by 1835 "The Muslim criminal law which the British had inherited and claimed to administer, had been so overlaid by Regulation Law that it was unrecognizable" (Stokes 1982, 223). In 1832 the British had discontinued the practice of *fatwa* entailed in the Muslim personal law.

The draft of the penal code of 1835 had to wait for more than twenty years before it was enacted in 1860 as the general criminal law of India. In its formulation Macaulay was influenced by the British utilitarians, especially by Jeremy Bentham. The utilitarian search for firm rules was also part of an authoritarian project. James Mill, who was directly involved in the administration of India, had argued that India desperately needed a common code, and this blessing could be conferred on her not by any popular government but by an "absolute government" (Stokes 1982, 219). In fact, it is the authoritarian conception which had led Mill to favor the establishment of a Law Commission with as few constitutive members as possible. The making of law here was confined to an elitist process and was not meant to be part of what Habermas (1996) would call a public discursive formation of will. Such an elitist character of law-making continues even more than one hundred and fifty years after the establishment of the first law commission of India. As Upendra Baxi writes about the contemporary scene, "law-making remains more or less the exclusive prerogative of a small cross-section of elites. This necessarily affects both the quality of the law enacted and its social communication, diffusion, acceptance, and effectivity…" (Baxi 1982, 45).

After the Sepoy Mutiny of 1857 which was in fact the first Indian war of independence, during which Hindus and Muslims fought against the colonial rule of the East India Company, India came under the direct rule of the British Crown in 1858. (So far it was being ruled by the East India Company.) In 1864, there was a major reform of the judicial system. The reform abolished the Hindu and Muslim law officers in the various courts of India. The codification of law and the consolidation of the court system were further intensified in the quarter century after the takeover of India by the Crown. While the law applied in the courts before 1860 was extremely varied, by 1882 "there was virtually complete codification of all fields of commercial, criminal and procedural law" excepting the personal laws of Hindus and Muslims (Galanter 1989, 18). While Hindu and Muslim laws previously applied to a variety of topics, now they became confined "to the personal law matters (family law inheritance, succession, caste, religious endowments)" (Galanter 1989, 18). Moreover, the new codes in place "did not represent any fusion with indigenous law" (Galanter 1989, 18). Rather they transformed indigenous law. The administration of law in the process moved from informed tribunal into the government courts, "curtailing the applicability of indigenous law" and transforming it in the course of its being administered by the government's courts (Galanter 1989, 18–19).

The transformation of the rule of law that took place in this colonial encounter is viewed through the prism of Henry Maine's differential historical divide of "from status to contract." But for some critical students of Indian history and society, the rule of law in the colonial period fixated boundaries of self and group in a tight manner. This becomes clear when we look into the reification of village, caste and tribe that took place during the British rule. As Richard Smith tells us, "As a unit of administration, the village community had been idealised as a 'petty commonwealth' or 'a little republic' at a time when new territories were being brought under the British rule... 'Caste,' on the other hand, was a different kind of concept, with different possible official uses. More a unit of knowledge about Indian society than a unit of administration, its great virtue was that it embraced the whole of India and all sections of Indian society. Even if it could not be made the basis for the extraction of revenue [it was important for a bounded construction of Indian society]" (Smith 1985, 172). In the process of the reification of caste which was appropriated within the "rule by reports," "The notional individual was stripped of the universality of his social roles within a 'village community' and clothed instead by a garment specific to India, 'caste.' The Government may thereby have figured a direct link with each individual, but an individual's right now depended irredeemably on his status in society. *One could almost say that, within the rule of law, the movement from contract to status had come full circle*" (Smith 1985, 173, emphasis added).[2]

These newly formulated codes and laws were applied in the lives of people in a complex manner. Arjun Appadurai (1983, 173) presents us an ethno-historical description of this complex working of the rule of law in colonial India in the field of the administration of temples. In the pre-British period, the kings were only the administrators of temples, not the legislators, and so there was no law of endowment in the field of temple administration. But with the formalization of rule of law under colonialism, temples began to be administered on the basis of the English model of a "charitable trust" (Appadurai 1983, 173). But "[the] English model of the Trust, whereby endowed property was transferred to, and vested in, a trustee for the benefit of other so-called 'beneficiaries', was clearly not applicable to the Hindu temple, where property was clearly vested in the idol and was only managed in its behalf, by the trustee" (Appadurai 1983, 173). It was probably because of such persistent ambiguities that religious endowments were explicitly exempted from the scope of the Indian Trusts Act, which was passed in 1882. Nevertheless, "for lack of a systematic alternative, the English model of trust continued by analogy, to inform the judgments of the Anglo-Indian courts..." (Appadurai 1983, 174). Appadurai helps us understand the impact of the colonial rule of law on the administration of temples in India: "... the judicial activity of the English courts in Madras between 1878 and 1925 had two far-reaching effects on the Sri Partasarati Svami Temple [of Triplicane, Madras, the temple on which Appadurai had carried out ethno-historical research]: first, the notion of a *Tenkalai* community (the community of worshippers built around the temple), was elaborated, refined and codified; at the same time, and paradoxically, various subgroups and individuals within the *Tenkalai* community were encouraged to emphasize the heterogeneity of their interests and to formulate their *special* rights in a mutually antagonistic way, thus making authority in the temple even more fragile than it had previously been. The court's effort to classify, define, and demarcate the concrete meaning of the concept of the 'Tenkalai' community of Triplicane generated more tensions than it resolved. The 'schemes' for the governance of the temple and the judgements and the precedents created by the court provided more opportunities for litigants to reflexively refine their self-conceptions and their political aspirations. The legal 'texts' encouraged the multiplication of ideas of the 'past' as well as model of the 'future' in respect to temple" (Appadurai 1983, 178–9).

However, it must be noted that during British colonialism all parts of India were not under the direct rule of the British. There were in fact two Indias: the British India and the princely India. The later, consisting of a third of the Indian subcontinent, was ruled by the native princes and constituted relatively autonomous domains. In these princely states sometimes progressive legislations were introduced, especially in the domains of family and personal laws. During colonialism Hindus and Muslims were governed by their respective personal laws, which were gender-biased and discriminatory towards women, but British rulers did not want to interfere in these personal laws. But rulers of princely states undertook some steps to redress such gender-oppressive personal laws. For example, the princely state of Baroda was the first state to introduce provisions for divorce. Similar progressive legislations during the colonial period took place in the princely state of Mysore, as social historian Janaki Nair writes: "Mysore introduced, and took several measures to implement an Infant Marriage Prevention Act as early as 1894, without the bitter debates that occurred in British India over the Age of Consent Act. A bill according rights to women under Hindu Law, which extended property rights, granted maintenance, adoption and related rights, became law with relatively little opposition in 1933, a full four years before even a partial bill was passed in the Central Legislature" (1996, 42).

Bernard Cohn writes about experimenting with establishing a formal rule of law in India within the hundred years between Warren Hasting's attempts in 1772 to the last quarter of the nineteenth century: "…publication of authoritative decisions in English had completely transformed 'Hindu law' into a form of English case law. Today when one picks up a book on Hindu law, one is confronted with a forest of citations referring to previous judges' decisions – as in all Anglo-Saxon-derived legal systems – and it is left to the skills of judges and lawyers, based on their time-honored abilities to find precedent, to make the law. What had started with Warren Hastings and Sir William Jones as a search for the 'ancient Indian constitution' ended up with what they had so much wanted to avoid – with English law as the law of India" (Cohn 1997, 75). This last sentence of Cohn provides an important continuum between the colonial and postcolonial moments.

The Post-colonial Experiments

The legal system built under colonialism in India continued after India's independence. In the Constituent Assembly which debated for two years (1947–9) the vision and text of the new constitution there was no concerted effort to institute an indigenous law based on the *Dharmasastras* (Austin 2000). Neither was there any spokesman for the revival of local customary law as such. Gandhi, the leader of the Indian struggle for freedom, was a great critic of the Western mode of life, including law. Gandhi had preferred the village as a unit of justice rather than individual, but an attempt made by Gandhians to "form a polity based on village autonomy and self-sufficiency was rejected by the Assembly which opted for a federal and parliamentary republic with centralized bureaucratic administration" (Galanter 1989, 40). As Marc Galanter writes about this formative period of constitutional law in post-colonial, independent India: "The only concession to the Gandhians was a directive principle in favour of village *panchayats* as units of local self-government. The existing legal system was retained intact, new powers were granted to the judiciary and its independence enhanced by elaborate protections" (Galanter 1989, 40). While making village *panchayats* a unit of local administration was earlier a part of the Directive Principle of State Policy, since 1992, after the 72nd and 73rd amendments to the constitution, it was now constitutionally mandatory to hold elections to the *panchayats* at regular intervals and share power with the representatives of *panchayats*.

The founding of the new Constitution of India was a moment of decisive significance in Indian society and history. The Indian constitution provided an alternative to the *Dharmasastras* as the foundation of the rule of law. The normative dissonance that the constitution introduces in traditional Indian society is best described by Andre Béteille: "The Hindu society is a harmonic system where inequality exists and is perceived to be legitimate whereas the Constitution ushers in a disharmonic system where inequalities exist but they are no longer legitimate" (as quoted in Baxi 1982, 339). The constitution guarantees secularism and promises a life of socio-economic equality and dignity to all its citizens. From the beginning, the Constitution of India has been a document of hope for fuller democratic realization. The rule of law enshrined in the Indian constitution not only created the autonomy of the domain of law but had a strong imperative for using law as an instrument for social transformation and the creation of a just social order. Jawaharlal Nehru, the first prime minister of India, particularly led the state to use law and constitution for the sake of socio-economic transformation. Much of the blueprint for socio-economic change was put under the Directive Principle of State Policy. As Rajeev Dhavan, an insightful commentator on this issue, tells us, "The upshot of all this was the creation of a positivistic welfare state that demanded enormous legal empowerment to effect the social and economic transformation of India. If 'law' had any role to play, it had to be functionally geared towards achieving this politically ordained social change" (Dhavan 2000, 322). During the founding of the constitution, "there was broad social and political consensus on the view that the only way India could dispense substantive *socio-economic* justice for its people was not just

through planned development, but by an effective transformation of Indian society"
(Dhavan 2000, 321) and law was to be an instrument in this transformation.

This desire to use the constitution for ensuring socio-economic justice continues to
inspire many efforts right up to the present. A recent effort is the institution of public
interest litigation in which the Supreme Court of India has revitalized the judiciary
as an instrument of governance. In public interest litigations, concerned actors –
citizens and other voluntary organizations – can bring to the notice of the Supreme
Court or the High Courts of the states any issues which need immediate attention
and redressal on behalf of the affected parties. As Sangeeta Ahuja, who has studied
this development, writes, "Public Interest Litigation (PIL) in the late 1970s was first
envisaged by its proponents as a way of ensuring that justice was made available to
those without the knowledge of resources to approach the courts and as a forum for the
resolution of public importance. Many of the earliest PIL cases detailed the conditions
in prisons and instances where fundamental rights had been abused" (Ahuja 1997, 1–2).
Justice P. N. Bhagwati, a former Chief Justice of Supreme Court of India, who had
played an important role in instituting Public Interest Litigation, says, "Public Interest
Litigation is brought before the Court not for the purpose of enforcing the right of
one individual against another as happens in the case of ordinary litigation, but it is
intended to promote and vindicate public interest which demands that violations of
constitutional and legal rights of large number of people who are poor, ignorant or in a
socially or economically backward position should not go unnoticed and unredressed"
(Ahuja 1997, 1–2). In the last two decades, the Supreme Court of India has addressed
public interest litigation in diverse areas: environment and environmental pollution,
corruption, and human rights abuses.

At this point, we can spend a little time on the Supreme Court of India as the
highest institution of rule of law of the land. From the beginning, the Supreme Court
of India has embodied two different orientations – conservative and radical. In the
founding years of the constitution, Prime Minister Nehru expressed dissatisfaction
with the attitudes of some Supreme Court judges, who gave primacy to the right to
property rather than right to equality in their interpretation of the constitution. Nehru
was keen to abolish *zamindari*, or landlordship, and in this task the Supreme Court's
primacy on property created stumbling blocks. The Supreme Court today continues
to embody these two tensions. In some cases the Supreme Court has approved radical
efforts on the part of the legislature, such as providing constitutional approval to
the 1990 governmental notification for implementing the Mandal Commission's
recommendations for job reservation for economically and socially backward
classes. Reservation in education and employment was earlier confined to the most
backward and downtrodden castes and tribes, known as the Scheduled Castes and
the Scheduled Tribes, but the new government legislation extended the reservation
to other economically and socially backward castes. While in the first phase of post-
independent India the judiciary was thought of as an institution of government, in
the second phase the judiciary was looked at as an "institution in the constitutional
polarity to the government" and now it is being looked at as an "institution of

governance in its own right" (Dhavan 2000). The working of the public interest litigation in the last twenty years is a reflection of the transition of the judiciary as an autonomous institution of governance. Here the Supreme Court has made some bold though controversial decisions, such as the closing of polluting industries in the capital city of Delhi. In post-independent India, the judiciary has been governed by not only "structural accountability" but also "value accountability": "Since democratic structures are essentially majoritarian in nature, it is felt that decisions should not only be democratically accountable in structural terms, but also 'value accountable,' so that the ends of justice are fairly met" (Dhavan 2000, 337).

The British were committed to a statute-based legal system compared to the value-based legal system of traditional Indian society. But in the working of the contemporary institutions of law in Indian society it is not correct to say that the value-based legal system has been totally replaced by the statue-based law. Though the constitution has replaced the *Dharmasastra*, judges continue to adopt a *Dharmasastric* approach to the constitution in that they stress the inviolable basic structure of the constitution consisting of democracy and secularism. As Rajeev Dhavan writes, "Even though Indian law is now statute-based and thoroughly 'western' in its approach, it should not surprise us if the basic instinct of Indian judges is to retain a *Dharmasastric* approach to otherwise Anglophone laws. This might explain their affinity to widely stated doctrines of judicial reviews including the famous basic structure doctrine, which powerfully restates the case for constitutionalism in ways that it has never been stated" (Dhavan 2000, 317). For some observers of the Indian juridical scene such as Chris Fuller, the way Indian judges work is similar to a great extent to the working of traditional *pundits*, the interpreters of the sacred texts. For Fuller, "The certainty of modern law is an ideal, but precedent (like legislation) is always in practice subject to judicial interpretation. This was known long before Dworkin placed such stress on the role of interpretation in the legal process. Once the flexibility of modern law is taken into account, the contrast between modern and traditional law becomes but a matter of degree, just as the difference between modern judicial reasoning and classical Hindu religious inter-pretation[3] is formally slight" (Fuller 1988, 246–7).

Establishment of a uniform civil code has been part of the directive principle of the state policy of the constitution. As we have briefly encountered, Hindus, Muslims and Christians followed their differential personal laws during the colonial rule. In fact, during the moments of colonial appropriation there took place Brahminization and Islamization of the personal laws of Hindus and Muslims respectively, as the colonial administrators ascertained and fixed their personal laws "from their scriptural texts" (Parashar 1992, 66). After independence and the institution of the constitution, personal laws among the Hindu were greatly modified. The Indian Parliament from 1955–6 passed a series of acts known collectively as the Hindu code, which effect a wholesale and drastic reform of Hindu law: "Hindu social arrangements are for the first time moved entirely within the ambit of legislative regulation; appeal to the sastric tradition is almost entirely dispensed with" (Galanter 1989, 29). Furthermore, "The code makes acceptance of Parliament as a kind of central legislative body for

Hindus in matters of family and social life" (Galanter 1989, 30). But for students of critical family law reform in India such as Archana Parashar, the reform of Hindu personal law did not embody gender equality in a full and substantive manner: "While reforms made to Hindu law were designed to give women more legal rights, it was never the intention to give complete legal equality to women" (Parashar 1992, 76). Furthermore, "By projecting the aim of incorporating sex equality and uniformity in Hindu law as desirable goals, the political leaders used law reform as an instrument of political development rather than as a means of ensuring legal equality per se" (Parashar 1992, 76).

But Muslims and Christians continue with their earlier personal laws with very little modification, though recently the government has sought to introduce new personal laws in the case of Christians, making it easier for Christian women to obtain a divorce. As Dieter Conrad, who has studied the constitutional problem of personal law in the context of the rule of law in India, writes, "There is within the Indian legal system, a wide area where constitutional rules don't apply, or rather are not applied by either the legislature or the courts. The area in question is not just one among the many-sided ramifications of law and social life, but concerns the core of the individual's position as a person in society. The crucial issue is…the position of women who in all the personal laws, though in varying degrees are subjected to discriminatory treatment" (Conrad 1998, 227). For example, males could practice polygamy under the Muslim personal law, but not females, and on the Hindu side even after the Hindu Code of 1955, daughters continue to be excluded from coparcenary in the law of *mitakhara* joint family.[4]

The existence of such gender-discriminatory personal laws continues to challenge law and society in India for a further deepening and universalization of the rule of law. But the formation of a uniform civil code, which is what this expected measure of universalization is called in India, has to come to terms with the fact that "major sections of citizens do regard their personal laws as an essential part of their religion" (Conrad 1998, 229). This factor, says the Supreme Court, has to be taken into account "in determining the scope of permissible legislation" (Conrad 1998, 229).

The case of Shah Bano, a deserted Muslim woman, dramatically presents the difficulties surrounding the formulation of a uniform civil code. Shah Bano, a poor Muslim woman, had applied to the Court for maintenance from her former husband, and the Supreme Court of India upheld in 1985 the decision of the High Court which directed him to pay maintenance to his divorced wife. But members of the Muslim Personal Law Board of India objected to the Supreme Court judgment as a gross interference with Muslim personal laws, and soon conservative political and religious forces, in the name of representing and protecting minority religious interest, exerted political pressure on the Government. The Government under the leadership of then-Prime Minister Rajiv Gandhi, instead of using this occasion for a broad-based dialogue on reform, introduced new legislation which nullified the decision of the Supreme Court. This is a controversial legislation which denies justice to Muslim women. This is a case of the triumph of conservative male Muslim religious and political leaders who claim that they are the spokespeople for the entire Muslim population. These leaders resist the formulation of a uniform civil code on the supposed ground that it would interfere with their religious personal laws. But religious leaders need to reinterpret religious laws in the light of contemporary challenges. The key issue here is, can freedom of religion be used to suppress the constitutionally guaranteed right to equality on the part of individuals, particularly women? The real issue here is the "conflict between the rights of minorities and rights of women of minority communities" (Parashar 1992, 229). The representatives of religious minorities do not represent the voice of suppressed groups within their communities. In this context, a variety of positions are offered. For radical critics such as Parashar, the category of personal law itself should be abolished (Parashar 1992, 258). But some others, such as Dieter Conrad, plead for introducing "individual choice" in matters of the status governed by personal law, along the lines of the Special Marriage Act (1954) or the optional clause in the Muslim Personal Law (Shariat) Application Act (1937). For Conrad, "..a legitimating element of individual option would ensure that personal law is not simply enforced as an ascriptive status on grounds of religious affiliation alone… At the same time paradoxically, peculiarities of the hierarchical law could be more easily justified, if accepted in an act of deliberate individual choice (Conrad 1998, 230).

Critical Reflections on Rule of Law in Contemporary Indian Society

Sociologist Andre Béteille is a keen and critical commentator on the rule of law in Indian society. For Béteille, in what he calls the populist interpretation and mobilization of democracy, Indian activists, scholars and citizens have not paid enough attention to the need for following scrupulously rules and procedures (Béteille 1999a). For Béteille, who provides a constitutionalist procedural approach to democracy, democracy hangs by the thread of procedure, but the general tendency in "our society is for life to be regulated by persons rather than by rules" (Béteille 1999b, 200; also see Béteille 2008, 2011). For Béteille, who builds upon Irawati Karve's view that Indian civilization has been shaped by the principle of accretion (in accretion, there is continuous accumulation of rules without the elimination of the old ones), "When we add new rules, we do not necessarily discard old ones, so that other rule becomes crowded with obsolete, anachronistic and inconsistent rules. In India administration by impersonal rules resists systematization because that demands continuous elimination of old and anachronistic rules" (Béteille 1999b, 228).

Béteille's contention that Indians have difficulty in subjecting themselves to a rule of law is corroborated by other critical commentators such as Satish Saberwal and Upendra Baxi. For Saberwal, "Indian society has not been historically inclined towards working with general rules: in Manu's codes, for instance, punishment depends on the culprit's caste status" (Saberwal 1988, 16). For Upendra Baxi, "Indian political elite and upper middle classes have not internalized the value of legalism" (Baxi 1982, 7). What Upendra Baxi, the critical legal theorist of India, wrote thirty years ago holds good even today: a large segment of the Indian population feels that "rule following is not merely unjustified but counterproductive in terms of their interest" (Baxi 1982, 7). Corruption and governmental lawlessness, where states violate laws (especially with regard to human rights abuses) and where the governments default "in the implementation of their statutory obligations" (Baxi 1982, 28) are further challenges to the establishment of rule of law in India.

Béteille draws our attention to the distinction between the Directive Principles of State Policy and the Fundamental Rights enshrined in the constitution. "All Fundamental Rights, including the right to equality, are enforceable by the courts. As against these, the Directive Principles of State Policy are not enforceable by the Courts although they are of great social and political significance" (Béteille 1997, 192). But over the years the primacy of Fundamental Rights has been relativized to accommodate striving for social justice and egalitarian policies. As Béteille writes, "Almost immediately after the new Constitution was adopted, two major instruments of the policy for greater equality, agrarian reform on the one hand and benign quotas on the other, came up against the processes of Fundamental Rights. These provisions had to be realigned by the First Amendment to the Constitution so as to accommodate policies designed to reduce disparities between classes and disparities between castes" (Béteille 1997, 202). In such a process, equality as a right has given way to equality as a policy where the individual right to equality and equal opportunity are compromised. Béteille is particularly critical of the introduction of reservation in education and job for socially and economically backward castes, which for him makes a mockery of the individual right to equality, especially equality of opportunity.

But while Béteille seems to lament the dilution of equality as a right by the populist mobilizations of equality, policy interlocutors such as Upendra Baxi on the other hand applaud the transformation of constitutional imperatives into concrete measures for the realization of the socio-economic rights of people. Baxi, however draws our attention to the way existing legal institutions create hurdles for the realization of the emancipatory and normative promises of the constitution. For example, "the Constitution and the law have generally strong redistributive thrust" (Baxi 1982, 30); yet "the orientation of the major institutions of Indian Legal System is towards maintenance and even aggravation of the status quo. The legal institutions generally decelerate and even prevent the inherent dynamism of constitutional aspirations towards a just social order" (Baxi 1982, 30). However, for critical students of law and society such as Rajeev Dhavan, the constitutional promises for a just world order are themselves half-hearted. In the words of Dhavan: "There was never any great dissonance between Nehru's developmental plan for the Indian people and the positivist theory of law that the British had bequeathed to the courts of independent India. The fact that the Constituent Assembly had scripted a judicially enforceable bill of rights into the text of the constitution did not disturb the positivist credentials of Indian law. The fundamental rights guaranteed to the citizen had been perceived as essentially "legal rights" granted by a super statue: each one of the rights had been hedged in by limitations and was interpreted like any other statute" (Dhavan 2000, 32).

Baxi also draws our attention to the continuance of the "the colonial model of reactive mobilisation of law rather than pro-active mobilisation" (Baxi 1982, 47). He also urges us to realize the problem of access to the rule of law: "The state legal system, pervasive in urban areas, is only slenderly present in rural areas. The low visibility of the state legal system and its slender presence renders official law (its values and processes) inaccessible and even irrelevant for people" (Baxi 1982, 345). The exorbitant court fee that people have to pay also discourages them from taking part in the rule of law. Of course in this regard, there emerged some efforts to make the law more accessible. Forty years ago *Nyaya Panchayats* were established to redress this balance, but these did not make much headway (Baxi 1982; Galanter 1989). Even in the new Panchayat Raj System, the task of realizing justice at the local level has not made much headway.

A decade ago, India was ruled by a coalition of parties which were part of what was called the National Democratic Alliance, and its leading partner was the Bharatiya Janata Party, which is actively sympathetic to the agenda of Hindu fundamentalist forces. The churning of the Indian political and social system in the recent years has led to the demise of one-party dominance in India's political and electoral firmament. This has led to apparent political instability at the centre. For instance, in the last five years alone, three general elections have been conducted for the Indian Parliament – in 1996, 1998 and 1999. After the general election in 1999, the then-ruling coalition established a constitution review committee to review the constitution. The review is meant to look into "salient issues in the area of governance, primarily federalism reforms [pertaining to the relation between the Center and States, which is still characterized by unfairness with regard to sharing of economic resources and political power], attainment of political stability for the present and future, Union Governments in an era of fractious coalitions" (Baxi 2000, 892). While the review commission is likely to examine the issue of the conversion of some Directive Principles into Fundamental Rights (especially the right to a primary education), the widespread fear and uproar in contemporary Indian society is that the present review of the constitution is a surreptitious attempt on the part of the ruling party to do away with the basic structure of the Indian constitution, such as secularism and parliamentary democracy. For Upendra Baxi, there is no need for a constitution review panel as the constitution has allowed numerous changes within it through amendments. But while the constitution allows changes *in* it it does not allow change *of* it: "Changes *of* Constitution are not allowed any scope by the present Indian Constitutionalism which denies legitimacy for its profound subversion" (Baxi 2000, 891).

The need to be vigilant about any subversion to constitution is presented in a passionately engaged manner by none other than K. R. Narayanan, the then-President of India. Narayanan was born into a poor untouchable family in Kerala and had difficulty in going to primary school in his locality. He was the President of the Republic of India towards the end of the 1990s and his journey from an untouchable hamlet in Kerala to the office of the President of the Republic symbolizes the social transformation that has taken place in post-independent India, in which the Constitution of India has played an important role. Narayanan urges those in Indian society who are bent on changing the constitution to ponder whether they have failed the constitution or the Constitution has failed them. In his address to the nation on the eve of the Golden Jubilee of the founding of Indian Constitution on 25 January 2001, Narayanan affirmed that "We cannot ignore the social commitments enshrined in our Constitution." He spoke about those in Indian society who wanted to subvert the emancipatory promises of the constitution: "Let us remember, it is under the flexible and spacious provisions of our Constitution that democracy has flourished during the last fifty years. Today India has been acknowledged as a great democracy – indeed the greatest democracy in the world and the Indian Constitution as the embodiment of the political, social and economic rights of people" (Narayanan 2001).

By Way of Conclusion: Rule of Law and the Calling of Self-Transformation

In this chapter, we have covered a long historical terrain of more than five thousand years while pointing out the way Indian society has related to the rule of law at various moments of her journey. We have looked at the idea of the rule of law in classical Indian tradition, and its workings under the constitution of independent India. The present Constitution of India has sought to create a more equal and just rule of law between individuals and groups than what existed under traditional authorities such as *Manusmriti*. The constitution strives to eliminate the humiliation that people suffered under the traditional social system of caste and patriarchy, thus creating new ground for the realization of human dignity. The realization of both formal and substantive equality that is possible under the rule of law in contemporary Indian society can facilitate a more creative flourishing of a life of *dharma* or righteous conduct in self and society. In the first section of this chapter we have seen how self-rule is central to realization of order in both self and society. But self-rule is facilitated by the existence of a just social, institutional and legal order which grants legal equality to individuals irrespective class, caste, religion and gender. Modern law thus can create an appropriate sociological condition for the realization of a life of *dharma* in self and society.

But though modern rules of law are necessary, they are not sufficient for the realization of self-rule, self-governance and order in society. It is here that modern rules of law both in contemporary India and the West can learn from aspects of Indian traditions, which emphasize self-development and self-transformation. In fact, it is the practice of continued self-transformation which realizes a Beyond in thinking about the rule of law, self and society, and the spiritual traditions of India continuously challenge us to invite and incorporate this beyond in our routines of law. As J. D. M. Derrett writes: "...the unbroken tradition of Hindu legal scholarship has emphasized the concept that Hindu law concerns itself with eternity and with morality judged against the greater background, and not with material, temporary considerations" (Derrett 1968, 101). For Shasheej Hegde, "Rules and laws in Indian traditions point towards a morality of subjectivation, a morality that extends beyond the space of power" (Hegde 1998, 11). There is an imperative/prescriptive dimension of the rule of law in

Indian tradition, but this "may neither be merely foisted on the practices of groups and institutions as extrinsic constraints, nor be made merely instrumental to their exercise or the principle of universalization that this could help realize must however be friends on a clarification of the *moral* point of view" (Hegde 1998, 116). The epithets "legal and moral are taken to be broadly coeval" and in Indian traditions "looked at as complementary modes of marking power" (Hegde 1998, 99). The transformational supplement of morality in the working of the rule of law, where morality means much more than obeying societal norms but acting righteously in accordance with one's conscience, has an epochal significance now. As Veena Das writes: "Texts (including the *Dharmasastras* which lay out rules of conduct) do not prescribe behavior in the sense of laying out areas of obligation as much as describing codes of conduct considered to be exemplary or desirable…by characterizing this as a purely *Brahmanic* conception, one loses the opportunity of treating it as an important conceptual resource" (quoted in Hegde 1998, 102).

The rules of law in modern Western tradition began with an emancipatory promise, but even by the mid-nineteenth century in the West law as emancipation was over-ridden by law as regulation. The crisis facing the rule of law in the contemporary world, both in India and in the West is "the collapse of emancipation into regulation" (Santos 1995), and the task here is to rethink and revitalize the emancipatory dimension of the rule of law. But this calls for not only incorporating the old models of emancipation, where emancipation entailed struggles with the external oppressive other, but also imagining, embodying and realizing emancipation in a new way, where emancipation from societal oppression and the consequent empowerment is accompanied by emancipation from one's egotistic passion and desire to control other people, and an aspiration to contribute to a participatory and transformational creation of society as a space of spiritual freedom and shared intersubjectivity (see Giri 1998; Laclau 1992). Working on this new challenge of emancipation, at the core of which lies work on self-development, self-transcendence on self-transformation, requires a new view of the subject and also society. Santos, who urges us to realize that "the collapse of emancipation into regulation symbolizes the exhaustion of paradigm of modernity" makes this connection clear: "A narrow view of ourselves tends to encourage even a narrower view of the other" (Santos 1995, xi). For Santos, the new paradigm of law that is emerging in the context of the contemporary crisis of modernist legalism entails a triple transformation where "power becomes shared authority," "despotic law becomes democratic law," and "knowledge as regulation becomes knowledge-as-emancipation" (Santos 1995, 482). But for the realization of this triple transformation, there is the need for the realization of a new subjectivity: the task is to invent a "subjectivity constituted by the topos of a prudent knowledge for a decent life" (Santos 1995, 489). And as Paul Ricouer would urge us to realize in his recent provocative interpretation of justice, "…the question with a juridical form who is the subject of rights? is not to be distinguished in the final analysis from the question with a moral form who is the subject worthy of esteem and respect?" (Ricouer 2001, 1).

For Santos, the "emergent subjectivity" of law lives in the frontier and to "live in the frontier is to live in abeyance, in an empty space, in a time between times"

(Santos 1995, 491). Living in an empty space and empty time calls for realizing the dialectic between time and eternity, tradition and modernity, and here openness to emptiness as an integral dimension of space, time, being and society in Indian socio-spiritual traditions can help us in bringing emancipation to the heart of the rule of law. The "emergent subjectivity" of law requires an emergent ethics where *a priori* rules and regulations are not enough for making prudent judgments with regard to dealing with dilemmatic situations in law, ethics and morality, and also for living a life of justice and responsibility. The task here is to bring the dimension of responsibility as unconditional obligation to the working of the rules of law, where responsibility as obligation "overflows the framework of compensation and punishment" (Ricouer 2000, 12; also see Dallmayr 2007). A life of responsibility calls for prudent judgment, which in turn calls for continuous guidance of the conscience.[5] But in modern Western legal and political tradition, exemplified in the works of Kant, Rawls and Habermas, the voice of conscience has all the features of social legality internalized as pure morality. But in bringing conscience to the heart of law, we have to realize that conscience is not just a product of society. It is the voice of conscience which "[tells] me that all other life is as important as my own" (Ricouer 2000, 152). Here an ontologically responsive interpretation of conscience for a just working of the rule of law is crucial, and here the Indian approach to the rules of law through *dharma* can help us.

In his critical reflection on law and society in India, Andre Béteille writes, "Individual rights do not have the same depth and firmness in India, the same anchorage in its social structure, that they do in the United States" (1997, 198). But this relativization of individual rights in the contemporary Indian legal systems can help us work out a much more balanced relationship between individual rights and group rights. Modern Western legal tradition has granted unquestioned primacy to individual rights, but with the social and theoretical revolution of postmodernism and multiculturalism, legal systems in the West are slowly opening themselves to recognizing and instituting group rights. But the realization of a proper balance between individual and group rights is still a great challenge, and here experiments in the West can learn from Indian experiments with policies of compensatory discrimination which have sought to work out a balance between individual rights and group rights.[6] The Indian experiment on arriving at a creative and transformative relationship between the individual and society in both tradition and modernity is still incomplete, but it has all along striven to relativize the egoistic primacy of either group right or individual right, society or individual, by bringing a dimension of transcendental beyond to the routines of rule and law. The spiritual traditions of India have all along emphasized that society is not merely a contract. This is an immensely helpful insight in rethinking and reconstituting law and society in the contemporary order. As Paul Ricouer challenges us:

> The question is worth asking: what is it that makes society more than a system of distribution? Or better: What is it that makes distribution a means of cooperation? Here is where a more substantial element than pure procedural justice has to be taken into account, namely, something like a common good, consisting in shared

values. We are then dealing with a communitarian dimension underlying the purely procedural dimension of the social structure. Perhaps we may even find in the metaphor of sharing the two aspects I am here trying to coordinate in terms of each other. In sharing there are shares, that is, these things that separate us. My share is not yours. But sharing is also what makes us share, that is, in the strong sense of the term, share in…

I conclude then that the act of judging has as its horizon a fragile equilibrium of these two elements of sharing: that which separates my share or part from yours and that which, on the other hand, means that each of us shares in, takes part in society (Ricouer 2000, 132).

Notes

1 Coomaraswamy further tells us, "The Inner Sage who may be called the chaplain within you, to whom the *Purohita*, who is the chaplain of the King's house, corresponds in the civil realm" (Coomaraswamy 1978, 85).

2 David Washbrook makes almost a similar observation: "If the public side of the law sought to subordinate the rule of 'Indian status' to that of British contract' and to free the individual in a world of amoral market relations, the personal side entrenched ascriptive (caste, religious and familial) status as the basis of individual right" (Washbrook 1981, 654).

3 "Hindu scriptural discourse is not and never monolithic.. and it does perennially generate reinterpretations of itself…" (Fuller 1988, 241). In Lingat's words, "The role of interpretation amounts to this: it offers society the means whereby it can rediscover itself" (as quoted in Fuller 1988, 241).

4 In traditional Indian society the rights of most Hindu women were governed by the Mitakshara and Dayabhaga systems of law. The Mitakshara conferred coparcenary rights at birth on sons but the Dayabhaga system ensured no such birth right. Thus the chances of a woman "inheriting property under the Dayabhaga was slightly better" (Nair 1996, 196–7). The Hindu Code of 1955 did not make a difference to inheritance of property on the part of Hindu women living under the Mitakshara system of law.

5 In this context what Ricouer writes deserves our careful consideration:

> Finally, it is to the virtue of prudence that we are led once more by the dilemma arising from the question of the side effects of action, among which fall its harmful effects. But it is then no longer a question of prudence in the weak sense of prevention, but one of *prudentia*, heir to the Greek virtue of *phronesis*, in other words, the sense of moral judgment in some specific circumstance. It is to such prudence, in the strong sense of the word, that is assigned the task of recognizing among the innumerable consequences of action those for which we can legitimately be held responsible, in the name of an ethic of the mean. It is in the end this appeal to judgment that constitutes the strongest plea in favor of maintaining the idea of imputability in the face of the assaults from those of solidarity and risk. (2000, 35)

6 Galanter writes,

> Compensatory discrimination offers a way to leaven our formalism without entirely abandoning its comforts. The Indian example is instructive: India has managed to pursue a commitment to substantive justice without allowing that commitment to dissolve competing commitments to formal equality that make law viable in a diverse society with

limited consensus. The Indian experience displays a principled eclecticism that avoids suppressing the altruistic fraternal impulse that animates compensatory policies, but that also avoids being enslaved by it. From afar it reflects to us a tempered legalism – one which we find more congenial in practice than theory. (Galanter 1989, 567)

References

Ahuja, Sangeeta. 1997. *People, Law and Justice: A Casebook of Public Interest Litigation*. New Delhi: Orient Longman.
Appadurai, Arjun. 1983. *Worship and Conflict under Colonial Rule: A South Indian Case*. Delhi: Orient Longman.
Austin, Granville. 1999. *Working a Democratic Constitution: The Indian Experience*. Delhi: Oxford University Press.
Bauman, Zygmunt. 1987. *Legislators and Interpreters: On Modernity, Postmodernity and the Intellectuals*. Cambridge: Polity Press.
Baxi, Upendra. 1982. *The Crisis of the Indian Legal System*. Delhi: Vikash.
_____. 2000. "Kar Seva of the Indian Constituton? Reflections on Proposals for Review of the Constitution." *Economic and Political Weekly* 35 (11): 891–5.
Béteille, Andre. 1991/1997. *Society and Politics in India: Essays in a Comparative Perspective*. New Delhi: Oxford University Press.
_____. 1999a. "Citizenship, State and Civil Society." *Economic and Political Weekly* 34 (36).
_____. 1999b. "Experience of Governance: A Sociological View." In R. K. Darr, ed., *Experience and the IAS*. New Delhi: Tata McGraw Hall.
_____. 2008. "Constitutional Morality." *Economic and Political Weekly* 43 (40): 35–42.
_____. 2011. "The Institutions of Democracy." *Economic and Political Weekly* 46 (29): 75–84.
Brennan, Teressa. 1993. *History After Lacan*. London: Routledge.
Cohn, Bernard S. 1997. *Colonialism and its Forms of Knowledge*. Delhi: Oxford University Press.
Conrad, Dieter. 1998. "Rule of Law and Constitutional Problems of Personal Laws in India." In Satish Saberwal and Heiko Sievers, eds, *Rules, Laws, Constitutions*. New Delhi: Sage Publications.
Coomaraswamy, A. K. 1978. *Spiritual Authority and Temporal Power in the Indian Theory of Government*. Delhi: Munshiram Manoharlal.
Dallmayr, Fred. 1997. "What is Swaraj? Lessons from Gandhi." Manuscript.
_____. 2007. "Love and Justice: A Memorial Tribute to Paul Ricoeur." In *In Search of the Good Life: A Pedagogy for Troubled Times*, 221–35. Lexington: University of Kentucky Press.
Derrett, J. D. M. 1968. *Religion, Law and the State in India*. London: Faber & Faber.
Dhagamwar, Vasudha. 1989. *Towards the Uniform Civil Code*. Bombay: N. M. Tripathi Pvt. Ltd.
Dhavan, Rajeev. 2000. "Judges and Indian Democracy: The Lesser Evil?" In Francine R. Frankel et al., eds, *Transforming India: Social and Political Dynamics of Democracy*. Delhi: Oxford University Press.
Dirks, Nicholas B. 1986 "From Little King to Landlord: Property, Law, and the Gift under the Madras Permanent Settlement." *Comparative Studies in Society and History* 28 (2): 307–33.
Foucault, Michel. 1986. *The Care of the Self*. New York: Pantheon.
Fuller, Chris. 1988. "Hinduism and Scriptural Authority in Modern Indian Law." *Comparative Studies in Society and History* 30: 225–48.
Galanter, Marc. 1984. *Competing Equalities: Law and the Backward Classes in India*. Delhi: Oxford University Press.
_____. 1989. *Law and Society in Modern India*. Delhi: Oxford University Press.
Giri, Ananta Kumar. 1998. "Moral Consciousness and Communicative Action: From Discourse Ethics to Spiritual Transformation." *History of the Human Sciences* 11 (3): 87–113.

_____. 2002 "Rethinking Systems as Frames of Coordination: Dialogical Intersubjectivity and Creativity of Action." In *Conversations and Transformations: Towards a New Ethics of Self and Society*. Lanham, MD: Lexington Books.

Giri, Ananta Kumar and van Ufford, Philip Quarles. 2000. "Reconstituting Development as a Shared Responsibility: Ethics, Aesthetics, and a Creative Shaping of Human Possibilities." Madras Institute of Development Studies Working Paper.

Habermas, Jürgen. 1996. *Between Facts and Norms: Contributions towards a Discourse Theory of Law and Democracy*. Cambridge: Polity Press.

Hegde, Sasheej. 1998. "Rules and Laws in Indian Traditions: A Reconstructive Appropriation." In Satish Saberwal and Heiko Sievers, eds, *Rules, Laws, Constitutions*. New Delhi: Sage Publications.

Laclau, Ernesto. 1992. "Beyond Empancipation." In Jan N. Pieterse, ed., *Emancipations, Modern and Postmodern*. London: Sage Publications.

Lingat, Robert. 1973. *The Classical Law of India*. New Delhi: Thompson Press.

Nair, Janaki. 1996. *Women and Law in Colonial India: A Social History*. New Delhi: Kali for Women.

Nandy, Ashis. 1995. "The Other Within: The Strange Case of Radhabinod Pal's Judgment of Culpability." In *The Savage Freud*, 53–80. Delhi: Oxford University Press.

Narayanan, K. R. 2001. President's address to the nation. 25 January.

Parashar, Archana. 1992. *Women and Family Law Reform in India: Uniform Civil Code and Gender Equality*. New Delhi: Sage Publications.

Ramanujan, A. K. 1989. "Is there an Indian way of thinking? An informal essay." *Contributions to Indian Sociology* (n.s.) 23: 41–58.

Ricouer, Paul. 2000. *The Just*. Chicago: University of Chicago Press.

Roy, Ramashray. 1999. *Beyond Ego's Domain: Being and Order in the Veda*. Delhi: Shipra Publications.

Saberwal, Satish. 1998. "Introduction: Why Do We Need Rules and Laws?" In Satish Saberwal and Hieko Sievers, eds, *Rules, Laws, Constitutions*. New Delhi: Sage Publications.

Santos, B. 1995. *Toward a New Common Sense: Law, Science and Politics in the Paradigmatic Transition*. London: Routledge.

Smith, Richard S. 1985. "Rule-by-Records and Rule-by-Reports: Complimentary Aspects of the British Imperial Rule of Law." *Contributions to Indian Sociology* (n.s.) 19 (1): 153–76.

Spellman, J. W. 1964. *Political Theory of Ancient India: A Study of Kingship from the Earliest Times to circa A.D. 300*. Oxford: Clarendon Press.

Stokes, Eric. 1982. *English Utilitarians and India*. Delhi: Oxford University Press.

Sri Aurobindo. 1948. *The Synthesis of Yoga*. Pondicherry: Sri Aurobindo Ashram.

Washbrook, David. 1981. "Law, State and Agrarian Society in Colonial India." *Modern Asian Studies* 15 (3): 649–721.

Chapter Nine

COMPASSION AND CONFRONTATION: DIALOGIC EXPERIMENTS WITH TRADITIONS AND PATHWAYS TO NEW FUTURES

Introduction and Invitation

Compassion is a key theme and foundation of life in paths of Buddha. It means to share in the suffering and joy of others. According to the Dalai Lama, this is the foundation of Buddhism, especially Tibetan Buddhism. Compassion heals and makes new ways of human development and social transformations possible. But compassion needs to be accompanied by confrontation: the courage to confront those parts of self and society which do not help us to blossom and realize our potential. In my recent visit to China and Tibet (July–August 2009) I saw images of Buddha as well as the Goddess Tara with swords in their hands. This is an example of compassion being accompanied by confrontation. The present chapter discusses compassionate confrontation as an important part of experiment with traditions in Buddhism and explores the contribution of Kashmir, especially the traditions of Kashmir Saivism, on Buddhism in realizing paths of compassionate confrontation.

Dynamic Harmony and Dynamic *Sunyata* and Pathways of Compassionate Confrontation

Compassion and confrontation are meditative verbs of co-realizations. It is compassion that enables us to confront even our friends, not only our enemies, giving rise to emergent pathways of compassionate confrontation. Compassionate confrontation is pulsated by the simultaneous flows of dynamic harmony and dynamic *sunyata*, or dynamic emptiness. The realization of dynamic harmony is an important part of creative experiments with Buddhist traditions. In his study of Japanese religion, where Buddhism has interacted with Shintoism and Confucianism, the great sociologist of religion Robert Bellah tells us that while Japanese religion is concerned with harmony – harmony among persons and harmony with nature – this not static but dynamic. For Bellah,

> What has been said about the unity of man, nature and divinity should not be interpreted as a static identity. Rather it is a harmony in tension. The gratitude

one owes to superordinate benevolent entities is not an easy obligation but may involve the instant sacrifice of one's deepest interests or even of one's life. Union with the ground of being is not attained in a state of coma but very often as the result of some sudden shock in daily living. Something unexpected, some seeming disharmony, is more apt to reveal the Truth than any formal orderly teaching. Japanese art and aesthetic attitude toward nature are also concerned with the unexpected… (1957/1985, 62–3)

Compassion here is not imprisoned in the logic status-quo but animated by a spirit to unsettle the existing harmony and invite the unexpected in a spirit of dynamic harmony. Realization of dynamic harmony is also an animated aspiration in paths of Kashmiri Saivism. As Harish Deheja writes about it:

Kashmir Saivism postulates that Parama Shiva contains the entire universe, pulsating within it, just as the seed of the mighty *nyagrodha* potentially contains the entire tree. At the immanent level, the transcendent *prakashavimarshamaya* splits into *prakasha* and *vimarsha*, Shiva and Shakti, *aham* and *idam*, I and this, subject and object, held together in pulsating, *dynamic harmony*… At every level there is differentiation into subject and object, *aham* and *idam*, but the differentiation is based in, and unified by, the non-duality of consciousness. (2006, 422, emphasis added)

Kashmiri Saivism seeks to realize dynamic harmony by realizing differentiation without dualism. Realization of non-duality is also an animated goal in the paths of the Buddha, and Kashmiri Saivism possibly has contributed to this pursuit of non-duality the work of dynamic consciousness. There is an occasion for mutual learning on the part of Buddhism and Kashimiri Saivism, as interested seekers can learn from experiments in these traditions. It must be noted here that differentiation and integration are perennial human concerns, and these also have been key themes in social and political theory in the last three or four hundred years. In our recent theoretical discourses, Niklas Luhman urges us to realize the need for distinction, for example, between the system and its environment; Derrida urges us to understand the work of difference which is not just mere difference but has the capacity to resist temporal and spatial incorporation; and Parsons and Habermas in their own different ways emphasize the significance of integration and communication. All theses attempts can be enriched by the quest from Kashmiri Saivism to realize differentiation without dualism. The Buddhist quest for non-duality (see Loy 1988) can also be enriched by it. It can also help us to rethink identity and difference in contemporary social and political theory.

Complex Histories of Influences and Violations

In order to understand the influence of Kashmiri Saivism on Buddhism, we need to understand that the field of influence is not only a discursive one but also a socio-political one. While the *sadhana* of dynamic of consciousness in Kashmir Saivism has influenced Buddhism, the political organization of it has also led to the annihilation of Buddhism from the Kashmir Valley. We can note what F. M. Hassnain writes about this in his book *Buddhism in Kashmir*:

> With Avanthiraman who came to power in 855 AD, Vaishnavism and Shaktaism got prominence in Kashmir. He patronized Saivism which was propounded by Vasugupta, the author of *Sivasutras*. Henceforth the masses were attracted towards Saivism. Now was the time to completely wipe out the Buddhist faith from Kashmir. Shankaravarman, the next ruler, either confiscated lands and *viharas* or plundered these shrines. During the rule of Khemagupta, the remaining *viharas* were either burnt or appropriated. He burnt the most significant *vihara* of Jayendra. Out of the burned material, he built a Siva temple. (Hassnain 1973, 28–9)

But while the political organization of Saivism in Kashmir valley led to annihilation of Buddhism, the history of the impact of the political organization of Islam seems to be different. Here what Sarao writes deserves our careful attention:

> Rinchana, the son of a Buddhist Ladakhi chief, moved into the Kasmira valley along with his followers and captured the throne of Kasmira by the end of 1320. Rinchana accepted Islam under the influence of Sharafuddin, adopted the Muslim name of Sadruddin, and established a *khanqah* with a *langar-khannah* (free kitchen) for the comfort of the travelers and the poor. It has been suggested that Richana's conversion to Islam was neither an isolated case nor was it merely a matter of political expediency. According to Aziz Ahmad, "The very fact of the conversion of the Buddhist Rinchana to Islam shows that Buddhism was no longer available as a power-base, possibly not even as the religion of any significant number of households, though it might have stayed on in monasteries, whereas a sizeable converted Muslim nucleus had already grown in urban centers." Islam does not appear to have received any special favours under Rinchana and the following kings including Shah Mir (1339–1342), Jamshed (1342–1343), Alauddin (1343–1354), Shihabuddin (1354–1373), so much so that when Shihabuddin's Hindu minister, Udaysri suggested the melting of a grand brass image of Buddha for coining it into money, it was turned down. On the whole, there is a clear indication in the sources that as far as Islam was concerned, Buddhism was not in any way persecuted. However, some Buddhists appear to have adopted Islam as a result of peaceful activities of Sufi saints, particularly those belonging to Rsi Silsilah. Nuruddin, the son of a Hindu convert, was the founder of an indigenous order of Muslim mystics (Rsi Silsilah) who made the Rsi movement socially important in Kashmira. These Rsis developed their ideas in their Hindu and Buddhist surroundings. The extreme asceticism, self-mortification, long fasts, sexual abstinence, and seclusion, which marked the early life of Nuuddin, and indeed, the lives of his followers, helped in blurring

the differences in the minds of common masses between Islam and Hinduism or Buddhism. (Sarao 2009, 3–4)

Thus Buddhism has been variously influenced by the rise of other religious systems in the Kashmir valley such as Saivism and Islam. In case of Saivism, its impact has been one of violation and erasure too, as there had been other kinds of impact as discussed before. We need to acknowledge this history of violation and violence so that we can cultivate our pathways to the future in a spirit of creativity and dialogue.[1] Without being a prisoner of the past, we can acknowledge the violence that has been unleashed in the past, and the violence and injury we continue to inflict upon each other. Such acknowledgment helps us to move towards a field of non-violence and compassion, a compassion which however is neither paternalistic nor *status quo* driven but has the courage to confront the violent histories of the past and present. Learning from our complex histories, we can cultivate compassionate confrontation as a path before Buddhism, Islam and Saivism.

Compassionate Confrontation

In compassionate confrontation, compassion is not simply confined to feeling empathetic towards others but involves taking steps to make life better. It is linked to what Thai political scientist Vira Somboon (2002) calls creating opportunities for all: "The practice of generosity in contemporary world may be entangled to include sharing of opportunities for all." It is manifested in a variety of attempts at what is called Engaged Buddhism, such as the Sarvodaya Sramadana movement in Sri Lanka, where the ideal of compassion is said to be put into practices of self-development. Compassion is also essential for security, human as well as social (see Ogata and Sen 2003). But compassion does not mean letting oneself be run over by others (what is called "idiotic compassion" by Buddhist monk Prema Chodron) (see Tagesson 2009).

Confrontation in compassionate confrontation is linked to what is called a loving quarrel or loving struggle for the transformation of self, others and the world. But we struggle not only for our existence, for the survival of the fittest; we struggle to excel, not just for individual achievement, but for mutual excellence and shared excellence (see Das 2006, Dallmayr 2001).

Compassionate confrontation thus redefines our concept of struggle. It is then linked to such discourses like *jihad* and *nirvana* in transformative ways. It involves practical *jihad*, where *jihad* means the practical struggle in daily life to lead a life free from the temptation to degrade oneself or others. It also involves multi-dimensional initiatives in practical nirvana where the objective is to realize *nirvana* in our moments of existence and in our everyday life. We realize it by leading a life which is not governed by temptation but one of noble truths in everyday life. We continuously strive to overcome our temptation[2] and lead a life of noble truths despite our many failures in our everyday life, and this constitutes practical nirvana.

Compassionate Confrontation, Meditative Pluralizations and Pathways to a New Future

Kashmir is celebrated as a land of pluralism, but this pluralism has also been marked by a history of violence. In this context we need to cultivate pluralism as an ongoing transformation involving dialogue, learning and meditation. Compassionate confrontation needs to be followed by practices of meditative pluralizations. Kashmir had acted like a motherly passage, a nurturing way for the flow of Buddhism to Ladakh, Tibet, China and Central Asia. But what is the impact of the traditions in these societies on Buddhism? What is the impact of Confucianism on Buddhism? How do we make sense of the fact that the Avalokiteshvara Buddha is represented in a feminine way in China and known as Guanyin and sometimes as the mother goddess Mazhou?

All these questions call for further intellectual and practical pursuits in learning, dialogue and transformations. Going beyond closure of nation-states and traditions, with our locus being in a place like Kashmir, we need to take part in border-crossing dialogues among Confucianism, Buddhism, Kashmiri Saivism, Advaita Vedanta, Islam and Christianity. For example, even students of Confucianism rarely think of dialogue, say, between Confucianism and Advaita Vedanta, or Confucianism and Kashmiri Saivism. But with Kashmir as our motherly and nurturing locus of dialogue, we can carry out such dialogues and experiments in border-crossing learning. Such dialogues have a global relevance today, and their insights could enrich all of us seeking souls and movements around the world. Needless to say such dialogues are facilitated by political transformations, such as transformations of the exclusionary claims of nation-states as well as transformation of the self. It also calls for hard intellectual labor and expansion of the heart. But how many of us in these fields are really prepared to undertake such tasks of dialogic experiments with traditions, learning across borders and paths of meditative pluralization into future?

Notes

1 As Jürgen Habermas would urge us to realize, when we acknowledge violence in the past and failure of traditions can we move towards autonomy and freedom.

2 This continuous striving to overcome temptation is expressed in the following poem, originally written by the author in the Odia language and then translated:

> Oh Buddha
> I, Buddha, touch your lotus heart
> Oh Tara, Tara of Heart
> Being a breast I salute your breast
> My love for breast gets transformed
> Desires become white flowers
> Insects become roses
> They kiss, Oh Buddha, you and me
> Tara and all beings

References

Bellah, Robert N. 1957/1985. *Tokugawa Religion*. Glencoe, NY: Free Press.

Dallmayr, Fred. 2001. *Achieving Our World*. Lanham, MD: Rowman & Littlefield.

Das, Chittaranjan. 2006. *Bira Jodha Kari* [Being a Heroic Warrior]. Bhubaneswar: Suhrut Gosthi.

Deheja, Harsha V. 2006. "Kashmir Saivism: A Note." In Makarand Paranjape, ed., *Abhinavagupta: Reconsiderations*, 414–28. Delhi: Samvad India.

Hassnain, F. M. 1973. *Buddhism in Kashmir*. New Delhi: Light Life Publishers.

Loy, David. 1988. *Nonduality: A Study of Comparative Philosophy*. New York: Humanities Press.

Ogata, Sadako and Amartya Sen. 2003. *The Commission on Human Security Now*. New York: United Nations.

Sarao, K. T. S. 2009. "Xuanzhang to Akbar: An Examination of the Decline of Buddhism in the Kashmira Valley." Paper presented at the seminar on "The Contribution of Kashmir to Buddhist Thought," 14–16 September, Central Institute of Buddhist Studies, Choglamsar, Leh.

Sombūn, Wīra. 2002. *Ariyavinaya in the Age of Extreme Modernism*. Bangkok: Komol Keemthong Foundation.

Tagesson, Helena. 2009. "A Yearning of the Heart: Spirituality and Politics." In Ananta Kumar Giri, ed., *The Modern Prince and the Modern Sage: Transforming Power and Freedom*. Delhi: Sage.

Chapter Ten

RETHINKING PLURALISM AND RIGHTS: MEDITATIVE VERBS OF CO-REALIZATIONS AND THE CHALLENGES OF TRANSFORMATIONS

Does the collapse of "logocentrism" anchored in the cogito, really compel us to abandon every type of 'humanism' or commitment to humanity even when it transgresses human self-indulgence? In the political domain: does the rejection or critique of liberal universalism inevitably force us to embrace the alternative of parochialism and hateful xenophobia? Is it not possible – indeed are there not good practical and philosophical reasons to cherish cultural and ethnic diversity while at the same time opposing the blandishments of both cosmopolitanism and local narcissism?

—Fred Dallmayr, "Truth and Difference: Lessons from Herder" (1998)

The very notion of human rights (or the "rights of man") is generally presented as the gift of the West to the rest. The non-Western traditions are usually considered bereft of notions of human rights… [But] this disables any intercultural, multi-civilizational discourse on the genealogy of human rights. The originary claims concerning the invention of "human rights" in the West lead to a continuing insistence on the oft-reiterated absence of human rights traditions in the "non-West." From this it is but a short practical step for the "West" to impart, by coercive and "persuasive" means, to others the gift of human rights. This leads to a rank denial, even in a post-colonial and post-socialist age, of equal discursive dignity to other cultures and civilizations. It also imparts a loss of reflexivity, in terms of intercultural learning, for the Euro-American traditions of human rights… The future of human rights is serviced only when theory and practice develops the narrative potential to pluralize the originary metanarratives of the past of human rights beyond the time and space of European Imagination, even in its critical postmodern incarnations.

—Upendra Baxi, *The Future of Human Rights* (2002, 24–6)

The critical struggle of our day is not between believers and non-believers, but between an ethos of existential revenge and one of care for the diversity of life and future of the earth. The struggle, manifest in economic and religious life, goes on within as well as between us.

—William Connolly, "The Ethics of Revenge" (2007, 97)

The Problem

Pluralism and human rights are epochal challenges now, and they challenge established modes of discourse and practice including our conceptions of the normative. Both of these face challenges of multi-dimensional transformations in self and society. A key challenge here is to broaden our conceptions and realizations of law and rights. In his critical reflection on law and society in India, Andre Béteille writes, "Individual rights do not have the same depth and firmness in India, the same anchorage in its social structure, than they do in the United States" (1997, 198). But this relativization of individual right in contemporary Indian legal systems can help us work out a much more balanced relationship between individual rights and group rights. Modern Western legal tradition has granted unquestioned primacy to individual rights, but with the social and theoretical moves of postmodernism and multiculturalism, legal systems in the West are slowly opening themselves to recognizing and instituting group rights and people's rights, as Upendra Baxi and Manoranjan Mohanty would challenge us (cf. Mohanty et al. 1998). This also challenges us to go beyond the individualist premise of both pluralism and rights. But as we pluralize our conceptions of laws and rights, there is a transformational challenge to pluralize our pluralist imagination itself, as our established conceptions of pluralism are state-centered and suffer from the problem of Western, and now Euro-American, ethnocentrism. Now discourses of multiculturalism and toleration are being globalized, but the globalization of these benevolent ideals reflects both the limits and possibilities of their genealogies and the locations of the performances, for example the contemporary Euro-American world. The discourse and practice of pluralism here has followed a stable trajectory, and toleration carries the original violence of killing the Native Americans, or colonizing the world and then tolerating the other. Even the Habermasian discourse of inclusion of the other does not interrogate this original violence and does not go beyond a dualistic model of self and other which is at the root of contemporary notions of rights and pluralism (cf. Habermas 1998). It is against this background that the present essay seeks to explore the pathways of a non-dual pluralism and mode of embodiment of responsibility.

Pluralizing the established pluralist imagination, which is based upon a stable conception of self (which is in turn predicated upon a dualist division between the private and the public), a stable model of expected inter-group relations under the benevolent and panoptic gaze of the state, and a notion of a public sphere which is one-dimensional, calls for a multi-dimensional vision and the practice of state, inter-group relations, public sphere, intersubjectivity; and much more significant, a plural or multi-dimensional conception of the self which William Connolly calls "plurivocity of being" (Connolly 1999). Thus we need now a radically pluralized multi-dimensional public sphere beyond the rationalist Habermasian one-dimensional one, and a multi-dimensional "plurivocity of being." In this essay, I present an outline of such a new pluralist imagination in both self and society. But my plurivocity of being differs from Connolly's Nietzchian conceptualization, as it is conceptualized not only in terms of the infra-rational but also by the work of what Sri Aurobindo (1962) calls "supramental," the work of a transcendental self which, while using reason, puts reason in its place. The self also has a transcendental dimension apart from its location in ego, social roles and other sources of identity, and it is possible to see a connection between the transcendental dimension of the self and many transnational social movements which urge us to embody a new mode of responsibility to self, society, world and cosmos. A plural conception of being is crucial for rethinking rights and laws, as it urges us to realize that the self is not only a bearer of rights and the subject of justice but also a practitioner of responsibility.

Towards a New Normative Pluralism: The Contemporary Challenges of Rethinking and Reconstitution

In recent political theory, Connolly has presented us with pathways of multi-dimensionally creative pluralism. Connolly urges us to understand the limits of conventional pluralism: "A conventional pluralist celebrates diversity within settled contexts of conflict and collective action… But what about the larger contexts within which the pattern of diversity is set? How plural or monistic are they? To what extent does a cultural presumption of normal individual or the pre-existing subject precede and confine conventional pluralism?" (Connolly 1995, xiii). Speaking of his own home experience, which should inspire all of us concerned to engage ourselves in a self-critical reflection, Connolly tells us, "The American pluralist imagination, in particular, remains too stingy, cramped, and defensive for the world now we inhabit. These stingy dispositions sustain operational standards of identity, nature, reason, territory, sovereignty and justice that need to be reworked" (1995, xii–xiii). For Connolly, in rethinking pluralism it is important to pluralize our accepted frames of identity: nation-state, ethnic identity, a normal model of heterosexuality, or a stable self. Connolly also urges us to understand the distinction between pluralism and pluralization and the work of critical social, political and cultural movements in pluralization as a continued process of broadening the accepted horizons of plurality. There is a need to "translate the pluralist appreciation of established diversity into active cultivation of generosity to contemporary movements of pluralization" (1995, xv). On the part of actors in state and civil society, it is essential to develop "an ethos of critical responsiveness" to such movements "seeking to redefine their relational identities" (Connolly 1995, xix).

Rethinking pluralism then calls for cultivating an ethos of pluralization, which in turn calls for the plural conception of the individual: A normal individual is not only a Kantian and Habermasian rational self, there is also a Nietzschian rebellion against reason which the pluralist imagination must be open to.[1] Connolly calls this "plurivocity of being." Though Connolly's "plurivocity of being" does not include within itself a supra-rational critique of reason as suggested by Sri Aurobindo, his conception of the "plurivocity of being" still has rich possibilities. Connolly seeks to introduce ontological nurturance in the practice and perspective of normative pluralism. Thus Connolly calls for cultivating an ethos of pluralization which "pursues an ethic of cultivation rather than a morality of contract or command; it judges the ethos it cultivates to exceed any fixed code of morality; and it cultivates critical responsiveness to difference in ways that disturb traditional virtues of community and the normal individual" (1995, xxiv). The practice of cultivating an ethos of pluralization in Connolly reaches a new height and depth when he urges us to cultivate a spirit of gratitude which need not be theistic and anxiously opposed to religion or any theistic cultivation of life: "[A] nontheistic gratitude for the rich diversity of being provides an ethical source from which a modified vision of pluralism might emerge, one in which [a] larger variety of identities strive to find ways to coexist on the same territory, combining together from time to time to support the general material and spiritual conditions of this very cultural diversity" (Connolly 1995, 32).

Thus realization of pluralism calls for crossing over many traditional boundaries in modernist thought and practice. In his work *Neuropolitics: Thinking, Culture, Speed*, Connolly (2002) urges us to understand the connection between mystical states and deep pluralism. Mysticism is an experience of crossing conventional boundaries of mind and identity, and finds "expression as a radiant feeling of joy and generosity" (Connolly 2002, 126). Connolly sends us his invitation: "We are, so it seems, to honor our existential faith in the first instance, according to whatever work it takes to do so, and there to cultivate self-modesty about its applicability to others in order to promote deep pluralism. We are, that is, not only to be born again, but also grow up a second time. The latter we do by working on ourselves – within those very religious and secular constitutions through which the first faith was consolidated – to activate the visceral appreciation of the contestability of that faith and to cultivate a presumption of receptive generosity of other faiths" (Connolly 2002, 127–8). But Connolly makes clear that such a multi-dimensional cultivation of pluralism is not an abdication of critical political action:

A public ethos of deep pluralism does not eliminate politics from life or sink into a tub of beautiful souls. It is itself an effect of micro- and macro-politics. It forms the lifeblood of democratic politics by folding creativity and generosity into intra-cultural negotiations over issues unsusceptible to settlement through pre-existing procedure, principle, or interest aggregation alone. On this reading, arts of the self, micro-politics, private and public deliberation, a generous ethos of engagement, and macro-political action are interconnected, even though valuable dissonances and disturbances well up between them. (Connolly 2002, 137)

What Connolly writes below provides us pathways of a multi-dimensional pluralism:

A pluralizing culture embodies a *micropolitics* of action by the self on itself and the small-scale assemblage upon itself, a *politics of disturbance* through which sedimented identities and moralities are rendered more alert to the deleterious effects of their naturalization upon difference, *a politics of enactment* through which new possibilities of being are propelled into established constellations, *a politics of representational assemblages* through which general policies are processed through the state, a *politics of interstate relations,* and a *politics of nonstatist, cross-national movements* through which external/internal pressure is placed on corporate and state-centered priorities. (1995, xxi)

Connolly's outline of a new vision of normative pluralism has inspiring pedigrees both in Western as well as non-Western imaginations and social experiments. In the Western tradition we are reminded of the pathway of "cooperative pluralism" that Herder had charted, and the vision of a non-assimilationist and non-dual pluralism that Uberoi outlines building upon both Gandhi and the hermetic tradition of Europe (cf. Dallmayr 1998; Uberoi 2002). For Herder, cultural and historical diversity do not entirely cancel a certain commonality, a link fashioned by universal human sympathy (Dallmayr 1998, 34). His project of cooperative pluralism was accompanied by a trenchant critique of state and militarism. Herder's project of cooperative pluralism finds a creative resonance in Uberoi's project of non-dual pluralism. Building on both Goethe and Gandhi, he writes in his *European Modernity: Truth, Science and Method,*

> ...under a regime of pluralist non-dualism, all human differences and partitions are negotiable in civil society as a "community of sovereignties" because no one reality or truth falsifies another... In effect our common humanity thereby returns to the perennial fashion of the Hermetic tradition of Europe, and produces neither simple homogeneity (equality) nor heterogeneity (inequality) but a new non-dualist axis of correlation and mediation, correspondence and complementarity. (Uberoi 2002, 130)

All these creative experiments in pluralism find a resonance in Dallmayr's project of integral pluralism, which pleads for units of pluralism to go beyond their logic of monadism, self-justification and closure, and communicate with each other. For Dallmayr, "pluralism harbors a danger that curiously approximates it again to the monistic temptation. Carried to the extreme of radical fragmentation or dispersal, pluralism – despite its protestations – shades over into an assembly of fixed and self-enclosed monadic units exhibiting the same static quality as its counterpart" (Dallmayr 2010, 8–9). He elaborates his project with a discussion of the work of Gandhi, Dewey, Gadamer, Merleau-Ponty and Raimundo Panikkar, among others. Specifically taking cues from Merleau-Ponty, Dallmayr offers integral pluralism as a form of communication which is more than a mere sharing of ideas "but a 'community of *doing*'... a sharing of practices, which includes a willingness to learn about unfamiliar practices, rituals, rites, and customs," which "in turn, involves a form of existential participation or engagement – a participation in past memories, present agonies, and future hopes and aspirations" (Dallmayr 2010, 122).

Dallmayr's project of integral pluralism can be linked to the Bahudha[2] pathway of pluralism in Indian traditions, which is evident in such lines as *Ekam Sat Vipra Vahuda Vadanti* – "Truth is one but the Wise speak it differently" (Rig Veda 1.164.46). But the Bahudha approach also offers a multi-sided view of Truth as, for instance, in the mode of reasoning and acting called *Anekantavada*, which urges us to realize that Truth has many dimensions and any one-sided exclusionary construction of it leads to violence. Anekantavada was nourished in Jain traditions and it is directly "related to Mahavira's philosophy of non-violence" (Singh 2008, 96).[3] As V. P. Singh interprets this pathway, "We have to recognize that ordinary violence is rooted in dogmatic but mistaken knowledge claims that fail to recognize other legitimate perspectives. Anekantavada provides us with an alternative epistemology to support dialogue among people of diverse viewpoints... It does not mean conceding that all views are valid. It does suggest, however, that logic and evidence determine the validity of a given view" (2008, 97). For Singh, "Anekantavada allows us to accept a pluralistic approach to reality" (2008, 97). Anekantavada and the broader bahudha approach to pluralism emphasize public policy of harmony and the crucial significance of education in this project.

Many other thinkers in the recent times have also elaborated concretely the economic and political implications of rethinking pluralism. In her work *Mayan Visions: The Quest for Autonomy in an Age of Globalization*, anthropologist June Nash (2001) shows how realization of pluralism in the face of a monological corporate globalization calls for sustaining and developing plural bases of production and cultural reproduction. Speaking of the Zapatista's revolution in Mexico to reclaim their land and to have autonomous development, Nash urges us to realize that the Zapatistas are "hatching the foundation for a pluricultural coexistence based on their existence as distinct indigenous entities within regions characterized by a multiplicity of languages and customs" (2001, 244). The Zapatistas urge us to take note of the pluricultural premises of economy, governance and the "global significance of autonomy in the constitution of a pluricultural state" (Nash 2001, 244).

To this pluralized vision of economy and governance, Will Kymlicka and his followers in the evolving global discourse of multiculturalism add the issue of a multicultural plural political organization. For Kymlicka (1995), "Many liberals hoped that the new emphasis on 'human rights' would resolve minority conflicts" (Kymlicka 1995, 2). "However, it has become increasingly clear that minority rights cannot be subsumed under the category of human rights. Traditional human rights standards are simply unable to resolve some of the most important and controversial questions relating to cultural minorities: which languages should be recognized in Parliaments, bureaucrats and courts" (Kymlicka 1995, 4). But Kymlicka himself writes, "Though it is important to supplement traditional human rights with minority rights but minority rights need to coexist with human rights [and be] limited by principles of individual liberty, democracy and social justice" (1995, 6).

Gurpreet Mahajan, an Indian political theorist, also presents us with some new challenges in thinking about pluralism. She urges us to understand the core significance of non-discrimination in democracy and how pursuit of pluralism and cultural diversity ought to be accompanied by commitment to a principle of non-discrimination. Mahajan writes, "…in a multi-cultural democratic polity, the pursuit of cultural diversity needs to be mediated through the concern of non-discrimination vis-à-vis assimilation, likewise the principle of non-discrimination needs to be given priority vis-à-vis the unconditional pursuit of cultural diversity" (Mahajan 2002, 215). For her "special rights [for minorities] have to be structured in a way that takes cognisance of…the undetermined nature of cultures" (Mahajan 2002, 215). She urges us to go beyond the state-centric view of pluralism and statist guarantee of special community rights in the name of pluralism. Furthermore, community rights and individual rights need not be seen in opposition:

> Against the backdrop of a homogenizing nation-state that almost always embodies the culture of the majority, cultural community rights and individual rights have been transformed into binary opposites. It is assumed that discrimination of minorities can only be overcome by granting special community rights. It appears that individual rights have little or no role to play in this. [But] the two are not mutually exclusive. While special rights given to cultural communities can help to correct the majoritarian biases of the nation-state and enable minorities to retain their identity, individual rights are essential, and indispensable, for protecting minorities from discrimination by the actions of other groups in society. (Mahajan 2002, 204)

Both Kymlicka and Mahajan call for the need to combine individual rights and community rights, but they need to touch upon the obligation that individuals and communities have to learn from each other, enter each other and tolerate each other at a deeper level of self, not only as a politically mandated thing. In this context, Michael Walzer brings up the issue of individual responsibility in an interesting manner. He writes, "As an American Jew, I grew up thinking of myself as an object of toleration. It was only much later that I recognized myself as a subject too, an agent called upon to tolerate others, including fellow Jews whose idea of what Jewishness meant differed radically from my own" (Walzer 1997, xi).

Rethinking Rights as a Verb: Beyond Universalism and Particularism and a Non-dual Embodiment of Responsibility

Dominant conceptions of pluralism are founded upon a rights-based approach, and though thinkers such as Connolly urge us to overcome their legalistic binding by cultivating an ethos of pluralization, there is still the stupendous task of overcoming the pervasive influence and valorization of rights discourse. This discourse lacks a perspective and practice of responsibility. The discourse had emerged in the midst of modernist revolutions and now it needs to be supplemented, not replaced, by a radical practice and a perspective of responsibility, especially as rights-based approaches are inadequate to come to terms with challenges such as environmental disasters and human responsibility to nature (Strydom 2000).

When once asked about the issue of rights, Gandhi said, "I do not know what rights means I only know duties." Though the discourse of duty and obligation has been used by hierarchical systems of caste, colonialism and gender to deny the rights of individuals, going to the other extreme of only rights is fraught with dangers. Moreover, different cultures have different conceptions of the relationship between rights and duties that a discourse of pluralism and human rights needs to open itself to. African philosopher Kwasi Wiredu helps us understand this: "On the face of it, the normative layer in the Akan (an African tribe) concept of person brings only obligation to the individual. In fact, however, these obligations are matched by a whole series of rights that accrue to the individual simply because s/he lives in a society in which every one has these obligations" (Wiredu 1996, 160). From this Wiredu goes on to elaborate the rights that are respected in the Akan land in Nigeria: a) the right to trial, b) the right to land, and c) religious freedom. On the first issue of the right to trial, Wiredu tells us, "...it was an absolute principle of Akan justice that no human being could be punished without trial" (1996, 164). On the right to land, Wiredu tells us, "Any human being was held, by virtue of his blood principle (*mogya*), to be entitled to some land. For the duration of his life any Akan had the right to the use of a piece of lineage land. However land was supposed to belong to the whole lineage, conceived as including the ancestors, the living members and those yet to be born" (Wiredu 1996, 165).[4]

Wiredu writes, "...so long as a custom has a rationale, it has at least, a qualified universality via its trans-cultural universality" (1996, 32). While rights such as rights to land, free trial and religious freedom embody universalizing human rights in Akan culture, certain aspects of Akan culture do not embody this. One such relates to the traditional belief and custom that a person should be killed to accompany the dead chief in his journey to the other world. Here Wiredu urges his fellow Akans, and us, to apply an internal critical perspective of sympathetic universality in valuing such customs:

> Equal respect is a requirement of sympathetic impartiality. Now the fact is that, in spite of the profound respect that the Akans had for their chiefs, few cherished the notion of being killed in order to have the honor of serving their chiefs on their last journey. Accordingly, sympathetic impartiality should have destroyed that custom before birth. In general, no rights can justifiably be superseded in a manner oblivious to the principle of sympathetic impartiality. (Wiredu 1996, 170)

For Wiredu, "A successful excercise in conceptual decolonization will usually be an unmasking of a spurious universal" (1996, 5). Shiv Visvanathan also urges us to go beyond the spurious divide between the West and non-West, universal and particular, in thinking about rights. Visvanathan writes, "...the question is not whether rights is universal but whether the notion of rights is inventive enough to be life-giving. Also, does the framework of rights, to use a Heideggerian term, provide a proper sense of *dwelling* to these societies" (Visvanathan 1996, 113). Visvanathan further challenges us to realize: "Saying rights is only a Western invention creates a stereotypical view of rights. It misses the creative acts of translation that the rights language is creating… When Castro says that the whole world has a right to Cuban research on sugar, he is challenging the dominant ideology of the rights, creating a dialogue of rights reminding the West of worlds it has forgotten…" (Visvanathan 1996, 117). For Visvanathan, "The notion of rights is only a thin layer…protecting the isolated I in the world of the nation-state. But what has been destroyed in a deep way is the commons of nature and communities between state and citizen" (Visvanathan 1996, 125).[5] He further argues: "A right is not a linear index. It is also what Mary Daly calls a knot, a myriad set of connections, a labyrynth, a maze. What Gandhi said of khadi should be equally true of rights. Khadi, he claimed, is not about cloth but about love, freedom and self-reliance" (Visvanathan 1996, 141).

Visvanathan quotes Wayne Booth, who tells us in his Oxford Amnesty Lectures, "human rights is an affirmation of the mystery, the inexhaustibility of personhood" (1996, 143). For Visvanathan, "we need to recover the 'I' as a bundle of possibilities that the Enlightenment has suppressed so unhistorically…" (1996, 142). The "I" in this Enlightenment discourse has been imprisoned within an ideology of possessive individualism and blindness of anthropocentrism, and now both the "I" and the notion of being human have to be broadened; they must be thought of as verbs rather than as a possessive pronoun and nouns. The challenge here is to rethink human rights as a verb, and for this we need to "provincialize Europe" (cf. Chakraborty 2001), realizing that its construction of human rights is only one path, and undertake a cross-civilization journey in order to realize that human rights as a verb is intimately connected with the practice and perspective of the commons and is intimately tied to the calling of responsibility. The challenge for us is to realize that a theory of rights without an ethics of caring would be fatal.

Cultivating Pluralism and Rights as Meditative Verbs of Co-realizations: The Calling of Non-dual Responsibility and the Development of Human Civilization

Human rights are verbs, and so are processes of pluralization.[6] But are they only activistic verbs?[7] Engagement with rights helps us realize that these are not simply activistic but also meditative. Both rights and pluralism go beyond mere epistemic pluralism and involve continuous questing and ontological transformation. It is a work of ontological epistemology of action, meditation, participation and transformation. While conventional pluralism emphasizes action with very little attention to the need for meditation, creative and transformative pluralization calls for action, mediations and meditations. Pluralization here embodies meditative verbs of co-realization of different parts of the interacting field of pluralism. It embodies a new art of border crossing between individuals and groups and their cultures and world views.

Pioneers of a new normative pluralism such as Connolly plead for the pluralization of self and society. But having a pluralized conception of self and society is only the first step, and it is crucial to interpenetrate this plurivocity with a vision and practice of responsibility, because it is responsibility which enables us to have a proper relationship of autonomy and interpenetration between different domains, dimensions, levels and realities, conceptualized aprioristically as dualistic. For many, an invocation of pluralism spells danger for the realization of rights, as in the name of pluralism we can easily justify violations of rights and human dignity. This concern is not unfounded, as many dictators around the world have used a version of pluralism and relativism to justify their suppression of rights. In this context, a key challenge is to have a logic of pluralism which is beyond the established binary logic of universalism and particularism (cf. Cistelecan 2011). We need a multi-valued logic in thinking about and realizing creatively the relationship between the "universal" and "particular" (Mohanty 2000a). Our basic problem is that the universal and particular are conceptualized in a closed manner, and now we should think about the particular and the universal in an emergent and open-ended way. What we conceptualize as local and particular has already within itself an opening for the universal – there is an emergent dimension within it. We need to develop a notion of emergent universalism and emergent particularism to help us go beyond the dualism of universalism and particularism.[8]

Similarly, pluralism is also a meditative verb embodying simultaneously action, meditation, mediation and transformations. This is suggested in Wilfred's (2008, 93) recent explorations of the paths of what he calls "contemplative pluralism," which helps us go beyond the violence emanating from an imperialistic universalism and an annihilating particularism.[9] We find it in the works of savants such as Raimundo Panikkar. Panikkar was born into a Catholic family. He studied the Vedas, starting his initial journey as a Catholic priest, and his *The Vedic Experience Mantramanjari: An Anthopology of the Vedas for Modern Man and Contemporary Celebration* (Panikkar 1977) is a testament to a meditative and contemplative pluralization he undertook, which is an invitation for all of us concerned. For Panikkar, "...we can [and should] be Christians, while also being Jews and Muslims, Buddhists and Taoists...since in our innermost beings we carry the legacy of religions from which we have lived and we seek to live. We can only become better Christians through being, at the same time, in our hearts Buddhists or Muslims...in an *interior dialogue* that respects the difference among religions, without trying to level them all by force but leaving them to purify themselves through mutual contact" (Pikaza 2010, 119–20).

Going beyond violence and realizing non-violence in discourse and practice is an important normative challenge here; in fact, we can rethink the very notion of the normative from an ideal of and striving for non-violence. Mohanty (2000b) makes this connection between non-violence in philosophical discourse, modes of reasoning and modes of action. Non-violence is a key theme in the strivings of Gandhi and it is my submission that normative pluralism and human rights now need to be broadened and deepened by a new notion of the normative emanating from our ideals and practices of non-violent imagination and social struggles. But the normative ideal of non-violence is also dear to critical philosophers in the contemporary West such as Vattimo (1999), Ricouer (2000) and Habermas. Consider here the following lines of Habermas: "Only when philosophy discovers in the dialectical course of history the traces of violence that deform repeated attempts at dialogue and recurrently closes off the path to unconstrained communication does it further the process whose suspension it otherwise legitimates: mankind's evolution toward autonomy and responsibility" (Habermas 1971, 315). Norberto Bobbio urges us to see this violence in both war and poverty, and while rethinking pluralism and rights we could provisionally conclude with his passionate calling for development of human civilization:

> The implementation of a better system for protecting human rights is linked to the global development of human civilization. If the problem is taken in isolation, then there is a risk not only that it will not be resolved, but that its true significance will not even be understood. One cannot abstract the problem of human rights from the great problems of our time, which are war and poverty, the abstract contrast between the excess of *power* which created the conditions for a genocidal war and the excess of *impotence* which has condemned the great majority of humanity to hunger. This is the only context in which we can approach the problems of human rights realistically. We must not be so pessimistic that we give up in despair, but neither must we be so optimistic that we become over-confident. (Bobbio 1999, 30; also see Samaddar 2011)

Notes

1 Speaking of the plural conception of an individual, we also need to be open to the trans-individual and non-individual dimensions in an individual. The first point is made by Buddhist thinker Sulak Sivaraksha, and the second point is made by Chantal Mouffe (cf. Clammer 2008; Baxi 2011). For understanding the trans-individual dimension of individual which can help us in rethinking the individualist framing of human rights in modernity, what Clammer writes deserves our careful consideration:

> In much the same way that Louis Dumont has argued that Western individualism has its roots in Christianity and that the consequences of this individualism are profound for the arrangement of society and assumptions about how relationships within it work, so Sulak is arguing for a 'trans-individualism' that arises from Buddhist roots, and which has profound implications for the ordering of society. (2008, 190)

2 As V. P. Singh tells us about the Bahudha approach:

> Etymologically speaking, the word *Bahu*, and *dha* is suffixed to it to make it an adverb. "Bahu" denotes many ways or parts or forms of directions. It is used to express manifoldness, much, and repeatedly. When the word is used with the root *kri*, it means to make manifold or multiply. *Bahudha* is also used an expression of intermittent continuity in various time frames. (Singh 2008, xi –xii)

3 In this context, what K. S. Singh (2011), the heart-touching anthropologist and seeker of pluralism, writes in his posthumous work also deserves our careful attention:

> It should be noted that while diversity of perceptions, approaches, and practices are recognized by some schools including those of the idealist philosophy, it is Anekantavada described by S. Radhakrishnan as a doctrine of realistic pluralism that tries to explore diversity logically and in depth.

...there are three tenets of Anekantavada. One, that there is a possibility of many perceptions of an object; two that everything is relative and multi-dimensional; and three, that there is an in-built co-existence of opposites, that one dimension is as possible as another and it is only in relation to other factors like time, place, and context that one dimension gains predominance over another. All this is subsumed under the doctrine of *syadavada* or *saptabhangi*. From the acceptance of the multi-dimensional nature of objects and their probability is derived the moral imperative of *ahimsa* or non-violence.

4 The dialogue that Wiredu undertakes between human rights discourse and Akan perspectives finds a creative resonance in the dialogue that Damien Keown recently undertakes between human rights and Buddhism:

Human rights can be extrapolated from Buddhist moral teachings...using the logic of moral relationships to illumine what is due under *Dharma*. A direct translation of the first four precepts yields a right to life, a right not to have one's property stolen, a right to fidelity in marriage, and a right not to be lied to. Many other human rights, such as the rights to liberty and security can either be deduced from or are extant within the general corpus of Buddhist moral teachings. A right not to be held in slavery, for example, is implicit in the canonical prohibition on trade in living beings. These rights are extrapolation of what is due under *Dharma*; they have not been "imported" into Buddhism but were always implicitly present. (Keown 2007, 266)

The exploration that Keown undertakes between Buddhism and human rights brings us to the complex terrain of the relationship between religious traditions and the striving for human rights in our plural worlds. While the dominant story in the Euro-American world is that of religions opposing human rights in the medieval and early modern periods, there is also a much more creative relationship between striving for human rights and the struggle for reform in religious traditions in Europe and around the world. As Banchoff and Wuthnow tell us in an impressive recent volume on the subject:

The movement from the Middle Ages to Modernity via the wars of religion and Enlightenment was not a simple story of the eclipse of religious authority by a new discourse about individual freedom, self-determination, and human rights. It is better read as the story of struggles within and across religious and non-religious communities about how to adapt to the rise of modernity, with its markets, laws and individualist ethos. For centuries, scholars, leaders, and followers across traditions have differed on core issues, including whether democracy – the rule of the people – is compatible with God's rule, and whether respect for the rights of individuals is compatible with duties to the wider social and moral order. (Banchoff and Wuthnow 2011, 5)

5 Herbert Reid and Betsy Taylor (2010) in their inspiring work, *Recovering the Commons: Democracy, Place, and Global Justice*, also draw our attention to the significance of the commons in rethinking rights and realizing justice. They also propose a folded ontology of the individual in place of the flat of ontology of the modern self, what they call "ecological ontology." This ecological ontology can help us realize rights as part of striving for common goods and an ecology of well-being which can also be linked to what M. S. Swaminathan calls the "ecology of hope" (cf. Ikeka and Swaminathan 2005).

6 Betsy Taylor explores the implications of my concept of knowledge as verb. For her, it urges us not only to look at and realize persons, institutions and discourse as "'verb', an unfolding

over time" but also those arising "in the synapses of self with other, self with world, and self with self" (2011, 112).

7 This seems to be the case with majority of scholars in this field. For instance, Gayatri Chakravorty Spivak tells us, "Activate is the key word here." As she writes: "Human rights activism should be supplemented by an education that should suture the habits of democracy into earlier cultural formation. I think that the real effort should be to access and activate..." (Spivak 2011, 96).

8 In this context, what Maria Christina Astorga writes deserves our attention:

> What we aim at is a culturally-inclusive universalism, where universal human values find valency and legitimacy in cultures and cultural values grounded in universal human rights. For culturally-inclusive universalism to be achieved, there must be a continuing cross-cultural conversation and education at the level of both theory and practice. (2010, 95)

9 In the words of Wilfred,

> We need a contemplative approach to pluralism rather than a systemic or epistemic one. Epistemic pluralism is operative when pluralism is structured into a system, and the differences are viewed but as various expressions of a well-defined unified concept, doctrine, etc.... The plurality resulting from the difference of gender, culture, soil, language, and historical spaces are such that they do not permit us to conclude as if the differences are variations of one single concept, or to force them all into the procrustean bed in the name of a common ground... Contemplative pluralism does not deny the need for unity behind plurality but simply says that the unity is not to be viewed as something already available or given...but as something hidden and forming an object of our continuous quest that is refreshing and transforming. (2008, 93)

References

Astorga, Maria Christina. 2010. "Human Rights from an Asian Perspective: The Challenge of Diversity and the Limits to Universality." *Concilium* 2010 (3): 88–98.
Banchoff, Thomas and Robert Wuthnow, eds. 2011. *Religion and the Global Politics of Human Rights*. New York: Oxford University Press.
Baxi, Upendra. 2011. "Critiquing Rights: The Politics of Identity and Difference." In Aakash Singh Rathore and Alex Cistelecan, eds, *Wronging Rights? Philosophical Challenges for Human Rights*, 61–78. Delhi: Routledge.
_____. 2007. *Human Rights in a Posthuman World*. Delhi: Oxford University Press.
_____. 2000. *The Future of Human Rights*. Delhi: Oxford University Press.
Béteille, Andre. 1997. *Society and Politics in India*. Delhi: Oxford University Press.
Bobbio, Norbert. 1999. *The Age of Rights*. Cambridge: Polity Press.
Cistelecan, Alex. 2011. "Which Critique of Human Rights? Evaluating the Postcolonial and the Post-Althusserian Alternatives." In Aakash Singh Rathore and Alex Cistelecan, eds, *Wronging Rights? Philosophical Challenges for Human Rights*, 3–20. Delhi: Routledge.
Chakrabarty, Dipesh. 2001. *Provincializing Europe: Postcolonial Thought and Historical Difference*. Princeton: Princeton University Press.
Clammer, John R. 2008. *Diaspora and Belief: Globalisation, Religion and Identity in Postcolonial Asia*. Delhi: Shipra.
Connolly, William E. 1995. *The Ethos of Pluralization*. Minneapolis: University of Minnesota Press.
_____. 1999. *Why I Am Not a Secularist*. Minneapolis: University of Minnesota Press.
_____. 2002. *Neuropolitics: Thinking, Culture, Speed*. Minneapolis: University of Minnesota Press.

_____. 2007. "The Ethos of Revenge." *Communication and Critical Cultural Studies* 4 (1): 93–7.

Dallmayr, Fred. 1998. *Alternative Visions: Pathways in the Global Village*. Lanham, MD: Rowman & Littlefield.

_____. 2010. *Integral Pluralism: Beyond Culture Wars*. Lexington: University of Kentucky Press.

Geertz, Clifford. 1983. *Local Knowledge: Further Essays in Interpretive Anthropology*. New York: Basic Books.

Habermas, Jürgen. 1971. *Knowledge and Human Interest*. Boston: Beacon Press.

_____. 1998. *The Inclusion of the Other: Studies in Political Theory*. Cambridge: Polity Press.

Keown, Damien. 2007. "Are there 'Human Rights' in Buddhism?" In Purushottam Bilmoria, Joseph Prabhu and Renuka Sharma, eds, *Indian Ethics: Classical Traditions and Contemporary Challenges*, 231–68. Delhi: Oxford University Press.

Kymplicka, Will. 1995. *Multicultural Citizenship: A Liberal Theory of Minority Rights*. Oxford: Clarendon Press.

Mahajan, Gurpreet. 2002. *The Multicultural Path: Issues of Diversity and Discrimination in Democracy*. New Delhi: Sage.

Mohanty, J. N. 2000a. *Self and Other: Philosophical Essays*. Delhi: Oxford University Press.

_____. 2000b. "Gandhi's Truth." In Krishna Roy, ed., *Fusion of Horizons: Socio-Spiritual Heritage of India*. New Delhi: Allied Publishers.

Mohanty, Manoranjan et al., eds. 1998. *People's Rights: Social Movements and the State in the Third World*. Delhi: Sage.

Pikaza, Xavier. 2010. "Raimon Panikkar (1918–2010)." *Concilium* 2010 (5): 117–20.

Nash, June C. 2001. *Mayan Visions: The Quest for Autonomy in an Age of Globalization*. New York: Routledge.

Rathore, Aakash Sing and Alex Cistelecan. 2011. *Wronging Rights? Philosophical Challenges for Human Rights*. Delhi: Routledge.

Reid, Herbert and Betsy Taylor. 2010. *Recovering the Commons: Democracy, Place and Global Justice*. Champaign: University of Illinois Press.

Ricouer, Paul. 2000. *The Just*. Chicago: University of Chicago Press.

Samaddar, Ranabir. 2011. "Rights after Globalisation." In Ray Chaudhury, Sabysachi Basu and Ishita Dey, eds, *Sustainability of Rights After Globalisation*, 212–37. Delhi: Sage.

Singh, K. S. 2011. *Diversity, Identity, and Linkages: Explorations in Historical Ethnography*. Delhi: Oxford University Press.

Singh, V. P. 2008. *Bahudha and the Post 9/11 World*. Delhi: Oxford University Press.

Spivak, G. C. 2011. "Righting Wrongs." In ." In Aakash Singh Rathore and Alex Cistelecan, eds, *Wronging Rights? Philosophical Challenges for Human Rights*, 79–104. Delhi: Routledge.

Sri Aurobindo. 1962. *Human Cycles*. Pondicherry: Sri Aurobindo Ashram.

Strydom, Piet. 2000. *Discourse and Knowledge: The Making of Enlightenment Sociology*. Liverpool: Liverpool University Press.

Swaminathan, M. S. and Daisaku Ikeda. 2005. *Revolutions: To Green the Environment, to Grow the Human Heart: A Dialogue Between M. S. Swaminathan and Daisaku Ikeda*. Chennai: East-West Books.

Taylor, Betsy. 2011. "Civil Society, Social Movements and Alternative Development: Implications of Giri's Notion of Knowledge." *Sociological Bulletin* 60 (1).

Uberoi, J. P. S. 2002. *The European Modernity: Truth, Science and Method*. Delhi: Oxford University Press.

Vattimo, Gianni. 1999. *Belief*. Cambridge: Polity Press.

Visvanathan, Shiv. 1996. "On Unravelling Rights." *Studies in Humanities and Social Sciences* 2 (2): 109–49.

Walzer, Michael. 1997. *On Toleration*. New Haven: Yale University Press.

Wilfred, Felix. 2008. "Christological Pluralism: Some Reflections." *Concilium* 3: 84–94.

Wiredu, Kwasi. 1996. *Cultural Universals and Particulars*. Bloomington: Indiana University Press.

Chapter Eleven

THE CALLING OF A NEW CRITICAL THEORY: SELF-DEVELOPMENT, INCLUSION OF THE OTHER AND PLANETARY REALIZATIONS

Oh Friend, Oh Dear Soul,
You asked, you asked
The embrace of my heart
Our questions are not only questions
Nor are they bombs nor edges of the sword
Our questions are flows – one and many
Flows of our hearts
In between flowers and hammers
Our questions are our stories
Of bathing together and searching together
Of Being Drowned and Rising Again

—A poem originally written in Odia by the author
and self-translated into English (2008)

The social process of the discursive construction of reality is a transformative cognitive process. On the one hand, it draws on existing knowledge and cognitive structures and, on the other, it generates new knowledge and new cognitive structures and brings about their selective coordination.

—Piet Strydom, *Risk, Environment and Society* (2002, 150)

I have sought to draw art and craft together, because all techniques contain expressive implications. This is true of making a pot; it is also equally true of raising a child.

—Richard Sennett, *The Craftsman* (2008, 290)

Introduction and Invitation

Piet Strydom is a creative and critical seeker of our contemporary world who has asked many questions and has also created spaces of mutual learning and collective blossoming. Strydom originally comes from South Africa, and his critique of the then-prevailing apartheid regime made him homeless. He first came to England and then settled down in Ireland, where he has taught at the pre-eminent University College Cork for more than three decades. While teaching at Cork, he embodied a new mode of critique and creativity, which has presented his students and fellow learners a critical and creative way of blossoming beyond the gaze of the authorities, and some of his students are now leading practitioners of social theory.[1]

Strydom has made valuable contributions to continental traditions of critical social theory which have many insights for all seekers of knowledge and human liberation beyond the Euro-American world. His concept of "triple contingency" and his other ideas, such as "triple contingency learning," resonance, socio-cognitive critique, and emergent frames of co-responsibility, are valuable contributions to critical theory. As a heart-touching teacher and fellow seeker, Strydom has inspired so many of us around the world to explore new horizons of learning. What is touching is the way Strydom combines critical engagement with a deep passion for emergent normativity, one which invites us to take sociological analytics to a new normative heights and depths. In outlining the contours of a new socio-cognitive critique in his book *Risk, Environment and Society*, Strydom pleads for a non-judgmental critical engagement: "Far from judging and condemning the ideology of a particular actor or agent…it is a matter of closely studying a variety of related cognitive processes and structures. Included are the frames and normative codes of all participants, despite their conflicting interpretations of it…" (Strydom 2002, 156). In his pioneering work, *Discourse and Knowledge: The Making of Enlightenment Sociology*, Strydom urges us to understand the limits of the rights and justice frames of modernity and open ourselves to the emergent frames of co-responsibility. In his recent essay, "Risk Communication: World Creation Through Collective Learning Under Complex Contingent Conditions," Strydom (2006) tells us how "different configurations of public spheres allow distinct learning processes" and invites us to accept the challenge of triple contingency learning: "Triple contingency learning represents the collective learning mechanism which brings us closest to the communicative self-constitution and self-organization of society… It harbors the 'cosmopolitan' promise of a transformative moment in which a 'creative combination of different forces' occurs" (2006, 9).

Continuing this inspiring spirit of a deeper normative critique and transformation, Strydom urges us to go beyond the contest of faculties, especially arts and sciences, and nurture a different relationship with science, scholarship and time. For Strydom, "Science is a much slower field than politics, not to mention economics" (2004b, 8). When science is "being steadily accelerated and stresses up well beyond its own time culture" social scientists have to contribute to the epochal need of "the unhastening or deceleration of science" (Strydom 2004b, 8).

In reflecting upon the issue of contest of faculties between arts and sciences, Strydom invites us to a new "chrono-politics." But this needs to be part of a multi-dimensional striving to cultivate a new relationship with time and generate a space of mutual nurturance and generosity – a new *chrono-spirituality*. Cultivating a new relationship with time calls for appropriate self-cultivation and spaces of value formation, along with structural transformations of the organizations of living. It also calls for cultivating a mode of non-anxiety vis-à-vis our living and the flow of time. This is not only a political process but also a spiritual process where spirituality refers to a continued quest for the critique, transformation, and overcoming of boundaries which have been turned into prisons, and the creation of relationships of beauty and dignity. Similarly, the emergent frames of responsibility are not only socio-political but also socio-spiritual, and responsibility does not emerge only in public spheres but also involves practices of self-development and transformation which are not reducible to the public. Strydom's preference for the concept of "co-responsibility" that he adapted from from Karl-Otto Apel, over and above the more usual "collective responsibility," is "precisely to make room for the individual who also has to come to embody personally the responsibility that is required at the macro-level" (personal communication; also see Strydom 2009). What Strydom wrote to me recently on this issue is helpful to understand his project:

> My account [of responsibility] covers all the different dimensions, including different versions of the personal or individual, but the main point…is of course to argue about the new development of a macro-ethic. But the fact that it is macro does not mean that it is only macro. From the cognitive view that I hold, there is always mediation between the micro (individual, personal), meso (e.g. groups, institutions and social movements) and the macro (societal) levels. At the individual or personal level, the cognitive structures cover all the dimensions, from the intellectual (epistemic), through the moral (conscience) to the ethical/aesthetic/conative – and at this latter level of emotional and motivational identity formation lies, in my view, the well-spring of what you call the spiritual. I've never excluded this dimension. All I haven't been doing is to explicitly elaborate, as you do, the theme of the cultivation of this dimension in itself and its relation to the other dimensions.

At the same time, emergent frames of responsibility are not only socio-political but also spiritual, and responsibility does not emerge only in public spheres of even Strydom's reformulated concept of public communication, but also involves practices of self-development and transformation which are not reducible to the public. These are also not solely epistemic processes; they involve ontological processes of self-cultivation and self-transformation. Strydom's inspiring critical theory, like much of continental critical theory, is still primarily epistemic, and its brilliance can now be transformed into manifold creative pathways of an ontological epistemology of participation, going beyond the dualism of ontology and epistemology (see the previous chapter). Strydom's deep engagement with the environmental challenges of our times calls for a foundational border crossing, for example transforming anthropocentrism to a new political and spiritual struggle for dignity of life and "cross-species dignity" (cf. Giri 2006, Nussbaum 2006). Strydom's plea for a non-judgmental critical theory – one which listens to all contending voices rather than quickly identifies with an *a priori* "legitimationist" perspective (this is how Strydom (1999) characterizes Habermas's approach to the public sphere) – reflects an openness to "multi-valued logic" (cf. Mohanty 2000). Strydom's critical theory can realize much of its potential by building on and contributing to self-development, the inclusion of the other and planetary realizations.

The Calling of a New Critical Theory: Learning with Piet Strydom

In the concluding chapter of his *Risk, Environment and Society*, entitled "Towards a New Critical Theory," Strydom writes,

> Since the late 1980s, finally, I have sought to extrapolate and develop what I provisionally call the new cognitive sociology from the cognitive turn in sociology and subsequent advances. Rather than concentrating on practices as such, whether communication, discursive negotiation, strategizing, competition, conflict or networking, none of which is of course jettisoned, the focal concern here is the variable structural models of practical action. (2002, 149)

In developing a new critical theory at the heart of which lies what he calls "socio-cognitive critique," Strydom (2002) creatively builds on both what he calls the new cognitive revolution and social constructivism, and, at the same time, imparts to this confluence his own characteristic originality. For Strydom, the cognitive turn questions,

> …the function of norms in social action and interaction by rejecting the traditional assumptions of norms as being consistent and extending a determining influence. Instead, it emphasized the need to develop a sensitivity for and an ability to identify the whole range of culturally defined alternatives to practices and the construction and organization of society. Casualties of the change were such modernist notions as the unitary concept of modernity, the linear concept of progress, the progressivist or developmental concept of evolution, the identification of modernity and universalism and so forth. (Strydom 2002, 180)

Such questioning resonates with some of the most important themes in contemporary critical theory such contingency, disjunction between facts and norms, the work of antinomies in self, culture and society, and critique of linearity (Giri 2007; Béteille 2000). Strydom gives a cognitive thrust to social constructivism: "Constructivism, in my view, is best seen from a cognitive theoretical point of view that acknowledges both intersubjective understanding and the objectivity of reality with which we maintain pragmatic relations" (2002, 151). Thus, with care, Strydom prepares the following pathways of "socio-cognitive critique":

a) It is based upon a "relational conception of the social world, with the emphasis therefore being less on static substances and entities…" (2002, 153);

b) It is both a "critique of the status quo and a critique of utopianism" (2002, 153);

c) "To fulfill the requirements of socio-cognitive critique, the whole network of different cognitive processes and structures is investigated." Socio-cognitive critique advances an "understanding of the critical task of sociology" by "distinguishing different types of cognitive structures or models" (2002, 157);

d) Socio-cognitive critique leads to generation of explanatory models which in turn has "epistemic authority." "But the sociologist has no exclusive possession of epistemic authority. Observers and commentators as well as the observing, evaluating and judging public to the very degrees enjoy this same privilege. In fact, often the epistemic authority of the sociologist depends on such a third point of view" (2002, 157).

Socio-cognitive critique is thus related to the work of "triple contingency" in the self, culture and society, and this mode of critique itself is also a mode of triple contingency learning. As stated before, triple contingency learning is a multilateral learning process in which participating actors and institutions learn from and with each other in a multigonal way, embodying an emergent self-constitution and self-organization of society. Socio-cognitive critique is thus a creative process of self-creation of society. Furthermore, socio-cognitive critique not only emerges out of vibrant public communication but also makes sociology public:

> The public role of sociology commences with the making visible of the whole spectrum of different experiences, perceptions, frames and knowledges. This is achieved by locating and heightening the tensions and relating the intersecting lines of creativity and conflict to each other. By adopting such a minimalist mediating role, sociology's aim is to break down the ethnocentricity of perspectives and to contribute to the development of reciprocal perspectives. (Strydom 2002, 158)

The new critical theory that Strydom puts forward with care is born of decades of work. "Triple Contingency" is at the core of Strydom's new critical theory which, for him, can take us from the "neo-classical" to the "post-classical" phase of theorizing (Strydom 2009, xxiii). For Strydom, "…the concept of double contingency needs to make way for a more adequate replacement – namely triple contingency. In the first scenario, two social actors, communicatively acting subjects or black boxes, A and B, face or encounter one another or enter into some relation with each other as 'I' and 'Thou.' In the basic situation of triple contingency, by contrast, there is a third perspective borne by C, who observes what A and B are saying. By so doing C has a constitutive impact on the social situation" (Strydom 1999, 8). Though this third point of view at an earlier stage of Strydom's formulation "represents society" (1999, 8), at a later stage it represents a discursively engaged and learning public which is not just a representation of society and is not bound to a society's "internal mode of justification" (personal communication). Strydom also asks a bold question: "the third point of view: within or beyond society?" and suggests that triple contingency is a product of immanent transcendence. For Strydom, immanent transcendence refers to "the relation between immanence and transcendence as defining of the process of the constitution of social reality, and in particular transcendence as it is represented by counterfactuals" (personal communication). Furthermore, "Critical theory has a stereoscopic perspective: it never focuses only on immanence (the empirical situation), but at the same time and even more importantly on those ideas of reason, normative ideas or cultural models in the form of counterfactuals which have an immanent foothold in people's pragmatic presupposition, assumptions, expectations, anticipations, visions of what ought to be, etc., yet transcend the situation as something unrealised and even unrealisable, but as such nevertheless still structure the situation since people to varying degrees allow themselves to be led by such counterfactuals and try to live up to them and to actualise and realise them immanently" (Strydom 1999, 8). But such a work of immanent transcendence can also involve what can be called transcendental immanence, where transcendence cannot be solely located within society and exists and rises from many other spheres such as the divine, nature and in creative engagements such as art and music. The prophetic traditions in many religions and spiritual pathways have embodied a critique of existing society, and here critique is a work of transcendental immanence and not solely that of immanent transcendence (Quarles van Ufford and Giri 2003, Toynbee 1956 and Vattimo 1999).

Strydom's pioneering concept of triple contingency urges us to explore the ontology of the third so that it again is not related to the first and the second in a dualistic mode and with *a priori* judgment. The third point does not represent only the observing third actor C who is observing A and B, but A and B also have the need to cultivate an observant self in their own selves. For the realization of triple contingency we thus need cultivation of a third observing mode of being and becoming within both the first and the second. In this context the question that Bourdieu asks to participant observation is relevant: "How can one be both subject and object, the one who acts and the one who is, as it were, watching himself acting?" (Bourdieu 2003, 282). Bourdieu himself does not address this issue, as he is primarily confined within "epistemic reflexivity" without accompanying ontological nurturance. But to be able to act and observe one's own action requires cultivation of what is called *sakhi purusha* (witnessing self) in Indian spiritual traditions and what Adam Smith (1976) calls the "impartial spectator." The work of triple contingency thus involves cultivation of an observant self in our own selves. It also calls for giving birth to the third in the life of first and second and in the margins in between, thus heightening the need for participants in and practitioners of triple contingency to be creative mothers of an emergent third in the initial lives of the first and the second.

Though Strydom creatively builds upon Habermas, he nonetheless raises some significant questions to Habermasian critical theory. For Strydom, Habermas does not really understand the distinction between public sphere and public: "...while writing eloquently about double contingency as well as the public sphere, Habermas surprisingly [fails] to capture the role of public in communication societies in a comparably sharp... manner" (2001, 166). For Strydom, Habermas gives priority to "the moral philosophical third point of view to the exclusion of the third perspective of members of society or citizenry" (Strydom 2001, 183). Strydom applies a constructivist and cognitive approach to triple contingency. He considers the Habermasian approach to public sphere and triple contingency "legitimationist" when Habermas privileges social movements in the discursive construction of important concerns of society. But for Strydom, we cannot privilege only social movements: "…other actors or agents who participate in the process of social construction, such as industry, the state, science, the legal profession and the media, should likewise be regarded as vehicles of cognitive processes" (2002, 150–51). Furthermore, for Strydom, in Habermas, "the cognitive is narrowly understood in terms of the individual mind rather than in terms of the more sociologically relevant phenomenon of social knowledge and cultural models" (1999, 12).

Responsibility is an important aspect of the critical theory of Strydom. Building upon philosopher Karl-Otto Apel, Strydom presents responsibility as co-responsibility, which is in tune with his other related strivings in critical theoretical engagement, such as resonance and the public. Strydom (2000) challenges us to acknowledge the limits of the rights and justice frames of modernity, and to transformationally supplement (not replace) them with the emergent visions and practices of responsibility. For Strydom, the rights frame emerged in the early modern revolutions (e.g., the Dutch Revolt of the Netherlands, the English Revolution and the French Revolution). The justice frame arose in the wake of industrial revolution in "late eighteenth century England and continued unabated yet in a sublimated form until the second half of the twentieth century, focused on the problem complex of exploitation, pauperisation and loss of identity…" (Strydom 2000, 20). These two discourses have inspired and influenced socio-political movements in the modern world, but they have now their limits to come to terms with the emergent challenge and calling of responsibility. For example, to come to terms with environmental crisis and the attendant calling of responsibility, the discourses of rights and justice and politics and policies revolving around them have limits. In the face of such challenges, in Strydom's pregnant formulations, "The theory of justice is today making way for another, still newer semantics in the form of the moral theory of responsibility which is crystallizing around a number of intertwined debates about the problem of risk" (Strydom 2000, 20).

Reflecting upon our contemporary condition of risk, and inviting us to his emergent frame of responsibility, Strydom writes,

[T]he competition and conflict point to a new evolutionary departure. The production of risks as well as the authoritarian paternalism by means of which they are institutionally being dealt with have both been revealed as being guided by structures that indeed originated from evolutionary learning processes [but] yet do not possess the universal cognitive import we have assumed until recently. Since these cognitive structures have contributed to both the generation of environmental crisis and to its poor management, they are in need of revision and fine-tuning. The limits around science, technology, industry, capitalism and state or, more generally, the experimenting society must be redrawn in a more precise manner by a new guiding and direction-giving structures developed in practical discourse. Collective responsibility, or co-responsibility, stands for this sort of cognitive structures. (Strydom 2002, 153)

But risk communication is not simply about "problem-solving" but of "creating and bringing a world into being" (Strydom 2006, 4). Risk communication, as the much broader genre of public communication, involves "learning under contingent conditions" where "different configurations of public sphere allow distinct learning processes" (Strydom 2006, 6). Resonance plays an important role in such processes of communication and mutual learning. Strydom quite creatively presents six concentric circles of resonance at work in contemporary communicative societies:

> The smallest circle…represents the formal political or decision-making institutions… The second circle…covers institutions such as statutory bodies, foundations, universities, chambers and so forth which fulfill delegated state functions or have been granted self-administration rights. They could likewise provide the necessary basis for system or institutional resonance. The third circle, representing civil society where it meets the public sphere, embraces a diversity of radically different social actors or agents, from active citizens, associations, organizations and social movements, on the one hand, to business organizations and corporations, on the other. Here business organizations and corporations make available the resonance structure of system or institutional resonance, while active citizens and the associations and organizations growing out of civil society serve as the structural basis of Habermas's civil society resonance and, directly corresponding to it, what Eder conceives as "extra-constitutional resonance." The fourth concentric circle represents the life world in which civil society and, by extension, the public sphere are rooted. The penultimate or fifth circle represents the cultural foundations of the life world, civil society and the public sphere, and as such it provides the cultural resources – i.e. cultural models, schemes, codes, or Gamson's themes and counter themes – upon which actors or agents draw and which they activate in public communication. The sixth and last concentric circle, however, brings to the fore a resonance structure that is of still greater significance, particularly in contemporary communication society, yet is often forgotten, perhaps because it is theoretically not well understood. It represents the public in the sense of the lay egalitarian public audience who observes the actors, agents or players in the public arena, evaluates and judges them, and thus takes a position on the relevance and value of their respective contributions to public communication. (Strydom 2004a, 7–8)

New Critical Theory and the Calling of Transformations

In presenting the picture of resonance, Strydom uses the notion of "concentric circles" and this is a creative one. But these circles are not interpenetrative. "Concentric circles" are also "interpenetrative circles" embodying a multi-dimensional ontology of autonomy and interpenetration (see the previous chapter). In fact the participants in public communication, including the conditions of triple contingency, are not isolated agents. The reciprocal perspectives that Strydom aspires to are possible because of an ontology of autonomy and interpenetration that characterizes the fields that Strydom talks about. Therefore, Strydom now needs to transform his concentric circles into interpenetrative ones. The public resonance that Strydom so inspiringly wants to generate needs adequate self-development, such as self-transformation and the capacity to listen (Giri 2007d). Just "performative competence" to argue in the public is not enough for resonance to realize its potential. Without developing the capacity of participating agents to listen, restrain the propensity to lecture, and overcome the egocentric, ethnocentric and anthropocentric perspectives, public resonance as multi-dimensional striving cannot really realize itself.

This calls for a multi-dimensional perspective which is in tune with Strydom's own admirable aspiration to go beyond any *a priori* and one-dimensional privileging. If socio-cognitive critique has to be open to all contending frames and models of discursive articulations and social constructions, then it needs a multi-valued logic instead of the binary logic of "either or" which dominates modernist epistemology. Strydom's critical engagement indeed strives to go beyond a simple "either or" logic (for example the state versus social movements) in the field of risk communication. But while his "multi-logical thinking goes back to Peirce and Apel's three-place theory of signs and the ontological dimensions of firstness, secondness and thirdness" (Giri 2009, xi), it can now invite a planetary border crossing in cultivating pathways of multi-valued logic: for example, inviting the Jain tradition of *anekanta vada* (many paths of truth), Gandhian pathways of non-violence and Husserlian pathways of overlapping contents. Multi-valued logic is not solely discursive and is based upon non-violence in ontology and intersubjective relations and non-injury in modes of thinking, especially epistemic engagement. Multi-valued logic is itself a work of the ontological epistemology of participation, where epistemic engagement with the partial nature of our truth claims, including attribution of falsity, is accompanied by appropriate ontological preparation which facilitates such an epistemic engagement and modes of reasoning (cf. Giri 2006, Clammer et al. 2003).

Strydom's socio-cognitive critique rightly pleads for inviting multi-dimensional perspective, but such a mode of engagement calls for an appropriate ontology of reality. I suggest that this is an ontology of multi-dimensionality which is, at the same time, an ontology of autonomy and interpenetration. Here we can take Strydom's own example of the field of the resonant public. To the six circles that Strydom presents, let us include the circle of self and present these seven circles not only as concentric circles but also as interpenetrative circles. The ontology of the public consists of, at least, these seven domains of vision and practice characterized by a multi-dimensional ontology of autonomy and interpenetration.

For Strydom (2002), "socio-cognitive critique" provides "epistemic authority," which is not only the exclusive possession of the sociologist; it also animates all discerning participants. But how do we come to terms with the possible dangers of authoritarianism in epistemic authority? Does not epistemic authority invite a critique and transformation, parallel to the critique of authorities such as religious authorities and ethnographic authorities, that we face in transformative movements? Should not epistemic authority be accompanied by an integrally connected move of epistemic humility?

An important challenge here is the challenge of participation. How can our mode of critical engagement be simultaneously critical and participatory, avoiding the pitfalls of a spectatorial and judgmental critique from above or afar? Commenting on Habermas's legitimationist approach to the public sphere where he already identifies with normative social movements, Strydom writes, "Constructivism, by its very nature, forbids the social scientist to adopt an identificatory procedure" (1999, 14). But Strydom still leaves untouched the challenge of participation. In order for critique to be transformative, it needs to be simultaneously critical and participatory, and here the pathway of an ontological epistemology of participation can suggest a way out. This can help both observing social scientists and participating activists overcome their initial arrogance and closure, transform their self-identity and learn with each other (see Giri 2004b).

Strydom's socio-cognitive critique builds upon potentials in contemporary cognitive social theory. But if cognition is not related again, in a spirit of autonomy and interpenetration, to other domains of life, such as emotion, it can be limiting. There is possibly an evolutionary challenge before humanity to combine cognition with emotion and generate knowledge which also flows from the feelings of our heart. A new critical theory could help us in this evolutionary journey in self and society.

Strydom's socio-cognitive critique emerges in the backdrop of what he calls contemporary experimenting knowledge society. He urges us to understand plural knowledges in our contemporary societies: scientific knowledge, legal knowledge, social knowledge, cultural knowledge and democratic common sense (Strydom 2004b, 6). But we do not find here self-knowledge. Critical theory involves the critique of knowledge, of knowledge and power. But this critique also involves a foundational critique of knowledge itself; for example, knowledge not only as emancipatory but also blinding.[2] It also needs to involve a foundational critique of the self; for example, critique and transformation of the limitations of our own egocentricity born of our confinement within only one dimension of self – be it role occupant, unconscious or transcendental.

Strydom has urged us to understand the significance of responsibility in sociology. His attention to responsibility has the potentially to transform theories of justice such as John Rawls'. Strydom discusses responsibility primarily as a frame in tune with his cognitive sociology. But how do we cultivate responsibility as modes of being and becoming in self and society? Here, again, is responsibility only a matter of frame or framing, or does it also involve appropriate self-preparation? What are the ethical and aesthetic dimensions of responsibility? Furthermore, what is the link between suffering and responsibility? For the embodiment of responsibility, are we not invited to co-suffer with our fellow beings, as Levinas and Gandhi in their different ways have urged us to realize (cf. Giri 2002 and Quarles van Ufford and Giri 2003)? Strydom talks about co-responsibility, and here we are called upon to embody it also through co-suffering, and thus contribute to mutual transformation and world transformation.

Endeetic Critique and the Quest for Meaning

Along with explorations of collective learning and triple contingencies as fields of socio-cognitive critique, in his recent work, Strydom (2009) cultivates pathways of an *endeetic* critique which has an epochal relevance for all of us, as it asks the question of ends and challenges us to remain vigilant about the displacement of ends by means which constitutes a pathology of not only different paths of modernities, but also in the modernization theory itself.[3] As Strydom tells us, in modernity there have been different kinds of movements, and what are usually labeled as counter-movements were not just irrational but were "involved in endeavors to realize a different or an alternative modernity."

At the contemporary juncture, Strydom urges us to realize that our explorations of alternative modernities involve questions of a new relationship between humans and nature, nature and society. We are invited and challenged to ask the question of our ends and be practitioners of what Strydom calls *endeetic* critique, which is "directed at what is unquestioningly taken for granted in modern society, namely an exploitative relation to nature, and hence at the *endeetic* foundations of economics, politics, labour and social life in general – that is, foundations as determined by the prevailing definition of human needs." Strydom presents us with some new social movements promoting a new radical expressive revolution which urges us to express ourselves authentically beyond the societal and contemporary definition of needs. They create a space for not only reiteration of existing needs but for the birth of new flames of aspirations in self and society. The latter has a spiritual dimension which, though not explored within the boundary of this name by Strydom, nonetheless is suggested in his pathway of *endeetic* critique, which asks questions about the meaning of our lives, the ends of our means and the nature of our needs. If we combine the paths of socio-cognitive critique and *endeetic* critique it has enormous enriching potential theoretically and practically.

Strydom's explorations of *endeetic* critique, which reflects on the quest for meaning, resonates with some of the inspiring contemporary savants of this as well as the last century. Authentic expression of the self in the spaces of the public, but not necessarily confined to them, resonates with Victor Frankl's pathways of logotherapy where we are invited to explore and realize that "deep down man is dominated neither by the will to pleasure nor by the will to power but by will to meaning: his deep-seated striving and struggling for a higher and ultimate meaning to his existence" (Frankl 1967, 117). Strydom does explore varieties of the quest for meaning in our contemporary world, and his bringing together of the cognitive, constructivist and expressive approach to understanding and living is itself an example of a remarkable quest for meaning. But this quest for meaning does meet with many shadows,[4] darkness and violence, where both self and even the emergent public (not just an existing crowd but participants in collective learning, social movements and observing situations of triple contingency) can and do suffer from self-delusion as well as a collective delusion, what Frankl calls the "collective neuroses of the present day" (Frankl 1967, 117). Strydom's new horizons of critical theory can also invite this as an issue to cope with and transform, which in turn calls for a new practice of therapy and healing where a critique of self and society, and the practice of sociology as creative criticism nurtured by both socio-cognitive critique and *endeetic* critique, can contribute to acknowledgment of our multiple sufferings – self as well as social – and also accompanying strivings to heal and to blossom together, realizing that in between there are not only flowers but also hammers. Srydom's treatment of the public could now invite the need to realize the delusions that the public itself can suffer from and the consequent need for the enlightenment of the public as well as public healing which can come from many sources – for instance art and social criticism, as well as spiritual mobilizations.

Strydom's work also resonates with the work of some other critical and creative sociologists such as Robert Bellah, who talks about a new paradigm of cultivation which seeks to heal the "split between the imaginative and the cognitive, the intellectual and the emotional..." (1970, 245) and pays attention to the needs of others (Bellah et al. 1991). Resonating with Strydom's concerns about ends, attention in this paradigm of cultivation is different from "distraction" and "obsession." For example, some of us are obsessed with power, money and sensual pleasure. For Bellah et al., "Attending means to concern ourselves with the larger meanings of things in the longer run, rather than with short-term payoffs" (Bellah et al. 1991, 273). And in Strydom, learning this art of cultivation is itself a collective learning which involves not only the self and the other but also an observant and emergent public. At the same time, it is fruitful to cultivate paths and patterns of cultivation in the spaces of what Strydom calls collective learning and triple contingency. Thus collective learning and triple contingency are also spaces and times of the cultivation of attending to one another and discovering the difference between attention and distraction. This also involves compassion and confrontation: compassionately understanding as well as confronting each other and all concerned.

Strydom's *endeedtic* critique (i.e. a critique concerned with the issue of the meaning of our ends and needs) also reminds us of the famous question that Maitreyee asked about the ends of our strivings thousands of years ago. Amartya Sen renders this immortal question of Maitreyee in the following way:

> It is not unusual for couples to discuss the possibility of earning more money but a conversation on this subject from around the eighth century B.C. is of special interest. As that conversation is recounted in the Sanskrit text *Brihadaranyaka Upanishad*, a woman named Maitreyee and her husband, Yajnavalkya, proceed rapidly to a bigger issue than the ways and means of becoming more wealthy: How far would wealth go to help them get what they want? Maitreyee wonders whether it could be the case that if "the whole earth, full of wealth" were to belong just to her, she could achieve immortality through it. "No," responds Yajnavalkya, "like the life of rich people will be your life. But there is no hope of immortality by wealth." Maitreyee remarks, "What should I do with that by which I do not become immortal?" (Sen 1999, 1)

Maitreyee's question is a question of *purusartha* (the ends and meaning of human lives – this is an important vision and practice of being human and realizing one's potential in society in Indian tradition) urging us to ask about the relationship between *artha* (wealth) and *moksha* (salvation), which has layers of symbolic and worldly meaning. Sen translates its worldly meaning in this way: "If we have reasons to want more wealth, we have to ask: What are precisely these reasons, how do they work, on what are they contingent and what are the things we can 'do' with more wealth" (Sen 1999, 2). Sri Aurobindo (1957), in his *Thoughts and Aphorisms*, has said there are eternities and eternities, and similarly Maitreyee's concern with immortality means immortalities and immortalities which can be creatively translated to our contemporary condition of collective learning and triple contingencies. Contributing to the self-critical and public discourse of the meaning and ends of human life and the public that Strydom presents with his *endeetic* critique and in the spirit of Maitreyee, we can ask, "What do we have to do with that kind of life, society, humanity and pursuit of wealth which does not ensure self-development, inclusion of the other and planetary blossoming?"

The Calling of a New Critical Theory: Self-Development, Inclusion of the Other and Planetary Realizations

Asking such questions urges us to use new terms of discourse for critical theory such as self-development, inclusion of the other, planetary realizations and a new *purusartha*. Critical theory is not only an epistemic engagement, it is simultaneously an ontological engagement; it is a dynamic work of an ontological epistemology of participation. Self-development is a neglected theme in critical theory, as it is in the broader discourse of social theory and human development. Building upon the creative work of savants and inspiring seekers such as Strydom, we can work towards a new critical theory which contributes to and builds upon self-development, inclusion of the other and planetary realizations.

Self-development here refers to multi-dimensional self-development of both the critics and the actors. What is the self? Does self refer only to the egoistic dimension of individual? Does it mean only *homo sociologicus*, *homo economicus*, or the *"techno-practitioner?"* The self is all these but at the same time is not exhausted by them and has a transcendental dimension, a dimension of transcendental and transversal connectivity to the other, society, nature, the world and the cosmos; what Roy Bhaskar (2002) calls "transcendentally really self." Self-development means the development of all these dimensions of self in a spirit of autonomy, interpenetration and non-dual realizations. Self-development thus includes processes of capacitation in various techno-practical fields of life such as economy, polity, organization, state, civil society, and now in the field of interlinked globality and cosmic humanity. Self-development involves the capacity for freedom as well as responsibility, and the deepening and broadening of these from their earlier state-centeredness to embody the aspirations of a global humanity.

An important challenge here is to overcome the binding of the concentration of power and to strive towards realization of what Dallmayr (2001), building on Heidegger, calls "the power free existence." This also involves a critique of the logic of sovereignty at the level of self and nation-state, and striving towards the realization of "sacred non-sovereignty" (cf. Dallmayr 2006) as well as shared sovereignties. This aspect of self-development has a longer lineage in philosophical and spiritual traditions of the West as well as the rest of the world, for example in the Christian concept of "kenosis," or self-emptying (cf. Vattimo 1999), the Confucian emphasis on self-cultivation (cf. de Bary 1991) and Foucault's plea for the development of self-restraint on the parts of holders of power (1986; also see Toynbee 1956).

The project of self-development is linked with a project of the inclusion of the other, which in Habermas's recent formulations is not just universalistic but sensitive to difference, defending "a morality of equal respect and solidaristic responsibility for everybody" (Habermas 1998, 5). But both the projects of self-development and the inclusion of the other can be locked in a self-justificatory closure, for example authenticity in the case of the former and emancipation in case of the latter. The movement of self-study in India, Swadhyaya, can do a lot in terms of the inclusion of the other, especially the low caste (cf. Giri 2008). Similarly, the project of inclusion of the other as articulated by Habermas needs a lot more self-development in order to realize its own aspiration of respecting the otherness of the other. Critical theory as inclusion of the other involves interrogation and transformation of presuppositions of both the self and the other, thus making the project of the inclusion of the other neither an assimilative nor a paternalistic one but an emergent and transformative one. It also involves interrogation of the presuppositions of critical theory itself and its participation in cross-cultural and planetary conversations.[5]

Inclusion of the other thus is a multi-dimensional process of dialogue and transformations involving dialogues across and within cultures, religions and civilizations. It also involves initiatives and struggles to build inclusive economies, polities, and communicating publics from the local to the global. In his critical theory Strydom is concerned about the inclusion of the other, and this concern can be further realized by taking part in transcivilizational dialogues and related processes of transformations.

Self-development and the inclusion of the other today have also to take part in planetary realizations. Writes Alberto Melucci in his *The Playing Self: Person and Meaning in the Planetary Society*, "We live on a planet that has become a global society... An ecology of economic, political, and technological choices cannot operate independently of an ecology of the everyday, *of the words and gestures with which we call into being* or annihilate the inner planet..." (1996, 69, emphasis added). Planetary realizations also involve realization of the inner planet "consisting of the biological, emotional and cognitive structures that underlie the experience and relations of us all" (Melucci 1996, 56). Planetary realizations are not unitary and simplistic processes: they involve complexity, difference and uncertainty which demand "[from] individuals the capacity to *change form* (the literal meaning of metamorphosis)..." (Melucci 1996, 2–3).

The metamorphosis of planetary realizations involves the transformation of our existing modes of knowledge, such as anthropocentrism, ethnocentrism (both Orientalism as well as Occidentalism) and nation-state centered rationality. It also involves transcivilizational dialogues and planetary conversations. Strydom's reflections on risk, environment and responsibility can be looked at from the emergent calling of planetary realizations, which involve the transformation of anthropocentrism, post-national transformations[6] and cosmopolitan learning.[7] Critical theory as planetary realizations also involves transcivilizational dialogues and planetary conversations about the foundational assumptions and themes of critical theory such as justification, argumentation, triple contingency learning, human interest and human liberation.

Notes

1 The most widely known among Strydom's students is Gerard Delanty, the author of many books on social theory and the philosophy of social science, who currently teaches sociology at the University of Sussex and is the founding editor of the *European Journal of Social Theory*. But other students also continue his creative and critical work in important ways, including Catherine Brennan of Massey University, New Zealand; John Farrell, an academic translator in Frankfurt, Germany; Marie Mater of Houston Baptist University, Texas, USA; Gerard Mullally of University College Cork; Orla O'Donnell of the University of Limerick, Ireland; Patrick O'Mahony of University College Cork; Séamus Ó'Tuama of University College Cork; Louise Ryan of City University London; and Tracey Skillington of University College Cork.

2 But in a recent communication Strydom writes:

> Critical theory started out as a critique of knowledge, e.g. Kant's critique of pure reason, Marx's critique of political economy, and so its goes on. Horkheimer's famous introduction of the very concept of critical theory was prompted by and took the form of a critique of knowledge and knowledge production processes. Habermas brought ideology critique to bear on science itself by criticising 'scientism' and, further, criticising the 'positivist' and 'scientistic' residues in critical theory itself, and in a recent book he wrote an article on 'Die Falsche im Eigenen' (On What is False in Our Own Tradition).
>
> Throughout my own work, I am acutely aware that critical theory has to maintain a self-critical relation to itself. In philosophy of social science materials I have always taken the view that the different philosophies have their own liabilities: if the science tradition's liability is elitism, technocracy and expertocracy, and if the interpretative tradition's is nativism, ethnocentrism and political naiveté, then *the liability of the critical tradition is dogmatism against which it must at all time guard*.
>
> But possibly there is still need for more foundational critique of our own self – presuppositions and traditions – and practice of transformative cross-cultural learning here. (Emphases added; see Strydom 2009, xxii)

3 What Bellah writes in his paperback edition in 1985 to his book *Tokugawa Religion* (first published in 1957), in which he adopted an uncritical modernization approach this context, deserves our careful consideration:

> However, the greatest weakness of the book has nothing to do with Japan but with a weakness in the modernization theory I was using: I failed to see that the endless accumulation of wealth and power does not lead to the good society but undermines the condition necessary for any viable society at all. I suffered myself from the displacement of ends by means, or the attempt to make means to ends, which is the very source of the pathology of modernization... What would it mean to reverse the functionalization of religion, the reduction of the realm of ultimate ends to the status

of means? What would it look like if religion set the ends, and the means – wealth and power – that have usurped the status of the ends, were reduced to the status of means again? (1957/1985, xix, xx)

4 In this context what Austin Harrington writes in his concluding essay, "Social Theory for the Twenty-First Century" in his edited book *Modern Social Theory*, deserves our careful attention:

> There are illusions, prejudices, and lies to be purged from the spaces of our public and private lives. But we also have to accept that the answers to our problems are not always unambiguous or clearly given. When the ancient Greek philosopher Plato compared ignorance to the perception of shadows on the walls of a cave lit by a dim fire, he made an assumption of the ultimate separateness of truth and enlightenment from the daily contexts of life in which people ordinarily experience the world. Today this kind of assumption is not possible for us. Today our reality is intrinsically a reality of shadowy appearances, and shifting forms, of mediated images and messy contradictions. (Harrington 2005, 314)

5 In his recent book, Strydom writes, "It should be emphasized, however, that whatever the theoretical dynamics exhibited by the conceptualization of the methodology of critique may be, the abiding theoretical core of critical theory, nevertheless, remains constant throughout. This core is to be found in the left- or young-Hegelian heritage which secures the uniqueness of critical theory" (2009, xxi). However what Strydom writes in a recent communication deserves our careful consideration:

> Everybody and every tradition starts somewhere and is grounded somewhere. The left-Hegelian tradition had always been and still is the basic anchor point of critical theory. But the left-Hegelian tradition is not just a Continental (German) tradition represented by the left-Hegelians from Marx via Lukács to the first, second and third generations of critical theorists. The same tradition is also represented by Peirce, the founder of pragmatism or pragmaticism, as well as by Kierkegaard who was exclusively focused on the cultivation of the self. It is much broader that the run-of-the-mill impression. Of course critical theory is open to questioning, learning, border-crossing etc., but does that mean that it has to surrender it most basic insight? That insight is 'immanent transcendence', which is precisely what allows it to mediate its own self with the transcendent Other. Surely, if the individual is to cultivate itself and thereby also becomes able to open up, then the same must hold of a tradition.
>
> But the question here is not of surrender of insight but that of foundational interrogation, border-crossing and broadening. (Strydom 2009, xxi–xxii)

6 In this context, what Strydom writes deserves our careful attention:

> Faced with this multi-leveled problematic situation, social and political theory is required today, at least to begin with, to find a theoretical point of articulation of these different apparently disparate dimensions: the gap between function systems and normative claims; the typical modern problems of individualization and social exclusion following this lack of coordination; the globalization of these very problems which are now manifest in the form of global risk society, world poverty and intercultural clashes; and the failure of globalization to mature into adequate worldhood. Such a theoretical means of mediation would entail mitigating long-standing internal divisions –e.g., micro and macro, life world and system or agency and structure, and in particular immanent social obligations and context-transcending

normative guidelines – and concurrent tendencies towards one-sidedness. There is no doubt that social and political theory can neglect or ignore any aspect of the diverse range of significant phenomena and developments characteristic of our time only at its peril. The question of how social and political theory could be brought, for instance, to adopt a more consistent global and cosmopolitan perspective or to recognize its own normative poverty, or how one version of political theory could be encouraged to reconsider, for example, its national fixation or ethnocentrism and another opened up so as to acknowledge its ecological blindness, is of central theoretical importance. (2009, 2)

7 In his recent works, Strydom (2009 and forthcoming) elaborates pathways of cosmopolitan learning. In a forthcoming essay, Strydom tells us:

> …cosmopolitanism is a meta-rule that emerges from social practices and the development of society to form part of the cognitive order of modernity and, by extension, of the emerging world society. In turn, this cognitive cultural structure has the at least potential recursive effect of generating and regulating the continuation of social practices and the further development of society.
>
> Whereas the development of society is the objective multilevel process of the opening up and globalisation of the economic, political, social, legal and cultural forms of society, cosmopolitanism is the internally experienced sense of the openness of social relations and society which is carried by collective learning processes. However, learning depends on competition, contestation and conflict between social actors who take for granted and share the cognitive order, including the idea of cosmopolitanism, but interpret it according to different values, act upon it in terms of different norms and therefore try to realise it in contrary ways.

References

Ankersmit, Frank R. 2002. *Political Representation*. Stanford: Stanford University Press.
Béteille, Andre. 2000. *Antinomies of Society: Essays on Ideologies and Institutions*. Delhi: Oxford University Press.
Bellah, Robert N. 1957/1985. *Tokugawa Religion*. Glencoe, NY: Free Press.
Bellah, Robert N. et al. 1991. *The Good Society*. New York: Alfred A. Knopf.
Bhaskar, Roy. 2002. *Reflections on Meta-Reality: Transcendence, Emancipation, and Everyday Life*. Delhi: Sage.
Bourdieu, Pierre. 2003. "Participant Objectivation." *Journal of Royal Anthropological Institute* n.s. 9: 281–94.
Clammer, John et al., eds. 2003. *Figured Worlds: Ontological Obstacles in Intercultural Relations*. Toronto: University of Toronto Press.
Dallmayr, Fred. 1984. *Polis and Praxis: Exercises in Contemporary Political Theory*. Cambridge, MA: MIT Press.
_____, ed. 1999. *Border Crossings: Toward a Comparative Political Theory*. Lanham, MD: Lexington Books.
_____. 2001. "Resisting Totalizing Uniformity: Martin Heidegger on the *Macht* and *Machenschaft*." In *Achieving Our World: Toward a Global and Plural Democracy*. Lanham, MD: Rowman & Littlefield.
_____. 2006. *Small Wonder: Global Power and its Discontents*. Rowman & Littlefield.
de Bary, William Theodore. 1991. *The Trouble with Confucianism*. Cambridge, MA: Harvard University Press.
Foucault, Michel. 1986. *Care of the Self*. New York: Pantheon.

Frankl, Victor. 1967. *Psychotherapy and Existentialism: Selected Papers on Logotherapy.* Harmondsworth: Penguin Books.

Giri, Ananta Kumar. 2002. *Conversations and Transformations: Towards a New Ethics of Self and Society.* Lanham, MD: Lexington Books.

_____, ed. 2004. *Creative Social Research: Rethinking Theories and Methods.* Lanham, MD: Lexington Books.

_____. 2004b. *Reflections and Mobilizations: Dialogues with Movements and Voluntary Organizations.* Delhi: Sage Publications.

_____. 2009. "Foreword." In Piet Strydom, *New Horizons of Critical Theory: Collective Learning and Triple Contingency.* Delhi: Shipra.

Greco, John. 2001. "Virtues and Rules in Epistemology." In Abrol Fairweather and Linda Zagzebski, eds, *Virtue Epistemology: Essays on Epistemic Virtue and Responsibility,* 117–41. Oxford: Oxford University Press.

Habermas, Jürgen. 1998. *The Inclusion of the Other: Studies in Political Theory.* Cambridge: Polity Press.

Harrington, Austin, ed. 2005. *Modern Social Theory: An Introduction.* Oxford: Oxford University Press.

Melucci, Alberto. 1996. *Playing Self: Person and Self in the Planetary Society.* Cambridge: Cambridge University Press.

Mohanty, J. N. 2000. *The Self and Its Other: Philosophical Essays.* Delhi: Oxford University Press.

Nussbaum, Martha. 2006. *Frontiers of Justice: Disability, Nationality, Species Membership.* Cambridge, MA: Harvard University Press.

Quarles van Ufford, Andrew and Ananta Kumar Giri, eds. 2003. *A Moral Critique of Development: In Search of Global Responsibilities.* London: Routledge.

Sen, Amartya. 1999. *Development as Freedom.* New York: Alfred A. Knopf.

Sennett, Richard. 2008. *The Craftsman.* Stanford: Yale University Press.

Smith, Adam. 1976. *The Theory of Moral Sentiments.* Oxford: Oxford University Press.

Strydom, Piet. 1999. "Triple Contingency: The Theoretical Problem of the Public in Communication Societies." *Philosophy and Social Criticism* 25 (2): 1–25.

_____. 2000. *Discourse and Knowledge: The Making of Enlightenment Sociology.* Liverpool: Liverpool University Press.

_____. 2001. "The Problem of Triple Contingency in Habermas." *Sociological Theory* 19: 165–88.

_____. 2002. *Risk, Environment and Society.* Buckingham: Open University Press.

_____. 2004a. "Resonance: Triggering a Dormant Dimension of the Public Sphere." Manuscript.

_____. 2004b. "The 'Contest of Faculties' and Cultures of Time: Sociological Reflections on the Relation of the Natural and Social Sciences." In *The Science Faculty Public Service,* 3 February, University College Cork, Ireland.

_____. 2006. "Risk communication as world creation through collective learning under complex contingent conditions." In *New Perspectives on Risk Communication,* 31 August–2 September, Gothenburg, Sweden.

_____. 2009. *New Horizons of Critical Theory: Collective Learning and Triple Contingency.* Delhi: Shipra Publications.

_____. "Cosmopolitanism, the Cognitive Order of Modernity, and Conflicting Models of World Openness: On the Prospects of Collective Learning." In Ananta Kumar Giri, ed., *Cosmopolitanism and Beyond: Towards a Multiverse of Transformations.* Forthcoming.

Toynbee, Arnold J. 1956. *An Historian's Approach to Religion.* Oxford: Oxford University Press.

Vattimo, Giani. 1999. *Belief.* Cambridge: Polity Press.

Part III

ASPIRATIONS AND STRUGGLES FOR
LIBERATION: TOWARDS PLANETARY
REALIZATIONS

Chapter Twelve

RETHINKING THE POLITICS AND ETHICS OF CONSUMPTION: DIALOGUES WITH "SWADESHI" MOVEMENTS AND GANDHI

Boycott is much more than a mere economical device, it is a rediscovery of national self-respect... The American struggle with England began in an enthusiastic and determined boycott of British goods enforced by much the same methods as the Indian boycott but with a much more stringent and effective organization. The Italian uprising of 1848 was heralded by the boycott of Austrian cigarettes and the tobacco riots of Milan. The boycott was the indispensable weapon of the Parnell movement in Ireland, and boycott and Swadeshi are the leading cries of Sinn Fein... In India also Boycott began as an assertion of national self-respect... The economical boycott has been on the whole an immense success... But now the whole weight of bureaucratic power is being brought to bear in order to shatter the boycott, and if we intend to save it we must oppose the organized force of bureaucracy by the organized will of people.

—Sri Aurobindo, *Bande Mataram* (1907, 501–2)

By patronizing foreign cloth we have committed a deep sin. [In taking the Swadeshi vow] we desire to do penance for our sins, that we desire to resuscitate the almost lost art of hand-weaving, and that we are determined to save our Hindustan crores of rupees which go out of it annually in exchange for the cloth we receive... The Swadeshi vow is not derived from any extraneous happening, whereas boycott is a purely worldly and political weapon. It is rooted in ill-will and a desire for punishment... One who wishes to be a Satyagrahi forever cannot participate in any boycott movement and a perpetual Satyagraha is impossible without Swadeshi.

—M. K. Gandhi, *The Swadeshi Vow* (1919, 196–7)

It is the greatest delusion to suppose that the duty of Swadeshi begins and ends with merely spinning some yarn and wearing Khadi made from it. Khadi is the first indispensable step towards the discharge of Swadeshi *dharma* to society. But one often meets men, who wear Khadi, while in all other things they indulge their taste for foreign manufactures. Such men cannot be said to be practicing Swadeshi. They are simply following the fashion. A votary of Swadeshi will carefully study his environment, and try to help his neighbors wherever possible, by giving preference to local manufactures, even if they are of an inferior grade or dearer in price than things manufactured elsewhere. He will try to remedy their defects, but will not because of their defects give them up in favor of foreign manufactures.

But even Swadeshi, like any other good thing, can be ridden to death if it is made a fetish. That is a danger which must be guarded against. To reject foreign manufactures merely because they are foreign, and to go on wasting national time and money in the promotion in one's country of manufacturers for which it is not suited would be criminal folly, and a negation of the Swadeshi spirit. A true votary of Swadeshi will never harbor ill-will towards the foreigner: he will not be actuated by antagonism towards anybody on earth. Swadeshism is not a cult of hatred. It is a doctrine of selfless service, that has its roots in the purest *ahimsa*, i.e., Love.

—M. K. Gandhi, *From Yeravda Mandir* (1932, 38)

Even though Gandhi's call to limit wants may seem utopian and the likelihood of its being accepted remote, the urgency of his message becomes all the more pressing with each passing year… Today's consumer society has little sense of obligation to the environment, and Gandhi wants to challenge this kind of moral apathy. He finds that modern consumption rests on a hubris that threatens to destroy both consumers and those who serve them. However, the ethic of limited consumption Gandhi wants to encourage seems to have little prospect of succeeding today. Recognizing the magnitude of the task, he believes a voluntary limitation of consumption is more likely to thrive if people have a cosmological outlook rather than a narrowly individualistic one. Persons who see interconnectedness and interdependency are more likely to recognize than someone whose sole point of reference is the isolated, "independent" self.

—Ronald J. Terchek, *Gandhi: Struggling for Autonomy* (1999, 235)[1]

The Problem

Consumption provides us with many important challenges now. The contemporary facts of consumption urge us to rethink the ethics and politics of it.[2] Concern with political consumerism tends to argue how appropriate consumption linked to life-style politics can have a politically significant critical function. But there are two related problems with such a contemporary approach to consumption. First, it is concerned with consumption without relating it to production, and second, the politics of consumption in the practice of political consumerism is not accompanied by a project of ethics. The present chapter seeks to rethink the politics and ethics of consumption by relating the critique of consumption to the critique of production and the potential this conjoint critique has for transforming the systemic condition of consumption. It also explores the ethical challenge of consumption – the way an alternative consumption practice is related to an ethical practice of self, intersubjectivity and community. It rethinks the politics and ethics of consumption by carrying out a dialogue with Swadeshi movements and Gandhi.

The Swadeshi movements of India were/are an important example of political consumerism. Swadeshi means "of one's locale or country," and the Swadeshi movements during India's freedom struggle mobilized against the logic of imperialistic consumption and strove for a meaningful relationship between consumption and production. Gandhi also provides an important challenge to rethink the politics and ethics of consumption. For him, Swadeshi, a pattern of consumption and style of life which gives primacy to local goods and is not enamored of foreign goods, is not possible without Swaraj, or self-rule/self-government, and Satyagraha, or desire and striving for truth. An appropriate style of consumption for Gandhi is not confined to only nihilistic efforts (i.e. to keep oneself austere and to cut oneself off from the world of luxuries and imported goods and commodities) but is primarily linked to an affirmative effort to reconstruct and transform self and society.

The Swadeshi Movements, Ethico-political Mobilization and the Critique of Consumption

The Swadeshi movement was the most important anti-colonial movement to take place in India after the Sepoy Mutiny of 1857, India's first struggle for independence. It began in Bengal in 1905 and then spread to the other parts of the country. The boycott of British goods was an important part of this struggle. Historian Sumit Sarkar gives us a helpful definition: "In its specifically economic aspect, Swadeshi may be defined as the sentiment – closely associated with many phases of Indian nationalism – that indigenous goods should be preferred by consumers even if they are more expensive than and inferior in quality to their imported substitutes, and that it was patriotic duty of men with capital to pioneer such industries even though profits initially might be minimal or non-existent" (1973, 92). The Swadeshi movement began as a protest against the partition of Bengal. Sri Aurobindo was one of the most important leaders of this movement during this phase of India's struggle for freedom. To him, the boycott of British goods "is much more than a mere economical device, it is a rediscovery of national spirit" (Sarkar 1973, 92). For this recovery of national spirit, the boycott of British goods was accompanied by efforts to establish Swadeshi education (i.e. nationalist education), and Indians themselves to establish industrial units of production. In this way, the critique of consumption became linked to a project of production, and also to a wider project of social reconstruction. Sri Aurobindo writes in *Bande Mataram* about the Swadeshi movement that followed the partition of Bengal:

> Ever since the Partition days, India has pressed on this path, the boycott of foreign goods, the return of weaver to his loom, the dissociation of the people

from the government...the foundation of the National Council of Education, of National schools, the institution of technical education, the insolvency of dealers in British goods, the social ex-communications of anti-boycotters. (Sri Aurobindo 1973, 482)

Sarkar also helps us understand how the Swadeshi boycott of British goods was a total social movement where critique of consumption was linked to a project of production. In his words, "The *Swadeshi* mood did bring about a significant revival of the handloom, silk-weaving, and some other traditional artisan crafts" (Sarkar 1985, 116). The Swadeshi movement also led to labor unrest: "In September 1905, the entire Swadeshi public hailed a walkout of 247 Bengali clerks of Burn Company in Howrah to protest against a new work regulation felt to be derogatory..." (Sarkar 1985, 118). According to Sarkar, the Swadeshi movement established different associations, or *Samitis*: "The sudden emergence of the *Samitis* or national volunteer movement was one of the major achievements of the Swadeshi age... Most Samitis were quite open bodies engaged in a variety of activities: physical and moral training of members, social work during famines...preaching the Swadeshi message through multifarious farms, organising crafts, schools, arbitration courts and village societies and implementing the technique of passive resistance" (Sarkar 1985, 119). For Sri Aurobindo, "The return to the land is as essential to our salvation as the development of Swadeshi. In national education there must be provision for agricultural training" (Sri Aurobindo 1973, 737).

Bonfires of foreign cloth was an important part of the Swadeshi movement. For example, such bonfires were organized and a Swadeshi Vastu Pracharan Sabha (Society for Promotion of Swadeshi Goods) was set up in Bombay city to spread the new message. Though the Bombay industrialists did not want to sell at a lower rate, in the wake of the Swadeshi, "[an] industrial conference for the promotion of industry came to be organised along with the Congress conference" (Sri Aurobindo 1973, 136).

In his study of the Swadeshi movement, Sarkar also tells us that, "If Swadeshi was to become a viable proposition in Bengal, the development of new productive capacity was the obvious prerequisite" (Sarkar 1973, 120). For Sarkar, "this took two forms – the revival of traditional handicrafts, and the starting of modern industries" (Sarkar 1973, 120). "A considerable number of small and medium-sized consumer goods industries sprang up in the wake of the Swadeshi movement" (Sarkar 1973, 128). "By 1907–8, the emphasis in Swadeshi efforts was shifting from industrial production towards banking, insurance and inland trade, where profits seemed much easier to make and capital was correspondingly less shy" (Sarkar 1973, 131–2). This phase also witnessed the establishment of new industries such as Bengal Chemicals by Prafulla Chandra Roy. For Sarkar, "the new demand created by Swadeshi did provide a very important stimulus to handloom weaving" (Sarkar 1973, 121). Furthermore, "The nationalist movement sought to check the swadeshi profiteers through cost-price hawking by volunteers. In one case, the volunteers of Samitis had hawked Rs. 700 worth of Swadeshi goods at cost price in the course of a fortnight" (Sarkar 1973, 118).

For Sarkar, Swadeshi did make an impact on the purchases that people made, and their purchases of foreign goods came down. But Sarkar goes on to add, "It is a significant commentary on the social character of the movement that the boycott should have achieved its most spectacular early success in boots and shoes and cigarettes" (1973, 148). The Swadeshi movement of Bengal was not sensitive to the problems of the poor, especially the poor Muslim artisans and weavers. The artisans and weavers continued to be bound to landlords and moneylenders, and Swadeshi movement made no effort to break this vicious circle. For example, "We never hear of efforts to organize artisan cooperatives" (Sarkar 1973, 123).

The Swadeshi movement was the first effort of its kind in broadening the base of the anti-colonial nationalist struggle. Before it politics was entirely "the preserve of the English educated elite" (Sarkar 1973, 252). But, according to Sumit Sarkar, "1905 changed all that, at least for some years. Organisationally too 1905 marks the beginning of a new age. In place of the 'ring of lawyers' monopolizing the politics in muffasil (rural areas), we have the sudden emergence of the samiti or 'national volunteer movement'" (Sarkar 1973, 252). This broadening involved the use of new techniques of mass contact and the development of new forms of organization. Poet Rabindranath Tagore played an important part in this broadening. In his "Swadeshi Samaj" address of 1904, Tagore presented an agenda of "a variety of imaginative forms of popular education, including the use of traditional folk media (the mela, the jatra and the kathakata) as well as the modern audio-visual methods of magic-lantern talks" for the propagation of Swadeshi ideals (Sarkar 1973, 153). He was for innovative mass education and for undertaking constructive work in the villages. He insisted that the medium of instruction in Swadeshi education should be the mother tongue. "Rabindranath made the interesting point that the foreign medium had actually hindered the assimilation of progressive Western values in two ways – by confining the benefits of education to a small minority, and by rendering superficial the enlightenment of even that narrow elite" (Sarkar 1973, 152–3).

It must be noted that soon leaders of the boycott movement realized that the realization of economic swadeshi is not possible without political independence. "So the emphasis shifted soon enough from constructive swadeshi to the new politics of passive resistance of which economic boycott and the promotion of indigenous industries formed just a part and no more" (Sarkar 1973, 99). Sri Aurobindo played an important part in this shift and anticipated Gandhi. In the words of Sarkar:

But the classic statement of course came from Aurobindo in April 1907 – clearly demarcating "passive resistance" from "petitioning," "self-development and self-help," and also from "aggressive resistance" or "armed revolt;" explaining the term to imply an "organized and relentless boycott" of British goods, officialized education, justice and executive administration backed up by the positive development of alternatives in the form of Swadeshi, national education, arbitration courts and leagues of mutual defence; enunciating also a programme of civil disobedience of unjust punitive laws and enforcing passive resistance through the machinery of a "social boycott" of traitors… The whole future political programme of Gandhism is virtually sketched out for us here… (1973, 69)

The above comment of Sarkar helps us make the transition from Sri Aurobindo to Gandhi. There took place a shift in the meaning of Swadeshi after fifteen years when Gandhi emerged as the leader of India's freedom struggle. The Swadeshi boycott of foreign goods here gets linked up to an act of production and reconstruction in the life of self and society. For Gandhi, swadeshi is not simply a matter of anti-colonial political agitation; it is a chosen vocation for a life of dignity and autonomy on the part of individuals and communities. Therefore Gandhi talks about the Swadeshi vow on the part of individuals, following which is the Swadeshi pledge of Gandhi which galvanized millions: "With God as my witness, I solemnly declare that from today I shall confine myself, for my personal requirements, to the use of cloth manufactured in India from Indian cotton, silk and wool; and I shall together abstain from using foreign cloth, and I shall destroy all foreign cloth in my possession." It is perhaps for this reason that historian Judith M. Brown writes, "The most striking aspects of the whole Swadeshi campaign were not only the large bonfires of cloth which took place throughout India, but also the way Khadi became a virtual uniform for nationalist politicians" (Brown 1972, 314–15). Wearing Khadi even now symbolizes, even if at an unconscious level, the striving for a life of purity (Chakraborty 1999). In Gandhi, Swadeshi meets both Swaraj – the struggle for autonomy – and Satyagraha – striving for truth.

Gandhi urged people to weave their own clothes; thus his critique of imperialistic consumption has a much more intimate ontological grounding in production, where the Swadeshi and Satyagrahi self produces his or her own cloth to begin with. For Gandhi, Swadeshi cannot be propagated by increasing the consumption of mill cloth in place of imported cloth: "he alone really encourages Swadeshi who spins and weaves, if only to produce a yard of cloth and no more… If only people try, any man or woman can learn spinning in no more than a day" (Gandhi 1915–17, 339). For Gandhi, cloth woven at home is purer than that purchased from the market, and weaving our own cloth not only saves us from "many an unnecessary need" but it makes our life "one song of joy and beauty" (Gandhi 1919, 200). Gandhi draws our attention to the beauty and purity involved in this process. In his discussion with women in a women's meet in Surat on May 26, 1919, Gandhi argues that as women would like to prepare their own food they should also spin their own cloth. "If all women cannot do this" they should have a weaver of their own in the same way they have a "washerman and a barber" (Gandhi 1919, 325). Thus Gandhi's agenda of Swadeshi makes the struggle of Swadeshi much more down-to-earth than a mere concern with the boycott of foreign goods, and is also intimately tied at the level both of the self and society to the production and the striving to build a dignified and decent local economy.

Gandhi urges us to realize the distinction between boycott and Swadeshi and the connection between Swadeshi and Satyagraha. For him, "In proclaiming a boycott of British goods, we expose ourselves to the charge of desiring to punish the English but we have no quarrel with them; our quarrel is with the governors. And, according to the law of Satyagraha, we may not harbor any ill will even against the rulers, and as we may harbor no ill will, I cannot see the propriety of resorting to boycott" (Gandhi 1919, 197). In Gandhi, Swadeshi is not just an immediate political agitation and is not limited only to the famous agitation against the Rowlatt Act of 1919, which tried to curtail the freedom of Indians (cf. Kumar 1971). For Gandhi, the struggle for Swadeshi would continue "even after the repeal of the Rowlatt agitation" (Gandhi 1919, 306). "We shall appeal to our English brethren also to join us in this Swadeshi vow" (Gandhi 1919, 306).

But Gandhi urges us to realize the self-transformation that is required to make Swadeshi a reality. "The mill-owners will have to fix their rates in a patriotic spirit... Swadeshi cannot advance unless thousands of petty shopkeepers from whom the poor millions buy introduce honesty to their dealings" (Gandhi 1919, 306).

Cambridge historian C. A. Bayly provides us with some new perspectives for understanding the Swadeshi movement. For him, "The Swadeshi movement which in its radical form was complemented by a boycott of foreign goods, bears comparison with other nativist upsurges in Asia and Africa that rejected European products or refused to produce European crops as symbols of local or national oppression" (Bayly 1998, 197). For Bayly, before the visible Swadeshi movements in the first decades of twentieth century, it had been "propagated for several decades by Indian businessmen and mill owners to promote their own products in difficult commercial environment" (1998, 198). Furthermore, "Swadeshi was also heir to a movement of artistic revival, which sought to protect the values of indigenous craft traditions against the impersonality of all mill production" (Bayly 1998, 198). But for Bayly, it is Gandhi who transformed the meaning of Swadeshi in a radical manner. In his words:

> Whereas the Bengali swadeshi leaders of 1905–10 had in general used homespun as a political symbol, Gandhi emphasized its nature as a talisman and pronounced the creation of cloth through spinning to be a prayer. The production of cloth in villages by spinning and weaving was to transform the moral fibre of the nation in a quite literal sense. (1998, 200)

Thus the political mobilization for Swadeshi goods got an ethical, moral and ontological deepening in the vision and experiments of Gandhi. After about a century of this struggle, in what way do we now make sense of the agenda of Swadeshi? In the face of contemporary globalization, which seeks to consume local worlds of production and consumption, Gandhi's agenda has an urgent salience. In the midst of globalization, individuals and societies now feel the need for nurturing a local space as a humane space for production and consumption (cf. Harvey 2000), and here Swadeshi can be redefined as a struggle to preserve and transform the local space of humane production and consumption. For the people whose livelihoods are being lost to globalization, preserving their local space of production and consumption is a question of life and death. The dialectic between localization and globalization that the contemporary processes of change unleashes makes the struggle for Swadeshi urgent in the lives of millions of marginalized people, but now Swadeshi needs to be redefined in terms of the struggle for autonomy and Swaraj, and for this those struggling have to be prepared to undergo suffering and pain. It is perhaps for this reason that the two recent writers on the subject tell us: "The subject of Swadeshi is indeed profound at a deeper, non-manifest level… Although it is pertinent to note here that Gandhi emphasized the economic aspect of Swadeshi (charkah, Khadi, etc.) as a beginning to get rid of the oppressive industrial culture which had reduced human needs to moronic vacuity, Khadi was, however, to him only the first step towards the ultimate. His most critical point was that for standing by this '*swa*' (self), one has to be ready for tremendous suffering and pain" (Kedia and Sinha 1994, 92). About the contemporary significance of Swadeshi, V. Krishna Ananth also writes,

> The logic which was of critical importance to the Gandhian approach to swadeshi was that industrial activity in the country should be labour-intensive; now the population having crossed the one-billion mark is a reality the nation and its planner cannot gloss over. There is no way that a specified number of people can be wished away because the idea of globalization appeals to a section consisting the ruling elite, a section of the middle classes and those aspiring to reach these levels in their own way. (2000)

In contemporary India, Swadeshi manifests itself in various movements and voluntary organizations who are fighting against the usurpation and destruction of local resources and spaces by the forces of the state and multinational capitalism. It is interesting to note that a scholar has included *Narmada Bachao Andolan*, a people's movement fighting against the construction of the mega Narmada Dam (which would displace thousands of people), as an instance of contemporary Swadeshi movement. Writes Subhendu Ranjan Raj in his essay, "Swadeshi in the Context of Globalisation: A Grassroot Development Perspective": "Today Swadeshi has come to mean taking effective steps to save our people from the onslaught of the predatory protectionist overtures of the West along with our state to protect our intellectual, cultural and resource heritage" (Raj 2000, 82). For Raj, in the contemporary context, Swadeshi includes "the rights of choosing what should be sustainable development for us" and harps on "not only providing for indigenous technology but also on how the fruits of development should not be usurped by the West, or members of the ruling class in India" (2000, 82).

Not only are several left-leaning social movements fighting for Swadeshi in contemporary India, but also right wing groups such as the Hindu fundamentalist conglomeration the Sangha Parivara. Swadeshi Jagran Manch (SJM) is an umbrella organization of the latter, and it is a critic of globalization. Though its political wing, the Bhratiya Janata Party, is the leading partner of India's ruling coalition, SJM is fighting against multinational companies. On its website SJM has posted an article by Gandhian economist Ramesh Diwan entitled "Economic Reforms, Swadeshi and Foreign Investments" in which Diwan writes, "…as the government opened the country to FDI [foreign direct investment], it also had to promote consumerism considered as a necessary condition. Consumerism impacts domestic savings negatively. It is not incidental that the savings-income ratio in India has declined steadily over the last four years; from 24% in 1990–91 to 20% in 1993–94" (Diwan 1995). For Diwan, "FDI, so far, seems to be interested not in production but control. FDI attracted to consumption goods production, such as cola, fired chicken, potatoes, does not add to the technological base of the economy." For Diwan, "Swadeshi and economic reform follow from different paradigms… Swadeshi promotes personal character, family and community. Economic reform induces corruption and individualism" (1995).

SJM uses the name of Gandhi but does not combine the critique of globalized consumption with Satyagraha, the seeking of truth. It does not have a critique of an urge to dominate minorities on the part of the majoritarian Hindu forces in Indian society. There is no scheme of voluntary poverty in the contemporary SJM, and a scheme of what Habermas (1998) calls "inclusion of the other" is also missing. It must be noted here that the first phase of the Swadeshi movement of India in Bengal had a problem in bringing the Muslims of India in its fold in the boycott of foreign goods. Apart from Hindu nationalism, there was a class dimension at work. A majority of the Muslims of Bengal were poor tenants and laborers, while the proponents of Swadeshi were landlords and the middle class, who found Swadeshi goods to be more expensive. But during the Swadeshi movement the poor were forced to buy expensive and low quality goods, which led to tensions between rich and poor, and Hindus and Muslims. In his Swadeshi struggle Gandhi was sensitive to this. He urged the local producers not to exploit the poor in the name of Swadeshi, and he fought for and gave his life for the establishment of Hindu–Muslim unity. The contemporary SJM has a narrow view of Swadeshi as fight against multinational corporations, and lacks both a class critique of contemporary systems of consumption and an ethical/moral critique of majoritarianism from the point of view of a Gandhian path of the inclusion of and love for the other.

In rethinking the politics and ethics of consumption, dialogues with the Swadeshi movements and Gandhi enable us to rethink the subject of political consumerism as it concerns nurturing and transforming spaces of production, and not simply consumption choices. But many of our contemporary interlocutors look at consumption as divorced from production and limit themselves only to issues of life style choices; but in such life styles, we do not witness preeminence accorded to either labor or to production. But to rethink the politics and ethics of consumption is to bring back the centrality of production and labor. Ulrich Beck (2000), famous for his sociology of "risk society," now urges us to recreate civil society through the practices of civil labor. In civil labor what is emphasized is the sharing of time and labor that is outside of the media of money and market (cf. Gorz 2000; Offe and Heinze 1992). Gandhi's project of Satyagraha makes civil labor capable of undergoing pain and contributes to a regeneration of the local civil space as a space of production and consumption, which also embodies the spirit of Swadeshi. The project of civil labor must have a spiritual foundation, and it is witnessed in the experiments of Swadhyaya – a socio-spiritual movement in contemporary India – which generates impersonal wealth in communities through the practices of *shramabhakti*, or devotional labor. In Swadhyaya there is an urge to meet unconditionally members of society, and this creates networks of trust and relationships; in fact this contributes to a spiritual creation and regeneration of social capital. This spiritual social capital then becomes a creative input in the nurturing of local spaces and the creation of alternative communities, where people find an alternative to the dominant clinical obsession with consumption by being in fellowship with each other and working towards the common good.

Gandhi makes a distinction between need and greed, and his oft-quoted line is, "The world has enough for everybody's need but not for everybody's greed." But in what way do we draw the distinction between need and greed now? For some commentators on consumption, it is not possible now to condemn all consumption as an expression of human greed (Crocker 1998). For example, David Crocker, building on Amartya Sen's notion of capability, urges us to understand the link between "consumption, well-being and capability" (Crocker 1998). But Crocker himself speaks about an "ethic of responsible consumption" and consumption choice.[3] The exercise of this choice and the embodiment of this responsibility is a matter of contextual judgment and a reflective process in which there is a creative play of conscience (cf. Ricouer 2000). For our personal choice to reflect a sense of justice, it is helpful to remember Gandhi's suggestion of remembering the face of the poorest of the poor:

> I will give you a talisman. Whenever you are in doubt, or when the self becomes too much with you, apply the following test. Recall the face of the poorest and weakest man whom you may have seen, and ask yourself if the step you contemplate is going to be of any use to him. (Gandhi, as quoted in Chambers et al. 1989, 241)

Thus rethinking the politics and ethics of consumption urges us to realize our responsibility and be attentive to others. Here we can link Gandhi with Levinas, as Levinas urges us to be aware of our responsibility to the other through an ethics of the face. In the words of Levinas, "The approach to the face is the most basic mode of responsibility. As such, the fact of the other is verticality and uprightness; it spells a relation of rectitude. *The face is not in front of me but above me…the face is the other who asks me not to let him die alone, as if to do so were to become an accomplice in his death*" (Levinas 1995, 189). But living such a life of responsibility calls for appropriate self-development and work on the self – a calling about which Levinas, unlike Gandhi, is not much aware (cf. Giri 1998). Thus in rethinking the ethics of consumption, there is a need to interpenetrate or intertwine ethics with an aesthetic of self-cultivation and self-development (cf. Foucault 1986; Giri and van Ufford 2000). The intertwining of ethics and aesthetics also calls for the creation of spaces of intersubjectivity where we are able to make responsible consumption choices; a space where consumption in itself is not given a transcendent value but becomes part of an integral seeking of meaning and dignity in self and society (cf. Joas 2000). Living a life of austere consumption or responsible consumption – a style of consumption which embodies attentiveness to the needs of the other – is facilitated by the existence of alterative communities, alternative institutions in society, and by being part of a vibrant community of friendship at a personal level. One reason behind the mindless consumption of the rich few now is that they do not know other worthwhile sources of satisfaction, pleasure and happiness, and if people learn to find happiness in relationships of friendship and by being part of community-building efforts via the sharing of time and labor, they will not consume for the sake of consumption.

The agenda of political consumerism now requires both political struggles and ethico-moral striving, and this is the lesson we get from dialogues with the Swadeshi movements and Gandhi. The Swadeshi movement began with the boycott of foreign goods and then it became part of a larger project of the struggle for autonomy and the striving for truth – Swaraj and Satyagraha. Through both critical politics and aesthetic ethics we must transform the contemporary discourse of political consumerism into responsible consumption and a democratic experimentation with self, society, nature and the cosmos, and in this we can derive inspiration from both Gandhi[4] and Foucault. As we began with Gandhi, let us conclude with the passion of Foucault:

> What strikes me is the fact that in our society art is now only linked to objects, rather than to individual or life itself. But could we ourselves, each one of us, make of our lives a work of art? Why should a lamp or a house become the object of art and not our own life?

Notes

1 We can also note here what Paul Watchel writes about consumer society:

> What we need is an image of an alternative that is not just a bitter necessity but holds out promise of a genuinely better life. The image of belt-tightening is one that issues from within our *present* set of assumptions: it equates conservation, recycling, and fewer gadgets with having "less." A notion of "standard of living" more rooted in our actual psychological experience points in quite a different direction and challenges the idea that altering our present way of life means settling for less. It encourages us to think beyond material goods as the defining essence of good life and to focus instead on the quality of our relations with others; on the clarity and intensity of our experiences, and on emotional freedom; and on the ethical, spiritual, and communal dimensions that give the entire enterprise meaning. (1998, 199)

2 What Tyler Wigg Stevensson writes deserves our careful consideration: "…the quest for personal identity in the Cold War led to a consumerist sense of personal meaning… Because we lack strong inherited stories, we are left with the burden of constructing our sense of meaning and place in the world. By and large, we have done so with the tools that lay closest at hand – consumer goods" (2007, 27).

3 Ramachandra Guha also speaks about "responsible consumption" and pleads for a creative anthropocentrism forging a "more peaceable and sustainable relationship between humans and other species with which we must share this earth" (Guha 2006, 32). He further writes, "The social needs and demands of the economy have to be made consistent with the natural

constraints of ecology; and both have to be harmonized with the political imperatives of democracy" (Guha 2006, 248).

4 As Guha writes:

> Sometime in the middle decades of the twenty-first century, Galbraith's great unanswered question, "How much should a country consume?" – with its Gandhian corollary, "How much should a person consume?" – will come finally to dominate the intellectual and political debates of the time. (2006, 250)

References

Ananth, V. Krishna. 2000. "Swadeshi, not just a sentiment." *The Hindu*, 26 December.

Bayly, C. A. 1998. *Origins of Nationality in South Asia: Patriotism and Ethical Government in the Making of Modern India*. Delhi: Oxford University Press.

Brown, Judith M. 1972. *Gandhi's Rise to Power: Indian Politics 1915–1972*. Manchester: University of Manchester Press.

Chakraborty, Dipesh. 1999. "Clothing the Political Man: A Reading of the Use of Khadi in Indian Public Life." *Journal of Human Values* 5 (1): 3–13.

Chambers, Robert et al. 1984. *To the Hands of the Poor*. London: Intermediate Technology Publications.

Crocker, David. 1998. "Consumption, Well-Being and Capability." In David A. Crocker and Toby Linden, eds, *The Ethics of Consumption: The Good Life, Justice and Global Stewardship*. Lanham, MD: Rowman & Littlefield Publishers.

Diwan, Romesh. 1995. "Economic Reforms, Swadeshi and Foreign   Investment." *The Hindu*, 31 October.

Fouault, Michel. 1986. *Care of the Self*. New York: Pantheon.

Gandhi, Mohandas K. 1915–1917. *The Collected Works of Mahatma Gandhi*, vol. 13. Government of India: Publications Division.

_____. 1918–1919. *The Collected Works of Mahatma Gandhi*, vol. 15. Government of India: Publications Division.

_____. 1932. *From Yeravda Mandir*. Ahmedabad: Navjivan Trust.

Gorz, André. 1999. *Reclaiming Work: Beyond the Wage-Based Society*. Cambridge: Polity Press.

Guha, Ramachandra. 2006. *How Much Should a Person Consume? Thinking Through the Environment*. Delhi: Permanent Black.

Harvey, David. 2000. *Spaces of Hope*. Edinburgh: Edinburgh University Press.

Joas, Hans. 2000. *The Genesis of Values*. Cambridge: Polity Press.

Kedia, Kusumlata and Aruna Sinha. 1994. "Swadeshi: A Question of Interpretation." *Gandhi Marg*, April–June, 86–92.

Kumar, Ravinder, ed. 1971. *Essays on Gandhian Politics: The Rowlatt Satyagraha of 1919*. Oxford: Clarendon Press.

Levinas, Emmanuel. 1995. "Ethics of the Infinite." In Richard Kearney, *States of Mind: Dialogues with Contemporary Thinkers on the European Mind*, 177–99. Manchester: Manchester University Press.

Offe, Claus and Rolf G. Heinze. 1992. *Beyond Employment*. Cambridge: Polity Press.

Raj, Subhendu Ranjan. 2000. "Swadeshi in the Context of Globalisation: A Grassroot Development Perspective." *Gandhi Marg*, April–June, 77–83.

Ricouer, Paul. 2000. *The Just*. Chicago: University of Chicago Press.

Sarkar, Sumit. 1973. *The Swadeshi Movement in Bengal: 1903–1908*. Delhi: People's Publishing House.

_____. 1983. *Modern India: 1885–1947*. Delhi: Macmillan India Ltd.

Sri Aurobindo. 1973. *Bande Mataram: Early Political Writings*. Pondicherry: Sri Aurobindo Ashram.

Stevenson, Tyler Wigg. 2007. *Brand Jesus: Christianity in a Consumerist Age*. New York: Seabury Books.

Terchek, Ronald J. 1998. *Gandhi: Struggling for Autonomy*. New Delhi: Vistaar Publications.

Watchel, Paul L. 1998. "Alternatives to the Consumer Society." In David Crocker and Toby Linden, eds, *The Ethics of Consumption*. Lanham, MD: Rowman & Littlefield.

Chapter Thirteen

SWARAJ AS BLOSSOMING: COMPASSION, CONFRONTATION AND A NEW ART OF INTEGRATION

Communication is always ambiguous and always an expression of latent violence. But when this description of violence is ontologized, when one sees "nothing but" violence in it, one misses the essential point, namely, that the critical power to put a stop to violence without reproducing it in new forms can only dwell in the telos of mutual understanding and our orientation to this goal.

—Jürgen Habermas, *The Divided West* (2006, 18)

Compassion brings inner strength, and compassion also brings truth… Compassion involves a feeling of closeness to others, a respect and affection that is not based on others' attitudes towards us. We tend to feel affection for people who are important to us. That kind of close feeling does not extend to our enemies – those who think ill of us. Genuine compassion, on the other hand, sees that others, just like us, want a happy and successful life and do not want to suffer. That kind of feeling and concern can be extended to friend and enemy alike, regardless of their feelings towards us. That's genuine compassion.

—The Dalai Lama, *The Middle Way: Faith Grounded in Reason* (2009, 2–3)

This implies *integration* in the sense of all relating to all, as opposed to fragmentation, and *holism*, the use of many faculties in all parties, as opposed to segmentation.

—Johan Galtung and Graeme MacQueen,
Globalizing God: Religion, Spirituality and Peace (2008, 18)

An Introduction and Invitation

Hind Swaraj is an open dialogue in which not only the Reader and Editor[1] speak to each other with compassion but all of us, the whole humanity, are invited to join this journey of co-walking and the realization of fuller humanization and divinization (Gandhi 1938). It is an open text, a very different kind of manifesto. In the known and valorized manifestos of modernity we have a parade of assertions, but in *Hind Swaraj* there is no such one-sided assertion and preaching from a pulpit. This is a revolutionary departure from modernistic models of pedagogy, human emancipation and national liberation, where the architects of liberation preach to the unenlightened as an all-knower, redeemer and deliverer. But in *Hind Swaraj* Gandhi is not speaking as an all-knower and a redeemer. This is also a revolutionary departure from tradition, for example the tradition of dialogue or of the lack of it in India. Let us realize together the dialogue between Krishna and Arjuna in *Srimad Bhagavad Gita* and the dialogue between the Editor and Reader in *Hind Swaraj*. Krishna does not address with compassion the question of the consequences of death and destruction that Arjuna raises and asserts only his own logic, which then leads Arjuna to surrender his questioning self and take part in the battle of mutual annihilation with the Kurukshetra (cf. Sen 2009). In *Hind Swaraj* there is a dialogue between the Editor and the Reader in which both question each other, and the Reader does not surrender to Gandhi as the only prophet of redemption and deliverer of Truth. It concludes with a call for further co-learning: "We have to learn, and to teach others, that we do not want the tyranny of either English or Indian rule" (Gandhi 1938, 85).

The dialogue between Reader and Editor can also be read together with other texts of reflections on politics, the self, society and the cosmos. Here we can read *Hind Swaraj* together with these two texts – John Rawls' (1971) *A Theory of Justice* and Ramachandra Gandhi's (1993) *Sita's Kitchen*.[2] The dialogue that takes place in Rawls' original position is a dialogue in blindness and ignorance in which the participants do not know each other and are blind to each other. There is no self in Rawls' original position which one can touch, smell and embrace. Compared to this, the dialogue that takes place in the forest in Ramachandra Gandhi's *Sita's Kitchen* has a face to it. But in the portrayal of the participants in the dialogue, Ramachandra Gandhi does not present all the participants with compassion. For example, his portrayal of Ajita Kesakambalin and Makhali Gosala as proponents of what Ramachandra Gandhi calls nihilism lacks compassion and seems to be a reiteration of *a priori* judgmental condemnation. Compared to texts such as *Srimad Bhagavad Gita*, *A Theory of Justice* and *Sita's Kitchen*, *Hind Swaraj* is an embodiment of a different journey.

Hind Swaraj is not only a text of conversation but also one of co-walking. It is a prayer and not an ordinary conversation. It is a prayerful conversation and a walking meditation. Most of us used to our academic habit of talking while seated in a chair and across the table may not envision *Hind Swaraj* as a co-walking meditation in which the Reader and the Editor are walking slowly – "ruminating while walking" (cf. Thoreau 1975)[3] – and meditating together. Through such co-walking and meditation emerge collaborative practices of mediations and transformations.

Hind Swaraj is also a co-walking in compassion and confrontation. In this Gandhi is treating his co-walker with compassion and both of them are confronting each other and the world. This confrontation is not violent but non-violent. Gandhi presents soul force and truth force as the forces with which to practice compassion and confrontation.

In our engagement with *Hind Swaraj* we are also invited to co-walk with Gandhi in our own ways. But as we co-walk it is helpful to ask the following questions: Who is the Editor in *Hind Swaraj*? Who is the Reader? Is Gandhi's voice heard only in the voice of the Editor? Is there not a part of Gandhi's self in the self of the Reader? Is the Reader only the other or doesn't he express part of Gandhi's self? In other words, is the dialogue only between the self and the other? Is it also not between different parts of oneself, for example a part of the self which wants to use brute force to realize Swaraj and a part of the self which wants to use truth force? One can argue that since the Reader and the Editor express some aspects of the same self, it is easier for Gandhi to use the language of compassion while dealing with the Reader. But it is not necessary that one deal with the other within with compassion. Psychoanalysis has helped us realize how often we deal with the other part of our self with violence and a lack of compassion which then gives rise to interpersonal violence and violence in society.

With this prelude, in my co-walking with Gandhi and *Hind Swaraj*, I wish to reconstitute and realize Swaraj not only as self-rule but also as the blossoming of self, the other and the world. An uncritical and mechanical rendering of Swaraj as self-rule does not address the problem that self-rule is not always accompanied by visions and practices of co-determination, co-constitution and co-responsibility. Swaraj as self-rule and self-determination needs to be accompanied by Swaraj as mutual blossoming, co-determination and co-responsibilization. Swaraj has been politically understood in a language of national self-determination, but today we need a new realization of Swaraj which is not just an extension of national self-determination or civilizational self-congratulation, but a multi-dimensional field of blossoming, co-determination, co-creation, co-responsibilization and realization of shared sovereignties.[4] We realize Swaraj as a field of shared sovereignties through cultivation of the non-sovereign dimension in us. In modernity we have considered sovereignty as sacred, which has led to a political theology of war and mutual destruction, but in Swaraj as blossoming we also cultivate a non-sovereign dimension in each of us – self, society, culture, nation-state and the world – which is sacred (cf. Dallmayr 2005; Giri 2009a). When we cultivate the non-sovereign dimension in ourselves we realize that we are not the masters of the other and the world and we do not exist to colonize and annihilate. We realize that we are servants and marked by a fundamental fragility of life and hence we are non-sovereign. Cultivation of non-sovereignty is a multi-dimensional political and spiritual task, and it is linked to our calling of responsibility.

Swaraj as blossoming through the cultivation of non-sovereignty and shared sovereignties is accompanied by a new art of integration which is neither totalizing nor totalitarian; nor is it strong. It is a field not of totality but a quest for infinity. It is an art of weak integration in which Swaraj as blossoming (realized through compassion and confrontation) generates practices of soulful togetherness and zones of proximal development (to put it in the words of educationist Leo Vygotsky; cf. Holzman) – spiritual, political, economic – in which the contending parties transform their initial isolation, help each other to develop their potential. They become part of a new wholeness, a wholeness which is a walk and a prayer with the Infinite in the self, other and the world, rather than a violent assertion of one-sided totality.

Swaraj as Blossoming

The usual definition of Swaraj is self-rule, but what are the meanings of self and rule? Is rule in the logic of government and governmentality the same as the practice of rule in Swaraj? Gandhian Swaraj involves transformation of the very logic, telos, means and ends of rule, including transformation of the vision and practice of power and freedom. Power in Swaraj is not the ability to exercise one's will over and against the will of others; rather it is the ability to walk and work together in compassion and confrontation for the realization of the potential of the self, the other and the world. Swaraj is thus a multi-valued, multi-dimensional and multi-layered process of blossoming in which the self, the other and the world first realize their bondage and struggle and strive together for unfolding their potential for blossoming, freedom and responsibility.

Gandhi himself says that by Swaraj he does not mean parliamentary Swaraj. "Real home-rule is self-rule or self-control [and] the way to it is passive resistance: that is soul-force or love-force" (1938, 90).[5] Gandhi also famously said having *Hind Swaraj* is not just replacing British rulers with Indian rules and making India an Englistan (1938, 26).[6] Another issue we need to bear in mind is that when Gandhi wrote *Hind Swaraj* in 1908 he had not articulated what the Indian National Congress adopted in its 1929 Lahore session: *Purna Swaraj*, total independence from the British Empire.[7]

In *Hind Swaraj*, Gandhi offers us a plural vision of Hind, or India. Note here Gandhi's insistence that nation and religion are not synonymous[8] *Hind Swaraj* is a foundational critique of modern civilization which erases the plural in the name of the singular conflations of multiple kinds, such as nation and language or nation and religion. But the plural understanding of the self and the other now needs to be cultivated at the very heart of the project of Swaraj. In *Hind Swaraj*, Gandhi hints at several places that the *Swa*, or self, is not singular and does not exist in dualistic opposition to the other. Here Gandhi's critique of egoism does contribute to a plural realization of self. Nevertheless, in its free-floating formulation in *Hind Swaraj* and in its common sense rendering, Swaraj as self-rule does not always contain a project of the pluralization of the very self striving towards self-rule. In other words, the self in Swaraj is not always realized as a plurivocity of Being (cf. Connolly 1999). But building on Gandhi and post-Gandhian developments in transformative philosophy and creative experimentations, we now need to interrogate a linear rendering of Swaraj as self-rule without at the same time making the self undertake a journey of what I have elsewhere called meditative verbs of pluralizations (Giri 2010a). Self in Swaraj takes part in meditative verbs of pluralizations by realizing the plural dimension in the self, the other, society and the world, which helps it overcome imprisonment in a fixed embeddedness of the self and the other and realize an emergent blossoming of all concerned.[9]

An uncritical rendering of Swaraj as self-rule leaves it entrapped in a logic of sovereignty – self, national, nation-state. Swaraj as blossoming interrogates and transforms such an imprisonment and makes it a field of the creative sharing of sovereignties (cf. Giri 2009). Even in the field of national self-determination, considering the very crisis of the model of the nation-state and the uncritical reproduction of the same exclusionary logic in contending and contesting projects of national self-determination, we need to reconstitute Swaraj as not just self-rule but mutual blossoming, co-determination, co-creative constitution and shared sovereignties. For this we need to cultivate the non-sovereign aspect of our self, society, nation and the world. This makes us realize that we are not the masters of the world but rather its servants, and our sovereignty is always fragile and ever calling for responses of responsibility. Through cultivation of non-sovereignty which has a dimension of sacredness (cf. Dallmayr 2005), we realize our own sovereignty and, at the same time, transform our singular and exclusivist sovereignty into creative fields of shared sovereignties. In this cultivation of non-sovereignty and shared sovereignties, both compassion and confrontation can help us. It is compassion which helps us realize that we need to fulfill our responsibility to others in terms of their claims to our sovereignty, and with this we need to confront our own sovereignty self-critically as well as with creative kindness so that our sovereignty becomes part of shared sovereignties. Swaraj as blossoming entails such processes of compassion, confrontation and transformations of self and sovereignty.

Hind Swaraj is now part of an interlinked project of *Jag Swaraj*, or Swaraj of the world.[10] Thus Swaraj as blossoming is part of planetary blossoming. This is facilitated by the transformation of the continuing condition of colonialism, the nation-state, the capitalist economy, control over the mind, and the transformation of consciousness, including slavish surrender to money and sex.[11] Swaraj as planetary blossoming is thus linked to these projects of planetary realizations such as post-national formations, the realization of the higher creative self within oneself who is not a slave of money, power and sex and also the overcoming of anthropocentrism.

Swaraj as blossoming involves global learning, cross-cultural and transcivilizational dialogues. But in the field of transcivilizational dialogue and co-learning, how do we walk with Gandhi's *Hind Swaraj*? Gandhi's views on civilization are quite complex. At a meta level Gandhi links civilization to the project of *dharma*: "Civilization is that mode of conduct which points to man the path of duty. Performance of duty and observance of morality are convertible terms. To observe morality is to attain mastery over our mind and passions. So doing, we know ourselves. The Gujarati equivalent for civilization means 'good conduct.'" (1938, 53). This indeed is a unique definition of civilization and thinking with and beyond Gandhi it can be applied as a global heuristic to understand the quality of all civilizations, Indian or modern. But instead of proceeding with *a priori* conclusions, as Gandhi seems to have done with such statements that modern civilization is concerned with bodily comforts and Indian civilization with our moral self,[12] we need to ask what the quality of good conduct in theory and practice in civilizations – Indian or modern – is. We are also familiar with Gandhi's quip about Western civilization; that this is a good idea. Gandhi's view has been interpreted in this way: for Gandhi, civilization is not a noun, much less a possessive pronoun, but a verb (cf. Dallmayr 2002). Taking the same line of interpretation, interrogation and reconstitution, shouldn't we look at all civilizations, Indian or modern, as a good idea?

It is in this context that we would have to learn with Gandhi about the profound critique of modern civilization that he offers in *Hind Swaraj*:

This civilization is irreligion, and it has taken such a hold on the people in Europe that those who are in it appear to be half mad. They lack real physical strength and courage. They keep up their energy by intoxication. They can hardly be happy in solitude. Women, who should be the queens of households, wander in the streets or they slave away in factories. For the sake of a pittance, half a million women in England alone are labouring under trying circumstances in factories or similar institutions. This awful fact is one of the causes of the daily suffrage movement.

Gandhi here bases his critique of modern civilization on the basis of the condition of life of men and women, especially laboring men and women. But in his portrayal of Indian civilization, where is such a picture of laboring bodies, especially low caste bodies and women?[13] If the suffering of such people makes modern civilization Satanic then does not the suffering of people in Indian civilization under the domination of caste, class and gender also make Indian civilization Satanic? Gandhi himself says in *Hind Swaraj* that all "civilizations have been on their trial"[14] and with this attitude of trial, self-questioning and mutual questioning we can now practice the art of transcivilizational dialogue and co-learning. Here we have to realize that an uncritical extension of Gandhi's term "Satanic" for the critique of other civilizations[15] may reiterate the current dangerous project of the clash of civilizations rather than cultivating dialogue among civilizations.

Swaraj as Blossoming and the Calling of Compassion and Confrontation

Hind Swaraj is a journey of compassion and confrontation. What strikes one is the compassion with which the Editor interacts with the Reader. It is worth noting the way the conversation takes place with deep compassion. The Editor says, "You are impatient. I cannot afford to be likewise… That you are prejudiced against me is not a matter of much anxiety" (Gandhi 1938, 18, 21). While explaining the meaning of Swaraj the Editor is telling the Reader, "There is need for patience. My views will develop of themselves in the course of this discourse. It is as difficult for me to understand the true nature of Swaraj as it seems to you to be easy. I shall, therefore, for the time being, content myself with endeavoring to show that what you call Swaraj is not truly Swaraj" (Gandhi 1938, 29). Towards the middle of the conversation in the chapter on brute force, when the Reader says, "Will you not admit that you are arguing against yourself? You know that what the English obtained in their own country they obtained by using brute force. I know you have argued that what they have obtained is useless, but that does not affect my argument," the Editor replies, "Your reasoning is plausible. It has deluded many. I have used similar arguments before now.

But I think I know better now, and I shall endeavor to undeceive you" In this there is both compassion and confrontation. There is compassion when the Editor is saying that he has used similar arguments in the past, thus establishing a sympathetic chord with the arguments of the Reader. At the same time, the Editor seeks to go beyond the existing mode of argument and wants to confront the Reader with further discussion about ends and means: "Your belief that there is no connection between the means and the end is a great mistake" (Gandhi 1938, 61).

The deployment of truth force or soul force and the vision and practice of passive resistance in *Hind Swaraj* is an act of compassion. At the same time, it is an act of confrontation, confronting the oppressor face to face and as a part of a wider structure of domination. In *Hind Swaraj* the Editor tells us, "Passive resistance is a method of securing rights by personal suffering; it is the reverse of resistance by arms. When I refuse to do a thing that is repugnant to my conscience, I use soul force" (Gandhi 1938, 69). The Editor further tells us, "If man will only realize that it is unmanly to obey laws that are unjust, no man's tyranny will enslave him. This is the key to self-rule or home-rule" (Gandhi 1938, 70). This reminds us of a long lineage of creative resistance beginning with the work of Étienne de La Boétie (1548) on voluntary servitude, through to Thoreau and Tolstoy.

While the agent of passive resistance in the above passage is the individual, Gandhi also presents us with instances of passive resistance as a collective act: "The fact is that, in India, the nation at large has generally used passive resistance in all departments of life. We cease to cooperate with our rulers when they displease us. This is passive resistance. I remember an instance when, in a small principality, the villagers were offended by some command issued by the prince. The former immediately began vacating the village. The prince became nervous, apologized to his subjects and withdrew his command" (Gandhi 1938, 72).

Passive resistance is an act of creative resistance and it is a process where the individual acts out of conscience, but there is also an act of cooperative and collective collaboration. Passive resistance as creative resistance becomes a field of co-nurturance, self-preparation and mutual energizing. An individualist translation of passive resistance can miss this collaborative, co-creative aspect of passive resistance. Passive resistance is a field and circle of mutual energizing in which passive resisters, inspired by their conscience, join together to confront the oppressors and the systems of oppression. The act of confrontation is also a field in which the resisters and oppressors confront each other, just as there is confrontation at the level of systems. Such confrontations interrogate the existing structures of domination and strive to create a new relationship of dignity and blossoming on the part of both the resisters and the oppressors individually as well as structurally. Probably keeping in mind this aspect of mutual blossoming, Gandhi tells us in *Hind Swaraj* that passive resistance "blesses him who uses it and him against whom it is used" (Gandhi 1938, 71–2).

We can also realize the work of passive resistance as a multi-dimensional field of creative resistance where resisters, by being together in a field of soulful togetherness of compassion and confrontation, help each other to develop their potential as well as the potential for fuller humanization and divinization on the part of the oppressors. To understand this we can make creative use of Vygotsky's concept of zones of proximal development. Creative resistance as a field becomes a zone of proximal development –spiritual, emotional, political, structural as well as soulful – on the part of all the participants in this field – resisters as well as all those with and against whom the resistance is offered. It is a field of performance (cf. Holzman 2009). In *Hind Swaraj*, because of the brevity of the text we do not get this extended realization of passive resistance as creative resistance which is animated by creative works such as music, song, drama and meditations. Creative resistance is a field of compassionate confrontation and is accompanied by meditation, mediation and transformations.

We can now meditate for a moment on the language of confrontation in *Hind Swaraj*. Gandhi does not mince words. He uses the language of prostitution to offer his critique of not only the institution of Parliament but also of professions such as law. As is well-known to readers of *Hind Swaraj*, Gandhi says, "That which you consider to be the Mother of Parliaments is like a sterile woman and a prostitute. Both of these are harsh terms but exactly fit the case" (1938, 27). In chapter eleven on "The Condition of India (Contd): Lawyers," Gandhi tells us in the voice of the Editor, "If pleaders were to abandon their profession, and consider it as degrading as prostitution, English rule would break up in a day" (Gandhi 1938, 50). But is this language of criticism fair towards the prostitutes? Doesn't it raise the problem of not only compassion but also justice? Prostitution is also a form of work, a work of labor; how would the sex workers of the world, present and past, including the one Gandhi tried to visit during his student days at London (cf. Gandhi 1929) , find such language? Wouldn't they raise the same issue of ends and means to the Editor that the Editor raises to the Reader in their conversation in *Hind Swaraj*?

Towards a New Art of Integration

Swaraj is a process and field of the blossoming of the self, the other and the world. It is a field of compassion and confrontation which helps us overcome our own isolation and fragmentation, and become connected again. This connection, however, is based upon beauty, dignity and dialogue. Thus the project of Swaraj is also part of a new art of integration. First of all, through creative resistance, the resisters and the oppressors become part of a field of compassion and confrontation which challenges them to be in communication and overcome their entrenched isolation, modes of thought and codes of conduct which give rise to systems of oppression. Through the process of realizing Swaraj new fields and processes of integration are cultivated and unfolded.

Swaraj as blossoming practices a new art of integration. While earlier models and practices of integration are modes of strong and totalizing integration, Swaraj as blossoming practices an art of weak integration. It also practices differential integration, which gives space and time for both the self and the other to blossom themselves with their unique potentiality, and at the same time be part of an emergent garland of connectedness, a web of solidarity – a solidarity which is always a process of becoming, a process of solidarizing rather than a continuation of existing mechanical solidarity which might hide structures of domination.

A new art of integration which is weak is facilitated by weakening our entrenched organizations and modes of belief. In my larger project on a new art of integration I argue that weak integration is facilitated by, among other processes, weak nationalism, weak ontology, weak religion and weak pedagogy (cf. Giri 2010b). Weak nationalism interrogates the construction of the nation-state as a naturalized entity propagating the cult of unitary strength at the expense of the plurivocity of beings, societies, languages, nations and cultures. Weak ontology urges us to realize that ontological cultivation is not only a cultivation of the mastery of the self but also a cultivation of its humility, fragility, weakness and servanthood, facilitating the blossoming of non-sovereignty and shared sovereignties (cf. Vattimo 1999). Weak ontology helps us realize that both identities and differences have inbuilt limitations and they ought to realize their own weaknesses as a starting point for communication and sharing through the cultivation of weak identity and weak differences. Weak religion as a companion in the journey of weak integration makes religious and theological systems weak rather than strong, which then facilitates border crossing and dialogues among religions and theological systems. Weak religion is also facilitated by the rise of practical spirituality in religions, which relativize pronounced religious beliefs and dogmas and lay stress on practice, especially transformative practice, to transform suffering.[16] Finally, weak pedagogy helps us realize that as educators we cannot perpetuate the logic of strength – that is, imposing our views on others, especially children – but rather persuade them to take part in collective transformative co-learning where as educators we realize, as Sri Aurobindo challenges us to realize, "nothing can be taught" (cf. Giri 2009b).

In all these aspects we can draw inspiration from Gandhi's *Hind Swaraj* as well as the larger vision, practice and life of Gandhi. Gandhi's inspiring mode of weak pedagogy embraces us when he writes, "I do not expect my views to be accepted all of a sudden. My duty is to place them before readers like yourself. Time can be trusted to do the rest" (1938, 55). Gandhi's nationalism, as well as that of his inspiring co-walkers in India's struggle for freedom such as Sri Aurobindo, Gopabandhu[17] and Tagore, is not the nationalism of a strong nation-state but the nationalism of an awakening self and grass-roots humanity realizing dignity, beauty and dialogue. Gandhi's religion is not a strong religion. Let us remember when Gandhi writes, "My first complaint is that India is becoming irreligious. Here I am not thinking of the Hindu or the Mohemedan or Zorastrian religion but of religion which underlies all religions" (1938, 36). What is this religion that underlies all religions? In *Hind Swaraj* one can read this as having faith in God and practicing compassion.[18] But the religion that underlies all religions also includes confrontation and creative resistance for the sake of the realization of beauty, dignity and dialogue. Gandhi's realization of God also has been a moving one. Towards the end of his life Gandhi realized that Truth as God is different from God as Truth. Such a position can be the foundation of a weak religion and a weak belief necessary for a new art of weak integration.

In *Hind Swaraj* through the practice of creative resistance we see the cultivation of a new strength – *weak strength*. It is a process of mutual energizing. The practitioner of creative resistance and Swaraj as blossoming is simultaneously a practitioner of a new art of cross-fertilization, critique, creativity and integration. The agent of Swaraj as blossoming is like an earthworm who tries to make the field of Swaraj fertile. At the same time she also works like a Socratic gadfly. While making the field fertile, she plants new seeds and nurtures the field like a gardener. She, together with others, cultivates the field of compassion and confrontation which gives rise to Swaraj as blossoming as a gardener. While working as an earthworm making the field fertile and as a gardener making the seeds blossom, a practitioner of Swaraj does not become confined to the field. She grows wings and flies between locations around the world. Though in *Hind Swaraj* there is a parochial assertion of the virtue of one's civilization, this needs to be supplemented with the larger vision of Gandhi where he is a bird and flying and cultivating not only with the *Bhagvad Gita* but also with the New Testament, Jesus, Thoreau, Ruskin and Tolstoy. Gandhi also wants to keep his doors and windows open. Swaraj as a blossoming of the self, the other and the world cultivates a new art of integration through such works as cross-fertilization, compassion and confrontation.

Notes

1 Those who have not read *Hind Swaraj* may note that Gandhi wrote this in the form of a dialogue between the Editor and the Reader in 1908 during his one week sea voyage from England to South Africa. Gandhi had originally written this in his mother language Gujarati. The Reader is asking the Editor many questions about Swaraj, or self-rule, as well as Indian home rule and other issues such as professions, modern civilization, education and machinery. The Editor is thinking together with the Reader with such questions and concerns and moving ahead.

2 Ramachandra Gandhi was a thoughtful philosopher from India who was also a grandson of Gandhi. *Sita's Kitchen* is a deep meditation on life in which the dialogue on the meaning of life is taking place in the forest between Buddha, a fugitive girl named Ananya and critics of Buddha such as Ajita Kesakambalin and Makhali Gosala. See Chapter Fifteen in this volume.

3 What Thoreau writes in his essay on walking is applicable to Gandhi and can be helpful in understanding walking meditation: "…you must walk like a camel…which ruminates when walking" (Thoreau 1975, 596).

4 According to Anuradha Veeravalli, Gandhi's project of Swaraj strikes at the roots of presuppositions of sovereignty in the modern nation-state. Gandhi proposes an alternative conception of sovereignty in *Hind Swaraj*. For Veeravalli,

> The theory of sovereignty proposed by Gandhi is based on the clear separation of origin, constitution, and methods of the state from that of civil society. Thus it is not surprising that Gandhi bases his understanding of swaraj…on three presuppositions fundamentally different from the accepted definitions of sovereignty in the modern nation-state: (1) it presupposed the necessary differentiation and separation of civil society from the state, in their origin and constitution. (2) The possibility of self-reform, rather than control over, or freedom from the other was seen as a necessary

condition of sovereignty. (3) It disposed of territory as a definitional condition of sovereignty; rather sovereignty defined the relation/frontier (not boundaries) between territories of different nations, and of self and other. Territory was neither an object of control, nor of acquisition or exploitation. The good of the self, or one's country rested in the good of the neighbor. (2011, 67)

5 Though Gandhi himself writes in the 1938 edition of *Hind Swaraj*, "But I would warn the reader against thinking that I am today aiming at the Swaraj described therein. I know that India is not ripe for it. It may seem an impertinence to say so. But such is my conviction. I am individually working for the self-rule pictured therein" (1938, 15–16).

6 In the words of Gandhi, "…we want English rule without the Englishman. You want the tiger's nature, but not the tiger; that is to say, you would make India English. And when it becomes English, it will be called not Hindustan but Englistan. This is not the Swaraj that I want" (1938, 26).

7 It was Sri Aurobindo, long ago, before Gandhi's *Hind Swaraj* had articulated total independence of India from the British rule. In his *Foundations of Indian Culture*, Sri Aurobindo (1972a) also talks about Indian civilization. It would be enriching to study together Sri Aurobindo's views on Indian civilization and Gandhi's, as well as their views on Swadeshi and Swaraj. Of course, one obvious contrast which is pertinent here is that Sri Aurobindo in his early political life supported political violence as a means to realize India's freedom (cf. Heehs 2008), but for Gandhi, as he makes it clear in *Hind Swaraj*, this was not acceptable. As he asks in *Hind Swaraj*: "Do you not tremble to free India by assassination?" (1938, 60). But beyond this there are remarkable similarities between Gandhi and Sri Aurobindo in their critique of the nation-state and cultivation of a different vision of a nation. Sri Aurobindo's *Bande Mataram* (1972b) is also a *Hind Swaraj*-like text in which Sri Aurobindo raised such issues as going back to the village and Hindu-Muslim unity long before Gandhi's *Hind Swaraj*. At the same time, Sri Aurobindo did not offer a wholesale condemnation of modern civilization, even though he, like Gandhi, had a civilizational approach, mainly drawing upon Indian spiritual traditions, to India and the world.

8 In the words of Gandhi, "If the Hindus believe that India should be only by Hindus, they are living in a dreamland. The Hindus, the Mahomedans, the Parsis and the Christians who have India as their country are fellow countrymen, and they will have to live in unity, of only for their own interest. In no part of the world are one nationality and one religion synonymous terms; nor has it ever been so in India" (1938, 43).

9 Here what philosopher R. Sunder Rajan writes helps us realize the emergent pluralization of the self, the other and the world: "Knowing or coming to understand others requires an aspect of renunciation, a capacity for loss of self-interest and preoccupation with oneself, of overcoming narcissism …to know the other in the sense of loving care requires upon our part a movement of the whole personality towards the mode of emergence; it involves an overcoming of the self-protective mechanism of embeddeness…" (1998, 80–81).

10 In the *Hind Swaraj* centenary seminar, "Social Development and Human Civilization in the 21st Century," 12–14 Feb 2009, Delhi, Professor Manoranjan Mohanty, the main organizer of the seminar, articulated such a project of Swaraj.

11 Gandhi writes, "Money renders a man helpless. The other thing which is equally harmful is sexual vice. Both are poison. A snake-bite is a lesser poison than these two, because the former merely destroys the body but the latter destroy body, mind and soul" (1938, 82).

12 In the words of Gandhi, "The tendency of the Indian civilization is to elevate the moral being, that of the Western civilization is to propagate immorality" (1938, 55). Furthermore, "Civilization seeks to increase bodily comforts, and it fails miserably even in doing so" (1938, 32–3).

13 In his *Letter to a Hindoo* Tolstoy (1908) had raised the issue of caste system. Gandhi refers to this in the list of books "for perusal to follow up" (1938, 91) and had also written an

introduction to this on 19 November 1909, but does not refer to this issue of caste and Indian civilization at all in his presentation of Indian civilization in *Hind Swaraj*.

14 Note here the following conversation in *Hind Swaraj*:

> Reader: If Indian civilization is, as you say, the best of all, how do you account for India's slavery?
>
> Editor: This civilization is unquestioningly the best, but it is to be observed that all civilizations have been on their trial. That civilization which is permanent outlives it. Because the sons of India were found wanting, its civilization has been placed in jeopardy. But it strength is to be seen in its ability to survive the shock. Moreover, the whole of India is not touched. Those alone who have been affected by Western civilization have become enslaved. (1938, 56)

15 Writing about modern civilization, Gandhi says, "According to the teaching of Mohammed this should be considered a Satanic civilization" (1938, 33).

16 Weak theology is at works in movements such as Habitat for Humanity (cf. Giri 2002) and Swadhyaya (cf. Giri 2008) where participants emphasize not so much belief or doctrinal content but the need for building homes and collective institutions of well-being.

17 Gopabandhu (1877–1928), a co-walker and co-fighter of Gandhi from Odisha, wrote an evocative essay called "*Odiyara Jatiyata*" (the Nationalism of Oriya) in which he wrote, "We are first of all human being, then Indian and then Odiya."

18 For Gandhi, "The poet Tulsidas has said: 'Of religion, pity, or love, is the root, as egoism of the body. Therefore, we should not abandon pity as long as we are alive. This appears to me to be a scientific truth. The force of love is the same as the force of soul or truth. We have the experience of working at every step" (1938, 67). Though Gandhi uses the word pity and not compassion, it does not have the usual connotation of pity and it does encompass compassion.

References

Connolly, William E. 1999. *Why I Am Not a Secularist*. Minneapolis: University of Minnesota Press.

Dalai Lama. 2009. *The Middle Way: Faith Grounded in Reason*. Boston: Wisdom.

Dallmayr, Fred. 2002. *Dialogue Among Civilizations*. New York: Palgrave Macmillan.

_____. 2005. *Small Wonder: Global Power and its Discontents*. Lanham, MD: Rowman & Littlefield.

Galtung, Johan and Graeme MacQueen. 2010. *Globalizing God: Religion, Spirituality and Peace*. TRANSCEND University Press.

Gandhi, M. K. 1909/1938. *Hind Swaraj*. Ahmedabad: Navajivan Publishing House.

_____. 1929. *The Story of My Experiments with Truth*. Ahmedabad: Navajivan Publishing House.

Gandhi, Ramachandra. 1993. *Sita's Kitchen: A Testimony of Faith and Inquiry*. Delhi: Penguin.

Giri, Ananta Kumar. 2002. *Building in the Margins of Shacks: The Vision and Projects of Habitat for Humanity*. Delhi: Orient Longman.

_____. 2008. *Self-Development and Social Transformations? The Vision and Experiments of the Socio-Spiritual Mobilization of Swadhyaya*. Jaipur: Rawat/ Lanham, MD: Lexington Books.

_____, ed. 2009a. *The Modern Prince and the Modern Sage: Transforming Power and Freedom*. Delhi: Sage.

_____. 2009b. *Learning the Art of Wholeness: Integral Education and Beyond*. Chennai: Madras Institute of Development Studies. Draft report of a project on integral education.

_____. 2010. "Towards A New Art of Integration." Paper presented at the International Symposium on "Learning Across Borders," University of Luxembourg.

_____. 2012. "Beyond Adaptation and Meditative Verbs of Pluraliztions." In *Sociology and Beyond: Windows and Horizons*. Jaipur: Rawat Publications.

Habermas, Jürgen. 2006. *The Divided West*. Cambridge: Polity Press.

Heehs, Peter. 2008. *The Lives of Sri Aurobindo*. New York: Columbia University Press.

Holzman, Lois. 2009. *Vygotsky at Work and Play*. London: Routledge.

La Boétie, Étienne de. 1548. *Discourse on Voluntary Servitude*. Originally published under the title *Anti-Dictator*. New York: Columbia University Press. Available at http://www.constitution. org/la-boetie/serve_vol.htm (accessed 23 May 2006).

Rawls, John. 1971. *A Theory of Justice*. Cambridge, MA: Harvard University Press.

Sen, Amartya. 2009. *The Idea of Justice*. Cambridge, MA: Harvard University Press.

Sri Aurobindo. 1972a. *Foundations of Indian Culture*. Pondicherry: Sri Aurobindo Ashram.

_____. 1972b. *Bande Mataram*. Pondicherry: Sri Aurobindo Ashram.

Thoreau, David. 1975. "Walking." In Carl Bode, ed., *The Portable Thoreau*. New York: Penguin.

Tolstoy, Leo. 1908. *Letter to a Hindoo*. Reprinted in *Letter to a Hindoo: Taraknath Das, Leo Tolstoy and Mahatma Gandhi*, ed. Chirstian Bartolf. Berlin: Gandhi Information Center, 2009.

Vattimo, Gianni. 1999. *Belief*. Cambridge: Polity Press.

Veeravalli, Anuradha. 2011. "Swaraj and Sovereignty." *Economic and Political Weekly* 46 (5): 65–9.

Chapter Fourteen

CIVIL SOCIETY AND THE CALLING OF SELF-DEVELOPMENT

If we divide the history of mankind into five periods, that is, the prehistoric, ancient, medieval, modern and post-modern, one can say that the history of civil society begins only when the institution of the sacred or the divine kingship begins to dissolve into two differentiated institutions at the dawn of the ancient, or at the very latest the medieval, period out of the past…

Even if this civil society was indeed the "child of the modern world," still it is the Christian society and its early modern reform that we may also have to consider, and not only the bourgeois society of modern capitalism. By this wider definition, the modern civil society was established or revived in Britain at any rate by the struggle of the Nonconformists, the new Christians, who together severed connection with the established Church of England when it accepted royal supremacy at the time of the Reformation… The new Christians wanted instead what we may call salvation through religion in society, with pluralist freedom of conscience and worship for all.

—J. P. S. Uberoi, "Civil Society" (2003, 115, 120)

There are groups as well as individuals all over the world who are increasingly conscious of their creative potentiality and wish to realise their aspirations. Contemporary history is about these multiple selves engaged in dynamic struggles. Some may be forward looking and emancipative while others may be regressive and irrational. But the overwhelming trend is likely to be one that demands respect for each self.

—Manoranjan Mohanty, "The Self as Center in the Emerging World
of the Twenty-first Century: A Sino-Indian Perspective" (2002, 1)

The Problem

It is Jürgen Habermas (1981) himself who quite some time ago had challenged us that now we need a new philosophy of science which is not scientistic. It is worth asking Habermas, and all of us sociologists for whom sociological engagement is nothing more than an elaboration of the agenda of modernity, whether we need an understanding of and relationship with modernity which is not modernistic.

This inquiry is at the core of understanding paths of civil society and experiments with modernities, not only in India but also in Europe, East Asia, Africa, Latin America and around the world. Both conceptions of civil society and modernity suffer from a profound modernistic bias which is part of the post-traditional telos of modernistic sociological theorizing.[1] The recent discourse of multiple modernities initiated by S. N. Eisenstadt (cf. Sachsenmaier et al. 2002) has suggested some new possibilities, but the approach of multiple modernities as that of the universalistic modernity of Habermas suffers from a modernistic bias when it comes to understanding tradition.[2] Prefiguring my argument I wish to submit that appreciating the significance of Indian modernities from Buddha to Gandhi challenges us to understand the relationship between modernity and tradition, state and society, and religion and secularism in a new way, through a multi-valued logic of autonomy and interpenetration rather than through the dualistic logic of modernity. Such a dualistic logic has impoverished our understanding of civil society and modernity in the West itself, not to speak of illuminating our historical paths and tryst with modernities in India.

The subject of Indian modernity is quite vast, and here I just wish to state that Indian modernities have emerged out of processes of criticism, creativity and struggles through history, as in the revolt of Buddha, the rise of Upanshishadic spirituality, *bhakti* movements in medieval India, movement for a new renaissance in the nineteenth century, and the multi-dimensional anti-colonial and post-colonial struggles for freedom.[3] Tryst with modernities in India have involved a transformative dialogue between reason and tradition, tradition and modernity, and rationality and spirituality which have shaped their paths, contents and visions. These modernities have generated their own public spaces of coming together, dialogues and public deliberations, which bear parallels to what is spoken of as civil society in the modern West. Civil society is not only an epistemic project, it is also an ontological project; in fact it is a project of ontological epistemology of participation going beyond the modernistic privileging of epistemology and dualism between ontology and epistemology. Taking inspiration from *bhakti* movements, Kabir, Nanak, Mira Bai, Sri Aurobindo and Gandhi, we can realize that the significance of Indian modernities lies in bringing to the fore strivings for multi-dimensional self-development where self-transformation contributes to world transformation, and where an aesthetics and ethics of servanthood is an important mark of being modern, rather than the will to power.

But such an open-ended approach to civil society and paths of Indian modernities seems to be missing from certain dominant sociological theorizing in India. For scholars such as Andre Béteille (2001) and Dipankar Gupta (1997), civil society is a modernist category of thought and practice guaranteed by state. Béteille writes, "...I will not try to give a definition of civil society but instead sketch out the context in which it may be meaningfully described. While doing so, I would like to repeat that civil society is a feature of the modern world, and it will serve little purpose to look for alternative forms of it in the medieval or ancient world" (Béteille 2001, 294). For Dipankar Gupta, "...if tradition is allowed to gain the upper hand then it is not civil society and with it the concomitant growth of freedom that develops" (Gupta 1997, 141).

In discussing the potential for the formation of civil society that the social mobilization of the Bharatiya Kisan Union of Mahendra Singh Tikait of Uttar Pradesh (BKU) offers, Gupta says, "When it comes to the laudable objective of curbing liquor and drug addiction, here too methods are traditional and repressive. Even if someone gives someone the legitimate contract to vend liquor, the outlet should be forcibly closed" (1997, 145). But Gupta does not look into the repressive apparatus of the state itself in flooding villages with liquor. While talking about Mahendra Singh Tikait, Gupta writes the following: "...many of his followers have told me that on several occasions the BKU chief leaves a meeting and goes to his prayer room where he is not to be disturbed" (1997, 60). But Gupta does not ask what significance prayer has in the leader of the movement's personal life or in his conduct in the public sphere. Such a derisive attitude is an instance of a modernistic bias and a disdainful attitude towards tradition. Understanding civil society and paths of modernities in India challenges us to overcome this.

Towards a Multi-dimensional and Multi-valued Understanding of Civil Society

We need a multi-dimensional understanding and realization of the sphere of civil society and its multiple activities, but for this we need to overcome the dualism between tradition and modernity, right and good (cf. Habermas 1990), civil society and good society (cf. Béteille 2001), and institutionalization and mobilization. I suggest that the field of civil society consists of an autonomous space but is interpenetrated by overlapping circles of society, religion, state, market, social movements/voluntary organizations and the self. Civil society is not only a space of "mediating institutions" (cf. Béteille 2001) but also of mobilization, where mobilization refers not only to socio-political mobilizations but also socio-spiritual mobilizations, including reflective mobilization of the self (cf. Giri 2004a).[4] In the same vein, state and civil society are not to be conflated with each other. Society and civil society are not synonymous – civil society refers to that conscious and mobilized aspect of society which strives to create a space for critical self-reflections and public deliberations. Despite contentions and struggles, state and civil society are related again in a logic of autonomy and interpenetration, and here social movements, different mediating institutions, and voluntary organizations play an important role. Civil society is also nourished by support from the market. Contributions from corporate leaders and other market leaders add to the resource base of civil society. In so far as the relationship between religion and civil society is concerned, one great challenge here is to overcome the dualism of religion and secularism. While for Béteille (2001), civil society is mainly a secular space, for Uberoi (1996) and Oommen (2001a) civil society is a space where religious associations and critical spiritual movements are also at work.[5] Civil society is also a space of work for the self; in fact the self is an actor in all the intersecting and interpenetrating dimensions of civil society – society, state, market and religion. The quality of the work of the self, its mobilization in civil society and its aforementioned intersecting dimensions determines the quality of civil society.

Critical spiritual movements such as the *bhakti* movements in Indian history have been important actors in articulating the paths of Indian modernities and generating a space of autonomy, self-realization, social transformation and world transformation. The *bhakti* movements created a new social space of caste and to some extent gender equality, and they embodied inter-religious dialogue. For Chittaranjan Das (1997), the Sant tradition is a product of creative and transformative dialogue and the encounter between Hinduism and Islam.[6] The participants of the Sant tradition and *bhakti* movements challenged people to go beyond accepted boundaries and generate a new space of togetherness.[7] The leaders of the *bhakti* movements wrote in the people's language, not in Sanskrit. Their literature has been one of love, protest and affirmation, and for understanding paths of modernities in India we need to understand the public sphere of creativity in language, religion and society that the *bhakti* movements created. This is not possible as long as we are bounded to an *a priori* dualistic logic of modernity and civil society which puts religion and civil society in two separate boxes.

Such an approach to civil society has a wider global significance; for example, understanding the relationship between Islam and civil society. As Nikamura Mitsuo writes, urging us to take Gellner's views on the impossibility of civil society and Islam only with a pinch of salt, "...for centuries Islamic civilizations have developed their own versions of civility and civil society which are different from the West. These have included the independence of Muslim communities (*ummah*) from the state under the spiritual leadership of the *ulama* (Islamic scholars), rule of law to protect personal life and property, religious and ethnic pluralism, consultative and consensus methods of decision-making. In short, there has been civility and [a] public sphere in [the] Islamic world to control the arbitrariness of state power and to guarantee the autonomy of diversified associational life" (Mitsuo 2001, 5). According to Madjid, "...the notion of civil society or civilized society coined in the constitution of Medina by the Prophet Muhammed makes a genuine part of the common heritage of mankind" (quoted in Mitsuo 2001, 5). Giving examples of voluntary organizations and political movements such as Nahdaltul Ulama and Muhamadiya, Mitsuo urges us to understand the religious resources for Muslim voluntarism in Indonesia. In his work on civil Islam in Indonesia, Robert Hefner (1998) also urges us to understand its role in the democratization of politics and society in Indonesia. But Hefner makes a larger point that calls for consideration from those of us who are bonded to a "post-traditional telos":

Viewed from the ground of everyday practice rather than the dizzying height of official canons, the normative diversity of traditional societies is far greater than most sociological models imply. As in China, Romania, and Islamic Indonesia, there are always "underdeveloped possibilities" – values and practices that hover closer to the social ground and carry unamplified possibilities. These low-lying precedents may not appear in high-flying discourse. Nevertheless, they are in some sense "available" for engagement and reflection, even if they have long been overlooked in public formulations. Under conditions of cultural globalization or cross-regional transfer, some legal actors may seize on exogamous idioms to [legitimatize] and elevate principles of social action (such as equality, participation etc.) already present in social life, if in an underdeveloped, subordinated, or politically bracketed manner. (1998, 20)

Here Hefner may have to consider that there are underdeveloped possibilities not only in so-called traditional societies but also in so-called modern societies. As there is underdeveloped possibility for participatory politics in the so-called traditional societies, there are underdeveloped possibilities for reflective mobilization of self in contemporary modern and post-modern societies as well.

While civil society and reflective mobilizations of the self have manifested themselves in a variety of societies, some of the unique features of their manifestation must not be lost sight of. This calls for a non-judgmental global comparative engagement with various manifestations of civil society, reflective mobilizations of self and spiritual movements in societies and histories. In India, socio-religious and socio-spiritual movements such as the *bhakti* movements generated new spaces of self and societal realization, but it did not offer a direct political confrontation of the governing regimes. In India public spheres and civil societies have not manifested themselves primarily in political terms, though in the public sphere itself participants had access to political rulers.[8] For S. N. Eisenstadt (2005), this contrasts with the Islamic public sphere which was driven by the primacy of the political. In Islamic public spheres and civil societies, a notion of political community was quite at the center, but this community, though autonomous, was still much more tightly controlled by the ruling political formation compared to the case of state and civil society in the modern West. But what is striking is that, though in Islamic civil society the political community and its autonomy was a key concern, in actual terms in India, without sharing this key preoccupation with the political, people had a "relatively widespread access to the political arena" (Eisenstadt 2005, 21) which makes the situation "very close to the ideal model of European civil society" (Eisenstadt 2005, 19).

But unlike both the modern European and Islamic cases, in the Indian engagement with civil society politics was not at the core. For Eisenstadt, "The political arena, the arena of rulership, did not constitute in 'historical India' – as it did in monolithic civilizations or in Confucianism – a major arena of the implementation of the transcendental visions predominant in this civilization" (Eisenstadt 2005, 20). Such a conception of the political was closely related to the theory and practice of sovereignty that developed in India. It emphasized "the multiple rights – usually defined in terms of various duties – of different groups and sectors of society rather than a unitary, quasi-ontological conception-real or ideal – of 'the state' or of 'society' – giving rise to what can be defined as fractured sovereignty" (Eisenstadt 2005, 21). In the pregnant phase of Eisenstadt, this was a condition of "non-ontologization of the political arena" (Eisenstadt 2005, 22).

The non-ontologization of the political and the work of fractured sovereignty in the Indian engagement with civil societies challenges us to rethink the primacy of the political and the cult of sovereignty in our dominant conceptions of state and civil society. Instead of looking at the Indian case as an aberration, this challenges us to make our conceptions of civil society a multiverse. It also challenges us to rethink our bondage to the cult of sovereignty that dominates European modernity. Transforming Eisenstadt's perspective of fractured sovereignty, we can say that civil society is not only a place of fractured sovereignties but also of shared sovereignties and sacred "non-sovereignty" (cf. Giri 2009; Dallmayr 2005). In order for civil society to be helpful in being a space of self-development and social transformation, the cult of absolute sovereignty at the level of state, society and self has to be transformed into a condition of shared sovereignties where all the interacting parties are interested in learning from each other in a spirit of mutual listening, co-laboring experiments, mutual interrogations and transformations. In this space, the interacting parties do not want to dominate each other with a will to power and mastery; they wish to serve each other for mutual growth and transformation. This second aspiration and activity makes this space a space of "sacred non-sovereignty" (cf. Dallmayr 2005) animated by a will to serve, nurture, share and co-create, rather than a will to dominate.

Towards a New Understanding of the Activities and Aspirations of Civil Society

If civil society is a multi-dimensional space of autonomy and interpenetration, what are some of its activities, works and aspirations? I suggest that these are love, labor, language, and rules/law.[9] To begin with the work of love in the sphere of civil society, Uberoi (1996) urges us to realize how the loving self-sacrifice of martyrs is crucial to the work of civil society.[10] For Uberoi, it is the martyr, rather than either the heroes or the victims, who constitute the universal foundation of civil society. Though Uberoi has not discussed the barbaric misuse of the ideology of martyrdom for annihilating men and women in religious traditions such as Sikhism and Islam, his emphasis on "loving self-sacrifice" is an important contribution to rethinking the modernist emasculation of civil society. For instance, one cannot understand the work of martyrs like Shankar Singh Guha Niyogi of the Chhattisgarh Mukti Morcha (CMM)[11] without understanding the dimension of loving self-sacrifice in civil society, not only as a space of association and mediation, but also as a site of struggle. As Chandhoke writes about the Chhattisgarh Mukti Morcha, "Despite the fact that CMM used only non-violent means of protest, such as peaceful demonstrations, *dharnas*, strikes, *morchas* and petitions – all of which are permissible in civil society – their protests were savagely put down. During a conversation with one of the CMM's leaders, I wondered whether it was not legitimate to use violence in a society where the regime virtually used violence against its own people. His answer was an emphatic no; violence, he argued, would impoverish the movement and denude it of any spirit of commitment" (Chandhoke 2003b, 206). Here the struggle is both a political struggle of democratization of state and society and the spiritual struggle of realizing "power free" existence (cf. Dallmayr 2001) , that is, not being a slave to the logic of power and using the instruments of power to oppress other people. This struggle is animated by the hope that the subaltern would embody a different subjectivity, and intersubjectivity and would not try to imbibe the same logic of dominant hegemony (Chakrabarty 2002). It is no wonder then that Chhattisgarh Mukti Morcha strives for a new meaning of "what it means to be a Chatisgarhi citizen. According to CMM, a Chatisgarhi citizen is one who works in the region and who does not exploit either the resources or the people for his or her personal benefit" (Chandhoke 2003b, 238).[12]

The relationship between the work of love and the work of civil society becomes clearer in an interesting essay by Veena Das entitled "The Small Community of Love." For Das, "One cannot base the little community of love on an appeal to law – you cannot wait, as Cavell says, for the perfect larger community before you form the smaller communities of love. Thus the constitutional promise about life, liberty, and pursuit of happiness has the public face of what it is to claim this in law and the private face of what it is to ask that human society contain the room for these small communities to be built" (2003). Elaborating on this further, Das writes, "In a conference I attended recently, someone asked if a song like, '*Tu Hindu banega na Musalman banega – Insaan ki aulad hai insaan banega*' from *Dhul ka Phul* was still possible. I thought of Mr. Insaniyat [humanity] and how he learnt that the claims of building small communities of love was also a way of learning to be Indian" (2003). In his article "Romantic Archives: Literature and the Politics of Identity in Bengal," Dipesh Chakrabarty also writes:

> What politics can we reconstitute out of our romantic investment in language? The politics I have in mind, however, is not programmatic. The making of a romantic literary legacy into a political archive is not something we can call into being. Romantic thoughts no longer furnish our analytical frameworks, but the inheritance of romanticism is built into the Bengali language. Our everyday and unavoidable transactions with the poetry of language may thus be compared to the practice of vigilant waiting. This vigilant and active waiting can itself be political. Listen to the romantic voice of a Bengali communist poet who captures its spirit:

> …When the rains depart
> We will put out in the sun
> Everything that is wet
> Woodchips and all
> Put out in the sun
> We shall
> Even our hearts. (2004, 682)

Continuing our exploration of the relationship between the work of love and work of civil society from a philosophical and theological perspective, Giani Vattimo (1999) tells us that we are all in need of forgiveness, not because we have fallen in love but because we have failed in love. Such a recognition of failure in love helps us to be repentant for our inability to transform situations of conflict and avert many social tragedies. Given the significance of the work of reconciliation and forgiveness in many societies, such as South Africa or India, after the violence of apartheid or communal conflicts, the work of love is quite central in civil society organizations working on post-conflict reconciliation.

From the aspiration and work of love in the sphere of civil society, let us come to the work of labor. Civil society is not only a sphere of public deliberations and discursive argumentations, it is also a sphere of labor where laboring bodies come together and build new spaces of habitation and hope. Gandhi's conception of bread labor helps us in understanding this link between the work of labor and work of civil society. So does Swadhyaya's (a socio-spiritual movement in contemporary India) vision and practice of *shramabhakti* – devotional labor (cf. Giri 2008). In Swadhyaya participants come together and build foundations of collective well-being through shared devotional labor, such as digging village wells. Similar is the work of Habitat for Humanity, a Christian socio-religious movement in the US which is working in many countries around the world, where volunteers of Habitat build houses together with prospective homeowners (Giri 2002a).

As civil society is also a sphere of institutions, rules and laws are quite central here, though it is important to acknowledge that civil society as a space of mobilization may challenge many of rules and laws within which civic institutions function.

Now to come to the theme of language in the work of civil society, in many ways it is quite central, as has been attested by theorists of civil society and the public sphere such as Habermas (1989). A Habermasian perspective on civil society helps us understand the key importance of communication, especially communicative action, in the working of civil society. In the history of India we find the struggle for people's languages beyond the language of the elites and the *pundits*. Movements such as the *bhakti* movements, as well as contemporary Dalit movements (cf. Narayan 2001; Pandian 1998), have played an important role in creating people's languages and literature which contributed to a new self-awareness among people, as well as new themes and spaces of discursive deliberation about the self, society and polity. For example, in Orissa Sarala Das wrote the epic *Mahabharata* in Odia and the Panchasakhas, or the "Five Friends," such as Achyutananda Das and Jagannath Das in the sixteenth century not only translated epics such as the *Ramayana* into Odia but also created life-elevating literature. They also contributed to building study centers known as *Bhagabata Ghara* for studying these works in villages (cf. Das 1997). These reading spaces, though limited by caste and gender inequality, contributed to the generation of new spaces of conviviality and conversations. But while understanding the relationship between language and civil society in these manifold ways, it is helpful at the same time to acknowledge the limits of language in the work of civil society. The language of civil society may be the heritage of a dominant language of class and culture, and here overcoming the limits of the dominant language calls for multi-dimensional cultural, political and social transformations.[13] While civil society is a sphere of critical deliberations, this very work itself calls for listening on the part of the participating actors, and this in turn calls for the ability to cultivate silence in discursive argumentations.

Civil Society and the Calling of Self-Development

Though the modernist discourse of civil society has been imprisoned within a predominantly statist and political model, it is Hegel himself who urges us to understand the link between civil society and self-development when he urges us to understand the significance of inner conscience in overcoming one's egotism in civil society (Dallmayr 1993; Giri 2002b). Hegel was aware of the crucial need for taming civil society. Hegel strives to tame civil society through "pedagogy or *bildung*" as well as by designing a "system of institutional mediations to consolidate incipient bonds between individuals in civil society" (Chandoke 2003c, 130). Before Hegel, the proponents of the Scottish Enlightenment, Adam Smith and Adam Ferguson, also urged us to understand the link between civil society and self-development. In the tradition of Scottish Enlightenment, "the idea of civil society came to rest on the notion of the autonomous and moral individual as standing at the foundation of social order" (Seligman 1995, 215). This individual in Smith, in the first instance, is "tempered by the instinct for approbation, sobered by the desire to be seen as praiseworthy"; she is also guided by "another consideration altogether, the workings of what Smith calls the 'impartial spectator'" (Chandhoke 2003c, 106). The impartial spectator needs not only to have sympathy for what it observes but also "compassion": "The compassion of the spectator must arise altogether from the consideration of what he himself would feel if he were reduced to the same unhappy or happy situation" (Chandhoke 2003c, 110). Recently Amartya Sen (2002) has argued that Adam Smith's notion of the impartial spectator suggests a different pathway of justice (in which the individual takes responsibility for justice) than the Rawlsian one. The space of civil society also calls for the development of the ability to be impartial spectators in and among the actors.

This capacity to be "impartial spectators" can be accompanied by efforts to put oneself in the shoes of the others through "sympathy" and compassion. This is also suggested in Edward Shils' plea for the development of the virtues of civility. As Béteille interprets:

> In his characterization of civil society, Shils assigns some importance to the virtues of civility. Civil society cannot prosper unless its members are able to put themselves, at least to some extent, in the position of their political opponents and their social inferiors. It is in this view of the subject…the idea of civil society comes closest to that of good society. (2001, 291)

Along with putting oneself into the shoes of one's opponents or inferiors, participation in the space of civil society also calls for the ability to listen rather than just talk and argue, to demonstrate one's performative competence in discursive argumentation. Though a Habermasian approach to civil society and the public sphere is open to the rise of post-conventional moral sensibility in self and society, Habermas has not paid enough attention to the need for the cultivation of the capacity for listening or to generating appropriate social and ontological conditions for listening. The challenge here is a deeper one, as it calls for a foundational border crossing that goes beyond a valorized linguistic pragmatics to the acknowledgment of the constitutive as well as the continued significance of silence in the work of discourse itself.

Such a border-crossing engagement calls for going beyond the modernist conception of the rational self and to realize what William Connolly (2001) calls "plurivocity of being." The Habermasian self, as with that of Bourdieu and most of us modernists, is mainly a techno-practitioner (cf. Faubion 1995), and here we need to realize that the self has also a transcendental dimension (i.e. that aspect of self which establishes friendship and solidarity across boundaries, for example between self and other). This is suggested in Spinoza's conception of trans-individuality (cf. Gatens and Llyod 1999) and Roy Bhaskar's (2002) recent discussion of the transcendentally real self as an inalienable dimension in the work of our everyday life. Self-development refers to the development of all the dimensions of self – sociological as well as transcendental. Considered from this broader understanding of self-development, much work needs to be done in theory and practice as even scholars who put the challenge of self at the core seem to take it for granted. Consider here the following reflections of Uberoi and Mohanty. For Uberoi, "In Gandhi's civil society the self would always look at the other in the eye as its second self, and offer dialogue and non-violent conversation without fear of the possible consequences" (2003, 124). For Mohanty, "In the conception of the creative self every entity grants other entities status for seeking creative fulfillment. In other words, *it is not placed as Self vs. Other. It is in a framework of Self and Self*" (2003, emphases in the original). But how does one treat the other as self and oneself as another? Does it call for ontological as well as social processes of self-development? Uberoi and Mohanty do not discuss the process of self-development and the inclusion of the other. Put briefly in tune with the multi-valued perspective of civil society presented earlier, such a mode of relationship on the part of self calls for ongoing practices of self-development on the part of actors and institutions, facilitated by participation in love, labor, language, and rules/laws.

Civil Society and Self-Development: Some Further Issues of Theory and Practice

Civil society as a space of creativity, public deliberation, self-cultivation, and socio-political and socio-spiritual struggle calls for continued self-development on the part of actors and institutions. As has already been suggested, some of the challenges of self-development in the sphere of civil society are the development of the capacity for listening, overcoming the logic of power and domination, creating a condition for critical reflection, and establishing relations of non-duality, non-domination and non-violence, not only between the self and the other but also as a foundation of social order. It should be clear that these are as much challenges for individuals as for institutions. Béteille looks at civil society as mainly consisting of mediating institutions, but does not explore the challenge of self-development and transformations, such as the realization of a reflective space of mutual learning and listening and dialogical democracy, that institutions of civil society face so that these institutions contribute to the multi-dimensional self-realization of actors rather than repressing or suppressing them.

Voluntary organizations and social movements are an important part of civil society. Often these organizations suffer from the problem of entrenched authoritarianism, and here self-development calls for the realization of dialogical democracy on the part of leaders and institutions. Those who work with them are often treated as bonded laborers and their need for self-development is not given sufficient attention (cf. Giri 2004). In my study of one such NGO, I found that the funds allocated for staff development remained unutilized for years. This organization, at the same time, continued to provide support to tribal people in their struggle against multinational mining companies at great risk to itself and its workers. According to one of the leaders of this organization, voluntary action has both a constructive and confrontational side. When it confronts the state and the market, its choice to confront cannot be solely an organizational choice. If there is not enough preparation in terms of courage and self-sacrifice, and an integral moral responsibility towards suffering humanity, it is difficult to be on the side of the people when actors are confronted with dire consequences (cf. Giri 2004).

Such a challenge of self-development confronts not only voluntary organizations but also social movements. Many a time social movements work as hegemonic entities suppressing the creative unfolding of its participants. In this context what Monanty writes deserves our careful consideration: "Self here is perceived as a creative self and not an obsessive self or exclusivist assertion of an identity… We have also seen people's movements functioning as monolithic movements not allowing democratic dissent within or not allowing freedom to the sub-groups within the movement" (2003, 17).

In the era of globalization, the challenge of self-development has more facets than just doing yoga. It requires personal knowledge of the shifting trajectories of state, market and the global system.[14] First of all, voluntary organizations, movements and institutions in civil society can learn from each other. Voluntary organizations in countries such as India are not condemned only to receive funds from donor agencies (such as HIVOS from The Netherlands and ACTIONAID from the UK) and execute programs among the poor in their localities. They should also go and study the nature of poverty in the UK and the Netherlands, thus creating a context for reciprocal learning. There has to be more people-to-people contact and learning, and when it happens, as in the global village program of Habitat for Humanity (cf. Giri 2002b) or in the mutual visitation of each other's groups in the slum dwellers' association of South Asia, it creates conditions for critical and reflective learning. As Arjun Appadurai (2002) tells us, when the leaders from slum improvement associations of Karachi visit their counterparts in Mumbai, they ask questions about funding and transparency which one does not ask so innocently in one's home locations. Such questions create the opportunity for critical self-reflection on the part of the host organization.

By Way of Conclusion

Self-development has been a neglected theme in the discourse of civil society. The present chapter has explored the links between civil society and self-development (i.e. how civil society has to contribute to self-development of individuals and institutions and how self-development is crucial to a revitalization of civil society). But understanding this link challenges us to develop a multi-dimensional and multi-valued understanding of civil society going beyond many modernistic dualisms such as private and public, tradition and modernity, civil society and good society, and religion and secularism. Such a multi-valued understanding not only helps in a new understanding of civil society, but also in understanding the paths of Indian modernities in particular and global modernities in general. It also provides a new aspiration, namely of self-development and social transformation for self and civil society, to live and strive towards.

Notes

1 For Giddens (1994), sociology is part of the post-traditional telos of modernity, and for Béteille (2002), sociology is a modern, not a postmodern or a traditional, discipline.
2 For example, following Max Weber, S. N. Eisenstadt, a key proponent of the multiple modernities approach, defines the core of modernity as the deconstruction of a God-ordained worldview held by all axial civilizations. "Since modern societies are no longer embedded in meaningful transcendental orders, they are in principle open to continuous transformation and adaptation" (Eisenstadt 2002,10).
3 For Uberoi, "The struggle to define and establish civil society in India during the modern period runs parallel to the rise, development and recognition of the vernaculars and vernacularism everywhere in language, labour and culture; and it is the story of religion and politics proceeding from Kabir (1440–1518) to the martyrdom of Mahatma Gandhi" (Uberoi 2003, 123). Uberoi himself says that civil society is not only a modernistic category, and we can explore struggles for Indian modernities and civil societies from the strivings of Buddha and his social struggles to build new critical spaces.
4 For Neera Chandhoke, "Civil society is not an institution; it is, rather, a process whereby the inhabitants of the sphere (i.e, civil society) constantly monitor both the state and monopoly of power within itself" (Chandhoke 2003a, 57). Chadhoke approaches civil society from the vantage point of continued mobilization, though she seems to be stressing more political mobilization and less reflective mobilization of the self. Similarly Oommen (2001a) has a mobilizational approach to civil society, while Béteille (2001) a predominantly institutional approach. This dualism between mobilization and institutionalization needs to be overcome for a fuller understanding of civil society.
5 Béteille asks, "How far do religious movements and assemblies for moral, ethical and spiritual discourses contribute to the formation of civil society?" and answers, "They may contribute a very great deal to the formation of the good society, depending, of course, on what one means by that phrase… I remain skeptical about what religious assemblies and movements can contribute directly to the formation of civil society, although their indirect contribution may be extremely valuable" (Béteille 2001, 307). But for Oommen, "…religious organizations were very much part of civil society in pre-independent India" (Oommen 2001a, 229). It is interesting to note here that both Uberoi and Oommen are not following any universalizing conception of modernity. Oommen (2001b) follows a "multiple modernities" perspective in his work, while Uberoi (2002) is one of the few proponents of Indian modernity.

CIVIL SOCIETY AND THE CALLING OF SELF-DEVELOPMENT   245

6 This is similar to Uberoi's (1996) argument about Sikhism that it is a product of dialogue between Hinduism and Islam.

7 As John S. Hawley writes of *bhakti* poets, "These poets' intimate involvement with their audiences – in their own life times, doubtless, but certainly down the generation as subsequent performers and their audiences – have taken up these roles – is the real democracy of *bhakti*" (Hawley 2005, 332).

8 In this context, what Eisenstadt writes about the *bhakti* movements is insightful: "Many of the visions promulgated by those movements emphasized equality, but it was above all equality in the cultural or religious arena, with respect to access to worship, and only to some extent in the definition of membership in the political community" (Eisenstadt 2005, 23).

9 This four dimensional conceptualization can be compared with the four dimensions of civil society articulated by Cohen and Arato (1992) – publicity, plurality, legality, and privacy. There are no references to love and labor in this framework, though the theme of privacy may touch upon the theme of love to some extent. But the theme of love in the present model also refers to socially transforming love.

10 In his reflections on civil society, Uberoi (1996) is not within the modernist trap. He neither considers civil society as a product of modernist transition in history (though he would not discount its significance in understanding the contour that civil society has taken in modern past and present) nor does he look at it through the dominant logic of power.

11 The Chhattisgarh Mukti Morcha is a multi-dimensional social movement of tribals and workers in the Chhattisgarh region of India fighting for dignity and rights, and its leader Shankar Singh Guha Niyogi was gunned down at the behest of the contractors and industrialists of the region.

12 The anonymous reader of this paper for *Sociological Bulletin* has raised the question of how appropriate it is to use this notion of a "Chatisgarhi citizen." Chandoke uses the word, but the way I understand the significance of such words is that it challenges us to realize a multi-layered conception of citizenship. We are not only citizens of our nation-states, we are also citizens of our significant communities of belonging, and this includes being citizens of the world. Today the rise of transnational civic movements and the emergent discourse and practice of cosmopolitanism challenges us to realize the limits of a nation-state centered discourse and practice of citizenship. This also challenges us to go beyond a purely *etic* use and understanding of categories such as citizenship and have an *emic* perspective which emerges from dialogues with people into conversations.

13 In her essay, "Language, Translation and Domination," Neera Chandhoke (2003c) speaks about the condition of tribals and their languages in the discourse of civil society in modern India. For a tribal, a particular piece of land belongs to him because the bones of his ancestors are buried there. But this language is not easily comprehensible in the dominant language of property rights that dominate state and civil society in modern India. The agents of state and civil society may negotiate with these subaltern languages but they do so from the perspective of the dominant language. For Chandhoke (2003c, 195), "…the more powerful language in civil society does not even have to practice savageness to bludgeon, club or hammer the less powerful language into insensibility, which is something that Habermas fears, and the he attempts to ward off through discourse ethics. The deliberative space of civil society has already been colonized, already saturated with power that privileges certain ideas of land proprietorship."

14 In this context, what Mohanty writes deserves our careful consideration:

The current historical situation is characterized by an ever-intensifying contradiction between hegemony and self-realisation. It manifests at every level, global, national and local in spatial terms and class, caste, race, ethnic, gender and such other terms of social relations. The former reflects struggles over political power vertically and the latter involves contests horizontally while all of them intersect at numerous levels. Global capitalism is the principal force whose influence decisively permeates all the contradictions at present. (2003, 15)

References

Appadurai, Arjun. 2002. "Deep Democracy: Urban Governmentality and the Horizon of Politics." *Public Culture* 14 (1): 21–47.

Arato, Andrew and Jean Cohen. 1992. *Civil Society and Political Theory*. Cambridge, MA: MIT Press.

Béteille, Andre. 2001. "Civil Society and Good Society." *Sociological Bulletin* 50 (2): 286–307.

———. 2002. *Sociology: Essays on Approach and Method*. Delhi: Oxford University Press.

Bhaskar, Roy. 2002. *Reflections on Meta-Reality: Transcendence, Everyday Life and Emancipations*. New Delhi: Sage Publications.

Chandhoke, Neera. 2003a. "A Critique of Civil Society as the Third Sphere." In Rajesh Tandon and Ranjita Mohanty, eds, *Does Civil Society Matter? Governance in Contemporary India*, 27–58. Tandon, Rajesh and Mohanty, Ranjita, eds. New Delhi: Sage.

———. 2003b. "When the Voiceless Speak: A Case Study of the Chatisgarh Mukti Morcha." In Rajesh Tandon and Ranjita Mohanty, eds, *Does Civil Society Matter? Governance in Contemporary India*, 198–242. New Delhi: Sage.

———. 2003c. *The Conceits of Civil Society*. Delhi: Sage Publications.

Chakrabarty, Dipesh. 2002. *Habitations of Modernity: Essays on the Wake of Subaltern Studies*. Chicago: University of Chicago Press.

———. 2004. "Romantic Archives: Literature and the Politics of Identity in Bengal." *Critical Inquiry* 30 (3): 654–83.

Connolly, William E. 2001. *The Ethos of Pluralization*. Minneapolis: University of Minnesota Press.

Dallmayr, Fred. 1993. *G. W. F. Hegel: Modernity and Politics*. Newbury Park, CA: Sage Publications.

———. 2001. *Achieving Our World: Toward a Global and Plural Democracy*. Lanham, MD: Rowman & Littlefield.

———. 2005. *Small Wonder: Global Power and Its Discontents*. Lanham, MD: Rowman & Littlefield.

Das, Chittaranjan. 1951/1997. *Achyutananda O Panchasakha Dharma* [Achyutananda and the Religion of the Panchasakhas]. Cuttack: S. B. Publications.

Das, Veena. 2003. "Small Community of Love." Available at http://www.india-seminar.com/2003/525/525%20veena%20das.htm (accessed 10 May 2012).

Eisenstadt, S. N. 2005. *Civil Society and Public Sphere in a Comparative Perspective*. Oct. 27. Warsaw: Institute of Sociology.

Faubion, James D., ed. 1995. *Rethinking the Subject: An Anthology of Contemporary European Social Theory*. Boulder: Westview Press.

Gatens, Moira and Genevieve Lloyd. 1999. *Collective Imaginings: Spinoza, Past and Present*. London: Routledge.

Giddens, Anthony. 1991. *Modernity and Self-Identity: Self and Society in the Late Modern Age*. Cambridge: Polity Press.

———. 1994. "Living in a Post-Traditional Society." In Ulrich Beck et al., eds, *Reflexive Modernization: Politics, Tradition and Aesthetics in the Modern Social Order*, 56–109. Cambridge: Polity Press.

Giri, Ananta Kumar. 2002a. *Building in the Margins of Shacks: The Vision and Projects of Habitat for Humanity*. Delhi: Orient Longman.

———. 2002b. "Rethinking Civil Society." In *Conversations and Transformations: Towards a New Ethics of Self and Society*, 287–314. Lanham, MD: Lexington Books.

———. 2004. *Reflections and Mobilizations: Dialogues with Movements and Voluntary Organizations*. Delhi: Sage Publications.

———. 2008. *Self-Development and Social Transformations? The Vision and Practice of the Self-Study Mobilization of Swadhyaya*. Lanham, MD: Lexington Books and Rawat Publicatons.

———. 2009. "Introduction." In Ananta Kumar Giri, ed., *The Modern Prince and the Modern Sage: Transforming Power and Freedom*. New Delhi: Sage Publications.

Gupta, Dipankar. 1997. *Rivalry and Brotherhood: Politics in the Life of Farmers in Northern India*. Delhi: Oxford University Press.

Habermas, Jürgen. 1981. *Philosophical-Political Profiles*. Cambridge: Polity Press.

———. 1989. *The Structural Transformation of the Public Sphere*. Cambridge, MA: MIT Press.

———. 1990. *Moral Consciousness and Communicative Action*. Cambridge: Polity Press.

Hawley, John Stratton. 2005. "Bhakti, Democracy and the Study of Religion." In *Three Bhakti Voices: Mirabai, Surdas, and Kabir in Their Times and Ours*. Delhi: Oxford University Press.

Hefner, Robert W. 1998. "On the History and Cross-Cultural Possibility of a Democratic Political Ideal." In Robert Hefner, ed., *Democratic Civility: The History and Cross-Cultural Possibility of a Modern Political Ideal*, 3–49. New Brunswick, NJ: Transaction Books.

Nakamura, Mitsuo. 2001. "Introduction." In Mitsuo Nakamura et al., eds, *Islam and Civil Society in Southeast Asia*, 1–30. Singapore: Institute of South East Asian Studies.

Mohanty, Manoranjan. 2002. "The Self as Center in the Emerging World of the Twenty-first Century: A Sino-Indian Perspective." *China Report* 38 (1): 1–10.

———. 2003. "Creative Self and its Enemies in the Emerging World." *Gandhian Perspectives* 11 (1–2): 15–21.

Narayan, Badri. 2001. *Documenting Dissent: Contesting Fables, Contested Memories and Dalit Political Discourse*. Shimla: Indian Institute of Advanced Studies.

Oommen, T. K. 2001a. "Civil Society: Religion, Caste and Language in India." *Sociological Bulletin* 50 (2): 221–35.

———. 2001b. "Multiple Modernities and the Rise of New Social Movements: The Case of India." *Indian Social Science Review* 3 (1): 1–16.

Pandian, M. S. S. 1998. "Stepping Outside History? New Dalit Writings from Tamil Nadu." In Partha Chatterjee, ed., *Wages of Freedom: Fifty Years of the Indian Nation-State*, 292–309. Delhi: Oxford University Press.

Sachsenmaier, Dominic et al., eds. 2002. *Reflections on Multiple Modernities: European, Chinese and Other Interpretations*. Leiden: Brill.

Seligman, Adam. 1995. "Animadversions Upon Civil Society and Civic Virtue in the Last Decade of the Twentieth Century." In John A. Hall, ed., *Civil Society: Theory, History, Comparison*. Cambridge: Polity Press.

Sen, Amartya. 2002. "Justice Across Borders." In Pablo de Greiff and Ciaran Cronin, eds, *Global Justice and Transnational Politics: Essays on the Moral and Political Challenges of Globalization*, 37–51. Cambridge, MA: MIT Press.

Tandon, Rajesh and Ranjita Mohanty, eds. 2003. *Does Civil Society Matter? Governance in Contemporary India*. New Delhi: Sage.

Uberoi, J. P. S. 1996. *Religion, Civil Society and State: A Study of Sikhism*. Delhi: Oxford University Press.

———. 2002. *The European Modernity: Truth, Science and Method*. Delhi: Oxford University Press.

———. 2003. "Civil Society." In Veena Das et al., eds, *The Oxford India Companion to Sociology and Social Anthropology*, 114–33. Delhi: Oxford University Press.

Wuthnow, Robert. 2004. *Saving America? Faith-Based Services and the Future of Civil Society*. Princeton: Princeton University Press.

Vattimo, Giani. 1999. *Belief*. Cambridge: Polity Press.

Chapter Fifteen

THE CALLING OF PRACTICAL SPIRITUALITY: TRANSFORMATIONS IN SCIENCE AND RELIGION AND NEW DIALOGUES ON SELF, TRANSCENDENCE AND SOCIETY

One conceives of truths not in terms of correspondence or satisfactions but as the pursuit of an ideal value which humanity tries to realize in and through time. The notion of transcendence enters just at this point to make the human seeking in and through time for an ideal or value which can never in principle be actualized or realized in time, however long we may conceive it to be. The idea of "transcendence" gives the seeking a "unity" which it would never have because of the very nature of "unendingness" of time on the one hand and of the "seeking" in it and through it, on the other.

—Daya Krisna, "Time, Truth and Transcendence" (1999, 324)

Sita's Kitchen is the entire field of her self-imaging Shakti, powerfully represented by the earth. It is on earth, in the embrace of the Divine Mother, that all are born, all creatures great and small; all forms manifest, noble or evil; and all are nourished... The truth of Rama is the truth of advaita, non-duality, the truth of singular self-consciousness and its cinematic field of self-imaging Shakti which is Samsara... Annihilationism (the readiness to destroy all life and civilization on earth) is the highest stage of development of dualism... Dualism is the conviction that self and not-self are everywhere pitted against one another.

—Ramachandra Gandhi, *Sita's Kitchen: A Testimony of Faith and Inquiry* (1993, 16, 18, 20)

Today we are so impressed with the progress of the physical sciences – originally derived from metaphysics – that we return the complement and derive our metaphysics from natural sciences. But the scientific worldview has its own metaphysical presuppositions which originated in ancient Greece as a way of looking at the world that came to fruition in Plato and especially Aristotle.

This dualistic view stands almost in dramatic opposition to a worldview based on the non-duality of the seer and the seen.

—David Loy, *Nonduality: A Study in Comparative Philosophy* (1988, 12)

Rta and *Satya* provide the cosmic foundation of the universe and may be apprehended by *tapasa* or disciplined "seeking" or *sadhana* and realized through them. The Sukta 10.191, the last *Sukta* of the *Rgveda*, suggests that this is not, and cannot be, something on the part of an individual alone, but is rather the "collective" enterprise of all "humankind" and names the "god" of this *Sukta* "Somjnanam" emphasizing the "Togetherness" of all "Being" and spelling it out as *Sam Gachhadhwam, Sam Vadadyam, Sambho Manasi Jayatam, Deva Bhagam Jathapurve Danjanatam Upasate.*

—Daya Krishna, "Rgveda: The *Mantra*, the *Sukta* and the *Mandala* or the *Rsi*, the *Devta*, the *Chanda*" (2006, 8)

Exploring Pathways of Practical Spirituality as a Tribute to the Strivings of Daya Krishna and Ramachandra Gandhi

Daya Krishna and Ramachandra Gandhi were inspiring seekers in the gardens of transformational knowledge, and in this journey of knowledge and human liberation it is enriching to walk together with them. Let us begin this dialogue with the following lines of Daya Krishna: "The development of new *purusarthas* (ideals of human flourishing and excellence) in the history of a culture or civilization would perhaps be one of the more important ways of looking at man's history as it will emphasize ways of making his life significant in the pursuit of new ends of a different kind... The emergence of any new *purusartha* on the horizon of human consciousness should be seen as a breakthrough in human history, providing the possibility of a new kind of pursuit not available earlier" (1997, 25). In Daya Krishna there is not only a critique of earlier models of *purusartha* as providing "no place for the independent life of reason as a separate value, or for that matter any other life which is not concerned primarily with *artha, dharma, kama* and *moksha*"[1] but also the seeking of a new *purusartha* which can help us realize life and society as a work of art, "meaningful and worthwhile in diverse ways" (Krishna 1991, 204). A seeking of a new *purusartha* beyond the violence of anthropocentrism and gender injustice and nurtured by the grace and compassion of non-duality and emptiness also animates the seeking of Ramachandra Gandhi (please see Dallmayr 2010). I wish to submit that it is practical spirituality which can contribute to the realization of a new *purusartha* of our times, involving transformations in science and religion and embodying a simultaneous multi-dimensional engagement with beauty, dignity and dialogue. Practical spirituality, whose contours I would soon elaborate only in an inviting, and not in a definitional way, is a way as well as an aspiration of self and social realization, of realizing Swaraj (self-rule) and *Samvad* (dialogue) and in the process fundamentally reconstituting these categories themselves. Swaraj, for example, may be seen as involving both the realization of autonomy as well as the embrace of the other, and *Samvad* is not only as a discursive activity taking place in the comfortable rooms in Jaipur or Shimla but also at work within the lives of millions of laboring men and women who are cooking their food by the road side.[2] In Ramachandra Gandhi's *Sita's Kitchen samvad* takes place in the forest, but there is no cooking in *Sita's Kitchen*. This *samvad* is also fictional[3] and not entirely compassionate to all the participants in the dialogue, such as Ajita Kesakambalin and Makhali Gosala. But practical spirituality seeks to transform these practices of dialogue as both normatively inspired aspirations and practical activities of laboring and cooking together. By exploring further its aspirational horizons and practical manifestations in religion and science, societies and histories, we can pay tribute not only to Daya Krishna and Ramachandra Gandhi, but also continue the inspiring works of these immortal companions of ours. This chapter does not discuss in detail the works of Daya Krishna and Ramachandra Gandhi but rather presents practical spirituality as a possible frame for understanding the significance of their works in a suggestive and not in an exhaustive way.

Practical Spirituality: An Introduction and Invitation

Practical spirituality involves a transformation of both science and religion, as well as the reconstitution of self, society and transcendence transforming the one-sidedness of what Day Krishna calls a "socio-centric perspective" on the one hand and "Atman-centric perspective" on the other (Krishna 1993). In the field of religion, practical spirituality emerges in a variety of transformative movements and seeking in self, culture and society, which interrogate existing structures of domination and strive for a new mode of self-realization, world-realization and God-realization. Practical spirituality seeks to transform religion in the direction of creative practice, everyday life and the struggle for justice and dignity. Practice here is not just practice in the conventional sense, for example in traditions of American pragmatism (cf. Aboulafia and Kemp 2002) or anthropological conceptions of practice as offered by Clifford Geertz (1973), Pierre Bourdieu (1971) and Jürgen Habermas (1971). These conceptions suffer from an entrenched dualism such as theory and practice and immanence and transcendence, and work with a notion of subject which is predominantly "techno-practitioner" and cut off from its integral links with transcendence. But practice in practical spirituality is simultaneously immanent and transcendent, and the actor here is simultaneously a "techno-practitioner" and a "transcendentally real self." Practical spirituality embodies immanent transcendence, as for example in music[4] or in the experience of transcendence in our various moments of everyday life – love, meditations, scientific engagements and other activities of life and in society (cf. Bhaskar 2002). As Daya Krishna says, "Practice itself though known to us intimately has an intrinsic inner mystery about it, and that is the transcendence in which we live even though we 'know' generally the 'practice-dimension' of it" (Krishna 1999, 336).

Practical spirituality emphasizes experience and realization – of the self, God and the world – in and through practice, but at the same time nurtures the humility not to reduce these only to practice. In its emphasis upon experience and realization, practical spirituality has close kinship with the spirit of science which embodies, in the words of Albert Einstein, a holy spirit of inquiry. In its emphasis upon practice, practical spirituality stresses that without taking part in practice we cannot realize truth, religious or otherwise. Practical spirituality involves manifold experiments with Truth as well as truths, where truth is not a thing but a landscape of meaning, experience and co-realization.

Practical spirituality also emphasizes transformative practice, which leads to self-transformation, cultural transformation and world transformation. For example poverty, inequality and oppression have been challenges with humanity for a long time, and here practical spirituality has generated a variety of transformative movements in its struggle against oppression and domination. There are movements of practical spirituality from different religions, as well as from traditions of emancipatory struggles such as the revolt against slavery, workers movements, women's movements, ecological movements and various other transformative struggles in discourse, society and history. Liberation theology in Islam, Buddhism and Christianity is a recent example of practical spirituality.[5] In Indian traditions practical spirituality has manifested itself in the Upanishads, the vision and practice of seekers such as Buddha, the *bhakti* movements, Swami Vivekananda's vision of practical Vedanta, Sri Aurobindo's strivings for *Life Divine* and Gandhi's experiments with Truth and struggles for liberation.[6] Movements such as the *bhakti* movements have involved struggles against caste and gender domination, along with new songs of self and social liberation. They have also embodied efforts to go beyond denominational concepts of truth and religion. They have involved not only struggles for justice but also border-crossing dialogues. We see this, for example, in the Sant tradition of India, which like Sufism and Sikshism is a product of a transformative dialogue between Hinduism and Islam (Das 1982, Uberoi 1996). Thus practical spirituality involves both struggles for dignity as well as new initiatives in transformative dialogues across borders. Dialogue is also a key concern in the strivings of Ramachandra Gandhi as he writes in *Sita's Kitchen*: "A non-dualist Church of Atman-Brahman Mary… would be a generous kitchen offering without exclusivist denial of the full range of truth's cuisine to spiritually hungry humanity…" (Gandhi 1993, 10).

Pathways of Practical Spirituality

In fact, practical spirituality involves both practical struggles for a better world and practical discourses for spiritual realization going beyond denominational fixation – not only in terms of boundaries among religions but also in terms of boundaries between science and religion, the material and the spiritual.[7] Practical spirituality urges us to realize that by undertaking concrete activities to ameliorate suffering we can realize God. From the Christian tradition theologian Johannes B. Metz (1981) urges us to realize that the Christian goal of unity of faith, or what is called ecumenism, cannot be solved at the level of doctrines alone. It can only be solved by undertaking concrete activities in addressing practical problems of life and society with the "Son of Man."

Habitat for Humanity is a movement within contemporary Christianity which tries to worship God by building houses with and for people. It is built on the foundations of "Economics of Jesus" and "Theology of the Hammer" (Giri 2002). We see a similar emphasis upon devotional labor and sharing in Swadhyaya, a socio-spiritual movement in contemporary India which can be looked at as an instance of practical spirituality from within contemporary Hinduism (Giri 2008a). Both Habitat for Humanity and Swadhyaya, despite their limitation of always having to uphold their own ideals, urge us to be more dialogical compared to their fundamentalist counterparts in Christianity and Hinduism. But the dialogical dimension of practical spirituality is multi-dimensional: it embodies not only dialogue between religions but also between religion and science and between the material and the transcendental. Swami Vivekananda has captured a bit of this sensibility in his vision of *practical vedanta*, which involves the realization of oneself as Divine,[8] as well as the struggle for justice and the movement towards dialogue.[9]

Practical spirituality emphasizes continuing practice, not only on euphoric moment of realization, enthusiasm and miraculous experience. As Robert Wuthnow tells us, drawing on his work with the spiritual quest of the artists: "Many artists speak of their work as a form of meditation. For some the sheer rhythm of the daily routine brings them closer to the essence of their being. Writing all morning or practicing for the next musical performance requires mental and emotional toughness… For spiritual dabblers the insight that these artists provide is that persistence and hard work may still be the best way to attain spiritual growth" (Wuthnow 2001, 10).

Practical spirituality accepts the brokenness of the world and does not want to assert any totalizing unity or totalitarian absorption (cf. Bellah 1970). At the same time, practical spirituality is a striving for wholeness in the midst of our inescapable brokenness and fragmentation in this world. This wholeness is emergent as it is manifested in the work of the artists. Artists strive to paint landscapes of emergent wholeness in the midst of fragmentation and brokenness. Artists incorporate "[their] experimental approach into one's spiritual quest" (Wuthnow 2001, 276).

An artist is a *bricoleur*, creating beauty and images of emergent coherence out of many fragments. "The creative scientist is also a *bricoleur*" (Bhaskar 2002, 394). There is an artistic dimension to the scientific quest, as there is to the spiritual quest, and in Ramachandra Gandhi it is an expression of the jewel of self-realization. The inspiration of art in creative spirituality makes transformative bridges between science and spirituality.

Practical spirituality involves a transformation in the conceptualization and realization of God. It submits that in order to be spiritual one need not believe in God nor be religious.[10] God in practical spirituality is not only in heaven but here on earth; she[11] is a presence in our heart and in every thing we see. In fact, Swami Vivekananda speaks about a practical God: "Where is there a more practical God than He whom I see before me – A God omnipresent in every being, more real than our senses?" (Vivekananda 1991, 305). In this context, Bhaskar's following proposals about God in his *From Science to Emancipation* deserves our careful consideration:

Ontological realism about God, that is a belief in the reality or experience of God is quite consistent with epistemological relativism;

Ontological immanence, that is the view that God is immanent within being, is consistent with episteme transcendence either in the sense of being unknown, God could be real even if we do not know it, or in the sense of being knowable in a way which is susceptible to the normal canons of our discursive intellect:

[Ontological ingredience] – if God is truly a kind of envelope which sustains and binds everything, then God in a certain way must be ingredient within us;

the proof of God's existence can only be experimental and practical. No one can prove to you that God exists. This can only come from your experience and practice;

[In this context, humanity's role is to increase the presence of the Divine in one's life, society and cosmos]. (Bhaskar 2002, 35; my paraphrasing in square brackets)

The above helps us rethink God and realize her in a new way. God in practical spirituality is not only a moral God, omnipotent, God with a capital G. God here is God with a small g.[12] God in practical spirituality is also not anthropocentric.[13] God in practical spirituality is not only a Father but also a Mother.[14] God is also a child who is eternally playing in creative works.

Practical spirituality involves a transformation of our conceptions of sin and evil. In practical spirituality evil is not the absence or the abandoned house of the Divine but a lesser manifestation of it. We find such a foundational rethinking of sin and evil in many different religious, spiritual and philosophical movements of the world. For Swami Vivekananda, "Sins are very low degrees of Self-manifestation" (Vivekananda 1991, 300). For him, "Vedanta recognizes no sin, it only recognizes error and the greatest error says the Vedanta is to say that you are weak, that you are a sinner" (Vivekananda 1991, 300). From a Christian perspective, Giani Vattimo (1999) redefines sin as failure in love.[15] For Vattimo, we have all sinned not because we have fallen in love but because we have failed in love. Love is not a conditional exchange but unconditional, and from this point of view we all can always be more unconditional in our loves, overcoming our integral original sin of not being quite up to mark in our practices of love. God is unconditional love. From the point of view of unconditional love, we fail in our lives of love, as the realization of unconditional love is always a journey. Given our human limitations, no matter what we do our love is always in need of much more intimate non-dual realization, and this becomes our condition of original sin. Thus our task is to overcome this through more love and grace and continue our strivings with gratitude, not simply for fear of punishment from a God conceived as a moral law commanding us not to do evil (cf. Dalferth 2006). Similarly, from the shores of contemporary critical philosophy, Giorgio Agamben (1993) redefines evil as a deficit of human existence, and anything that blocks the realization of fuller potential, including the potential of fuller God-realization and world-realization, is evil. Here Bhaskar (2002) also speaks about structural sin and ill-being, referring to such fields as contemporary capitalism, which leads to exploitation and blocks universal self-realization. Both Swami Vivekananda and Roy Bhaskar urge us to go beyond a facile dualism of good and evil which resonates with the non-dual strivings of Ramachandra Gandhi. He would consider sin as our lack of awareness of ourselves and realizing ourselves and running after desires which blocks such a self-realization. In *Sita's Kitchen*, "The missing slave girl is a powerful symbol both of the true extra dimension of existence, Atman, self, which we must seek and not the fulfillment of extra desires..." (1993, 29).

Non-dual Realizations and Practical Spirituality: Transformational Challenges before Science and Religion

The interrogation of the dualism of good and evil in practical spirituality, as it is accompanied by a transformational conception of God, points to non-dual realizations –science, religion and spirituality – as an important challenge in human life. In fact, transcendence in science and spirituality involves a critique of available dualisms such as sacred/profane and subject/object. The dualism between subject and object has been at the cornerstone of modern science. Recent developments in science, such as quantum physics and the system theory of pioneers such as Humberto Maturana, challenge us to understand the limitations of a spectatorial perspective in science and the dualism of subject and object. "In the words of a biologist, if you want to really understand about a tumor you have got to be a tumor" (Knor-Cetina 2001, 520).

The dualism between subject and object in modern science finds a parallel in the dualism between ontology and epistemology. Modern science, as a part of the agenda of modernity, has been primarily epistemic and procedural and has neglected ontological issues including nature of self and the quality of self-involvement in the practice of knowing. Moreover, there is a profound revolution in varieties of scientific engagements today – from biology to anthropology to the philosophy of science – where "to know is not only to know of" but also "knowing with" (Sunder Rajan 1998). "Knowing with" involves subject and object – epistemology and ontology – and embodies what may be called an *ontological epistemology of participation*. It embodies transformations in epistemology such as virtue epistemology which points to the quality of the knowing subject, and transformations in ontology – practical ontology – which moves from a preoccupation with a fixed subject to practical labors of love and learning. It also involves "weak ontology" characterized by humility (cf. Dallmayr 1991; Vattimo 1999).

Ontological epistemology of participation embodies multivalued logic in place of the dualistic logic of modern science. As J. N. Mohanty argues, "In multivalued logic every point of view is partly true, partly false and partly undecidable" (2000). This helps one not to be trapped in closure and to be engaged in science and spirituality as a continued journey. Multivalued logic draws inspiration from multiple traditions of science, philosophy and spirituality such as the Jaina tradition of *Anekantavada* (many paths to truth), Gandhian experiments with truth and non-violence, and Husserl's phenomenology of overlapping contents. Multivalued logic builds on non-injury in our mode of thinking and non-violence in our mode of relationship.[16] Multivalued logic as an integral part of an ontological epistemology of participation is also an aspect of the transformational dimensions of science and spirituality.

Non-duality is an important part of the ontological epistemology of participation in science and spirituality. Yoga helps us overcome our dualism and realize non-duality. As David Loy writes, "We may see the three traditional *yogas* as types of spiritual practice that work to transform different dualistic modes of experience onto their respective non-dual mode. *Jnana yoga* transforms or 'purifies' the dualistic intellect, *karma yoga* the dualistic physical body and *bhakti yoga* dualistic emotions" (Loy 1988, 27).[17]

The multivalued logic of practical spirituality transforms not only sciences but also religions: it helps sciences not to be dismissive about what they do not know and religions to be more exploratory, experimental and less assertive. It urges religions to be more dialogical – to recognize and know more about each other and to mutually interrogate each other with a smile.

The Calling of Practical Spirituality and Reconstitution of Self, Transcendence and Society

Practical spirituality seeks to go beyond a dualistic view of self and society. As suggested in the beginning of this chapter, practical spirituality goes beyond a dualistic view of self as either techno-practitioner or transcendental. It urges us to realize that we are both and yet more. For example, self is a field consisting simultaneously of autonomous and interpenetrating circles of techno-practice, transcendence and unconsciousness. In its conception and reconstitution of society, practical spirituality seeks to go beyond the dualism of the individual and society and realizes that this is an evolutionary journey involving evolutionary transformations of our conception and practice of society and self.[18] It seeks to realize that each society has a dimension of sociality and a dimension of *Atman* at the levels of both the individual and the collective going beyond what Daya Krishna (1993) would call the one-sided extremism of either an "Atman-centric perspective" or a "socio-centric perspective." Practical spirituality also strives to go beyond one-sided valorization of the self or the other as occurs with many of us, including Daya Krishna who is more on the side of the other and Ramachandra Gandhi who lies on the side of the self[19] to the point of disallowing the other to flourish or even to speak.[20] Practical spirituality can provide a compassionate critical framework for fellow seekers in understanding the limitation of these two companions of ours vis-à-vis their proclivity to a one-sided valorization of either other or self and the need to continuously strive to embody self-realization and to embrace the other in non-domineering and transformative ways.

Practical spirituality also seeks to overcome the dualism between immanence and transcendence by cultivating paths and fields of immanent transcendence, a cultivation which resonates with the spirit of Daya Krishna and Ramachandra Gandhi. In Daya Krishna it also involves a reconstitution of our understanding of the relation between relative and non-relative: "Relativity is the inevitable condition of everything that man claims either in the realm of knowing, or of feeling, or of willing, but this relativism makes sense only if it is seen in the light of the pursuit of that which itself is non-relative…" (Krishna 1999, 336).

Practical Spirituality, Practical Discourse and Democratic Transformations

Practical spirituality has implications for various domains and discourses of our lives such as secularism and democracy. It offers a new realization of secularism which embodies spiritual cultivation for mutual tolerance, learning and criticism, and it goes beyond the confrontation between science and religion which has characterized the first stage of modernist secularism (Annaim 1995, 2008; Giri 2005b). The dialogical dimension of practical spirituality is a helpful companion for reliving secularism in our turbulent world.

Practical spirituality also involves a radical reformation of the logic of power and the transformation of democracy. In their struggle for justice and dignity, movements of practical spirituality confront and interrogate power. However,they are not just preoccupied with capturing power as an instrument of domination, but seek to have power as a covenant to realize the common good as Hannah Arendt would put it (cf. Cohen and Arato 1995). These movements do not embody the logic of sovereignty of self and state in modernity, which has an inherent propensity to mastery, rather they embody the aspiration and the struggle for what Dallmayr (2005), reflecting on the struggle of Jesus calls "sacred non-sovereignty." While the logic of sovereignty, including the so-called democratic sovereignty in modernity, has a propensity to make us bare (cf. Agamben 1995) and denude us of our dignity and mutuality, practical spirituality as a struggle for "sacred non-sovereignty" embodies new ethics – the ethics and politics of servanthood in place of the politics of mastery.[21] Sacred non-sovereignty embodies what Ramachandra Gandhi calls the grace of emptiness and nothingness (Gandhi 1993, 29).

Practical spirituality as a struggle for dignity embodies a multi-dimensional partnership between God and man. This struggle challenges us to widen and deepen our vision and practice of democracy; democracy as not only a political mechanism but also as a spiritual struggle. Democracy as participation and reasoning in the public sphere must be supplemented with the practices of self-cultivation and the cultivation of generosity of being to go beyond the dualism of private and public.

Democracy as a mode of public reasoning and deliberation – embodying what Habermas (1990) calls practical discourse where actors are engaged in moral argumentation about the nature of self and society – is crucial for transforming the spiritual traditions of India which have been mostly authoritarian in their structural organization. While there has to be a transformative dialogue between practical discourse and practical spirituality, it must be emphasized that practical discourse in Habermas does not bow down before authority in a slavish manner, and it discovers moral insights from deliberation among its participants. Such public deliberation and democratic decision making seems to be missing in varieties of socio-spiritual mobilizations of India where democratic participation for value formation can be helpful (cf. Dreze and Sen 2002).

Swadhyaya is a socio-spiritual movement in contemporary India that is now riddled with power struggles involving crucial issues of the sole control of resources and doctrinal authority. After the passing away of its founder, the control of the organization fell on his daughter and this succession was not very different from the entrenched culture of dynastic succession in Indian religions and politics. The integral education movement in Orissa embodies aspirations of a practical spirituality as it works with children, parents and society for more joyful and integral learning by drawing inspiration from Sri Aurobindo and the Mother. However, it also faces the challenge of generating spaces for public deliberation where people in management with power and money can sit together with the teachers who join the movement out of devotion but are mostly without adequate resources (cf. Das 2001; Giri 2004).

Along with transforming secularism, democracy and authoritarianism, which is in tune with the spirit of both Daya Krishna and Ramachandra Gandhi, practical spirituality also draws our attention to the spiritual significance of food and to the link between food and freedom (cf. Sen 1999). It draws inspiration from texts such as *Taittereya Upanishad* where it is written, *Annam Brahmeti Vijanama* – "Know food as *Bhrahma*." Practical spirituality challenges us to understand the link between food and freedom and to realize the violation of the human and the divine when there is not adequate nourishment for us. It also invites us to cook together in *Sita's Kitchen* and sing new songs of self-discovery, mutual nourishment and intimacy.[22] It also challenges us to realize the significance of the body and understand that the aesthetics of spirituality are not only confined to places of worship, but they also touch our bathrooms thus overcoming the dualism between the temple and the toilet. In my field work with Swadhyaya, I found that while in the Swadhyaya orchards there is a separate special room for the leader which is rarely used, and the common bathrooms used by "devotee workers" are mostly dirty without even cleaning soap. This is a problem, as a senior Swadhyayee once told me in a conversation, not only in the rural projects such as *Brukhamandir* (tree temple) but also in Swadhyaya-run schools. In his recent reflections on religion, Jacques Derrida (1998) tells us that one who claims authority in the name of religion speaks Latin today. Those of us who valorize spirituality also need to ask ourselves whether we are claiming authority in the name of spirituality. We need not close our eyes to the fact that there is a problem of entrenched authoritarianism in spirituality as well. Practical spirituality has to transform this authoritarianism by taking part simultaneously in the political, moral and spiritual struggle in the new poetics and politics of transformation. *Bhakti* movements in medieval India were bound by a feudal order, but practical spirituality now calls for a new *bhakti* movement which embodies both democratic participation and a multi-dimensional generosity of being. In cultivating such a *bhakti* movement, not only for India but for the world, practical spirituality builds upon the strivings of both Daya Krishna and Ramachandra Gandhi.

This multi-dimensional struggle for transformation – food and freedom, universal co-realization, the transformation of existing institutions, and the creation of new institutions – calls for the embodiment of values such as voluntary poverty and voluntary optimism (cf. Das 2005). Both Daya Krishna and Ramachandra Gandhi are deeply concerned with the cultivation and nurturance of values. Practical spirituality strives to embody the values of voluntary poverty, voluntary co-sharing in both suffering and joy, and voluntary optimism. Humanity has flourished with the *sadhana* of selves and collectivities who have chosen to remain poor and enjoy the creative beauty of simplicity unencumbered by the many outward temptations of money and power, and who resist the pressure to conform from the priests, merchants and the kings. Similarly, voluntary optimism is an integral aspect of the journey of life, including its manifestation in practical spirituality. It is not a lack of acknowledgment of our failures but a continuing aspiration and drive despite our failure in order to realize beauty, dignity and dialogue, and therefore we do not easily become a victim of nihilism in a debilitating way. As Ramachandra Gandhi tells us in the attributed voice of Buddha in *Sita's Kitchen*, "Do not declare war against reality…because reality doesn't declare war against anything. The nihilism you preach and the self-centeredness you pardon are caricatures of the pacifying compassion of nothingness and the joyous explosiveness of self-realization" (1993, 45).

Notes

1 For Daya Krishna,

> The oft-repeated traditional theory of the *purusarthas*…is of little help in understanding the diversity and complexity of human seeking which makes human life so meaningful and worthwhile in diverse ways. The *kama*-centric and *artha*-centric theories of Freud and Marx are as mistaken as the *dharma*-centric thought of sociologists and anthropologists who try to understand man in terms of the roles that he plays, and society in terms of the norms of those roles and their interactive relationships. For all these theories, the independent seeking of any value which is different from these is an illusion, except in an instrumental sense… Fortunately for the Indian theory of *purusarthas*, it has postulated the ideal of *moksa* which is tangential to all the other *purusarthas*. But it too has no place for the independent life of reason as a separate value, or for that matter for any other life which is not concerned primarily with *artha*, *dharma*, *kama* and *moksa*. (Krisna 1991, 204–5)

It is worth probing if Daya Krishna had in mind independent pursuit of knowledge or science as having no place in the traditional theory of *purusartha*.

2 This also raises the question of the relationship between philosophy and fieldwork in our practice of dialogue. I do not know if Daya Krishna or Ramachandra Gandhi ever did fieldwork. Daya Krishna characterizes "Anthropology as a bonded science" and he could not liberate himself from this view of him emerging in the sixties in the context of views of anthropologists such as Lévi-Strauss. See Daya Krishna, "Anthropology: The Bonded Science" in his *The Art of the Conceptual* (Krishna 1989).

3 Gandhi himself calls this "speculative narrative" (1993, 24) and it is worth exploring how this is different from the fictional dialogue taking place in John Rawls' *A Theory of Justice* (1971).

4 Consider here the following lines of Luc Ferry: "When I hear a musical passage, it does not reduce to a series of related notes with no connection between them (actual immanence). On the contrary, it contributes – in an immanent way, apart from any rational operation – a certain structure that transcends this actual immanence, without being imposed on me from the outside like an argument from authority. This 'immanent transcendence' contains within itself, par excellence, the ultimate significance of lived experiences" (Ferry 2002, 26).

5 Liberation theology from Latin America is more widely known, but less known are movements of liberation theology in Islam and social engagement in Buddhism. Helpful here are the works of Farid Esack (1997), Abdullahi An-Naim (1995), Fred Dallmayr (2001) and Sulak Sivaraksha (2006).

6 This is not an exhaustive list, but only a few pointers.

7 As E. H. Cousins tells us in his *Global Spirituality*, "people of faith now rediscover the material dimensions of existence and their spiritual significance" (1985, 7).

8 Ramachandra Gandhi would urge us to realize that such a quest for self-knowledge and self-realization involves realizing oneself as empty as well as a Self, a realization which brings compassion to our lives (cf. Gandhi 1993, 29).

9 Though the dialogical dimension in Swami Vivekananda's practical vedanta seems to be imprisoned in fundamentalist interpretations, which would like to see his work only from a Hindu point of view.

10 Let us not forget here Buddhism, which is silent about God, and many atheists, who do not believe in God. The Buddha also did not use the word "self," and Gandhi's reflections on it deserves our careful consideration: The Buddha could have identified emptiness or *nirvana* or *dhamma* with *atman* or self, but did not do so because the atrophying self-consciousness of that age could have taken self to mean ego or body or mind, with disastrous consequences for his mission of compassion. (1993, 22)

11 In their work on critical realism and transcendence, Archer et al. (2004) prefer to use "He" in talking about God. The use of "she" here is an invitation, and it draws inspiration from traditions such as India's where God is thought of as *Brahma*, which is gender neutral.

12 Sulak Sivaraksha speaks about Buddhism with a small "b": "There is a need to practice Buddhism with a small 'b' (Engaged Buddhism). This means concentrating on the meaning of the Buddha's teaching (*nibbana* or freedom) and being less concerned with myths, culture and ceremony" (Sivaraksha 2006, 1). Dallmayr (2005) urges us to understand the political and spiritual significance of moving from the big God and inviting the "small" to our lives.

13 For Swami Vivekananda, "A God who is partial to his children called men, and cruel to his children called brute beasts, is worse than a demon" (Vivekananda 1991, 297). Realization of a non-anthropocentric god in practical spirituality can also draw inspiration from non-anthropocentric cultivation of human identity, divinity and spirituality in Ramachandra Gandhi.

14 In the Judeo-Christian tradition, the language of God the Father predominates. But this is not just in the patriarchal sense that we know. In this context what creative theologian S. Painadath writes vis-à-vis the mystical experience of Jesus deserves our careful attention:

> There are two primordial symbols to speak about the Divine in terms of a personal relation: father and mother. In most of the primal religions both the symbols are profusely used. In the semitic religions there is a dominance of the use of the symbol of father, while in Indian religions the mother symbol plays a significant role in speaking of God. Jesus belonged to the semitic spiritual hemisphere and hence his language has been considerably conditioned by the historical and cultural factors of his country. Therefore it is not surprising that Jesus never addressed God as *mother*. Does it therefore mean that the motherly dimension of God-experience has been lacking in his consciousness? Is language merely a product of the cultural psyche?... Deep within himself Jesus experienced the Divine as the Mother, though this experience has been articulated through the culturally conditioned symbol of the *Father*... When we are sensitive to the motherly dimension of his divine consciousness, we realize that Jesus was not in fact addressing a Father seated above him, but turning to the divine Mother dwelling within him. This is not just a question of shifting the

gender language, but an invitation to dive into the mystical depth of the experience of Jesus. (2007, 20–21, 22, 23)

15 For Ekhart Tolle, "...to sin means to miss the mark, as an archer who misses the target, to sin means to miss the point of human existence. It means to live unskillfully, blindly, and thus to suffer and cause suffering" (2005).

16 Non-duality and non-violence are also enduring concerns in Ramachandra Gandhi and the practice of multivalued logic can learn from him.

17 Bocchi and Ceruti also help us understand the significance of non-duality in our spiritual quest: "The dialogical and dynergic cosmology symbolized by the union of Shiva and Shakti and manifested in yoga has given rise to many philosophical systems of the two great spiritual traditions of classical India: Hinduism and Buddhism. Beyond all their differences and disagreements, they express a principle of 'duality within the non-duality.' The ultimate reality of the universe, the 'noumenon,' is defined precisely as 'non-dual': *a-dvaita* (a Hindu term) or *a-dvaya* (a Buddhist term)" (Bocchi and Ceruti 2002, 47).

18 For Sri Aurobindo:

> In the relations between the individual and the group, this constant tendency of Nature appears as the strife between two equally deep-rooted human tendencies: individualism and collectivism. On one side is the engrossing authority, perfection and development of the State, on the other the distinctive freedom, perfection and development of individual man. The State idea, the small or the vast living machine, and the human idea, the more and more distinct and luminous Person, the increasing God, stand in perpetual opposition. The size of the State makes no difference to the essence of the struggle and need make none to its characteristic circumstances. It was the family, the tribe or the city, the *polis*; it became the clan, the caste and the class, the *kula*, the *gens*. It is now the nation. Tomorrow or day after it may be all mankind. But even then the question will remain poised between man and humanity, between the self-liberating Person and the engrossing collectivity. (1962, 272–3)

19 The name of the protagonist in both *Sita's Kitchen* and *Muniya's Light* is *Ananya*, and Gandhi translates this as "no other." But Ananya also means unique including being uniquely different.

20 In his review of Gandhi's novel *Muniya's Light*, Makarand Paranjape writes, "[In the novel] the narrator's consciousness...dominates totally, not even allowing his beloved Muniya to come into her own or flower forth fully" (Paranjape 2008, 16). Gandhi considers the other as the apparent other and though he himself writes, "Apparent otherness is undoubtedly a disguise of Self but what a powerful disguise it is! Let us make no mistake about this, let us not sentimentally deny the terrifying face of world-appearance" (1993, 4). His relationship with the other needs a foundational transformation in terms of realizing the other as also uniquely different and not just apparently different as (Muniya/Ananya (?)) is also related to the self.

21 In our edited book *The Modern Prince and Modern Sage: Transforming Power and Freedom*, I and several of our co-collaborators are exploring this (Giri 2009).

22 Daya Krishna and Ramachandra Gandhi cook together in *Sita's Kitchen* and possibly listen to this poem of co-creativity which emerges from cooking together:

> Oh what a disaster!
> No onions
> I gave your list
> How could he forget
> I would kill my husband
> Now sending an SMS
> But here are colored onions in this corner

II

Onions and tomatoes
Got dressed
You said
Oh Director
Give me order
No Soul, no order
This is our meditation together
Together we blossom
But if you do not sing
Onions would be still in sleep
Tomatoes would be sad
You sang:
I may be worn
But my love
makes my body blossom
and my soul a fragrance

III

Do you write poems?
You became silent
How did you know?
Did Patrick tell you?
No just thought like this
After dinner
We sat beside the fire
I read a poem of embrace of fire and water
Of wave and flame
You laughed and laughed
Smiled with your heart
Tears flowed down
Tears from eternity
You read your poems
In French, Bulgarian and English
You, the sadhika of poems and life
Said
Oh Indian Orange
Let your journey be a bliss
Touch hearts and million hearts
Write new poems

References

Aboulafia, Myra Bookman and Catherine Kemp, eds. 2002. *Habermas and Pragmatism*. London: Routledge.

Agamben, Giorgio. 1993. *The Coming Community*. Minnesota: University of Minnesota Press
_____. 1995. *Homo Sacer: Sovereign Power and Bare Life*. Stanford: Stanford University Press.

Annaim, Abullahi. 1995. "Toward an Islamic Hermeneutics for Human Rights." In *Human Rights and Religious Values: An Uneasy Relationship?* Grand Rapids, MI: W. B. Eerdmans.
_____. 2008. *Islam and the Secular State: Negotiating the Future of Sharia*. Cambridge, MA: Harvard University Press.

Archer, Margaret et al. 2004. *Transcendence: Critical Realism and God*. London: Routledge.

Bellah, Robert. 1970. *Beyond Belief: Essays on Religion in a Post-Traditional World*. New York: Harper and Row.

Bhaskar, Roy. 2002. *From Science to Emancipation*. Delhi: Sage Publications.

Bocci, G. M. Ceruti. 2002. *The Narrative Universe*. Cresskill, NJ: Hampton Press.

Bourdieu, Pierre. 1971. *An Outline of a Theory of Practice*. Cambridge: Cambridge University Press.

Cohen, Jean and Andrew Arato. 1992. *Civil Society and Political Theory*. Cambridge, MA: MIT Press.

Cousins, E. H. 1985. *Global Spirituality*. Madras: University of Madras Press.

Dalferth, I. U. 2006. "Problems of Evil: Theodicy, Theology, and Hermeneutics." Paper

Dallmayr, Fred. 1991. *Between Frankfurt and Freiburg: Toward a Critical Ontology*. Amherst: University of Massachusetts Press.

_____. 2001. "Liberation Beyond Liberalism: New Perspectives from Buddhism and Islam." In *Rethinking Social Transformation*. Jaipur: Rawat Publications.

_____. 2005. *Small Wonder: Global Power and its Discontents*. Lanham, MD: Rowman & Littlefield.

_____. 2010. "Reason and Life World: Two Exemplary Indian Thinkers." In *Integral Pluralism*, 143–65. Lexington: University of Kentucky Press.

Das, Chittaranjan. 1982. *Santha Sahitya: Literature of the Saints*. Bhubaneswar: Orissa Sahitya Akademi.

_____. 2001. "Integral Education: The Vision and an Experiment." In Ananta Kumar Giri, ed., *Rethinking Social Transformation*. Jaipur: Rawat Publications.

_____. 2005. *Sataku Sata Ma:A Biography of Mother of Sri Aurobindo Ashram, Pondicherry*. Bhubaneswar: Suhrut Prakashan.

Derrida, Jacques. 1998. "Faith and Knowledge: Two Sources of 'Religion' at the Limits of Reason Alone." In Jacques Derrida and Gianni Vattimo, eds, *Religion*. Cambridge: Polity Press.

Dreze, Jean and Amartya Sen. 2002. *India: Development and Participation*. Delhi: Oxford University Press.

Esack, Farid. 1997. *Qur'an, Liberation and Pluralism: An Islamic Perspective on Inter-Religious Solidarity*. Oxford: Oneworld.

Faubion, James, ed. 1995. *Rethinking the Subject: An Anthology of Contemporary European Social Theory*. Boulder, CO: Westview Press.

Ferry, Luc. 2002. *Man Made God*. New York: Columbia Press.

Gandhi, Ramachandra. 1993. *Sita's Kitchen: A Testimony of Faith and Inquiry*. Delhi: Penguin Group.

Giri, Ananta Kumar. 2002. *Building in the Margins of Shacks: The Vision and Projects of Habitat for Humanity*. Delhi: Orient Longman.

_____. 2004. *Reflections and Mobilizations: Dialogues with Movements and Voluntary Organizations*. Delhi: Sage Publications.

_____. 2008. *Self-Development and Social Transformations? The Vision and Practice of the Socio-Spiritual Mobilization of Swadhyaya*. Jaipur: Rawat Publications.

_____. 2009. *The Modern Prince and Modern Sage: Transforming Power and Freedom*. Delhi: Sage Publications.

Giri, Ananta Kumar and Philip Quarles van Ufford. 2004. "A Moral Critique of Development: Ethics, Aesthetics and Responsibility." Department of Development and International Relations, Aalborg University, Working Paper Number 128.

Habermas, Jürgen. 1971. *Knowledge and Human Interest*. Boston: Beacon Press.

_____. 1990. *Moral Consciousness and Communicative Action*. Cambridge: Polity Press.

Knor-Cetina, Karin. 2001. "Post-Social Relations: Theorizing Society in a Post-Social Environment." In George Ritzer and Barry Smart, eds, *Handbook of Social Theory*. London: Sage Publications.

Krishna, Daya. 1989. *The Art of the Conceptual: Explorations in a Conceptual Maze Over Three Decades*. New Delhi: Oxford University Press.

_____. 1991. "Time, Truth and Transcendence." In Daya Krishna and K. Satchidananda Murty, ed., *History, Culture and Truth: Essays Presented to D. P. Chattopadhyaya*, 323–6. Delhi: Kalki Prakashan.

_____. 1993. *Social Philosophy: Past and Future*. Shimla: Indian Institute of Advanced Study.

_____. 1997. *Prolegomena to Any Future Historiography of Cultures and Civilizations*. New Delhi: Munshiram Manoharlal Publishers.

_____. 2006. "Rg Veda: The Mantra, the Sukta and the Mandala or the Rsi, the Devata, the Chanda: The Structure of the Text and the Problems Regarding it." *Journal of Indian Council of Philosophical Research* 23 (2): 1–13.

Loy, David. 1988. *Non-Duality: A Study in Comparative Philosophy*. New York: Humanity Press.

Metz, Johannes B. 1981. "Towards Second Reformation: The Future of Christianity in a Post-Bourgeoisie World." *Cross Currents* 31 (1).

Mohanty, J. N. 2000. *Self and Other: Philosophical Essays*. Delhi: Oxford University Press.

Painadath, S. P. S. J. 2007. *The Spiritual Journey: Towards an Indian Christian Spirituality*. Delhi: ISPCK.

Paranjape, Makarand. 2008. "Ramachandra Gandhi's 'Truth': Non-Dual Mediations and Meditations." Keynote address at a National Conference on Ramachandra Gandhi, Visva-Bharati, Santiniketan, 15–17 March.

Quarles van Ufford, Philip and Ananta Kumar Giri, eds. *A Moral Critique of Development: In Search of Global Responsibility*. London: Routledge.

Roy, Ramashray. 1999. *Beyond Ego's Domain: Being and Order in the Vedas*. Delhi: Shipra.

Sen, Amartya. 1999. "Food and Freedom." *World Development* 17: 76–81

Sivaraksa, Sulak. 2006. *Visioning New Life Together Among Asian Religions: A Buddhist Perspective*. Manuscript.

Sri Aurobindo. 1951. *The Life Divine*. Pondicherry: Sri Aurobindo Ashram Press.

_____. 1950. *Savitri*. Pondicherry: Sri Aurobindo Ashram Press.

_____. 1962. *Human Cycles*. Pondicherry: Sri Aurobindo Ashram Press.

Sunder Rajan, R. 1998. *Beyond the Crises of European Sciences*. Shimla: Indian Institute of Advanced Study.

Tolle, Eckhart. 2005. *A New Earth: Awakening to Your Life's Purpose*. New York: Penguin Group.

Tolstoy, Leo. 1997. "Letter to a Hindoo." In Christian Bartolf, ed., *Letter to a Hindoo: Taraknath Das, Leo Tolstoy and Mahatma Gandhi*. Berlin: Gandhi-Informations-Zentrum.

Tutu, Desmond. 2004. *God Has a Dream: A Vision of Hope for our Time*. London: Rider.

Uberoi, J. P. S. 1996. *Religion, Civil Society and State: A Study of Sikhism*. Delhi: Oxford University Press.

Vattimo, Gianni. *Belief*. Cambridge: Polity Press.

Vivekananda, Swami. 1991. *The Collected Works of Swami Vivekananda*. Calcutta: Advaita Ashram.

Wuthnow, Robert. 2001. *Creative Spirituality: The Way of the Artist*. Los Angeles: University of California Press.

Chapter Sixteen

SPIRITUAL CULTIVATION FOR A SECULAR SOCIETY

In order to be a Muslim by conviction and free choice, which is the only way one can be a Muslim, I need a secular state. By a secular state I mean one that is neutral regarding religious doctrine, one that doesn't claim or pretend to enforce Sharia – the religious law of Islam – simply because compliance of Sharia cannot be coerced by a fear of state institutions or faked to appease the officials… a secular state that facilitates the possibility of religious piety out of honest conviction.

— Abdullahi An-Naim, *Islam and the Secular State: Negotiating the Future of Sharia* (2008, 1)

Exiting from the palaces and mansions of the powerful, faith – joined by philosophical wisdom – is beginning to take shelter in inconspicuous smallness, in those recesses of ordinary life unavailable to co-optation.

— Fred Dallmayr, *Small Wonder: Global Power and Its Discontents* (2005, 4)

To undertake contemplative cultural critique is to engage in transcoding. For, notwithstanding the theological roots of Western rationality, the language and concepts of socio-cultural analysis are, for the most part, thoroughly secular. To bring the insights of spiritual and secular knowledge to bear on current phenomena thus requires one to translate between and across epistemes or ways of knowing. Many tend to see these two forms of knowledge as autonomous and incompatible, and choose to privilege one or the other. However, there is much that is common to the emancipatory streams within both knowledge traditions.

— Lata Mani (2009), *SacredSecular: Contemplative Cultural Critique* (2009, 2)

The arts are contributing to a deeper, maybe even spiritual, examination of life, so what it means to be human is expressed in a variety of cultural and literary revivals in different regions of the world. Thus, the postmodern world is turning out to be a post-secular world as well. It is giving rise to what is increasingly called postmodern theology and spirituality, which recognizes that identity is linked to relationships with the family, society, and the natural world, which can be seen as part of a larger divine reality.

—Scott M. Thomas, *The Global Resurgence of Religion and the Transformation of International Relations: The Struggle for the Soul of the Twenty-First Century* (2005, 45)

The Problem

Much water has flown down the Jordan, Jhelum, Ganges, Cauvery, Mahanadi, Thames, Rhines and Mississippi rivers since the dawn of humanity and the independence of India, and in recent years much discussion has taken place over the nature of secularism in India, including its uses and abuses. Broadly speaking, we can classify the various contending positions on secularism in India into three approaches: a) those who defend the secular character of the Indian Republic as enshrined in the Constitution of India; b) those who oppose it on the grounds that the practice of Indian state-led secularism has been a pseudo-secularism; and c) those who critique that secularism is Western in origin and we must have something in its place which is appropriate for a centuries-long tradition in India of already existent religious harmony and interreligious coexistence. While I do not want to spend much time on the second argument of pseudo-secularism, which has been offered by Hindu fundamentalist forces with an eye on religious minorities, I wish to address directly the first and third arguments and draw our attention to a dead-end in which both approaches are locked at present. I argue how both need to rethink secularism and reshape it with a spiritual cultivation of self and society. The defense of secularism in the face of the rising fundamentalism in Indian body polity – especially on the wake of the 1992 demolition of Babri Masjid in Ayodhya, which was a watershed in the history of secularism in post-independent India – by many left-wing scholars and constitutional experts has been mechanical, and it does not wish to make a dialogue with the transcendental dimension of religion. Religion is a false consciousness to these secularists, but even if it is a false consciousness it is a reality in the lives of millions of people in the Indian subcontinent as it is in many parts of the world, including the so-called secularized universe of North America and Western Europe. How do we come to terms with religion if we label it as a form of false consciousness from the beginning? It is probably for this reason that Andre Béteille, an ardent defender of secularism in contemporary India, tells us, "If civil society is pluralistic and tolerant in its very nature, then it would be absurd for it to wish to expel religious institutions from its fold or to denigrate its beliefs as a form of false consciousness" (Béteille 1996, 23). Béteille warns us against what he calls the "adoption of a militantly secular ideology," "Our constitution is based, I believe wisely, on the separation between religion and politics, and on their mutual toleration. Civil society must find ways of creating and nurturing secular institutions, but that objective is likely to be hindered by the adoption of a militantly secular ideology"(Béteille 1996, 23. Similarly, William Connolly, who is more self-critical about secularism than Béteille, argues from the other side of the Atlantic, "The historical *modus vivendi* of secularism, while seeking to chastise religious dogmatism, embodies unacknowledged elements of immodesty in itself. The very intensity of the struggle it wages against religious tolerance may widen blind spots with respect to itself'" (Connolly 1999, 4).

It is a fact that Hindus, Muslims, Christians, Jains, Buddhists, tribals and people of other religious faiths live in India, and the key question for an agenda of secularism is to ensure, facilitate and enhance toleration among people of different religious faiths. But the defenders of secularism have not told us how much to ensure and facilitate toleration not only as a static equilibrium, but also as a dynamic movement of life which creates "fusions of horizons" between the people who are part of this process of intersubjective and interreligious (also multireligious) interaction. Similarly, those who oppose secularism on the grounds that it originated in the socio-historical context of Western Europe, which has a monoculture of Christianity, is not applicable to our ethos of religious pluralism; present "Antisecular Manifestoes" (cf. Nandy 1985) do not say that they want our society and politics to be guided by religious authorities. In other words, their agenda is not one of a return to a theocracy or an "establishment of a Hindu state" (Madan 1992, 408). However, they do not spell out clearly their positive agenda or whether their desire to relate to religion authentically and sympathetically supports violence and authoritarianism perpetrated in the name of religion.

An example of this ambivalence is the work of Ashis Nandy and T. N. Madan, who are two of our main proponents of the third approach to secularism mentioned above. Both of them make a cultural critique of the agenda of secularism and rope in Gandhi in the process. For example, in his now-famous address "Secularism in its Place," first presented as the Anniversary Distinguished Lecture on the occasion of the 1987 Annual Meeting of the American Association of Asian Studies, Madan (1992) writes, "Perhaps men of religion such as Mahatma Gandhi would be our best teachers on the proper relation between religion and politics – values and interests – underlining not only the possibilities of interreligious understanding, which is not the same thing as an emaciated version of mutual tolerance or respect, but also opening out avenues of a spiritually justified limitation of the role of religious institutions in certain areas of contemporary life" (408). But Madan does not take further a spiritual critique of religion, which he just hints at with his phrase, "spiritually justified limitation of the role of religion" (Madan 1992, 408). If secularism now has to be redefined as "religious pluralism," as Madan argues (Madan 1997, 262), then how does it relate to non-religious participation in our public life and what is its ethos of engagement (ethics of self-cultivation, terms of public dialogue and politics of becoming)? (cf. Connolly 1999). Furthermore, Madan does not realize that the proposed intermixture of secularism and faith is not simply a given one – as Madan seems to be suggesting – but has to be an object of a spiritual *sadhana*. Madan does not explore the preparation in self and society that is required to make this possible. The Gandhian agenda of secularism is a transformative agenda of alternative practice and movement at the level of self, culture and society. In Gandhi's agenda, in order to be secular (i.e. to be able to accept each other coming from different backgrounds of religious faith) one has to be spiritual, but this spirituality is a matter of conscious striving, *sadhana* and struggle. It is an aspect of continuous self – cultivation in the life of both individuals and societies. Therefore, Gandhi used to have interfaith prayer meetings everyday. But this aspect of the Gandhian agenda of spiritual cultivation of self and society does not find much place in Madan's critique, even in his latest work *Modern Myth and Locked Minds* (cf. Madan 1997).

In this context of the dead-end in the discourse and practice of secularism, within Indian society specifically and the present-day world more generally, this chapter of our engagement in knowledge and human liberation explores the pathways of a spiritual reshaping of secularism from an emergent transdisciplinary perspective involving dialogues with sociology, anthropology, political theory, theology, philosophy and literature. Spiritual cultivation redefines secularism as genuine cohabitation, acceptance of each other and respect for each other (facilitated by appropriate ontological cultivation and intersubjective dialogue), non-violence and self-emptying, or *kenosis*, vis-à-vis one's will to power, domination and annihilation. It argues that both the critics and defenders of secularism need a radical spiritual supplement for a fuller realization of their potential and to prepare them against one-sided self-closure of and for a simultaneous critique of religious tradition and the secular state. Cultivation in spirituality would enable us to reconstitute secularism as genuine pluralism, both ontological and social, characterized by a striving for realization of non-duality between self and other, self and society, among religious groups, and between the religious spheres and the state. A spiritual cultivation would enable us to realize the plurivocal dimensions of our being as well as broaden and deepen civil society and the public sphere as a space of meditative and multi-dimensional pluralism. Our contemporary conceptions of civil society and the public sphere suffer from a rationalist and secularist blindness where sources from religions and spirituality are automatically excluded. A spiritual cultivation for a secular society contributes to a contemporary renewal of the public sphere beyond the rationalist gaze of Kant, Rawls and Habermas. Thus, starting with the specific debate about secularism in contemporary Indian society, this chapter touches on some of the broad themes of modernity, discusses the emergent evolutionary calling of practical spirituality, and points to the need for a realization of non-duality and transcendence in self, society and polity as a way of spiritualizing secularism, modernity, self and the public sphere. Spiritualization here is not bound to religion, belief in a personal God, theistic beliefs or other familiar orthodoxies but embodies a permanent critique of the violation of life and an incessant striving for the establishment of relationships of dignity.

Critiques of Secularism and the Calling of Spiritual Transformations

In the Indian context, Ashis Nandy and T. N. Madan have been at the forefront of presenting a cultural critique of secularism as a statist, hegemonic and culturally alien ideology. For Nandy (1985), much violence has been perpetrated by the secularist state and it is the ideology of secularism that not only makes us look at religion with suspicion, but also does not enable us to build on traditionally existent people's capacity for co-existence. Madan's critique of secularism also begins with such a view. The problem of secularism in India for Madan is the problem of a "modernist minority," which is "beset with deep anxieties about the future of secularism in the country and South Asia generally" who in their attempt to rescue secularism want to "foster modern scientific temper" as a foundation for secularism (Madan 1992, 396; 2011).

But in Madan's critique of secularism, the issue is not only between modernity and tradition, but also between different religious traditions in the way they classify the world. For Madan, the modernist ideology of secularism has its most comfortable home in Christian religious tradition, namely in its supposed neat distinction between the sacred and the secular. In other religious traditions such as Hinduism and Islam, although there is a distinction between the two religions, the secular is always hierarchically encompassed by the religious. Madan's argument is that since a majority of South Asian people are vibrant followers of other religions, they have a problem in feeling at home in the dichotomy between the sacred and the secular. In the words of Madan, "…the Hindu tradition does not provide us with a dualistic view of the kind that Christianity does. I find that a Hindu, or a Sikh or a Muslim for that matter, would find it more difficult to make sense of the notion of 'privatization of religion' than perhaps a Christian does" (Bhargava 1998, 319).

Madan's reflections on comparative religious approaches to secularity call for a deeper study of the religions, particularly of Christianity, which in the Indian context is a neglected domain of inquiry. It remains to be ethnographically validated if Protestant Christians are more secular or feel more at home with the ideology of secularism in a multi-religious society such as India or Western Europe and North America. Furthermore, in the last quarter-century we have witnessed intense mobilization against the global privatization of religion in which many Christian movements, including Protestant ones such as liberation theology and Habitat for Humanity, have been key actors (Beyer 1994 and Giri 2002a). For Madan, secularism is a gift of Christianity but Madan himself says that it is Protestantism which has made a more complete delivery of this gift possible. But even in understanding the post-Reformation ideal of secularism there is a problem here because it neglects the trajectory of what Charles Taylor (1996) calls Catholic modernity. It is the Catholic encounter with modernity, as Alexis de Tocqueville (1961) suggests from his encounter with the dialectic of individualism and equality in American democracy, which has struggled more on the side of equality rather than just feeling satisfied with possessive individualism.[1]

What should be taken note of here is that Gianni Vattimo, a present-day critical philosopher who comes into his Christian faith by taking both Nietzsche and Heidegger seriously, also makes a similar argument about secularism and Christianity. For Vattimo (1999), there is an intimate connection between the secular project and the Christian vocation in the world as Jesus Christ makes a break with violence. In making the connection between secularization and Christianity, Vattimo urges us to realize that secularization here is characterized by striving for non-violence or *kenosis*, which also means "self-abasing" oneself in love, and charity – namely interpretive charity with regard to supposedly sanctioned divine commands and laws. For Vattimo, secularization means working with a "non-violent and non-absolute God," a God who is "post-metaphysical." In the words of Vattimo, "If the natural sacred is the violent mechanism that Jesus came to unveil and undermine, it is possible that secularization – which also constitutes the Church's loss of temporal authority and human reason's increasing autonomy from its dependence upon an absolute God, a fearful Judge who so transcends our ideas about good and evil as to appear as a capricious or bizarre sovereign – is precisely a positive effect of Jesus' teaching, and not a way of moving away from it" (Vattimo 1999, 41, and Taylor 1996).

For Vattimo, non-violence inaugurated by Jesus' break with the supposed violence of the natural sacred is an important part of the secular vocation. As Madan's formulations suffer from a weak study of the anthropology and the theology of Christianity, Vattimo's formulations suffer from a messianic zeal of it and lack a cross-cultural and cross-religious realization that all sacred is not all violent. The God of Taittiriya Upanishad where God meditates upon himself to bring forth a world is not violent. But apart from this, Vattimo's reflections urge us to realize the many other dimensions in the connection between Christian vocation and secularization. Secularization here is not confined to the neat distinction between the sacred and the secular but points to normative ideals of non-violence, *kenosis*, and charity – ideals which call for appropriate self-realization and institutional transformations. These ideals, arguing with Vattimo against Vattimo, are not only the legacy of Christianity, but they also work as a critique of both religion and secularism as they are conventionally understood. If we understand secularism as *kenosis*, then one challenge of being secular is to empty oneself from one's will to power. Secularism as self-emptying of power poses enormous challenges to the prevalent conceptions of secularism and models of emancipation as empowerment, and it urges us to realize that emancipation as politics of empowerment must have within itself an ethics and spirituality of self-cultivation so that one does not become a slave to one's will to power in one's private life and the public sphere. Secularism as *kenosis* vis-à-vis one's will to power challenges us not to be obsessed with "exercising power over others," as Foucault urges in his *Care of the Self*, and to be concerned with discovering and realizing "what one is purely in relation to oneself" (Foucault 1986, 85). Secularism as *kenosis* can thus be linked to Foucauldian care of the self: "It is then a matter of forming and recognizing oneself as the subject of one's own actions, not through a system of signs denoting power over others, but through a relation that depends as little as possible on status and its external forms" (Foucault 1986, 85).

Madan concludes his address "Secularism in its Place" with a passionate plea to take both religion and secularism seriously. But the task of taking both religion and secularism seriously also entails a mutual critique and a foundational interrogation and broadening of the categories. In his critique, Madan presents us with a cross-cultural interrogation of what may be called the ideology of secularism. Secular ideology for Madan leads to "the marginalization of religious faith." The more foundational problem for Madan, which he expresses in the words of Fazlur Rahman, is that "Secularism destroys the sanctity and universality (transcendence) of all moral values" (Madan 1992, 402). But does secularism do this or have necessarily to do this? Does religion always promote moral values? Does the invocation of transcendence necessarily lead to human emancipation? What kinds of ultimate values lead to human annihilation, and what kind of ultimate values lead to human flourishing including a mutual sharing of each others ultimate values? If, as Vattimo (1999, 90) suggests, love is the ultimate value and all of us have sinned because we have failed in love, then should we be prepared to reject religions if they fail us in love?

Madan himself says that the religious traditions of South Asia are "totalizing in character, claiming all of a follower's life," but in our engagement with religion should we support its totalitarianism? I am sure for Madan that respect for religion does not mean support for a totalitarian determination of life in the name of religion. Taking religion seriously means engaging ourselves with a critique of it, certainly a connected critique to begin with. What we need here is a critique of religion, not only secularism, and from this critique realize the significance of secularism as it loosens the totalitarian hold of religion and contributes to the quest and realization of human freedom. As Thomas Pantham argues, "The problematic relationship between religion and politics in the West had its analogues in India too. Despite important philosophical or metaphysical differences between them, both European Christianity and Indian religions rationalized in their own ways, a feudal order of social inequalities prevailing during the medieval period" (Pantham 1999, 182). And in the medieval world, a radical interrogation of religion as a partner in social exploitation was articulated by varieties of socio-spiritual movements such as the Anabaptists in Europe (cf. Mauss 1979) and *bhakti* (devotional) movements in India. *Bhakti* movements were spiritually inspired socio-spiritual movements which fought against caste and gender hierarchy in medieval India. The work of spirituality in *bhakti* movements involved a critique of religion as a partner in the systemic oppression of society and the quest for an establishment of relationships of dignity. As critic and essayist Chittaranjan Das argues, "To go inside in the life of the spirit is also to expand oneself in terms of consciousness, to break down the separating wall between oneself and the all. Self-realization with the medieval saints of India was not a running away from the world to what is called to save one's soul; it is being reborn ego-less, so that you are able to look at the whole world in a different eye. You become a rebel because you want the relationships and arrangements of society to be determined anew" (Das 1982b, 80). Thus secularism as a fight for human emancipation and striving for realization of human freedom has also an origin in spiritual protests in India as well as in Europe and helps us to deconstruct religion as we take it seriously. In medieval India, *bhakti* movements characterized by a quest for love and non-violence have been the forbearers of secularism and modernity, what J. P. S. Uberoi (1996) calls Indian modernity, which started with Kabir and has found an ally in Gandhi, among others, in the midway. But what is interesting is that this spiritual origin of secularism buttresses the non-violent character of it, as pointed to us by Vattimo, and is characterized by a religion, spirituality and praxis of love. Spirituality as a movement of transformation in self and society and embodied in the life and work of

Antigone, Socrates, Buddha, Jesus, Kabir, Guru Nanak, Meister Eckhart, the *bhakti* movements, Ali Shariati, and innumerable movements of what can be called practical spirituality all over the world provides not only a critique of secularism, but also a radical interrogation of religion. It is my submission that both the critiques as well as the defense of secularism would be enriched by bringing the vision and practice of spirituality not only to our discourse, but also to our practice.

However, opening ourselves to such sources of secularism calls us to cross the borders of conventional academic boundaries. When we look at the discursive field of secularism, this seems to be a crucial challenge as it is bounded by a dualistic logic and is one-dimensional and mono-disciplinary. In contemporary Indian society and scholarship, it is a field which suffers from the blindness of disciplinary exclusivity, which affects both the critics and the defenders. The political scientists writing here talk mostly of state, to some extent of civil society, and of course always of constitution. Anthropologists such as Madan or cultural critics such as Nandy enter the field with an a priori privileging of the religious and faith in their capacity for tolerance in the pre-modern life-world. But if one of the tasks before us is an interpretative task of providing more clarity to the agenda of secularism, as Madan challenges us to do in the Indian context and Connolly in the Euro-American world, then what is called for is a creative embodiment of transdisciplinarity. This calls for political scientists to go beyond the secured logic of constitution and state and anthropologists to acknowledge, as Andre Béteille (1992, 2002) would urge, that contemporary Indian society is governed not only by *Dharmasastras*, but also by constitution. But again, the called for transdisciplinary participation here must have within it the perspective of spiritual movements and seekers and must cross the boundaries between sociology and spiritual seeking. A spiritual process of abandonment and creative exploration is central to the practice of transdiscplinarity, and the discursive field of secularism calls for a spiritual interrogation of our disciplinary homes in anthropology, sociology, philosophy, theology and even spirituality (Giri 2000).[2]

Such transdisciplinary participation has not only a semantic function or a scholastic utility, but it also has important implications for our art of learning and living within a secular society, which is understood as a plural society. Consider here Ashis Nandy's statement, "As far as public morality goes, statecraft in India may have something to learn from Hinduism, Islam or Sikhism; but Hinduism, Islam and Sikhism have very little to learn from the contribution from state secular practices" (Pantham 1999, 177). But do not Muslim males who do not give alimony to their divorced wives and caste Hindus who burn Dalits have something to learn from the Indian Constitution? Even do not the well-meaning Hindus, Muslims and Sikhs have something to learn from the secular principles of the Indian Constitution?

Thus in rethinking secularism the challenge is a multi-dimensional education – lateral as well as vertical – and a simultaneous critique of both religious tradition and modern state. Transdisciplinary participation in secularism with a radical spiritual supplement can prepare us against one-sided, confident self-closure and prepare us for a simultaneous critique of both religious traditions and the secular state. Gandhi can help us in not only discovering the religious resources for living in a secular society, but also in initiating a spiritual transformation of the telos and the machinery of modern state. For Gandhi, "the modern state itself needs to be 'civilized' by integrating it with spirituality or morality" (Pantham 1999, 183). As Thomas Pantham argues, "…Gandhi seems to have inaugurated a postliberal, ethical-secular trajectory of relationship between politics and religion in which their relative autonomy from each other is used in moral-political experiments or campaigns for the reconstruction of both the religious traditions and the modern State…" (Pantham 1999, 181). Unfortunately, this aspect of Gandhian critique of a moral transformation of state has not received much attention from either the critics or the defenders of secularism.

Gandhi is dear to many of us, but the question is how far, deep and up we wish to walk with him. One important implication of holding the hands of Gandhi is that we strive to learn about each other's religions. Madan finds this difficult and gives the analogy of difficulty of multilingual learning in India (Madan 1997, 277). But if secularism as a dignified mode of interreligious and plural existence has to succeed, then learning about each other's religion is a must. As Gandhi tells us:

> I hold that it is the duty of every cultured man or woman to read sympathetically the scriptures of the world. If we are to respect others' religions as we would have them respect our own, a friendly study of the world's religions is a sacred duty. We need not dread, upon our grown-up children, the influence of scriptures other than our own. We liberalize their outlook upon life by encouraging them to study freely all that is clean… For myself, I regard my study of and reverence for the Bible, the Qur'an, and the other scriptures to be wholly consistent with my claim to be a staunch Sanatani Hindu. He is no Sanatani Hindu who is narrow, bigoted, and considers evil to be good if it has the sanction of antiquity and is to be found supported in any Sanskrit book. (Sharma 1995, 89–90)

However, the invocation of Gandhi in the reshaping of secularism does not go unchallenged. Political scientist Paul Brass (1998) finds the invocation of Gandhi in the critique of secularism offered by Nandy and Madan problematic. For Brass, "The peaceful pursuit of interreligious dialogue through the 'recovery of religious tolerance' has no meaning for those groups who have seen themselves as oppressed and discriminated against in Hindu society: Muslims, backward castes, Scheduled Castes, and Scheduled Tribes" (Brass 1998, 493). But Brass helps us understand how, even for these groups, tolerance is possible without cultivation of the capacity of tolerance at the levels of individuals and groups. And here Gandhi is important because he urges us – through the example of his life and death – to be ever prepared for the knockings of the Other on our house and to open our doors. As J. P .S. Uberoi argues, "…Gandhi would always look the other in the eye as his second self and offer truthful dialogue and non-violent conversation without the fear of the possible consequences" (Uberoi 2002, 121). Gandhian agenda is not confined only to the search for "transcendent interreligious truths" as Brass makes it to be. Learning to hold the hands of the other from other religions here on Earth – in Noakhali, Delhi, in Sevagram, Lahore, and in Amritsar, India – is an important part of the Gandhian way of life.

Defense of Secularism: Towards a Spiritual Transformation of Justification and Application

Coexistence and tolerance are important aspects of the way of life which Gandhi inspires us to lead. Even the defenders of secularism in the Indian context are coming to realize that tolerance is the single most important task facing us now insofar as the issue of secularism is concerned. For example, in his recent insightful reflection on the predicament of secularism "Secularism and Its Discontents," Amartya Sen (1996) argues that the key question for an agenda of secularism is the question of the symmetric treatment of religions, groups, individuals and other autonomies. For Sen, a secular state has a moral duty to ensure such a symmetric treatment among religions, and he does not agree with the critics of secularism, such as Nandy, that such a practice is inevitably accompanied by an increase in the power of the state to perpetrate violence on people in the name of defending secularism.

But how do we cultivate and facilitate the capacity for symmetric and fair treatment to each other on the part of individuals and groups? Here, Sen does not go much deeper. He does not address the ontological preparation that is required for such a mode of life to exist in our society and politics. Similar is the problem with another thinker, Partha Chatterjee (1994), who titles his contribution on the subject as "Secularism and Toleration." But Chatterjee does not tell us how we can cultivate toleration among members of different religious faiths. And, like Sen, Chatterjee finds a panacea only in secular politics. For Chatterjee, by initiating politics of a representative democracy among the minorities to run their religious affairs, such as the Muslim Wakf Board or the Akal Takht, we can help initiate reform within these minorities and create more favorable conditions for inter-group toleration. But is this enough to ensure toleration? The practice of toleration requires preparation in the life of the individuals for another religion – another world – and this is not a matter of politics alone.

The same challenge of self-cultivation and transformation we find in the defense of secularism offered by other political scientists of India. They defend secularism as a part of democratic equality. Manoranjan Mohanty makes a distinction between secularism – hegemonic and democratic. Mohanty would agree with the critics of secularism, such as Madan and Nandy, that there is a danger in making it only an ideology of the state or an elite and would want secularism to be part of the ongoing democratic mobilization and transformation of Indian society. Neera Chandhoke (1999) continues the same engagement with democracy, although her views are a bit more constitutional than the mobilizational views of Mohanty, and defends secularism as the defense of minority rights, which is part of a broader agenda of democratic equality. For her, "...societies that are deeply polarized on the matter of religion, such as India or Northern Ireland, will need to institute protections for their minorities against majoritarianism" (Chandhoke 1999, 7). But Chandhoke also argues, implicitly suggesting the argument of Uberoi, that the problem of humanity cannot be solved "within a framework of majority and minority" (cf. Uberoi 2002, 120) because "... the right of a minority community to its own identity and practices has to be balanced with respect for the rights of other communities to their own identity and practices. ...*The struggle for recognition that is simultaneously a search for dignity, directs our attention to the intersubjective conditions of human realization*" (Chandhoke 1999, 19, emphasis added).

Rajeev Bhargava contributes important clarifications to this defense of secularism by redefining secularism contextually. He develops the notion of contextual secularism partly from the recognition of the problem that there is very little sensitivity to religious pluralism in the state-centric discourse of secularism, which was posed by Nandy and Madan. Contextual secularism recognizes that "many forms of separation lie between total exclusion and complete fusion" (Bhargava 1998, 516). Contextual secularism for Bhargava is political secularism, not ideological secularism, and "political secularism demands only that every one – believer or non-believer – gives up a bit of what is of exclusive importance in order to sustain that which is generally valuable..." (Bhargava 1998, 496).

But is politics enough to realize political secularism or do they need appropriate ethics and spirituality? Is realization of democratic equality possible only by institution of group rights in the constitution, or does it require appropriate self-cultivation and ontological preparation of self and society for inviting the other into the core of the "political" self? This requires not only a Rawlsian political liberalism and Habermasian inclusion of the other but also a spiritual praxis of self-opening and self-transformation, which is conspicuous by its absence in Rawls and Habermas (cf. Cohen 2001, Giri 2002b). Bhargava's conception of political secularism uncritically reflects a Rawlsian project of liberalism, but the challenge now is to realize the limits of Rawls. As Connolly urges us to realize, "*But secularism is the last historical moment in the politics of becoming Rawlsian categories authorize us to acknowledge.* Rawls wants us to freeze the liberal conception of the person and the secular conception of public space today while everything else in and around the culture undergoes change" (Connolly 1999, 66).

Chandhoke writes that "we need not value pluralism although we are faced with a plural society" (Chandhoke 1999, 297). This urges us to understand that even if we institute pluralism constitutionally, we may not embody a plural mode of being or what William Connolly calls "the ethos of pluralization" (Connolly 2001). As Connolly would suggest, in order to embody an ethos of pluralization we need to be self-reflective about the modernist privileging of epistemology and open ourselves to ontological journeys. However, this calls for not only a multi-dimensional conception of pluralism and public sphere, but also a multi-layered conception of being, which is suggested in Connolly's conception of "plurivocity of being." But Connolly's "plurivocity of being" stops at the foot hills of Nietzsche; thus, it is no wonder that the only other dimension of plurivocality of being that we are opened to in Connolly is the dimension of the infra-rational. But here a cross-cultural, transcivilizational, philosophical and spiritual engagement can help us realize that it is not only a Nietzschean and Deleuzian infra-rational which constitutes the other dimension of plurivocality of being, but also

Sri Aurobindo's suprarational and Roy Bhaskar's "transcendentally real self" (Bhaskar 2002, 139), which is characterized by striving for the realization of non-duality in a world of duality and strife. For Sri Aurobindo, the "suprarational dimension" of our being enables us to overcome the limitations of our mind, especially our "desire-mind," and enables us to "have the joy of contact in diverse oneness" (Sri Aurobindo 1950, 484).

A multi-dimensional, rich conception of self enables the realization of secularism as multi-dimensional pluralism by facilitating not only public contestations of one's fundamentals, but also a sharing of selves – a creative interpenetration between the self and other, or as Uberoi would say, an exchange not only of gifts, but of self (Uberoi 2002). And this sharing of self and society is pre-eminently a spiritual activity. Thus in the political reshaping of secularism as democratic equality, a spiritual foundation is helpful. But spiritual processes of transformation are not foundational only in a genealogical sense, but also in a critically constitutive sense of permanent critique and reconfiguration. Spirituality as a permanent critique of a violation of life and the destructive logic of power provides us with a much needed perspective of "limits;" for example, the realization of the "limits of politics" of both the confident and self-critical political scientists of our times (Lalcau 1992).[3] As Roberto M. Unger, a political and legal theorist, tells us, there are two kinds of sacred – a transcendental sacred and a social sacred – and whenever a system of power loses touch with the transcendental sacred, it can and very often will present oppression as manifestation and justification for the social sacred and there may not be any critical ground to critique such an unjust arrangement (Unger 1987). And here as Alberto Melucci, a sociologist, urges us to understand:

> Instrumental rationality has restored the world to mankind's scope of operation, but it also denies humanity all chances to transcend reality, it devalues everything that resists subsumption under the instrumental action. Society thus becomes a system of apparatuses identical with its own actions and intolerant of any diversity. The sacred thus emerges as an appeal to a possible other, as the voice of what is not but could be. Divested of the ritual trappings of the churches, the sacred thus becomes a purely cultural form of resistance which counters the presumption of power by affirming the right to desire – to hope that the world is more than what actually is. (Melucci 1996, 171)

Melucci's critique of instrumental rationality in modernity is in tune with Gandhi's critique and even has resonance in Weber. Madan helps us understand this by stating, "A Gandhian critique of secularism in terms of ultimate values and individual responsibility is in some respects similar to Max Weber's concern with the problem of value. What Gandhi and Weber are saying is that the secularized world is inherently unstable because it elevates to the realm of ultimate values the only value it knows and these are instrumental values" (Madan 1997, 237–8, Madan 2011). These critiques point to a spiritual horizon of secularism not as a way of providing a stable ground to the inherent instability of secularism but as a permanently moving frame of criticism. But understanding this requires not only a transformation in our political reasoning, but also a transformation in our sociological reasoning. Sociology has been a part of the project of modernity, which believes that it can "provide a privileged or authoritative interpretation of social events" by making it a hegemonic discourse while "all others, including religious utopias, are derivative" (Wuthnow 1991, 14). But opening ourselves to spiritual critique and transformation calls for us to "interpret the significance of contemporary movements in terms of the hopes and aspirations of their participants, including their hopes for salvation and spiritual renewal…" (Wuthnow 1991, 14).

The Calling of Mutual Learning and Cultivating Non-dual Pluralism

If toleration is the most important part of the agenda of secularism, we must lay its seed in our minds and hearts. In order to accomplish this, it is important for us to learn about each other andknow each other in an open-ended spirit of exploration, dialogue and the creation of a new ground of life. Such a mode of learning is pre-eminently a spiritual activity. Spirituality is about the quality of relationship between the self and the other (cf. Kurien 1996); in fact, spirituality lies in the heart of relationships or at the mid-point of relationships, to borrow a phrase from Martin Heidegger (cf. Dallmayr 1996). And to achieve a more dignified relationship, we must prepare ourselves by being engaged in the multifarious practices of education, self-cultivation or *Bildung* (cf. Dumont 1994) and understand the spiritual foundations of a secular society.

But now there is a shocking ignorance about each other's religion. In a society like contemporary India, we are not taught about other religions in schools because of the secular injunctions against it, nor do we have any opportunity for this in civil society. If we do not know anything about each other's religions then how can we accept each other's religions? It is true that knowing is not enough, but this is an important part of a more inclusive process of feeling and realization. So how do we learn about each other's religions? If Hindus learn about Islam only from the *Rashtriya Swayam Sevak Sangha* and the *Vishwa Hindu Parishad* (sectarian Hindu organizations) and Muslims learn about Hinduism only from sectarian Islamic organisations, then what is the nature of our knowledge of each other? Is this not knowledge of hatred only? Is there any knowledge here where we have already formulated our objects of knowledge in an a priori mode?

In this context, it is helpful to hear my discussion with a follower of a Hindu socio-spiritual movement. This movement is an exciting one, and it believes that we should accept all religions. *Sarva Dharma Sambhava* ("Goodwill towards all religions") is not enough; we must have *Sarva Dharma Swikara* – "acceptance of all religions." This movement also believes that Hindus should accept Jesus as the eleventh incarnation of God and Prophet Mohammed as the twelfth. But when I asked him if he knew anything about Jesus or Mohammed, he told me, "I am sorry that I do not know anything." I told him, "But the city in which you live has so many Muslims. Could not you make a little effort?" Then he told me, "Yes, there is an eagerness within me. But it stays at a subterranean level of my consciousness. It is helpful if we have organizations to activate this dormant eagerness within me?" Thus the challenge of education I am pleading for goes much deeper, and here we must have appropriate institutional conditions for learning both one's religion as well as that of one's neighbors at the level of state and civil society (Sharma 1996).

If secularism has to be redefined as pluralism and multiculturalism then we must confront the epistemic task of living in such a plural and multireligious society (cf. Mohanty 1998). As has been suggested, learning about other religions, cultures and communities is an important part of this epistemic engagement. But learning is not simply a question of epistemology, but involves ontological preparation and work on developing the self, culture and society.

To live in a multireligious, multicultural and plural society, we need a new ethics, politics and spirituality of self-cultivation. And it is this focus on self-cultivation that is missing in our discourse on both secularism and pluralism. In Indian sociology, T. K. Oommen (2002) is a passionate advocate of pluralism, but his view of pluralism remains at the boundaries of groups and it does not have a project of what can be called ontological pluralism. Ontological pluralism calls for the realization of non-dual plurivocality in our beings. Roy Bhaskar, a philosopher of critical realism who has taken critical realism to new depths and horizons of spiritual strivings, provides us with glimpses of non-dual self-realization as an important part of the realization of ontological and sociological pluralism (Bhaskar 2000, 2002). For Bhaskar, "the possibility of human emancipation depends upon expanding the zone of non-duality within our lives; and in the first instance upon shedding our own heteronomy so that we become in a way non-dual beings in a world of duality" (Bhaskar 2002, 11).

There are several implications of realization of non-duality for rethinking and reshaping secularism. One implication is that there is no point in thinking about the relationship between the religious and the secular in terms of an essential opposition. But the other implication for us in this path of engagement is to open ourselves up to emergent evolutionary occurrence and possibility. Reminiscent of Sri Aurobindo's words, Uberoi suggests that "...the theory of evolution means to us, not chiefly or only development of what is complex out of simple, but also the development of many varieties of existence out of the original few, and without humanity in anyway losing the unity of its universe of discourse" (Uberoi 2002, 130).

The Calling of an Emergent Evolution: Transcendence and Practical Spirituality

(a) The calling of a new transcendence

I would like to submit that the emergence of transcendence as an existence sphere and a value sphere of self and society along with "the standard threesome of science, morality and religion" (cf. Schrag 1997, 148) is an important part of the contemporary processes of spiritual evolution. Fred Dallmayr's following comments make this clear: "There are plenty of signs in our time that a narrowly confined immanence cannot satisfy human longings and aspirations. What needs to be recognized is that longing for transcendence, even a transcendental holism, are vibrantly alive today in many societies on the level of the ordinary life – world – far removed from traditional holistic power structures" (Dallmayr 2001, 17). And as Jean-Luc Nancy argues, "It is precisely the immanence of man to man, or it is man taken absolutely, considered as the immanent being par excellence, that constitutes the stumbling block to a thinking of community" (Dallmayr 1998, 281).

But the process of unification in the emergent sphere of transcendence, as it relates to other domains of our lives, is different from the familiar process of universalistic unification. It is not the simple formula of unity-in-diversity as Uberoi suggests. It is a process of unification where unity is always a deferred state. As Scharg urges, "…it is a dynamics of unification that is always an 'ing,' a process of unifying, rather than an 'ed,' a finalized result" (Schrag 1997, 129).

Schrag builds upon Kierkegaard and urges us to overcome the facile dualism between transcendence and immanence. What is helpful is that in contemporary philosophy and theology we have a passionate reformulation of not only the relationship between transcendence and immanence, but also the very categories themselves. Building on the philosophical and theological works of Jacques Derrida and Luce Irigaray, John D. Caputo writes, "The new idea of transcendence turns on a new and positive idea of the finite, not as confining limit, as in Kant's example of the dove that thinks it is confined by the air that sustains it… [Rather] transcendence [is] life in the elements, in the enveloping medium in which soul and body 'marry.' What then is God's transcendence? Who is the God who comes after metaphysics? Not a God of infinite distance from earth and flesh, but the infinite freedom to make God self-immanent in the finite, incarnate" (Caputo 2002, 14–15). Giving a new interpretation to Derrida's famous dictum "God is Wholly Other," Walter Lowe (2002) writes in his "Second Thoughts About Transcendence," "Surely we have the option of reading 'God is other' as 'God is different' and 'God as Wholly Other' as 'God differing-differently.' There would then be the conceptual space to conceive that 'divine transcendence' might refer, perhaps, to God's freedom. Then transcendence would cease to be the opposite of immanence; for a God of freedom would not be isolated in some lofty place but would be capable of being immanent precisely because of being transcendent, i.e. free" (Lowe 2002, 250).

For Derrida, there is no problem, and in fact it is a blessing, if we do not take the name of God. As Caputo (2002) interprets the Derridean pathway, "Save everything about God, save the name of God, lest it become an idol that blocks our way." This Derridean refusal and abandonment of God's name is noticed in the *bhakti* movements of India. Here Chittaranjan Das' work on *bhakti* movements and spiritual evolution deserves our careful attention. Das (1982a) tells us in his study of *bhakti* literature of India that Saint Pundarika Das of Karnataka has described Rama and Krishna as *Idli* and *Dosha* (items of food in South India) in his poems. In Orissa, while the Panchasakhas-Achyutananda Das, Balram Das, Arakhita Das, et al. have transcended many idols and arrived at Jagannatha as Brahma, the blind tribal poet, Bhima Bhoi, the spiritual prophet of the nineteenth century has transcended Jagannatha himself and made him a watchman in the house of Sunya ("Emptiness") (Das 2001). This abandonment of and refusal to name God has affinity with the path of spiritual seeking and enlightenment, which was charted by Buddha.

Luce Irigaray has been another source of inspiration in the contemporary rethinking of transcendence where transcendence refers to the air we breathe. Irigaray has been an important source of inspiration in rethinking religion as a process of being divine, reminding us of Sri Aurobindo's pathway of life-divine (cf. Jantzen 2002, Sri Aurobindo 1951). Irigaray provides us with a critique of religion, namely Christian religion, from the point of view of feminine spirituality. A female client in psychoanalysis tells Irigaray, "At the point in the mass when they, the (spiritual) father and son, are reciting together the ritual words of the consecration, saying 'This is my body, this is my blood,' I bleed" (cf. Jantzen 2002). Irigaray points to the shifting trajectory of Christian theology, and Felix Wilfred (1999) points to the Indian context's mystical dimensions. Wilfred presents us the agenda of a situated Christian theology, taking into consideration the cultural and spiritual aspirations of Asia. For Wilfred, Christianity in the new millennium, not only in India but around the world, should not only assert its prophetic truths, but also open itself up to the mysterious dimension of religion, spirituality and the human condition. In the words of Wilfred, "Christian attempts to cross over to the other, to the different, has been by and large from the pole of being or fullness. This naturally creates problems, which can be overcome by activating the ability to also cross over from the pole of nothingness or emptiness" (Wilfred 1999, xiii).

(b) The calling of practical spirituality

At this point, the work of German theologian Johannes B. Metz (1981) deserves our careful attention. He says that the quest for unity can not be achieved on the level of faith but must be a practical quest – the practical quest of addressing the concrete problems of men and women here on Earth. We can utilize this as a turning point for discussing practical spirituality as an emergent mode in many world religions now. Swami Vivekananda spoke about it more than one hundred years ago, and the previous chapter has described the emerging vision and practice of practical spirituality. (Please see the previous chapter on practical spirituality.)

What is to be noted is that practical spirituality can be looked at as an emerging global genre. Consider, for instance, the shifting contours of spirituality in contemporary American society. For Robert Wuthnow, in contemporary American society there is a shift from a "spirituality of dwelling" to a "spirituality of seeking" (Wuthnow 1998). "A spirituality of dwelling emphasizes habitation: God occupies a definite place in the universe" (Wuthnow 1998, 10). It "emphasizes an orderly, systematic understanding of life" (Wuthnow 1998, 8). But a spirituality of habitation and dwelling inadequately satisfies our multiple aspirations at present when the secured houses of our lives are in flux. This creates the context for the emergence of a "spirituality of seeking," which is "closely connected to the fact that people increasingly create a sense of personal identity through an active sequence of searching and selecting" (Wuthnow 1998, 18). But Wuthnow makes it clear that a spirituality of seeking in itself is inadequate in regard to challenges of self-development and responsibility to the other and the world, because it offers only "fleeting encounters with the sacred" (Wuthnow 1998, 8). Spirituality of seeking suffers from the danger of making seekers of spirituality satisfied with temporary spiritual sensations and needs to be supplemented by what Wuthnow calls "practice-oriented spirituality." Practice-oriented spirituality provides multiple grounds for combining spiritual practice and social service. Practice-oriented spirituality is not confined to moments of spiritual sensations but touches all aspects of our life: "...the point of spiritual practice is not to elevate an isolated set of activities over the rest of life but to electrify the spiritual impulse that animates all of life" (Wuthnow 1998, 198).

The significance of practical spirituality as a global genre is attested by many observers of the contemporary scene such as Peter Beyer (1994); he argues that "pure religion" is at a disadvantage in global society and the solution to its increasing and inevitable privatization lies in finding "effective religious applications." Thus, in order to be of interest to both believers and non-believers, religions have to undertake activities which ameliorate the conditions of poverty and suffering, build the foundations for what Giddens calls a "generative well-being" (Giddens 1994) and, through this act of building, encourage the participants to develop themselves ethically, morally and spiritually. But the practical activities of religion are not just "applied" where application is dissociated from what Kierkegaard (1962, Giri and Quarles von Ufford 2000) calls a transcendental inspiration of love. The applied activities of practical spirituality manifest themselves through various projects – life-projects, where the actors are committed to a cause and live in accordance with such a commitment, and social projects, where religious movements are engaged in a concrete activity such as building houses as in the case of Habitat for Humanity or building water-harvesting structures in case of Swadhyaya. However, these projects are not merely instances of "application"; they are manifestations of an integral mode of engagement where applied activities are nourished by a spiritual relationship with the Transcendent. Thus the applied projects of such movements of practical spirituality are different from projects of mere application, which is the case with many development projects of our times (cf. Quarles van Ufford and Giri 2003). Practice and practical work in such movements differ from the familiar anthropological category of practice outlined by Bourdieu (cf. Bourdieu 1971) and the notion of practical discourse presented by Habermas (1990); both of the categories refer only to rational strategies and rational deliberations of actors, and neither is linked to spiritual realization and transcendent self-awareness of the actors. The applied activities of movements of practical spirituality transcend the familiar dichotomies between transcendence and immanence; in fact, their projects of social action for the other, which are simultaneously initiatives in self-development, transcend the familiar dichotomies between transcendence and immanence and exist at the "mid-point" of the relationship between transcendence and immanence.

This crossing between the borders of transcendence and immanence also involves transformations in the ethico-moral horizons of religion. While in the past moral considerations meant "sin, ignorance, etc." (cf. Beyer 1990, 360), now the condition of our life and society – the nature of poverty, social justice and quality of our love – is the subject of ethico-moral engagement. Vattimo challenges us to "…stand in need of forgiveness; not because we have broken sacred principles that were metaphysically sanctioned, but rather because we have 'failed' toward those whom we are supposed to love" (Vattimo 1990, 90).

By Way of Conclusion: Spirituality as a Permanent Critique and Creativity

In this chapter we have explored different pathways of spiritual cultivation for the realization of plurivocal beings and a multi-dimensional, rich public sphere. We began this essay with a cautionary note from Jacques Derrida that we should be on our guard so that we do not authorize ourselves in the name of religion. In exploring spiritual cultivation for a secular society, am I authorizing myself in the name of spirituality? Here I have not provided a definition of spirituality, but spirituality for me lies within the in-between lines and embodies a permanent quest for the realization of relationships of dignity. But it would be a mistake to look at spirituality as a stable foundation, the ultimate truth, and a solution to all our problems. It is also important not to forget that spiritual movements, at times, are trapped within the logic of authoritarianism and individual salvation (cf. Krishna 1996). In this context, as we work on spiritual cultivation for a secular society, the challenge before spirituality now is to continue to fight for radical democracy and universality – a universality which transgresses the boundaries of self and other, creates new intimacies and solidarities across boundaries, and participates in the struggle for creation and nurturance of transformative institutions of justice, well-being and dignity.

Notes

1 Tocqueville writes, "If Catholicism predisposes the faithful to obedience, it certainly does not prepare them for inequality: but the contrary may be said of Protestantism, which generally tends to make men independent, more than to render them equal" (Tocqueville 1961, 356).

2 Of course, admirable exceptions in this field are J. P. S. Uberoi's (1996) *Religion, Civil Society and State: A Study of Sikhism* and Felix Wilfred's (2000) *Asian Dreams and Christian Hopes*, which embody a simultaneous and sometimes transgressive engagement with politics, religion, theology and spirituality.

3 This is as much a challenge for Neera Chanhoke and Rajeev Bhargava as for William Connolly. It is striking that Connolly's inspiring conception of "politics of being" has no engagement with the issue of self-cultivation in terms of, among others, developing *kenosis* vis-à-vis the will to power. Note here the way Connolly defines "politics of being" and compare this, without judgment, to the vocation of being, which is articulated by Roy Bhaskar and described later in Connolly's essay: "By the politics of becoming I mean that paradoxical politics by which new cultural identities are formed out of unexpected energies and institutionally congealed injuries.

The politics of becoming emerge out of the energies, suffering, and the lines of flight available to culturally defined differences in a particular institutional constellation" (Connolly 1999, 57).

References

An-Na'im, Abdullahi. 2008. *Islam and the Secular State: Negotiating the Future of Sharia*. Cambridge, MA: Harvard University Press.

Basu, Kaushik and Sanjay Subrahmanyam, ed. 1996. *Unravelling the Nation: Sectarian Conflict and India's Secular Identity*. New Delhi: Penguin Books.

Béteille, Andre. 1992. *Society and Politics in India: Essays in a Comparative Perspective*. Delhi: Oxford University Press.

_____. 1996. "Civil Society and its Institutions." Lecture at the First Fulbright Memorial, Calcutta.

_____. 2002. *Antinomies of Society*. Delhi: Oxford University Press.

Beyer, Peter F. 1994. *Religion and Globalization*. London: Sage Publications.

Bhargava, Rajeev, ed. 1998. *Secularism and Its Critics*. Delhi: Oxford University Press.

Bhaskar, Roy. 2000. *From East to West: The Odyssey of a Soul*. London: Routledge.

_____. 2002. *Reflections on Meta-Reality: Transcendence, Emancipation and Everyday Life*. New Delhi: Sage Publications.

Bourdieu, Pierre. 1971. *Outline of a Theory of Practice*. Cambridge: Cambridge University Press.

Brass, Paul R. 1998. "Secularism Out of Its Place." *Contributions to Indian Sociology* 32 (2): 485–505.

Caputo, John D. 2002. "Introduction: Who Comes After the God of Metaphysics?" In John D. Caputo, ed., *The Religious*. Oxford: Blackwell Publishing.

Chandhoke, Neera. 1999. *Beyond Secularism: The Rights of Religious Minorities*. Delhi: Oxford University Press.

Chatterjee, Partha. 1994. "Secularism and Toleration." *Economic and Political Weekly* 29 (28).

Cohen, G. A. 2001. *If You're Egalitarian, How Come You Are So Rich?*. Cambridge, MA: Harvard University Press.

Connolly, William. 1999. *Why I am not a Secularist*. Minneapolis: University of Minnesota Press.

_____. 2001. *The Ethos of Pluralization*. Minneapolis: University of Minnesota Press.

Dallmayr, Fred. 1996. *The Other Heidegger*. Ithaca, NY: Cornell University Press.

_____. 1998. *Alternative Visions: Pathways in the Global Village*. Lanham, MD: Rowman & Littlefield.

_____. 2001. "Global Modernities." University of Notre Dame, unpublished paper.

Das, Chittaranjan. 1982a. *Santha Sahitya: Literature of the Saints*. Bhubaneswar: Orissa Sahitya Akademi.

_____. 1982b. *A Glimpse into Oriya Literature*. Bhubaneswar: Orissa Sahitya Akademi.

_____. 1996. *Bhinna Jane Vivekananda: Another Vivekananda*. Cuttack: The Universe.

_____. 2001. *Dekhu Dekhu Keba Sahu: How Can One Tolerate All These One Sees*. Bhubaneswar: Siksha Sandhana.

De Tocqueville, Alexis. 1961. *Democracy in America, Volume 1*. New York: Schocken Books.

Derrida, Jacques. 1998. "Faith and Knowledge: Two Sources of 'Religion' at the Limits of Reason Alone." In Jacques Derrida and Giani Vattimo, eds, *Religion*. Cambridge: Polity Press.

Dumont, L. 1994. *German Ideology*. Chicago: University of Chicago Press.

Foucault, Michel. 1986. *Care of the Self*. New York: Pantheon.

Giddens, Anthony. 1994. *Beyond Left and Right: The Future of Radical Politics*. Cambridge: Polity Press.

Giri, Ananta Kumar. 1998. "The Quest for a Universal Morality: Jürgen Habermas and Sri Aurobindo." In *Global Transformations: Postmodernity and Beyond*. Jaipur and Delhi: Rawat Publications.

_____. 2000. "The Calling of a Creative Transdisciplinarity." *Futures* 34: 103–15.

_____. 2002a *Building in the Margins of Shacks: The Vision and Projects of Habitat for Humanity.* New Delhi: Orient Longman.

_____. 2002b. *Conversations and Transformations: Towards a New Ethics of Self and Society.* Lanham, MD: Lexington Books and Rowman & Littlefield.

Giri, Ananta Kumar and Philip Quarles van Ufford. 2000. *Reconstituting Development as a Shared Responsibility: Ethics, Aesthetics, and A Creative Shaping of Human Possibilities.* Madras Institute of Development Studies, unpublished paper.

Habermas, Jürgen. 1990. *Moral Consciousness and Communicative Action.* Cambridge: Polity Press.

Jantzen, Grace M. 2002. "'Barely By a Breath…': Irigary on Rethinking Religion." In John D. Caputo, *The Religious.* Oxford: Basil Blackwell.

Joas, Hans. 2000. *Genesis of Values.* Cambridge: Polity Press.

Kierkegaard, Soren. 1962. *Works of Love.* New York: Harper and Row.

Krishna, Daya. 1996. *The Problematic and Conceptual Structure of Classical Indian Thought about Man, Society, and Polity.* Delhi: Oxford University Press.

Kurien, C. T. 1996. "The Material and Spiritual in Social Life." Lecture at the 317th anniversary of St. Mary's Church, Chennai, 28 October.

Laclau, Ernesto. 1992. "Beyond Emancipation." *Development and Change* 23 (3): 121–37.

Lowe, Walter. 2002. "Second Thoughts About Transcendence." In John D. Caputo, ed., *The Religious.* Oxford: Basil Blackwell.

Madan, T. N. 1992. "Secularism in its Place." In T. N. Madan, ed., *Religion in India.* Delhi: Oxford University Press.

_____. 1997. *Modern Myths, Locked Minds.* Delhi: Oxford University Press.

_____. 2003. "Freedom of Religion." *Economic and Political Weekly* 38 (11): 1034–41.

_____. 2011. *Sociological Traditions.* Delhi: Sage Publications.

Mani, Lata. 2009. *Sacred Secular: Contemplative Cultural Critique.* Delhi: Routledge.

Matuštik, Martin J. 1997. *Postnational Identity: Critical Theory and Existential Philosophy in Habermas, Kierkegaard, and Havel.* New York: The Guilford Press.

Mauss, Marcel. 1979. "The Category of the Person." In Marcel Mauss, ed., *Sociology and Psychology: Essays.* London: Routledge and Kegan Paul.

Melucci, Alberto. 1996. *Challenging Codes.* Cambridge: Polity Press.

Metz, Johannes B. 1981. "Towards Second Reformation: The Future of Christianity in a Post Bourgeoisie World." *Cross Currents* 31 (1).

Mohanty, Manoranjan. 1989. "Secularism: Hegemonic and Democratic." *Economic and Political Weekly* 24 (22).

Mohanty, Satya P. 1998. *Literary Theory and the Claims of History.* Delhi: Oxford University Press.

Nandy, Ashis. 1985. "An Anti-Secular Manifesto." *Seminar* 314: 14–24.

Oommen, T. K. 2002. *Pluralism, Identity, Equality.* Delhi: Oxford University Press.

Pande, G. C. 1989. *The Meaning and Process of Culture as Philosophy of History.* Allahabad: Raka Prakashan.

Pantham, Thomas. 1999. "Indian Secularism and its Critics." In Fred Dallmayr, ed., *Border Crossings: Toward a Comparative Political Theory.* Lanham, MD: Lexington Books.

Quarles van Ufford, Philip and Ananta Kumar Giri, eds. 2003. *A Moral Critique of Development: In Search of Global Responsibilities.* London: Routledge.

Sen, Amartya. 1987. "Secularism and its Discontents." In Kaushik Basu et al., eds, *Unravelling the Nation.* New Delhi: Penguin Group.

Sharma, Arvind. 1995. *Hinduism for Our Times.* Delhi: Oxford University Press.

Sri Aurobindo. 1950. *The Synthesis of Yoga.* Pondicherry: Sri Aurobindo Ashram.

_____. 1951. *Life Divine.* Pondicherry: Sri Aurobindo Ashram.

Sunder Rajan, R. 1998. *Beyond the Crisis of European Sciences: New Beginnings.* Shimla: Indian Institute of Advanced Studies.

Taylor, Charles. 1996. *A Catholic Modernity?* Dayton, OH: University of Dayton Press.

Thomas, Scott M. 2005. *The Global Resurgence of Religion and the Transformation of International Relations: The Struggle for the Soul of the Twenty-First Century.* New York: Palgrave Macmillan.

Uberoi, J. P. S. 1984. *The Other Mind of Europe: Goethe as a Scientist.* Delhi: Oxford University Press.

———. 1996. *Religion, Civil Society and State: A Study of Sikhism.* Delhi: Oxford University Press.

———. 2002. *The European Modernity: Truth, Science and Method.* Delhi: Oxford University Press.

Unger, Roberto M. 1987. *False Necessity: Anti-Necessitarian Social Theory in the Service of Radical Democracy.* Cambridge: Cambridge University Press.

Van der Veer, Peter. 1996. *Religious Nationalism: Hindus and Muslims of India.* Delhi: Oxford University Press.

Vattimo, Gianni. 1999. *Belief.* Cambridge: Polity Press.

Vivekananda, Swami. 1991. *The Collected Works of Swami Vivekananda.* Calcutta: Ramakrishna Missions Publications.

Wilfred, Felix. 1999. "Introduction: The Art of Negotiating the Frontiers." In *Concilium*, Special Issue on "Frontier Violations."

———. 2000. *Asian Dreams and Christian Hopes.* Delhi: ISCPK.

Wuthnow, Robert. 1991. "Understanding Religion and Politics." *Daedalus* 120 (3): 1–20.

———. 1998. *After Heaven: Spirituality in America Since the 1950s.* Berkeley: University of California Press.

Chapter Seventeen

COSMOPOLITANISM AND BEYOND: TOWARDS PLANETARY REALIZATIONS

Only when philosophy discovers in the dialectical course of history the traces of violence that deform repeated attempts at dialogue and recurrently close off the path to unconstrained communication does it further the process whose suppression it otherwise legitimates: mankind's evolution toward autonomy and responsibility.

—Jürgen Habermas, *Knowledge and Human Interest* (1971, 315)

A lonely freedom cannot satisfy
A heart that has grown one with every heart
I am a deputy of the aspiring world
My spirit's liberty I ask for all.

—Sri Aurobindo, *Savitri*

We also need to consider how a deliberate engagement with the twentieth century's histories of suffering might furnish resources for the peaceful accommodation of otherness in relation to fundamental commonalty. In particular, we need to ask how an increased familiarity with the bloodstained workings of racism – and the distinctive achievements of the colonial governments it inspired and legitimated – might be made to yield lessons that could be applied more generally, in the demanding contemporary settings of multicultural social relations. This possibility should not imply the exaltation of victimage or the world-historic ranking of injustices that always seem to remain the unique property of their victims. Instead of these early choices, I will suggest that multi-cultural ethics and politics could be premised upon an agonistic, planetary humanism capable of comprehending the universality of our elementary vulnerability to the wrongs we visit upon each other.

—Paul Gilroy, *After Empire: Melancholia or Convivial Culture?* (2004, 25)

Introduction and Invitation

The vision that we are not just members of our tribes and nations but belong to the whole world – as the children of Mother Earth – has a long genealogy in many different cultures and traditions of the world; from the Stoic conception of human beings as citizens of the world in ancient Greece, to the Vedic vision of *Vasudhaiva Kutumbakam* (the *Vasudha*, meaningworld and Mother Earth), to the Buddha's interrogation of such conceptions of cosmopolitanism by submitting the ideal of universal self-realization, which is not confined to the human realm and has challenged seeking human beings to realize the *bodhisattva* nature of all beings. There is now a revival of cosmopolitanism in both discourse and practice. However, much of this revival draws inspiration from only one trajectory of cosmopolitanism – from Stoic cosmopolitanism to Kant and on to the "post-national" sensitivity of Habermas – but it does not build upon different traditions of cosmopolitan thinking and experimentation.

The contemporary revival is a response to the challenges of living in an interdependent world, and it reflects efforts to go beyond the limits of both relativism and universalism. As K. Anthony Appiah argues, "As a position in ethical theory, cosmopolitanism is distinct from relativism and universalism. It affirms the possibility of a mutual understanding between adherents to different moralities but without holding out the promise of any ultimate consensus" (Appiah 2006 quoted in Gray 2006). The revival of cosmopolitanism to which Martha Nussbaum, among others, has made significant contributions reflects an urge to go beyond the postmodern and multicultural imprisonment within cultural and other makers of difference and realize our common humanity. But the pointer to our common humanity by the prevalent discourses does not sufficiently embody the pain and suffering of crying humanity as it has been and is being subjected to a series of violations and colonial violence. Though Stoic cosmopolitanism has always emphasized education and "passional enlightenment" (Nussbaum 1997) as a way to cultivate cosmopolitanism, modern projects of cosmopolitanism, from Kant to Habermas to Ulrich Beck, have been primarily epistemic and have not sufficiently addressed the ontological challenges of appropriate self-preparation and self-transformation for belonging to and creating a cosmopolitan world. There is also the discourse of cosmopolitanism (see below) to counter the aforementioned elitist cosmopolitanism, but this discourse does not interrogate the foundations of contemporary cosmopolitanism itself; for example, it does not ask whether the cosmopolitanism is primarily epistemic, ethnocentric, anthropocentric or imperial.

This final chapter in our engagement with knowledge and human liberation discusses the issue of cosmopolitanism and explores the multiverse of transformations that it is confronted with. It submits that cosmopolitanization[1], an ongoing process of critique, creativity and border crossing, involves transformations in self, culture, society, economy and polity. Cosmopolitanization involves multi-dimensional processes of self-development, inclusion of the other and planetary realizations (Giri 2004a). In the field of self-development, cosmopolitanization involves the development of a transcendental self, transnational citizenship and cultivation of our cosmic humanity. Cosmopolitanization, as inclusion of the other, builds upon contemporary strivings in economics, politics, religions and spiritual mobilizations, which embody post-capitalist, post-national and post-religious spiritual formations (Bellah 1970, Habermas 1998,

Vattimo 1999 and 2002). Cosmopolitanization, as planetary realization, builds on post-anthropocentric and post-national transformations and urges us to realize that we are not only citizens of the world, but also children of the Mother Earth (Toynbee 1976). The chapter also discusses the issue of cosmopolitan responsibility and notes three major challenges – the realization of global justice, the realization of "cross-species dignity" (cf. Nussbaum 2006), and dialogue among civilizations, cultures, religions and traditions. It outlines the pathways of going beyond cosmopolitanism by striving for a post-colonial cosmopolis characterized by global justice, transcivilizational dialogues and dignity for all.

On Cosmopolitanism

Ethical cosmopolitanism refers to our belonging to the world in terms of some duties and obligations. For the Stoics, we are not just members of our city-states but citizens of the world. However, this does not mean building a world-state. As Nussbaum helps us understand, "The point is more radical still: that we should give our first moral allegiance to *no* mere form of government, no temporal power. We should give it instead to moral community made up by the humanity of all beings" (Nussbaum 1997, 8). This does not mean we should abandon local affiliations but that we should realize that as human beings we are "surrounded by a series of concentric circles" (Nussbaum 1997, 9). Stoic cosmopolitans acknowledged the divisive role of politics and challenged us to develop "empathetic understanding, whereby we come to respect the humanity of our political enemies" (Nussbaum 1997, 9). "A favoured exercise in this process of world thinking is to conceive of the entire world of human beings as a single body" (Nussbaum 1997, 9, 10). Stoic cosmopolitans were also concerned with peace, and they took "cosmopolitanism to require certain international limitations upon the conduct of warfare" (Nussbaum 1997, 9, 11).

In modern European thinking, Kant is the major proponent of cosmopolitanism. He challenged us to establish justice and perpetual peace beyond the boundaries of nation-states. For Kant, cosmopolitanism was not a specific political proposal but a regulative ideal of peace and justice. He built upon the Stoic tradition in important ways, but while the Stoics "linked the ideal of world citizenship to the goal of passional enlightenment," Kant's conception of personal and social enlightenment involves the "suppression of evil forces in human beings rather than their education" (Nussbaum 1997, 9, 21).

Many different traditions and experiments of our modern world have worked towards cosmopolitanism. In his *Geography of Human Life*, Japanese thinker Tsunesaburō Makiguchi "taught the importance of realizing that the individual human being is more than just a citizen of a nation state. We are all members of our local regions and at the same time citizens of the whole world" (Henderson and Ikeda 2004, 68). Makiguchi inspired the formation of a critical spiritual movement in Japanese Buddhism – Sōka Gakkai – which strives for value creation in our lives and around the world. The visions and practices of Sōka Gakkai are an important part of cosmopolitanism as planetary conversations that strive to carry out dialogues across religious, cultural and ideological boundaries. Its leader, Daisaku Ikeda, has carried out a series of dialogues on important themes, such as his famous dialogue with historian Arnold J. Toynbee, *Choose Life* (1976). Tagore, Gandhi and Sri Aurobindo have also embodied cosmopolitan dreams and strivings. In Gandhi's struggle, freedom from colonial rule is an integral part of realizing our common humanity and laying the foundation of a post-colonial cosmopolis. Tagore challenges us to overcome uncritical loyalty to nationalism and build a world not broken into fragments (cf. Bharucha 2006, Tagore 1917). Sri Aurobindo was a leader of the Indian freedom struggle in its early years, but he left it and dedicated himself to the spiritual evolution of humanity and the supramental realization of earth; he makes note of his studies in a series of important writings (see Sri Aurobindo 1951, 1962, 1970, 1971, 1992). Throughout his life, Aurobindo was a major experimenter in meditations on the ideal of human unity, and to whom struggle and *sadhana* brought a spiritual deepening and an expansion of the project of cosmopolitanism. He observes, "Even cosmopolitan habits of life are not uncommon and there are a fair number of [such] persons…[but] unless man in his heart is ready, a profound change in the world conditions cannot come" (Sri Aurobindo 1971, 528 and 531).

These cosmopolitan meditations find a resonance in many contemporary reflections. Ulrich Beck argues, "The national perspective is a monologic imagination, which excludes the otherness of the other. The cosmopolitan perspective is an alternative imagination, an imagination of alternative ways of life and rationalities, which includes the otherness of the other" (Beck 2002, 18; Beck 1998). Beck and others understand the long journey that must be undertaken for the realization of a cosmopolitan society. Ulf Hedetoft and Mette Hjort, who talk about the post-national self, write, "Our home may be open to the globe (liberal, tolerant, sensitive, multicultural), but the globe is not our home" (Hedetoft and Hjort 2002, xx). At the same time, there are attempts, however small, towards making our globe our home; here we see the emergence of both experiential cosmopolitanism and political cosmopolitanism. The former embodies an experience of the varieties of cultures of the world; for example, in food, drink and travel (what Beck calls the important fact of banal cosmopolitanism inspired by a new slogan: foods and drinks of the world unite!). The latter espouses varieties of justice at a global level, such as the work of ATTAC (Association for the Taxation of Financial Transactions and for Citizens' Action) in Europe, which is fighting for the realization of global justice (cf. their website http://www.attac.org). Political cosmopolitanism is facilitated by an experiential cosmopolitanism which "need not be as self-consciously expansive… It might rather involve a kind of piecemeal build up of sense of being at home in cosmopolis" (Hannerz 2002, 231; Dallmayr 2003).

Reflections on cosmopolitanism have been immensely enriched by the multi-faceted contributions of Martha Nussbaum over the years and most recently by the publication of her *Frontiers of Justice: Disability, Nationality, Species Membership* (Nussbaum 2006). In her work, Nussbaum meditates upon the challenge of global justice. She challenges us to realize the limitations of the social contract tradition in thinking about justice, because it privileges the principle of mutual advantage to the exclusion of those who cannot take part in such a contract such as disabled people and non-human animals. Nussbaum shows the limitations of Rawls's principles when she says that "Rawls treats the domestic principles of justice in both liberal and non liberal peoples as fixed and not up for grabs in the second stage contract [between states]" (Nussbaum 2006, 242). Nussbaum also critiques the Rawlsian analogy between state and person by stating, "There is a good reason to begin with persons and to give them salience in a theory of justice… We cannot say, in a similar way, that the state is a necessary moral starting point" (Nussbaum 2006, 236–7).

Nussbaum builds upon the capabilities approach (developed with the aid of Amartya Sen) by extending the frontiers of justice from Rawls's unproblematized nation-state to the global community and including the disabled and non-human animals. Her meditation on justice for the non-human animal seems to be the most profound revolution beyond the anthropocentrism of theories of justice in the Euro-American tradition.

Cosmopolitanism: Roots and Variants

The dominant discourses of cosmopolitanism in the Euro-American world have Stoic and Kantian roots. While both traditions have important lessons for inquiring souls all around the world, they also have some foundational limitations. There is the problem of sidelined politics in Stoic cosmopolitanism (Dallmayr 2004). Nussbaum herself points to the Stoic silence on the issue of colonial conquest; although it must not be forgotten that Diogenes, the father of Stoic cosmopolitanism, snubbed Emperor Alexander, and Seneca took part in anti-imperial movements in imperial Rome which cost him his life (cf. Dallmayr 2005). Speaking of the Kantian legacy of cosmopolitanism, Nussbaum writes that Kant's hope for human betterment "is, of course, a hope in and for reason" (Nussbaum 1997, 24). But is reason the only saviour here? The Kantian project of cosmopolitanism did not have a dimension of self-development and self-transformation. "The constitution of politics out of democracy, market and publicity is for Kant a work of art; it provides the framework in which the individual can be a good citizen without first being reformed into a good person" (Safranski 2005, 30). The challenge here is a simultaneous cultivation of good citizenship and ideal personhood – an agenda which is missing not only in Kant, but also in much of the tradition of Western democratic theory from Aristotle to Habermas (cf. Roy 1999). Gandhi helps us understand the limitation of Kantian cosmopolitanism. He challenges us to realize the limitation of reason alone in achieving peace and justice and to understand the significance of loving self-suffering and self-sacrifice (Giri 2002).

Kant's meditation on cosmopolitanism in his *Perpetual Peace* (1795) can be read alongside his texts on anthropology and geography. He writes in his *Geography* that "Burmese women wear indecent clothing and take pride in getting pregnant by Europeans" (quoted in Harvey 2000). His *Anthropology from a Pragmatic Point of View* (1798) has parallel ethnocentric comments about Native Americans. Harvey argues that Nussbaum needs to follow Kant "into the nether regions of his *Geography*" (Harvey 2000, 547). Harvey also interrogates Nussbaum's defence of universalism without considering its imperial potentials; he writes, "How easy it is to justify (as Ulrich Beck apparently does) those NATO bombs on Serbia as a grand effort to eradicate a particular geographical evil in the name of Kantian ethics" (Harvey 2000, 547)?

Fred Dallmayr is a proponent of an alternative cosmopolitanism that embodies varieties of cross-cultural learning and transcivilizational dialogues. He writes, "Nussbaum makes allowance for some human diversity; however, by defining reason as the universal human 'essence' her account renders differences non-essential and marginal" (Dallmayr 2004, 98). Dallmayr finds a streak of "top down universalism" and "global moralism" in not only Nussbaum, but also other proponents of global ethics such as Hans Kung. Dallmayr draws our attention to the work of Luce Irigaray as an example of an embodiment of a different approach to the issue of universality and cross-cultural learning. Irigaray challenges us to inhabit the space of "in-between-traditions" rather than a self-confident contrast between a triumphant universalism and a supposed particularism.[2] Interestingly, a sympathetic scholar of Nussbaum herself writes, "A more useful guide for feminist internationalism than the language of universals may be the idea of commitments developed through dialogues" (Charlesworth 2000, 76).

Let us come back to Beck's proposal about cosmopolitanism. For Beck, "Methodological cosmopolitanism rejects the either – or principle – and assembles a this-as-well-as-that principle…thinking and living in terms of *inclusive oppositions*" (Beck 2002, 19). But is this possible only epistemologically or does it also involve appropriate ontological nurturance? In this context, philosopher J. N. Mohanty argues that a "multi-valued logic"[3] of realizing that "every point of view is partly true, partly false and partly undecidable" (2000, 24) calls for a simultaneous practice of non-injury in thought and non-violence in practice and is facilitated by multiple traditions of human strivings. The Jaina tradition of *Anekantavada*,[4] Gandhian experiments with non-violence, and Husserlian phenomenology, especially the "Husserlian idea of overlapping contents" (Mohanty 2000, 24) are some examples of these traditions. The problem with Beck, as with many of the enthusiastic cosmopolitans of our times, is that they are not only self-confidently epistemic to the neglect of any project of ontological nurturance, but they also lack an engagement in transcivilizational and transcultural dialogues. They also do not open their projects to a quest of transcendence, even of a kind of immanent transcendence. Their cosmopolitan inclusion of the other lacks a spiritual striving. In Habermas – despite the best political intentions – it can lead to a not very generous approach to other cultures, religions and traditions. The celebrated philosopher of inclusion of the other writes, "We no longer confront other cultures as alien since their structures still remind us of previous phases of our own social development. What we *do* encounter as alien within other cultures is the stubborn distinctiveness of their religious cores" (Habermas 2002, 156). When pressed to the limits, despite his post-metaphysical thinking, Habermas acknowledges the significance of the Judeo-Christian tradition for the project of modernity,[5] but he seems not to be offering the same acknowledgment to other traditions such as Buddhism.[6]

Towards a Multiverse of Transformations

Contemporary discourses of cosmopolitanism are confronted with the challenge of a multiverse of transformations.[7] Nussbaum defends universal values, but a key challenge here is deciding our conception of the universal. Some conceptions of the universal are much more tyrannical and imperialistic than others. Rethinking cosmopolitanism involves rethinking universality. Here, instead of a one-dimensional conception of universality and the dualism between the universal and the particular, we can conceive emergent transversality.[8] Emergent transversality does not begin with an opposition between the universal and the particular. Instead, it seeks to explore and understand if there is a yearning for the universal in one particular culture and tradition. Emergent transversality draws inspiration from several contemporary efforts to rethink universality, such as the projects of relational universality by literary critic R. Radhakrishnan (2003) and dialectical universality by Roy Bhaskar (2002). For Bhaskar, "once you describe the world in an abstract universal way as consisting in constant conjunctions of events or actualized empirical uniformities then you put a halt to history" (Bhaskar 2002, 122). It reflects "ontological monovalence" and a sense of fatalism that the present society is the best of all possible worlds. Instead, "Universality had to be understood dialectically – that is universality together with differentiations and mediations, together with geo-historical trajectories…" (Bhaskar 2002).

When we consider geo-historical trajectories, we need to be aware that colonialism is not just a historical legacy. Colonialism is a continued experience for many of us as our life-world is being subjected to colonization by the system worlds of market, authoritarian state, and varieties of communitarian fundamentalism. It is in this context that the realization of a post-colonial condition is a subject of a continuing struggle. Overcoming the colonization of the life-world calls for the continuing struggle for realization of self-rule or what Gandhi called Swaraj. This is not a plea for possessive individualism but a struggle for autonomy and responsibility.

Gandhi brought together anti-colonial struggles for freedom with a cosmopolitan imperative of belonging to humanity. His struggle was not against the colonizer but against the colonial system, and through this he sought to free the colonizers themselves from their suppression and gain a fuller realization of their humanity. But this Gandhian legacy is rarely followed in contemporary discourses of post-colonialism, because the discourses are still imprisoned within the logic of anti-colonial anger and do not want dialogue with cosmopolitanism. Building a post-colonial cosmopolis, therefore, calls for a mutually transformative dialogue between post-colonial critical reflections and cosmopolitan meditations on our common humanity (cf. Chakraborty 2000, Guha 2002).

Cultivating this common humanity calls for appropriate self-development. Nussbaum understands the crucial significance of education. Elaborating on the Stoic agenda of education, she writes, "The hatred of members of other races and religions can be effectively addressed by forms of early education that address the cognitive roots of those passions…[and] that get children to view those people in the Stoic cosmopolitan ways as similarly human" (Nussbaum 1997, 22). She urges us to "devote sustained attention to moral sentiments and their cultivation – in child development, in public education, in public rhetoric, in the arts" (Nussbaum 2006, 414). She also draws our attention to the significance of art in moral education where "the artist's fine-tuned attention and responsiveness to human life is paradigmatic of a kind of precision of feeling and thought that a human being can cultivate" (Nussbaum 1990, 379).[9]

Transforming cosmopolitanism also entails transforming the perception of transcendence (Bhaskar, 2002). Nussbaum's new frontiers of justice call for "new ways of thinking about who the citizen is" (Nussbaum 2006, 2), but her notion of self is still predominantly Aristotelian. For her, the self is far richer artistically than the Aristotelian self of techno-practitioner, which is found in Bourdieu and Habermas (cf. Faubion 1995); nonetheless, it needs a transcendental supplementation. Nussbaum is comfortable with the conception of internal transcendence found in great art, but she does not go further.[10] Yet internal transcendence is also an integral part of the conceptualization and realization of transcendence in many different religious, philosophical and spiritual traditions of the world. Nussbaum extends her capability approach to the project of global justice and cosmopolitanism, but she does not sufficiently explore the corresponding challenge of transcendence that the capability approach is confronted with.

The project of self-development here calls for the development of a transcendental dimension within oneself which coexists with other dimensions such as the techno-practitioner. The transcendentally real self is not to be imported from heaven or religion. It is a reality, as well as a possibility, in human lives characterized by our yearning for love and establishing connections across the border (Bhaskar 2002). Amartya Sen (2002) draws our attention to the fact that global justice is not a question of institutional arrangement alone, but it also calls for the ability to sympathize with others across borders. Building upon Adam Smith's ideas in his *A Theory of Moral Sentiments* (1976), Sen suggests how the development of the "impartial spectator" within oneself is crucial to a realization of justice across borders (2009).

The project of self-development is integrally linked with the project of inclusion of the other. But this inclusion, as Habermas (1998) notes, needs to be "non-appropriating." Inclusion of the other is a multi-dimensional project in politics, economics, religion and spirituality. In politics, inclusion of the other calls for the simultaneous politics of recognition and empowerment (Andersson and Siim 2004), which are politics of openness and hospitality to aliens and minorities; in economics, the inclusion of the other requires building inclusive economics (Pani 2001); in religion, inclusion of the other is manifested in varieties of spiritual mobilizations, which go beyond the boundaries of religious systems; and in spirituality, inclusion of the other details varieties of efforts in non-dual realizations and some transformations that embody creative and practical spirituality.

Thus the project of cosmopolitanism today is confronted with the challenge of a transcivilizational, transreligious and transcultural dialogue. As shaping the individual for a cosmopolitan humanity is a core issue here,[11] the conception of the self and the individual becomes as important a subject of cosmopolitanism as transcivilizational and planetary conversations. In her work on capability, justice and cosmopolitanism, Nussbaum focuses on separate individuals. She writes:

> One might of course come to accept religious beliefs, in particular Buddhist beliefs, which do hold that people aren't really separate individuals at all and the whole idea that objects and people are different from one another is an illusion… Buddhism, [however], self-consciously portrays itself as a radical critique of ordinary practices… So a political focus on the individual is not insulting or unfair even to Buddhists, since it is meant to supply a basis for politics in the daily world, not in the world of enlightened meditation and reflection. (Nussbaum 2000, 58)

The issue, however, is what implication a Buddhist critique of ordinary life has for focusing on the individual. Does it not decentre the conception of the individual? (Dallmayr 2004).

Buddhism emphasizes the co-dependent origination of all beings and phenomena. Its implication for our conceptualization of the individual is that it is not helpful to assert a dualism between interdependence and autonomy; rather, our task is to understand the non-dual logic of autonomy and interconnection.[12] Writing of the 1980s, Nussbaum notes, "I was ill-advised about the problems of developing countries and, more generally, about non-western traditions and ways of life. My office neighbours from Sri Lanka and India could talk clearly about Sophocles and Aristotle, but I had absolutely nothing to say about *Mahabharata* or about Buddhist ethics" (Nussbaum 2000, viii).

After reading *Frontiers of Justice*, one wonders whether the situation is different now. By offering a political conception of justice for non-human animals, Nussbaum acknowledges how her own approach cannot fully address the issue of animal suffering, and she refers instead to utilitarianism. But she does not explore how this has been dealt with in traditions of Buddhism and Jainism. She writes, "We should begin our scrutiny of social contract theories by recognizing that these theories arise within a more general Stoic/Judeo-Christian culture" (Nussbaum 2006, 329). But it seems that Nussbaum does not take this critical inquiry further in the direction of cross-cultural learning and transreligious dialogue. It is no wonder then that she writes, "The capabilities approach does not urge uncritical nature worship" (Nussbaum 2006, 94). One wonders to what extent Nussbaum is aware of the influences placed on her from her own Judeo-Christian tradition and modernistic sensibility. An experiential dialogue with an Indian, Japanese or American-Indian view of nature may lead to a much more nuanced understanding of the relationships among man, nature and society (Clammer 2006).

On her remarkable idea of cross-species dignity, Nussbaum writes, "[This] is not a political idea that can be readily accepted by citizens who otherwise differ in metaphysical conception…we may rely instead, on the loose idea that all creatures are entitled to adequate opportunities for flourishing life" (Nussbaum 2006, 383–4). Furthermore, she states that "we must continue to emphasize that the principles we are advancing are political and not metaphysical; they are expressed in a practical (albeit moral) form that is metaphysically abstemious, intended not to conflict with key metaphysical doctrines of the major religions" (Nussbaum 2006, 301). But the religious traditions themselves may have been engaged in a foundational rethinking of a spiritual kind about the anthropocentric nature of their own metaphysics. Even though Gianni Vattimo's *After Christianity* (2002) does not interrogate fully the Judeo-Christian metaphysics of anthropocentrism, it is possible to find other critical spiritual movements in major world religions, including the Semitic, which go beyond anthropocentrism. Nussbaum thus need not stay at the gates of the custodians of systemic religious metaphysics, but instead she can explore varieties of critical and transformative spiritual movements of going "beyond belief" in these traditions (cf. Bellah 1970).

Beyond Cosmopolitanism: Towards Planetary Realizations

I have suggested that the dominant discourses of cosmopolitanism require a multiverse of transformations. One important challenge is to understand cosmopolitan responsibility, which calls for the realization of global justice, transcivilizational and planetary conversations, and non-anthropocentric and post-anthropocentric moves, in order to achieve cross-species dignity and the nurturing of our planet. Nussbaum has made important contributions to the issue of global justice and cross-species dignity, although there is also need for further transformation here. In *Frontiers of Justice*, Nussbaum is more open about the issue of global justice and to visionary movements, such as Martin Luther King's, which extend the frontiers of justice. She could pay further attention to grassroots transnational movements, such as ATTAC in Europe and the Landless People's Movement in Brazil, which are both struggling for realization of global justice, and to the emergent global public sphere and civil society. An engagement with emergent global civil society can redeem the elitist connotations of some dominant strands of cosmopolitanism (cf. Ezzat 2005, 54).

In this context, what Egyptian political theorist Hebba Ezzat writes about transnational movements deserves our careful attention; he claims that "Global civil transactions have a philosophical dimension and represent to many activists a search for meaning and identity that goes beyond the modernist philosophical notions of individualism as well as beyond modernity's central socio-political structure, namely the nation state" (Ezzat 2005, 40). Thus, critical conversation about the nature of subject and state is an integral part of the making of a post-colonial cosmopolis, and there is a need for much more interrogation and transformative conversation (Venn 2006). Despite her earlier critique of patriotism in *Frontiers of Justice*, Nussbaum writes, "National sovereignty... has moral importance, as a way people have of asserting their autonomy" (Nussbaum 2006, 314). But how does this also confront the challenge of the nation-state as an "island of problematic justice?" (Habermas 1990). How do we transform sovereignty into shared sovereignty? How do we cultivate what Dallmayr (2005) calls "sacred non-sovereignty," where a sovereign self is not preoccupied with power and mastery but with an ethic and spirituality of servanthood? Cosmopolitanism calls for a foundational critique of sovereignty at the levels of self, state, and society and for the realization of shared sovereignty and "sacred non-sovereignty," which embodies the multivalued logic of autonomy and interpenetration (Giri 2009, Hardt and Negri 2004).

Cosmopolitan realization thus has a spiritual dimension. This spiritual dimension seems not to have received enough attention in the dominant discourses of contemporary cosmopolitanism, such as those of Nussbaum, Beck and Habermas. Here we can compare Nussbaum's global capabilities list with another visionary document of creative global will formation – the Earth Charter. Fortunately for us, we have intimation of the interlinked spiritual horizon of a post-colonial cosmopolis in the work of savants such as Daisaku Ikeda, Johan Galtung and Fred Dallmayr. Ikeda's transformative conversations across boundaries and borders are valuable contributions to this generation's knowledge and their drive for a post-colonial cosmopolis.[13] Galtung founded the group TRANSCEND International, which is involved with peace education and reconciliation around the world. Dallmayr's work offers us a different vision of cosmopolitanism that embodies much more listening and learning rather than the self-confident triumphalism which marks much of the contemporary discourse of cosmopolitanism (Galtung and McQueen 2010, Dallmayr 1998, 2001, 2002, 2004, 2005). Dallmayr (1999, 2) urges us to see that "the reflective theorist in the global village must shun spectatorial allures and adopt the more modern stance of a participant in search for truth by opening mind and heart to the puzzling diversity of human experiences and traditions…and also to the possibility of jeopardising cherished preoccupations or beliefs."

One important area of transcivilizational dialogue and planetary conversation is the vision of cosmopolitanism itself – being a citizen of the world or being a member of the human family. The first vision of cosmopolitanism comes from the Greek tradition, which has influenced modern European conceptions of cosmopolitanism. The second vision of cosmopolitanism comes from Indian traditions as well as many other traditions of the world. The second vision also permeates many religious traditions such as Christianity, which emphasizes the significance of family (Tutu 2005). As Tutu writes, "How I pray that in our world we can learn to emulate a true family, perhaps then we could address the injustices that cause a small percentage of our world to consume the vast majority of its resources… God's dream wants us to be brothers and sisters, wants us to be family" (Tutu 2005, 23).

What is helpful is that both the traditions of cosmopolitanism – of citizenship and of human family – work with images of concentric circles. Now, this needs to be supplemented by a vision and practice of overlapping circles. In this area of emergent transversality, our vision and practice of being a cosmopolitan is that of being a citizen of the world as well as member of the human family. Such a multi-dimensional self-conceptualization and institutional figuration of cosmopolitanism would help us overcome the limitations of both polis and family, open them to mutual critique and transformation, and inspire them to embody a multivalued existence of autonomy, interpenetration and responsibility.

Thus cosmopolitanism as planetary conversations takes us beyond the cosmopolitanism we know. The Truth and Reconciliation Commission in South Africa contributed to overcoming hatred, anger and revenge in post-apartheid South Africa. Many people of East Asia now feel the need for a Truth and Reconciliation Commission in East Asia. In reality, we need a Truth and Reconciliation Commission in all regions of the world. These commissions could even be accompanied by some planetary truth and reconciliation commissions to address the issues and experiences of our common humanity; for example, the annihilation of cultures and people, colonialism, slavery, the Holocaust, the dropping of atom bombs in Hiroshima and Nagasaki, and the violence perpetrated by and in the name of modern science, technology, and nation-state. These examples point to our predicament of suffering. It is interesting that Nussbaum concludes her *Frontiers of Justice* with an inspiring self-critical admission that the capabilities approach is not fully adequate to deal with the issue of animal suffering. Suffering – animal and human – also raises issues about human finitude and fragility, especially the fragility of a predominantly political approach to knowledge, self, society, justice, cosmopolis and human liberation. As Arnold Toynbee challenges us:

> In human life, Suffering is the antithesis of Power, and it is also a more characteristic and more fundamental element in Life than Power is… Suffering is the essence of Life, because it is the inevitable product of an unresolvable tension between a living creature's essential impulse to try to make itself into the center of the Universe and its essential dependence on the rest of creation and on the Absolute Reality on which all creatures live and move and have their being. On the other hand, human power, in all its forms is limited and, in the last resort, illusory. Therefore any attitude towards Life that idolizes human power is bound to be a wrong attitude towards Suffering and, in consequence, a wrong attitude towards Life itself. (Toynbee 1956, 74)[14]

Notes

1 Ulrich Beck (2002) makes the helpful distinction between cosmopolitanism and cosmopolitanization. Also see Beck 2003 and 2004.
2 Irigaray (2002, 25 and 39) writes, "We avoid letting ourselves be moved, questioned, modified, enriched by the other as such…We flee dialogue with a *you* irreducible to us… The transcendence of the *you* as other is not yet, really, part of our culture."
3 Similar to the kind suggested in Beck, but Mohanty (2000) has talked about it in another context.
4 *Anekantavada* refers to a mode of thinking that truth has many dimensions and many roads of arrival.
5 As Habermas (2002, 148–9) writes, "For the normative self-understanding of modernity, Christianity has functioned as more than just a precursor or catalyst. Universalistic egalitarianism…is the direct legacy of the Judaic ethic of justice and Christian ethic of love."
6 Habermas is not alone amongst thinkers from the contemporary Euro-American world in this foundational exclusivity. Vattimo (1999 and 2002), for example, draws our attention to emergent movements of building a post-Christian world from within Christianity based upon

love and non-violence, but he seems to consider these as the unique heritage of Christianity rather than seeing similar developments in many religions in the world (cf. Giri 2002 and Toynbee 1956).

7 Safranski uses the term "multiverse" in his elaboration of Kant's project of cosmopolitanism: "[Plato's philosophy] generally treats multiplicity and historical becoming as symptoms of defective being... It was Kant who, in the eighteenth century, outlined a conception of world peace on an underlying assumption of multiplicity... The conclusion to be drawn from Kant's reflection is that there will be no homogeneous and political universe. Politically speaking, the world remains a 'multiverse'" (Safranski 2005, 28).

8 This is in tune with the conception of emergent ethics proposed by Philip Quarles van Ufford and myself in our collaborative work on developmental ethics (Quarles van Ufford and Giri 2003).

9 Nussbaum's focus on aesthetic education reminds us of Schiller's project of the "aesthetic education of man" (Safranski 2005, 66). But Safranski adds, "Schiller was aware that such aesthetic education cannot have a wide social impact and is not suitable as a political strategy; nor did he expect aesthetics to bring about a fundamental change in the different reality of his time. It was enough for him that the aesthetic sense offered some protection against the devastating effects of that reality" (Safranski 2005, 66–7).

10 Nussbaum writes:

> There is a great deal of room for transcendence of our ordinary humanity... transcendence, we might say, of an *internal* and human sort... There is so much to do in this area of human transcending (which I also imagine as a transcending by *descent*, delving more deeply into oneself and one's humanity, and becoming deeper and more spacious as a result) that if one really pursued that aim well and fully I suspect that there would be little time left to look about for any other sort. (1990, 379)

11 In this context, what Safranski writes deserves our careful attention:

> Each individual is the stage where the world makes its entrance, where it can make its appearance... To shape globalization is therefore still a task that can be handled if the other major task is not neglected: the task of individuality itself. For the individual is also the whole where heavens and earth touch. (2005, 41)

12 Desmond Tutu also brings a similar perspective from the African tradition of *Ubuntu* where "my humanity is caught up and inextricably bound up in yours." *Ubuntu* speaks about "wholeness; it speaks about compassion. A person with *Ubuntu* is welcoming, hospitable, warm and generous, willing to share" (Tutu 2005, 26).

13 See Ikeda and Galtung (1995); Gorbachev and Ikeda (2005); Henderson and Ikeda (2004); Ikeda and Teheranian (2002); Ikeda and Toynbee (1976); Swaminathan and Ikeda (2005). Particularly significant here is what Gorbachev tells us in his dialogue with Ikeda:

> Personally, I learned my first lessons in cosmopolitan education at home in Stavropol. It was not theory but the fundamental basics of life in the North Caucasus. There, people of many nationalities live side by side, sometimes in the same village or settlement. Preserving their own cultures and traditions, they help each other in times of trouble. (Gorbachev and Ikeda 2005, 97)

14 An acknowledgment of human, animal and non-human suffering, though not reducing these to simple generalizing types (acknowledging what Derrida calls "irreducible living multiplicity of mortals" (2008, 41)) as all animals are not the same, is an integral part of planetary realization.

References

Andersson, John and Birte Siim, eds. 2004. *The Politics of Inclusion and Empowerment: Gender, Class and Citizenship*. New York: Palgrave Macmillan.

Appiah, K. A. 2006. "The Case for Contamination." *New York Times*, 1 January.

Beck, Ulrich. 1998. "The Cosmopolitan Manifesto." *New Statesman*, 20 March.

_____. 2002. "The Cosmopolitan Society and its Enemies." *Theory, Culture & Society* 19 (1–2): 17–44.

_____. 2003. "Toward a New Critical Theory with a Cosmopolitan Intent." *Constellations* 10 (4): 453–68.

_____. 2004. "Cosmopolitan Realism: On the Distinction between Cosmopolitanism in Philosophy and Social Sciences." *Global Networks* 4 (2): 131–56.

Bellah, Robert N. 1970. *Beyond Belief: Essays on Religion in a Post-Traditional World*. New York: Harper and Row.

Bharucha, Rustom. 2006. *Another Asia: Rabindranath Tagore and Okakura Tanshin*. Delhi: Oxford University Press.

Bhaskar, Roy. 2002. *Reflections on Meta-Reality: Transcendence, Everyday Life and Emancipations*. New Delhi: Sage Publications.

Chakraborty, Dipesh. 2000. *Provincializing Europe*. Princeton: Princeton University Press.

Charlesworth, Hilary. 2000. "Martha Nussbaum's Feminist Internationalism." *Ethics* 111 (1): 64–78.

Clammer, John. "Nature, Culture and the Debate with Modernity: Japanese Critical Theory." In Ananta Kumar Giri, ed., *Social Theory and Asian Dialogues*. Forthcoming.

Dallmayr, Fred. 1998. *Alternative Visions: Pathways in the Global Village*. Lanham, MD: Rowman & Littlefield.

_____. 1999. *Border Crossing: Towards a Comparative Political Theory*. Lanham, MD: Lexington Books.

_____. 2001. *Achieving our World: Toward a Global and Plural Democracy*. Lanham, MD: Rowman & Littlefield.

_____. 2002. *Dialogue Among Civilizations*. New York: Palgrave Macmillan.

_____. 2003. "Cosmopolitanism: Moral and Political." *Political Theory* 31 (3): 421–42.

_____. 2004. *Peace Talks: Who Will Listen?* Notre Dame, IN: University of Notre Dame Press.

_____. 2005. *Small Wonders: Global Power and its Discontent*. Lanham, MD: Rowman & Littlefield.

Ezzat, Hebba. 2005. "Beyond Methodological Modernism: Towards a Multicultural Paradigm Shift in the Social Sciences." In Helmut Anheier et al., eds, *Global Civil Society 2004/2005*. London: Sage Publications.

Faubion, James D., ed. 1995. *Rethinking the Subject: An Anthology of Contemporary European Social Theory*. Boulder, CO: Westview Press.

Galtung, Johan and Graeme MacQueen. 2010. *Globalizing God: Religion, Spirituality and Peace*. Bergen: Kolofon and Transcend University Press.

Gilroy, Paul. 2004. *After Empire: Melancholia or Convivial Culture?* London: Routledge.

Giri, Ananta Kumar. 2002. *Conversations and Transformations: Toward a New Ethics of Self and Society*. Lanham, MD: Lexington Books.

_____. 2004a. "Self-Development, Inclusion of the Other and Planetary Realizations." In Oscar Salemink et al., eds, *Religion of Development, Development of Religion*. Delft: Eburon.

_____. 2004b. "Knowledge and Human Liberation: Jürgen Habermas, Sri Aurobindo and Beyond." *European Journal of Social Theory* 9 (2): 245–62.

_____. 2004c. *Reflections and Mobilizations: Dialogues with Movements and Voluntary Organizations*. New Delhi: Sage Publications.

_____. 2005. "Introduction, The Modern Prince and Modern Sage: Transforming Power and Freedom." *Asian Journal of Social Sciences* 33 (1): 1–3.

Gorbachev, Mikhail and Daisaku Ikeda. 2005. *Moral Lessons of The Twentieth Century: Gorbachev and Ikeda on Buddhism and Communism*. London: I.B. Tauris.

Gray, John. 2006. "Easier Said Than Done: A Review Article on K. Anthony Appiah's *Cosmopolitanism: Ethics in a World of Strangers*." *The Nation* 30, January.

Guha, Ranajit. 2002. *History at the Limit of World History*. New York: Columbia University Press.

Habermas, Jürgen. 1971. *Knowledge and Human Interest*. Boston: Beacon Press.

_____. 1990. *Moral Consciousness and Communicative Action*. Cambridge: Polity Press.

_____. 1998. *Inclusion of the Other: Studies in Political Theory*. Cambridge: Polity Press.

_____. 2002. *Religion and Rationality*. Cambridge, MA: MIT Press.

Hannerz, Ulf. 2002. "Where We Are and Who We Want To Be." In Ulf Hedetoft and Metter Hjort, eds, *The Postnational Self: Belonging and Identity*. Minneapolis: University of Minnesota Press.

Hardt, Michael and Antonio Negri. 2004. *Multitude*. London: Penguin Group.

Harvey, David. 2000. "Cosmopolitanism and the Banality of Geographical Evil." *Public Culture* 12 (2): 529–36.

Hedetoft, Ulf and Mette Hjort. 2002. "Introduction." In Ulf Hedetoft and Metter Hjort, eds, *The Postnational Self*. Minneapolis: University of Minnesota Press.

Henderson, Hazel and Daisaku Ikeda. 2004. *Planetary Citizenship: Your Values, Beliefs and Actions Can Shape a Sustainable World*. Santa Monica, CA: Middleway Press.

Ikeda, Daisaku and Johan Galtung. 1995. *Choose Peace*. London: Pluto Press.

Ikeda, Daisaku and Majid Teheranian. 2002. *Global Civilization: A Buddhist Islamic Dialogue*. London: British Academic Press

Ikeda, Daisaku and Arnold J. Toynbee. 1976. *Choose Life*. Oxford: Oxford University Press.

Irigaray, Luce. 2002. *Between East and West: From Singularity to Community*. New York: Columbia University Press.

Kant, Immanuel. 1795. "Perpetual Peace: A Philosophical Sketch." Available at http://www.mtholyoke.edu/acad/intrel/kant/kant1.htm (accessed 3 January 2013).

_____. 1798/2006. *Anthropology from a Pragmatic Point of View*, ed. Robert B. Louden and Manfred Kuehn. Cambridge: Cambridge University Press.

Mohanty, J. N. 2000. *Self and Other: Philosophical Essays*. Delhi: Oxford University Press.

Nederveen Pieterse, Jan. 2004.*Globalization and Culture: Global Melange*. Lanham, MD: Rowman & Littlefield.

Nussbaum, Martha. 1990. *Love's Knowledge: Essays on Philosophy and Literature*. New York: Oxford University Press.

_____. 1997. "Kant and Stoic Cosmopolitanism." *Journal of Political Philosophy* 5 (1): 1–25.

_____. 2000. *Women and Human Development: The Capabilities Approach*. New York: Cambridge University Press.

_____. 2006. *Frontiers of Justice: Disability, Nationality, Species Membership*. Cambridge, MA: Harvard University Press.

Pani, Narendra. 2001. *Inclusive Economics: Gandhian Method and Contemporary Policy*. Delhi: Sage Publications.

Quarles van Ufford, Philip and Ananta Kumar Giri, eds. 2003. *A Moral Critique of Development: In Search of Global Responsibilities*. London: Routledge.

Radhakrishnan, R. 2003. *Theory in an Uneven World*. Malden, MA: Blackwell Publishing.

Roy, Ramashray. 1999. *Beyond Ego's Domain: Being and Order in the Vedas*. New Delhi: Shipra Publications.

Safranski, Rudiger. 2005. *How Much Globalization Can We Bear?* Cambridge: Polity Press.

Sen, Amartya. 2002. "Justice Across Borders." In Pablo de Grieff and Ciaran P. Cronin, eds, *Global Justice and Transnational Politics: Essays on the Moral and Political Challenges of Globalization*, 37–51. Cambridge, MA: MIT Press.

Sri Aurobindo. 1951. *Savitri: A Legend and A Symbol*. Pondicherry: Sri Aurobindo Ashram.

———. 1962. *Human Cycles*. Pondicherry: Sri Aurobindo Ashram.

———. 1970. *Life Divine*. Pondicherry: Sri Aurobindo Ashram.

———. 1971. *Ideals of Human Unity*. Pondicherry: Sri Aurobindo Ashram.

———. 1992. *Synthesis of Yoga*. Pondicherry: Sri Aurobindo Ashram.

Swaminathan, M. S. and Daisaku Ikeda. 2005. *Revolutions: To Green the Environment, to Grow the Human Heart: A Dialogue Between M. S. Swaminathan and Daisaku Ikeda*. Chennai: East-West Books.

Tagore, Rabindra Nath. 1917. *Nationalism*. London: Macmillan.

Toynbee, Arnold J. 1956. *An Historian's Approach to Religion*. New York: Oxford University Press.

———. 1976. *Mankind and Mother Earth: A Narrative History*. Oxford: Oxford University Press.

Tutu, Desmond. 2005. *God Has a Dream*. London: Rider Books.

Vattimo, Gianni. 1999. *Belief*. Cambridge: Polity Press.

———. 2002. *After Christianity*. New York: Columbia University Press.

Venn, Couze. 2006. *The Postcolonial Challenge: Towards Alternative Visions*. London: Sage Publications.

Wuthnow, Robert. 2001. *Creative Spirituality: The Way of the Artist*. Berkeley, CA: University of California Press.

Afterword

KNOWLEDGE AND PRAXIS

Fred Dallmayr
University of Notre Dame

A transformative sociology? A transformative and transforming "knowledge" of social life? These phrases are signature notions of Ananta Kumar Giri. In a string of earlier publications, he has provided sketches adumbrating these notions. Now, in the present volume, he finally has enlisted all his rich intellectual resources in order to flesh out the meaning of an active kind of "knowledge" capable of promoting human "liberation" or emancipation. As one should note, liberation for Giri does not just denote deliverance from oppressive social and political structures, but also the overcoming of inner compulsions and addictions standing in the way of genuine human freedom. To this extent, liberation as used in this volume resonates with Gandhi's notion of self-rule (Swaraj) and also, more distantly, with the notion of *"cura sui"* as cultivated by the Roman Stoics.

Still, one may ask: a transformative and liberating "knowledge"? Does knowledge not always precede transformative practice? Does one not first have to know what it is that one wishes to change or liberate? As one can readily see, these questions lead back to an old philosophical conundrum that can be traced from the Greeks (especially Aristotle) down to Hegel and Marx: the so-called "theory-practice" nexus. Different philosophical traditions give different answers to this conundrum. In large measure, modern Western rationalism – from Descartes to Kant – places the accent squarely on knowledge or cognition, even a purely "transcendental" cognition entirely removed from practical or experiential contexts. On the other hand, Marx is famous for having assigned primacy to transformative social change over cognitive or theoretical interpretation. What seems to be lacking in such extreme formulations is attention to interconnections, to the mutual interpenetration of theory and practice, of lived contextual experience and cognitive detachment from context. Surely it seems plausible to assume that theoretical reflection is triggered by some dilemmas or traumas experienced in ordinary life – and that without this instigation theorizing would be empty and pointless. By the same token, having been triggered by lived dilemmas, reflection can be assumed to make a contribution to overcoming these dilemmas, thus paving the way to liberation. No doubt, this exit route is normally difficult and painful. The Greeks spoke of learning "the hard way" or through suffering (*pathei mathos*).

The close linkage between knowledge and transformative practice was a hallmark of John Dewey's pragmatism – whose legacy Giri invokes at the beginning of his Introduction. This legacy has often been thoroughly misunderstood. On one side, some philosophers have tried to blend pragmatism into traditional modes of cognition, and especially into conventional forms of epistemology (not far removed from Kantian epistemology, as outlined in the *First Critique*). Profiled against this "pure" theory of knowledge, practice appears as a derivative by-product of cognition and hence not in any way constitutive of knowledge. On the other hand, pragmatism is notorious for allegedly having equated knowing with doing and even "truth" with "what works." Through this construal, pragmatism slides inevitably into consequentialism and even a crude type of relativism, because the criteria for "what works" is not specified and hence is subjectively up for grabs. What is completely neglected in this reading is that "truth" is not a by-product of work but is inherently a "work" itself. Differently phrased: truth is not found by simply gazing at the stars but by human searchers allowing themselves to be "worked over" and thus undergoing a transformative learning experience.

The interlacing of knowledge and practice is not an exclusive Deweyan insight; it is also found in Indian thought, especially in the teachings of the Upanishads and the *Bhagavad Gita*. As Giri points out, the *Gita* is well known for its effort to link together three pathways to liberation (or *moksha*): *jñana*, *karma* and *bhakti* – usually translated as knowledge, action and devotion. Although it makes ample room for *jñana* or knowledge, the *Gita* does not allow cognition to overshadow or overwhelm action and devotion. Above all, action is not simply a derivative or marginal by-product of knowledge; rather, genuine knowledge is made manifest – and intrinsically or primordially made manifest – in right action. By the same token, faithful devotion is not dependent on intellectual insight or knowledge, nor is it seen as antithetical to, or basically at odds with, knowledge. To this extent, the *Gita* makes an important contribution to the resolution of profound dilemmas which have beleaguered Western thought: the compatibility or incompatibility between reason and faith, between philosophy and theology, between immanence and transcendence.

Closely linked with these dilemmas in Western thought has been the issue of the relation between orthodoxy and *orthopraxis*. The issue has gained particular prominence in recent times due to the upsurge of such perspectives as "political theology" and "liberation theology." In the opinion of some critical observers, the linkage of theology with political practice and liberation threatens the integrity and absolute truth quality of theological doctrines, that is, their "perennial" status outside of practical-temporal contexts. For defenders of these perspectives, in contrast, the removal of "God-talk" beyond practical human reach means to erect an abstract myth devoid of any redeeming and liberating quality; in fact, it is only through participating in God's ongoing self-disclosure – modeled by the image of the "suffering servant" – that religion can shield itself against idolatry and recover the living spirit of faith. To be sure, for defenders, not every type of activism is equally redeeming or liberating, but only a practice illuminated by its orientation toward goodness and divine grace. In the words of Gustavo Gutierrez, one of the "founders" of liberation theology, "The starting point for all theology is to be found in the *act* of faith. Rather than being a mere intellectual [or theoretical] adherence to the message, it should be a vital embracing of the gift of the Word as heard in the ecclesial community, as an encounter with God, and as love of one's brother and sister. It is about existence in its totality."[1]

As it happens, the relation between orthodoxy and *orthopraxis* has in recent times attracted the attention of numerous theologians and philosophers of religion. A prominent example is Clodovis Boff's book titled *Theology and Praxis: Epistemological Foundations*. In a chapter devoted to the "dialectic of theory and praxis," Boff explores and indicates precisely the mutual interpenetration of theological doctrine and liberating practice. Commenting on this text, one interpreter remarks pointedly that, for Boff, "human practice and involvement" is a basic "constituent of epistemology" or epistemic knowledge; at the same time, his dialectical method "potentially enables the integration of human practice into theoretical understanding."[2] By rejecting the need for full prior knowledge as a requisite for practice, Boff's text comes close to the tradition of "apophatic" theology – a tradition to which Giri refers when he quotes Felix Wilfred's statements about the "ineffable character" of our "human-divine existence" and the "darkness enveloping it." In turn, this tradition is close to the notion of an "apophatic anthropology" as articulated by Ivan Illich in these words: "Apophatic anthropology is the rigor of not talking about God, but actually living as Christ enfleshed has done."[3]

To conclude, let me add these statements by Denys Turner, which I find particularly illuminating on the issue of knowledge and praxis:

At the heart of any authentic spirituality is the means of its own self-critique, an apophatic putting into question of every possibility of "knowing" who God is, even the God we pray to. In the heart of every Christian faith and prayer [probably every faith and prayer] there is, as it were, a desolation, a sense of bewilderment and deprivation, even panic, at the loss of every familiar sign of God, at the requirement to "unknow" God – as the Meister Eckhart put it, for the sake of the "God beyond God." For it is somewhere within that desolation and negativity that the nexus is to be found which binds together the Christian rediscovery of justice with the poor and the rediscovery of the God who demands that justice. For in that bond of action and experience – "praxis" – is the discovery that, as the liberation theologians say, "knowing God is doing justice."[4]

Notes

1 Gustavo Gutierrez, "The Task and Content of Liberation Theology," trans. Judith Condor, in Christopher Rowland, ed., *The Cambridge Companion to Liberation Theology* (Cambridge: Cambridge University Press, 2007), 29.
2 Clodovis Boff, *Theology and Praxis: Epistemological Foundations*, trans. Robert R. Barr (Maryknoll, NY: Orbis, 1987). See also Zoe Bennett, "'Action is the Life of All': The Praxis-Based

Epistemology of Liberation Theology," in Rowland, ed., *The Cambridge Companion to Liberation Theology*, 49.

3 See Felix Wilfred, "Christological Pluralism: Some Reflections," *Concilium* 3 (2008): 84–94; Trent Schroyer, "Illich's Genealogy of Modern Certitudes," in *Beyond Western Economics* (London: Routledge, 2009).

4 Denys Turner, "Marxism, Liberation Theology and the Way of Negation," in Rowland, ed., *The Cambridge Companion to Liberation Theology*, 246. See also Turner, *The Darkness of God* (Cambridge: Cambridge University Press, 1995).

ADVANCE PRAISE

"This book by Ananta Kumar Giri is very timely as the author discusses one of the key trends of contemporary global changes – knowledge, human liberation and planetary realizations. Indeed, sometimes too much attention is paid to the economic and also political dimensions of globalization while the role and transformations of the 'human capital' do not get much attention. Giri shows that what is really becoming the greatest value nowadays is the intellectual and moral background of civilization concentrated in the person, that in the globalizing world knowledge is acquiring the status of a high value and as the most important precondition for social development. In this book high academic standard is combined with the clearly displayed humanistic position of the author who advocates for bridging the East and the West, the First, Second, and Third Worlds on the background of shared knowledge and morality that underpins it. In his humanistic socio-historical stance Giri, at all significant distinctions in approaches, resembles another searcher of the world civilization's foundations, Karl Jaspers. Indeed, Giri, an Indian who has worked intensively overseas, combines the East and the West in himself what makes his book even more interesting and instructive for the reader."

—Dmitri M. Bondarenko, Russian Academy of Sciences, Moscow

"Perspective taking with a deep knowledge of reality and an imaginary view of future is a major requirement of the *critical theory*, and it can be met only in a work like this book, and by a scholar like its author."

—Tong Shijun, Director of the Institute of Philosophy, Shanghai Academy of Social Sciences

"Ananta Kumar Giri's new book is an attempt at fostering epistemological awareness, making us conscious about the presuppositions within which we think and act. What it argues in particular is that this awareness is hidden in forms of knowledge that are permeated by power. Therefore we are forced to find this awareness by critical self-observation. To do so Giri draws on a series of, at first glance, highly divergent writers such as Habermas or Sri Aurobindo, an Indian social thinker and many others, to find a basis for this self-liberation. In addition, he adds what can be called an emotional component to this process of self-liberation, the quasi-religious idea of joy disentangled from repressive affects that permeate us through knowledge and acting. This book is to be recommended to all who want to have a look beyond what is normally discussed in treaties on epistemology. It makes us think more deeply about our normative presuppositions, about new foundations of a critical theory and about the role of religion in our craft as social and political theorists."

—*Klaus Eder, Professor of Sociology, Humboldt University, Berlin*

"*Knowledge and Human Liberation* not only calls for transcivilizational and transcultural dialogues but practices them in a beautiful and engaged manner. Ananta Kumar Giri juxtaposes for instance Jürgen Habermas with Sri Aurobindo, Martha Nussbaum with Mahatma Gandhi, and Fred Dallmayer with Daisaku Ikeda, drawing important lessons from each encounter. For him, personal self-development, global democracy and cultivation of our cosmic humanity go hand-in-hand. Giri is replacing anti-colonial anger with a dialogue on cosmopolitanism; and simultaneously reminds Western progressive cosmopolitans of their limited and biased understanding of other cultures. Warmly recommended reading for anyone interested in the future of humanity!"

—*Heikki Patomäki, Professor of International Relations, University of Helsinki*

"Ananta Kumar Giri's book is one of the first major works of a new era. The global South has passed through stages of copying, denying and outflanking the global North. Indian scholars have been busy trying to adapt modernization theory to India, to develop a nationalist frame of reference and to portray Indian traditions as an alternative to the modern West. In all of these attempts, the West has remained the frame of reference. We are now entering an era in which the global South is actually starting to develop new frames of reference. Giri's book is situated at this junction and in one important regard even beyond it. It calls for a global epistemology conceived as conversation of differing traditions and frames of references. The book exemplifies this conversation with regard to the European critical epistemology and Indian spirituality. This is a first step out of the impasse of the struggle of -isms and post-isms"

—*Boike Rehbein, Professor of Asian and African Societies, Humboldt University, Berlin*

"Going beyond the conventional functions of description, explanation and prediction of the knowledge enterprise, which is currently a tool of commercialization and political domination, Dr. Ananta Kumar Giri attempts to provide a framework for creating compassionate and transformative knowledge in which, the self, the other and the world (encapsulating both humanity and nature) are partners in producing knowledge so that knowledge becomes liberative. Admittedly, this book deserves to be widely read, discussed and commented."

—*T. K. Oommen, Professor Emeritus,*
Jawaharlal Nehru University, New Delhi

"One of the conditions under which knowledge can be a force for liberation from narrow concerns and false dichotomies has to be knowledge's own liberation. The issue then becomes how we can know what liberation might be. If anyone can at once pose and answer this question, it is Ananta Kumar Giri."

—Dame Marilyn Strathern, William Wyse
Professor of Social Anthropology (Emeritus), University of Cambridge

www.ingramcontent.com/pod-product-compliance
Lightning Source LLC
Chambersburg PA
CBHW022348280326
41935CB00007B/118